RACE RIOTS

To Roger
with warm regards
from Michael
9/26/2006

Race Riots

Comedy and Ethnicity in Modern British Fiction

Michael L. Ross

McGill-Queen's University Press
Montreal & Kingston • London • Ithaca

ISBN-13: 978-0-7735-3109-3 ISBN-10: 0-7735-3109-2

Legal deposit third quarter 2006
Bibliothèque nationale du Québec

Printed in Canada on acid-free paper that is 100% ancient forest free (100% post-consumer recycled), processed chlorine free.

McGill-Queen's University Press acknowledges the support of the Canada Council for the Arts for our publishing program. We also acknowledge the financial support of the Government of Canada through the Book Publishing Industry Development Program (BPIDP) for our publishing activities.

Library and Archives Canada Cataloguing in Publication

Ross, Michael L., 1936–
Race riots: comedy and ethnicity in modern British fiction/
Michael L. Ross.

Includes bibliographical references and index.
ISBN-13: 978-0–7735-3109-3 ISBN-10: 0-7735-3109-2

1. Racism in literature. 2. Stereotype (Psychology) in literature. 3. Comic, The, in literature. 4. Laughter in literature. 5. English fiction – History and criticism. I. Title.

PR830.C63R68 2006 823'.91093552 C2006–901537-6

This book was typeset by Interscript in 10/13 Palatino.

Contents

Illustrations

Acknowledgments

A number of colleagues and friends have read portions of this study at various stages of its composition; I am indebted to them for their suggestions and criticisms. Daniel Coleman, who shares many of my interests while pursuing them over a different terrain, valuably enlarged my awareness of relevant critical and theoretical texts and sharpened my perceptions of the sorts of issues involved in my analysis of material bearing on questions of race and nationality. I benefited equally from discussions with Sarah Brophy, who found time, despite a hectic schedule, to read draft versions of several chapters and to direct me to material I might otherwise have missed. Lynn Shakinovsky, who reads omnivorously in contemporary fiction, also provided me with suggestions regarding relevant texts. My long-time friend Ron Granofsky diverted his attention from the often uncomic D.H. Lawrence to listen and respond to my ideas about racial comedy. I had valuable conversations with Silvia Ross, Mark Chu (who is pursuing interests similar to mine, though in the field of Italian studies), and with Blake Morrison (who steered me toward the work of Howard Jacobson and William Boyd). Carl Spadoni, of Mills Library, McMaster University, went (as usual) out of his way to help me locate material in Mills Special Collections. I am also grateful to staff members at the Bodleian Library, Oxford University, for assistance in accessing the papers of Barbara Pym. Andrew Griffin, who served for several months as my research assistant on *Punch* humour, encouraged me both by his enthusiasm for my project and by his zealous and always perceptive survey of many numbers of the magazine. Nick Roberts, of the *Punch* archive in London, has been consistently generous in facilitating the reproduction of *Punch* drawings and in tracking down for me information I would otherwise have been hard put to obtain. Students in my seminars on modern British comic fiction at McMaster stimulated and sometimes profitably confused my thinking about comic texts and the problems of interpretation they present. Finally, as always I am enormously indebted to Lorraine York, who read my entire manuscript, parts of it – masochistically – more than once, and made acute criticisms, many of which are incorporated in this book. While she and the others I have named have contributed much to whatever merits this study may have, none of them, needless to say, bears any responsibility for its shortcomings.

Preface

I was moved to write this book by my growing interest in the relations between humour and power structures in society. The two subjects, I found, had for the most part been thought about in isolation from each other, and I felt that this intellectual firewall was arbitrary and stultifying. However, when I set out bravely to tear down the wall, I soon realized that the topic was too vast to be encompassed in a single study. It then occurred to me that the literary use of racially based humour, though still a dauntingly broad field, might provide a workable, less sprawling terrain for the sort of inquiry I had in mind. It promised to focus in a novel fashion the manifold and problematic ways in which humour can either enforce or undermine hegemonic social structures, often abasing "otherness" but sometimes embracing it. My hope is that my discussion of such issues, though necessarily restricted, will by extension shed light as well on humour aimed at other sorts of difference: those arising from gender, class, or sexual orientation.

Since the logic of this book's organization may not be obvious, a preliminary roadmap will perhaps be helpful. Because I endeavour to trace an evolution in literary modes of deploying racial comedy, my discussion follows a broadly but not scrupulously chronological path. The introduction, "Preliminary Convulsions," deals with basic philosophical issues connected with racial joking, including the controversy over so-called "political correctness."

Part 1, *Punch* Lines, begins with a departure from my overall focus on modern British fiction: a look at the nexus between humour and race in a famous text anticipating much that will come later: Shakespeare's play *The Tempest*. After some glances at modes of racial joking in fiction of several centuries, I go on to examine how such joking figured in *Punch*, the foremost British humour magazine, in the early decades of the twentieth century. My premise is that racial comedy in works of literature needs to be read in the context of more popular forms, though literary comedy troubles and complicates popular models rather than simply duplicating them. The texts I use to explore this relationship are "African" novels by Evelyn Waugh and Joyce Cary.

Part 2, Passages to Elsewhere, considers four writers whose treatment of racial humour subverts the paradigms found in Waugh and Cary: E.M. Forster, Muriel Spark, Barbara Pym, and Elizabeth Taylor. I argue that differences of sex and of sexual orientation help to account for these authors' resistance to established patterns of racial joking, and for their willingness to explore less conventional sources of humour.

In part 3, The Empire Laughs Back, I discuss novels by recent writers, all but one members of ethnic minorities, who undertake campaigns of radical revisionism against older traditions of British racial comedy. These texts regularly feature inversions of familiar comic paradigms; yet their humour is rendered both more complex and more problematic by their own occasional stereotyping of ethnic out-groups. My final treatment of a literary text *in extenso*, Matthew Kneale's *English Passengers*, looks back to *The Tempest*, arguing that Kneale's novel reverses Shakespeare's characterizations of Prospero and Caliban, subverting the classic colonialist model of power relations. My concluding chapter examines current developments in interracial comedy, focusing on three acclaimed twenty-first-century novels by young authors of mixed race, Zadie Smith's *White Teeth*, Hari Kunzru's *The Impressionist*, and Andrea Levy's *Small Island*. I suggest that the blurring of identities enacted in these works looks forward to a type of humour that jettisons stable concepts of nation and race, and that their self-consciousness about humour itself aligns them with postmodern tendencies that have come in recent decades to characterize British fiction in general.

RACE RIOTS

INTRODUCTION

Preliminary Convulsions

> It may be noted, by the way, that there is no better start for thinking than laughter. And, in particular, convulsion of the diaphragm usually provides better opportunities for thought than convulsion of the soul.
>
> Walter Benjamin, "The Author as Producer" (*Reflections* 236)

> Laughter is indeed the propriety of a Man, but just enough to distinguish him from his elder Brother, with four Legs. 'Tis a kind of Bastard-pleasure too, taken in at the Eyes of the vulgar gazers, and at the Ears of the beastly Audience.
>
> John Dryden, Translator's Preface to C.A. Du Fresnoy, *De Arte Graphica* (55–6)

In the long-running philosophical debate about the nature of humour, a gulf separates the Benjamins, who believe that the convulsion of laughter engenders thought, from the Drydens, who believe the contrary. My own deepest sympathies lie with Benjamin; but humour and my special concern, its relation to literature, are subjects too complex to be definitively settled in favour of either camp. What I would insist is that humour, whatever its value for starting thought, is itself a subject that demands to be thought about, rather than laughingly brushed aside. This study is written against what Paul Lewis calls "the common reluctance to take humor seriously" (170).

One good way to take humour seriously is to situate it within a broader sociopolitical context. The belief that humour by nature defies entrenched power structures has been tersely voiced by George Orwell: "A thing is funny when … it upsets the established order. Every joke is a tiny revolution" (*Collected Essays* III 325). Against such a view Wylie Sypher argues that "[i]n middle-class societies, particularly, the comic artist often reassures the majority that its standards are impregnable or that other standards are not 'normal' or 'sane'" (244). Ultimately, the attempt to categorize humour as embodying one sole, predictable tendency is futile; as Lewis wisely says, "[A] particular experience of humor can serve any cause – good or evil, constructive or destructive, conservative or radical ... [H]umor is not one but many things" (156).

What this study will assume, however, is that humour, whatever cause it serves, is in essence a social phenomenon. Henri Bergson, in his century-old but still foundational book on laughter, declares: "Our laughter is always the laughter of a group ... However spontaneous it seems, laughter always implies a kind of secret freemasonry, or even complicity, with other laughers, real or imaginary ... To understand laughter, we must put it back into its natural environment, which is society, and above all we must determine the utility of its function, which is a social one" (64–5). Sigmund Freud, though he likened "wit" (or humour) to dreams, followed Bergson in pointing out that whereas "[t]he dream is a perfectly asocial psychic product ... [w]it, on the other hand, is the most social of all those psychic functions whose aim is to give pleasure" (285–6). Freud's isolation of what he called "tendency wit" has a suggestive general relevance to my own inquiry, and his discussion of "hostile and obscene wit" (138 *et seq.*) offers provocative insights into the psychodynamics of aggressive humour. Characteristically, though, his attention is directed more toward sexual than toward racial joking; his analysis consequently has only a limited application to what will concern us here. The large questions still remain to be confronted: what sorts of social functions does laughter serve, and precisely what sort of pleasure does it yield?

Among later attempts to take humour seriously, one of the most fruitful is the work of the Russian theorist and critic Mikhail Bakhtin, whose exploration of the "carnivalesque" element in comic literature helps to illuminate my own main concern: the humorous treatment of race. Generally speaking, Bakhtin, like Orwell, sees the comic impulse both in life and in literature as a destabilizing, revitalizing force. As embodied in the ancient popular festivity of carnival, it "celebrates the destruction of the old and the birth of the new world – the new year, the new spring, the new kingdom" (*Rabelais* 410). Carnival mirth enacts renewal not through any systematic program but through its informal, spontaneous irreverence: "[F]estive folk laughter presents an element of victory not only over supernatural awe, over the sacred, over death; it also means the defeat of power, of earthly kings, of the earthly upper classes, of all that oppresses and restricts" (92). Goethe's account of the Roman carnival demonstrates, for Bakhtin, that "[i]n the world of carnival all hierarchies are cancelled. All castes and ages are equal" (251). Such popular festivities "were the second life of the people, who for a time entered the utopian realm of community, freedom, equality, and abundance" (9). Embedded in works of literature, such carnivalesque laughter "destroys the epic, and in general destroys any hierarchical (distancing and valorized) distance" (*Dialogic Imagination* 23). Unlike solemnity, "Laughter … overcomes fear, for it knows no inhibitions, no limitations. Its idiom is never used by violence and authority" (*Rabelais* 90); it "could never become an instrument to oppress and blind the people" (94). It opens the door to social and intellectual innovation; "[G]reat changes, even in the field of science, are always preceded by a certain carnival consciousness that prepares the way" (49).

Not surprisingly, Bakhtin's utopian view of laughter as progressive and anti-authoritarian has been disputed. Roger Sales argues that "[t]he release of emotions and grievances [during carnival] made them easier to police in the long run" (qtd in Stallybrass and White 13). Stallybrass and White raise a possibility that has a special salience to issues of racial humour: the populace's derision may be deflected from those in authority to those constructed as "inferiors": "[C]arnival often violently abuses and demonizes *weaker*, not stronger, social groups – women, ethnic and religious minorities, those who 'don't belong' – in a process of *displaced abjection*" (19).[1]

In works of comic fiction, carnivalesque laughter has recurrently been directed against "those who 'don't belong,'" a rhetorical strategy not envisioned by Bakhtin in his famous discussion of Rabelais. A term for such writing might be *hegemonic comedy*, for it engenders a type of unBakhtinian laughter – a "laughing down" – more apt to cement than to disturb the hierarchical lineaments of the entrenched social order. Much of the British humour I will examine in the chapters that follow – Shakespeare's play *The Tempest*, novels by Evelyn Waugh and Joyce Cary, jokes in *Punch* magazine – arguably fits this hegemonic paradigm. Such comedy tends to construe the folk-unruliness of carnival, which Bakhtin deemed healthy and progressive, as potentially dangerous *misrule*, a lack of "civilized" order requiring correction. A central thesis of this study will be that racially oriented British comedy undergoes a decisive change in direction during the course of the twentieth century. As one moves from the fiction of Waugh, Cary, Anthony Powell, and Ronald Firbank to more recent works by Muriel Spark, Samuel Selvon, Salman Rushdie, Hanif Kureishi, and others, a mode more closely resembling Bakhtin's cherished egalitarian carnivalesque gains ascendancy. This narrative of mutation parallels, and is conditioned by, profound alterations in the makeup of British society.

According to the theorist Elder Olson, "The basis of the ridiculous and the ludicrous … is the *unlike*" (18). Over centuries England's history and geography have bred in its people a firm, if misleading, sense of tribal homogeneity and of unlikeness to other breeds. The growth of the British Empire, while bringing about more frequent contact with "exotic" foreigners, tended to reinforce this myth of group sameness, especially vis-à-vis those who embodied visible unlikeness. These Others came, by a well-known logic of group psychology, to represent communally sanctioned joking targets.

Until the mid-twentieth century, however, interaction with "laughable" non-whites was largely confined to British colonial administrators and other personnel in remote reaches of the empire; by as late as 1950 there were no more than 100,000 people of colour in all of Britain (Daniel 9). Once more significant numbers of non-whites came to be present in the United Kingdom itself, discrimination, as surveys have demonstrated, "operate[d] ... on a substantial scale" (3). John Solomos notes that, from the mid-1940s on, "an increasingly racialised debate about immigration took place, focusing on the supposed 'social problems' of having too many black immigrants and the question of how they could be stopped from entering" (57). Still, as Solomos establishes, the attitudes that surfaced during that period had long been latent in the thinking of ordinary Britishers.

The literature and culture of Britain, like those of other European countries, have tended to assume whiteness as a norm and to define other ethnicities as curious aberrations. As Richard Dyer puts it, "For those in power in the West, as long as whiteness is felt to be the human condition, then it alone both defines normality and fully inhabits it ... [T]he equation of being white with being human secures a position of power. White people have power and believe that they think, feel and act like and for all people; white people, unable to see their particularity, cannot take account of other people's; white people create the dominant images of the world and don't quite see that they thus construct the world in their own image; white people set standards of humanity by which they are bound to succeed and others bound to fail" (9). Dyer goes on to point out that whites tend to be less vulnerable than other groups to deformation by stereotypes: "[S]tereotyping – complex and contradictory though it is ... – characterise[s] the representation of subordinated social groups and is one of the means by which they are categorised and kept in their place, whereas white people in white culture are given the illusion of their own infinite variety" (12). While Dyer's binary division may be overstated, it is reasonable to assume that the tendency to stereotype non-whites has had a distorting effect on white people's perceptions of them and ultimately on non-whites' perceptions of themselves.

Edward Said, in his influential study *Orientalism*, has shown how, in British imperial discourse, "the Oriental is *contained* and *represented* by dominating frameworks" (40). As Said argues, this discursive containment has had important political consequences. He quotes Arthur Balfour on the state of affairs in Egypt: "'You may look through the whole history of the Orientals in what is called, broadly speaking, the East, and you never find traces of self-government. All their great centuries – and they have been very great – have been passed under despotisms, under absolute government'" (32–3). According to Brian Street, the idea that "the native was ... not fit to rule himself and his laws were not binding on whites" had wide currency in imperial discourse (45). Balfour himself adduces the Egyptians' supposed incapacity to rule themselves to argue that they should be ruled by the British – absolutely (Said 33).

For Evelyn Baring Cromer, the virtual ruler of Egypt between 1883 and 1907, "'Want of accuracy, which easily degenerates into untruthfulness, is ... the main characteristic of the Oriental mind'" (qtd in Said 38). Cromer draws a firm distinction between the mental processes of "the European" and those of "the Oriental": "'The European is a close reasoner; his statements of fact are devoid of any ambiguity; he is a natural logician, albeit he may not have studied logic; he is by nature sceptical and requires proof before he can accept the truth of any proposition; his trained intelligence works like a piece of mechanism. The mind of the Oriental, on the other hand, like his picturesque streets, is eminently wanting in symmetry. His reasoning is of the most slipshod description'" (qtd in Said 38). Cromer's own logic – his heady generalizing on the basis of hypostatized national figments and glib analogies – itself now looks slipshod, but, as Said shows, it typifies Western thinking about the East during this period. There is a measure of plausibility in Said's own wholesale generalization that every European of the time was "a racist, an imperialist, and almost totally ethnocentric" (204).

Nor did such habits of thought fade away after the nineteenth century. Street points out how "three forces ... politics, science and literature, served to form an image which by 1920 was as hardened as that which [Philip] Curtin describes for 1850" (10). The traits assigned both to the colonized and their masters tended to be, as they were for Cromer, invariable:

> Since the races were ... divided up by various criteria and characteristics, a particular "character" could be attributed to a whole people on the strength of casual personal observations; a "race" might be gullible, faithful, brave, childlike, bloodthirsty, noble, etc. and these qualities were assumed to be hereditary. Likewise, the

Anglo-Saxon race had certain qualities which were inborn in all its members, and it was these qualities which enabled it to dominate the rest of the world.

"Primitive" man, on the other hand, spent his whole life in fear of spirits and mystical beings; his gullibility was exploited by self-seeking priests and kings, who manipulated religion to gain a hold on the minds of their simple subjects; he worshipped animals and trees, tried to control the mystical forces of nature by means of ceremony, ritual, taboos and sacrifices, and explained the wonders of the universe in imaginative but "unscientific" myths. (Street 7)

The ability to use science and technology, rather than ritual and taboos, to control the forces of nature became, from the late eighteenth century on, a talisman for distinguishing "advanced" Westerners from "primitive" natives. As Michael Adas notes, "Those involved in the colonies and intellectuals who dealt with colonial issues came to view scientific and technological achievements not only as the key attributes that set Europe off from all other civilizations, past and present, but as the most meaningful gauges by which non-Western societies might be evaluated, classified, and ranked" (144). The crucial impact of this technological bias on humour directed at non-Westerners will be discussed in later chapters.

Literature, through the work of writers like Rudyard Kipling and Rider Haggard, was instrumental in fixing images of the undiffereniated "native" in the popular mind: "Kipling and Haggard … were writing about very different parts of the world, yet, despite occasional acknowledgments of local difference, they share common attitudes of superiority to 'primitive' races that had been made respectable by anthropologists. The extent to which the theory that had been developed to deal with 'primitive' man made all 'primitive' men seem the same, is evident from the similar preconceptions with which the inhabitants of Borneo, Matabeleland and the Punjab are approached by English writers. There is a common body of expectations, a common mythology on which to draw, and differences of detail are subsumed beneath a common structure" (Street 15–16). This literary homogenizing of the "primitive" encourages a tendency that will surface repeatedly in the chapters to follow: the wholesale caricaturing of colonials, whatever their origin, as more or less interchangeable cultureless buffoons.

Richard Dyer outlines the mechanism whereby popular racial mythologies perpetuate distinctions between superior and inferior: "All concepts of *race*, emerging out of eighteenth-century materialism, are concepts of bodies, but all along they have had to be reconciled with notions of embodiment and incarnation. The latter become what distinguish white people, giving them a special relation to race. Black people can be reduced (in white culture) to their bodies and thus to race, but white people are something else that is realised in and yet is not reducible to the corporeal, or racial" (14–15). The reducing of black people to their bodies has a direct bearing on their presumed comic status. According to Henri Bergson, comedy results from the overwhelming of the "soul," or "living energy," by materiality: "The impression of the comic will be produced as soon as we have a clear apprehension of this putting of the one on the other ... [T]he general law of these phenomena may be formulated as follows: *Any incident is comic that calls our attention to the physical in a person, when it is the moral side that is concerned*" (93). Since, in Dyer's terms, non-whites are perceived as wholly defined by their physicality, they become, by Bergsonian logic, automatic candidates for comic treatment.

Another item of racial mythology that abets this reducing of non-whites to the risibly physical is the habit of regarding "natives" as linguistically impaired. As Said observes, the nineteenth-century orientalist Ernest Renan uses his scholarly expertise to link non-European verbal inadequacy to deficits of race and culture: "Read almost any page by Renan on Arabic, Hebrew, Aramaic, or proto-Semitic and you read a fact of power, by which the Orientalist philologist's authority summons out of the library at will examples of man's speech, and ranges them there surrounded by a suave European prose that points out defects, virtues, barbarisms, and shortcomings in the language, the people, and the civilization" (142). Such a linkage was widespread also in the thinking of less erudite colonizers, and it is frequently echoed in popular works of literature. The language of one African tribe, reports an author of exotic adventures, was "just about as comprehensible as the jabbering of apes" (qtd in Street 85).

The portraying of dark-skinned people as jabbering apes endowed with physicality but not mentality places them at a far remove from "suave Europeans." According to one long-familiar theory, the act of situating human individuals or groups out of reach of empathetic identification tends inevitably to produce them as legitimate objects of humour. Bergson, the best-known exponent of this "detachment" principle, points to "the *absence of feeling* which usually accompanies laughter. It seems as though the comic could not produce its disturbing effect unless it fell, so to say, on the surface of a soul that is thoroughly calm and unruffled. Indifference is its natural environment, for laughter has no greater foe than emotion. I do not mean that we could not laugh at a person who inspires us with pity, for instance, or even with affection, but in such a case we must, for a moment, put our affection out of court and impose silence upon our pity" (63). Much anecdotal evidence can be found to support Bergson's contention that laughter is incompatible with emotional involvement. A classic literary example is the cool, olympian mirth of Shakespeare's Puck at the blundering of love-besotted mortals. Another is the profound moment at the close of Chaucer's *Troilus and Criseyde*, when, after he has been slain in battle, the spirit of the passionate, jilted hero looks down on Earth: "And in himself he lough right at the wo / Of hem that wepten for his deeth so faste" (v 1821-2) – death, the arch-distancer, converts tragedy to comedy. A comparable if more light-hearted moment occurs in Mozart's comic opera *Così Fan Tutte*, where two pairs of young lovers, about to be sundered by the departure of the two men on (fictitious) military duty, sing in exquisite harmonies of their anguish at parting. Meanwhile, against their impassioned strains the *dégagé* old cynic Don Alfonso keeps repeating puckishly, in his *sotto voce* bass, "*Io crepo se non rido*" ("I'll die if I don't laugh").[2]

Nevertheless, Bergson's thesis invites obvious objections. Is there really no such thing as indulgent or compassionate laughter?[3] Counter-examples flock to mind, foremost among them, perhaps, the tramp persona in Charlie Chaplin films. Millions have found this endlessly battered but irrepressible figure an object at once of sympathy and humour, and the sympathy is inextricably *bound up with* the humour; those who laugh do not put affection out of court or impose silence on their pity; far from it. (A similarly blended response, balanced between amusement and compassion, is evoked by the high-modernist comedy of Leopold Bloom's Chaplinesque meanderings in James Joyce's *Ulysses*.) True, the occasional viewer may find Chaplin's tramp too poignant to be genuinely funny, a case showing that, if sufficiently keen, emotion can indeed thwart laughter and also that emotional distance is partly a function of individual sensibility. On the other hand, a character like Molière's miserly Harpagon typically provokes a Bergsonian type of laughter that is equally robust but much less personally implicating. The linkage between detachment and laughter, in short, is not governed by an iron, unalterable rule; it mutates according to a sliding scale of gradations.

A theory of humorous detachment more nuanced than Bergson's, then, is needed. Still, Bergson's position remains broadly relevant to racial humour of a condescending sort. Where there exists a vacuum of fellow-feeling, laughter tends to rush in to fill it. Street explains how popular accounts and fictions of "remote" places like Africa provided "emotional confirmation of the unreality of native lands which ... makes the inhabitants themselves appear more unapproachable and difficult to understand.

By emphasising, in this way, the gap between European and native, England and ... Africa, the popular writers created an emotional barrier against the understanding of 'primitive' peoples which affected the response and reports of future travellers" (26). I would add that readers' as well as travellers' responses were inevitably affected; though not humorous themselves, such writers helped open a path for comic treatment of "primitives" by enhancing the sense of their remoteness. Also, by promulgating a mythos according to which a so-called "Kaffir" (besides such other oddities as being "unable to wink") has a skin "insensible to pain" (qtd in Street 75), writers like John Buchan created an image of the native as curiously devoid of subjectivity. Such objectified people resemble those figures in animated cartoons who are continually victims of atrocious punishment but are never irreparably damaged. They are rendered automatically laughable because alienated from the range of our sympathy; it is not easy to extend fellow-feeling to those who cannot feel. Other behavioural patterns attributed to natives of several continents, such as lawlessness, servility to despots, and cannibalism, compounded their removal from the reach of Western reader identification. Little wonder that, as one writer incisively remarks, "There was ... a tendency to use comments on cultural differences to *provide comic relief* to the reader and simultaneously to re-affirm white racial and cultural superiority" (Cairns, qtd in Street 134; emphasis added).

One guarantor of such superiority was the prerogative of laughter itself. If, in terms of the racial mythos of empire, non-whites were the prescribed butts of humour, they were by the same token deemed incapable of originating it. "'We Orientals have no humour, ass iss well known,'" says Dr Veraswami in his stage-Indian accent in George Orwell's *Burmese Days* (42). ("'Lucky devils. It's been the ruin of us, our bloody sense of humour,'" replies Flory, the novel's jaded English protagonist.) According to one unidentified "old Oxonian," the "'utter and unmitigated savage'" does not play practical jokes, since "'the sense of humour, which is needed for a joke of any kind, is totally absent, possibly because the whole working life of a thorough savage is occupied with the tasks of procuring food and guarding himself from violence'" (qtd in Street 74). Such a view, taking humour as an implicit touchstone of the civilized, helps to place "savages" even further beyond the pale of European humanity. It also reinforces the native's eligibility for the position of comic object, since the humourless are targets of ridicule *par excellence*. It follows that those rare non-white fictional characters who are endowed with wit (a sinister example is the village official U Po Kyin in *Burmese Days*) may be thereby empowered to enact a subversive rupture of orthodox reader expectations. In general, however, coloured people seeking to attain white status tend to be viewed, both in life and in literature, as intrinsically comic. According to Stallybrass and White, "[T]he Other's mimicry of the polite is treated as absurd, the cause of derisive laughter, thus consolidating the sense that the civilized is always-already given, the essential and unchanging possession which distinguishes the European citizen from the West Indian and the Zulu, as well as from the marmoset and manteger" (41).

Nevertheless, the relation between colonizer and colonized was too complex to be captured by a schematic image of the laughing master lording it over the mocked, abjected subaltern. Frantz Fanon's 1952 book *Black Skin, White Masks*, according to Daniel Coleman, "initiated a projection / internalization theory that has proved powerfully influential in late twentieth-century discussions of racial, colonial, and sexual politics. Fanon considered racism a process whereby white Europeans projected their own 'darkest' fantasies and fears onto the dark-skinned others whom they encountered in their colonial and imperial quests" (58). Dyer cites more recent theorists to the effect that "projection of sexuality on to dark races was a means for whites to represent yet dissociate themselves from their own desires" (28). In fact a covert and at times overt connection between sexual impulses and dark-skin figures insistently in popular art and literature of the British imperial age. *Punch* political cartoons from the late nineteenth century and after repeatedly personify African and Asian nations (for example that "Jewel in the Crown," India) as voluptuous and often half-nude tawny females, typically being courted or protected by an emphatically male (and of course white) figure of John Bull. As Dyer cautions, "[W]hiteness never exists separately from specific class, gender or other socio-cultural inflections" (xv), a nexus vital to keep in mind when considering both *Punch*'s humour and the comic novels that will be our principal concern.

"Why do we laugh at a head of hair that has changed from dark to blond? What is there comic about a rubicund nose? And why does one laugh at a negro? The question would appear to be an embarrassing one ... " (Bergson 86). The concluding question is certainly more embarrassing today than it may have seemed one hundred years ago, when Henri Bergson posed it in his celebrated treatise on humour. The identity of the "one" who does the laughing has become problematic in ways the eminent philosopher would not have suspected. Before dismissing Bergson's attitude toward racial laughter as a period piece, however, one should note that such laughter, whether informal or literary, can still claim its proponents, some of them likewise eminent. It has, in fact, become fashionable of late to decry what the literary historian Martin Green terms "ideological squeamishness" (*Dreams* 392), more commonly known as "political correctness."

Mahadev Apte, author of what may be the first comparative anthropological study of humour, believes ethnic joking to be a normal, even universal, expression of collective culture: "Ethnic humor, like all other types of humor, is an integral part of expressive culture. It reflects a group's perception and evaluation of other groups' personality traits, customs, behavior patterns, and social institutions by the standards of ingroup culture, with its positive or negative attitudes toward others. Judgments proceed from intergroup interactions, but once established, they tend to become a part of cultural heritage and do not change substantively unless they are affected by significant historical events" (121). According to Apte, "Stereotypes are crucial to ethnic humor and its appreciation. Because they are widely accepted by members of individual cultures, they constitute a shared set of assumptions necessary for ethnic humor" (114). Apte grants that such stereotypes usually "have little or nothing to do with 'objective reality' or 'empirical truth,' and they may persist despite strong evidence to the contrary" (114). He nevertheless argues that "[e]njoyment of any humor, including ethnic humor, does not necessarily make individuals aggressive or hostile. Rather, a make-believe framework or state of mind is developed temporarily for sheer pleasure and is discarded when engagement in humorous exchange is over" (145). Apte's rationale for ethnocentric joking as inherently performative and therefore benign doubtless does apply to many occurrences of such humour. However, while it is unlikely that enjoying jokes "necessarily makes" anybody one thing or another, Apte's formulation overlooks the venom of aggression and hostility typically infusing racial humour.

Other commentators, unhampered by anthropological decorum, go Apte one better, warmly applauding the aggressive and hostile elements in such joking. The novelist and critic Malcolm Bradbury, reporting in the *Independent* on a 1995 humour conference, deplores the current tendency to be embarrassed by "incorrectness": "One of our preoccupations was that, in the age of new solemnities, laughter isn't what it was. The comic is improper and partial. It displays prejudices, personal and cultural. It targets minorities; there's always some group (Irish Poles) who are worse off and funnier than you. It tosses into the limbo of laughter people who now feel they have every right to assert their assertion, every case for opposing representations that deny or oppress them. This is the day of the guilty comedian, the humorist asked to contemplate his or her shame." Bradbury's case for unconstrained hostile laughter as a handy means of keeping upstarts in limbo is not unique; it is only an unusually forthright example of the arguments against "new solemnities" one regularly encounters. (Most frequently the group targeted is "assertive" women, but ethnic minorities are also fair game.) As his prime exemplar of the need for fearless "incorrect" humour Bradbury cites Evelyn Waugh, who "was, especially in his later years, outrageous, probably even to himself. He's also one of the greatest writers of the 20th century." Read in context, Bradbury's formulation implies that Waugh's greatness as a writer came about not *despite* his penchant for "outrageous" (i.e., "politically incorrect") humour but precisely *because* of it. Such a proposition, which is hardly self-explanatory, needs to be tested by careful inspection of Waugh's work, a project I will reserve for a later chapter.

A more fully articulated case for humour as a timely rebellion against creeping tolerance is Howard Jacobson's 1997 book *Seriously Funny*, a spirited and often witty engagement in the war with "ideological squeamishness." Jacobson, a well-known British novelist and essayist, would likely endorse the thesis that Evelyn Waugh's literary stature is enhanced, rather than diminished, by the gusto with which he deploys "politically incorrect" humour. For Jacobson, humour directed against stock objects of discrimination serves a therapeutic psychological and social function: "[I]f we once acknowledge that black and hostile comedy (laughing *at*, not laughing *with*) fulfils an important physiological function [as some medical findings may indicate], we are well on the way to understanding how it also fulfils an important social one" (31). Lauding the performances of English stand-up comic Bernard Manning, a noted adept in racial insult, he argues: "Comedy in a [Manchester] club like Bernard Manning's lances the boil. It enables the pus to run" (32). Presumably the metaphor is meant as a vivacious way of saying that Manning's jokes expose to the light of day festering racial ill-feeling and cleanse it through the agency of laughter.

One problem with such a diagnosis is its failure to track the direction in which the pus is running. A performance for a police gathering, which caused Manning to be slated by the press for his alleged overuse of the word "black," is justified for Jacobson on the grounds that "Manning was giving the policemen not just what they wanted but what they needed" (32). Such an act is a specimen of ritual drama: "And ... the play transfigures actuality. In the event of expression of hostilities ... the play is a substitute for the real thing. Saying the unsayable in place of, and in preference to, doing the undoable" (33). Jacobson does not consider the counter-argument that hearing the unsayable said publicly might conceivably encourage police officers to do the undoable when on duty in tense, racially mixed neighbourhoods. As Paul Lewis observes, "It is foolish, even dangerous, to insist that jokes about the worthlessness of out-group members, about the importance of oppressing or even annihilating these groups, must be harmless" (38).

Jacobson tends generally, like Bradbury, to identify comedy with the transgression of conventional boundaries. He points for support to folk ceremonies in which transgression becomes naturalized; but unlike the carnival described by Bakhtin, which features insouciant nose-thumbing aimed at exalted authority, the occasions cited by Jacobson – for example, the Hopi ritual involving clowns licenced to indulge in indecency and insult directed at tribal minorities (34) – punish the "lowliest" members of the group. Jacobson claims that the lone black policeman in Manning's audience took no offence: "The single black policeman at Manning's function also reported having enjoyed the fun. As a participant in the ritual, he grasped the difference between make-believe rudeness and the real thing. We are still in a theatre of cruelty; but it is cruelty not hate, and it is theatre not actuality" (34). Jacobson's distinctions between "pretend" and real rudeness, between mere cruelty and outright hatred, should not be rejected out of hand. His argument has much in common with Apte's anthropological account of joking, and it applies to some types of humour to be found in comic fiction. Nevertheless, such subtleties disregard obvious questions raised by the social context of the occasion Jacobson is addressing. Can one solitary, unprotesting black audience member really be taken to represent the reactions of his ethnic group as a whole? Would the single black policeman's imaginable options – say, taking vocal exception to Manning's humour – have been socially viable for him? For that matter, is the outnumbering of the black officer by a horde of white colleagues itself a fact to be shrugged off, or is it rather a symptom of troubling imbalance in a racially mixed metropolis where complaints about police discrimination are legion? The overtones of the whole situation seem far from harmlessly funny.

Jacobson denies that "jokes with an ethnic content promote the rhetoric of racism": "Of all the unquestioned assumptions on the politically correct agenda, this is the most indurated" (35). According to him, humour is inherently neutral: "[A] joke is a structured dialogue with itself ... it cannot, by its nature, be an expression of opinion" (36). The logic here is manifestly specious, since many race- and gender-based jokes undeniably imply opinions (normally, negative ones) about the target group. Legal proceedings may recognize the abusive subtexts of humorous discourse. Alison Ross notes that "in 1997 two Afro-Caribbean women won an appeal, claiming that their employers had failed to protect them from racial abuse and harassment. They were employed as waitresses at a function at which Bernard Manning made racially offensive remarks to them, encouraging members of his audience to join in the abuse" (103).

Jacobson would doubtless cite the women's victory as itself dispiriting evidence of an invasive "new solemnity" in the legal system. Unstinting in his claims for the legitimacy of Manning's brand of humour, he maintains "that there can be no drawing of lines [between the benign and the unacceptable] with comedy" (37-8) and roundly declares, "I, a Jew, feel far more threatened by those who would wipe out ethnic jokes than by those who unthinkingly make them" (35). Nobody loves a censor, but there is scant risk of ethnic jokes getting "wiped out," apart from those that – *pace* Jacobson – do cross the (admittedly somewhat fuzzy) line dividing good, or passable, fun from legally actionable hate-mongering. The issue is not, in any event, whether to permit or to suppress; the issue is whether to chuckle or to wince, and Jacobson's case for chuckling is on several grounds unpersuasive. His *ad hominem* argument based on his own ethnicity seems especially thin. A white, male, well-educated, middle-class writer, Jewish or gentile, enjoys a position of security and privilege in British society; he may be haunted by the memory of the Nazi Holocaust, but he runs no imminent risk of being subjected to anything comparable. He may not be invited to join the most "exclusive" London clubs, but he will not be obliged to scour their latrines, and he need not fear daily exposure to rejective mistreatment and derision, an immunity that a struggling Afro-Caribbean woman living in today's England might wistfully envy.

Generally speaking, what commentators like Jacobson and Bradbury fail to acknowledge is the contingent, *situational* nature of humour, its dependence for its effect on the context in which it takes place; on the circumstances, personalities, and social climate involved. (One obvious illustration would be the difference in resonance between a black comedian telling a "nigger" joke to an all-black audience and Bernard Manning telling the same joke to an audience that included only one person of colour.) For that matter, Jacobson's own theorizing reflects the sociohistorical context in which it occurred. John Solomos, writing about the growing resistance during the 1980s to the movement for racial equality in England, comments: "It is perhaps a sign of the nature of the present political climate that increasingly it is not racism which is presented as the central problem but the work of the anti-racists" (106).

Jacobson's position cannot, however, be discounted simply as a token of a passing political trend. He clearly views "incorrectness" as the very *essence* of humour, and this aligns him with a significant number of other humour theorists. Robert Heilman, an academic commentator, holds that comedy displays a spirit accepting of the world-as-it-is with all its diversity, including ethnic differences: "People are not of the same height or weight or color or race or strength or health or intelligence or point of view; we note this lack of uniformity, we may jest about it, but we do not reject people because of their divergencies. Par is the expectable; some men surpass, some fall short of, expectation. *Disparateness* defines, not an artificial collocation designed by a comic writer according to a recipe for laughter and allied responses, but a persistent state of human affairs. In our humanity, we differ from each other in candor, veracity, reliability, consistency, amiability, charitableness, thoughtfulness, urbanity, cooperativeness, responsiveness to the *sens commun*" (180–1). This stress on acceptance leads Heilman to take an interestingly counter-Bergsonian position on the issue of comic detachment. "To laugh at something," he argues, "is to take it to oneself rather than to declare it alien, unthinkable, unmentionable, unacknowledgeable, unacceptable, or exclusively terrible. To take it to oneself, even by transposing it into a key different from the common one, is to grow" (135). Paradoxically, however, Heilman's faith in the positivity of laughter, its intrinsic quality of acceptance, leads him to defend ethnic jokes against what he calls "the trendy populism of the 1970s," which "appears to be a protest against inequitable privilege" but "is at heart a rejection of the disparateness which manifests itself in superior taste or manners or perception" (246). He deplores "that solemn antiethnicism which pursues equality by rejecting ethnic and national comedy; it mistakes a sense of disparateness for a sense of superiority, that inferior man's self-defensiveness which will alas exist eternally to spark venemous jokes and will of course gain in underground strength if a society cuts off the legitimate comedy of ethnic disparateness" (246).

According to Heilman's logic, it would seem that *Amos 'n' Andy* is the sort of genial entertainment a society should cherish as a safeguard against truly nasty racial humour. Like Jacobson, though with more subtlety, he treats such comedy as a mechanism for "letting the pus run" by frankly acknowledging ethnic diversity and ethnic tensions. Once again, the basic problem with such theorizing is that it is hyper-generalized; the "ethnic and national comedy" to which Heilman gives blanket approval really comes in as many flavours as the mixed society he claims to celebrate. Precisely what makes some racial jokes venomous and others benign is an issue to which he gives scant attention. Like the other theorists I have been discussing, he declines to contextualize humour with reference to the power relations actually obtaining in society.

"[T]he creation and use of humor is an exercise of power: a force in controlling our responses to unexpected and dangerous happenings, a way of shaping the responses and attitudes of others and a tool in intergroup and intragroup dynamics" (Lewis 13). Paul Lewis's linkage of humour with power suggests an approach to the *realpolitik* of minority-scourging laughter more pragmatic than the formulations of Jacobson, Heilmann, and other deplorers of "political correctness." Lewis goes on to raise questions that will be central to my own analysis of racial humour: "Think of minstrel shows, or the comic blacks of early Hollywood films, or of the enduring popularity of ethnic jokes. If we ask 'Are these jokes funny?' we are asking the wrong question. Funny to whom? And why? How do these jokes embody or reinforce value systems; how do they serve psychic, social, cultural, or political objectives?" (13). According to George Frederickson, "[R]acism ... has two components: *difference* and *power*. It originates from a mind-set that regards 'them' as different from 'us' in ways that are permanent and unbridgeable. This sense of difference provides a motive or rationale for using our power advantage to treat the ethnoracial Other in ways that we would regard as cruel or unjust if applied to members of our own group" (9). Like Lewis, I would argue that one common way of exploiting such a "power advantage" is the exposure of the Other to demeaning humour.

The philosopher Ronald De Sousa has labelled jocularity of the Bernard Manning variety "phthonic laughter," identifying it as humour that expresses aggression and contempt toward an abjected individual or group.[4] He claims that such laughter can be distinguished by its component of malice "from wit and mere amusement," and he therefore considers it "particularly susceptible to moral condemnation" (Morreal 238). Instead of focusing on the function of such laughter in releasing *personal* tensions, De Sousa provocatively scrutinizes the *social* attitudes underlying it: "In contrast to the element of wit, the *phthonic* element in a joke requires *endorsement*. It does not allow of hypothetical laughter. The phthonic makes us laugh only insofar as the assumptions on which it is based are attitudes actually shared. Suspension of disbelief in the situation can and must be achieved for the purposes of the joke; suspension of attitudes cannot be" (Morreal 240). De Sousa elaborates: "We cannot come to find something funny by merely imagining that we share the phthonic assumptions" (Morreal 240). His categorical denial that one can willingly suspend one's tolerance, i.e., pose as a holder of ethnic or national prejudice "for the nonce" in order to relish a joke, is debatable, as Jacobson would doubtless be quick to object. Still, not everyone can engage with equanimity in chuckling Enoch Powell impersonation; many will balk at the idea of "performing" even as pro tem bigots.

In her book *Comedy: The Mastery of Discourse* (1992), the British theorist Susan Purdie focuses attention on how humour functions to confirm the abasement of targeted groups in society. She argues that "joking, precisely because it offers immediate individual psychic pleasure, is very likely to be at the service of entrenched social power" (126). "Carnival" – the sort of transgressive communal ritual that Bakhtin, and from his own standpoint Jacobson, see as empowering – has for Purdie "long-term effects" that are "constraining rather than liberating" (126), partly because it can act as a mechanism to channel and contain social unrest, diverting it from practical action. "Letting the pus run" may simply be an expedient designed to preserve the putrid status quo. According to Purdie's Foucaultian analysis, joking "always has unambiguous political effects which are produced on the back of its psychic operations" (125). These effects, for her, manifest themselves discursively. She reads joking as a claim to entitlement by those who enjoy "superior" social status, manifested by their "mastery of discourse": "[T]he capacity to joke is connected to possession of that 'proper' language which commands full subjectivity, for it is that full subjectivity which patriarchy consistently denies to women and, by extension, to its other abjected groups: blacks, gays, Jews, and so on. Such groups will simultaneously be denied the capacity to make jokes and also form the conventional targets of jokes" (128-9). Those configured as comic butts "are definitionally lower than, more discursively inept (often in specific ways) than, and above all *different from* Teller and Audience" (129). The latter pair profit from "the collusive discursive empowerment [at the expense of the butt] that shared joking creates" (130). While Purdie concedes that "[n]ot all joking involves conventional targets" (130), she maintains that the bulk of it does. Each society constructs its "'inept' speakers with particular 'weaknesses'"; in England, for example, Scots and Jews are identified as "mean" types who "'refuse the discourse of exchange'" (130).

Purdie's preoccupation with verbal empowerment and disempowerment leads her to downplay the role of extra-verbal, pre-existing power relations in society that might be analyzed in more purely structural terms. She maintains "that it is not any socioeconomic positioning which determines the constructions of groups as 'Irish-type' Butts, but rather that these Butts form a construct which joking demands: that of 'near neighbours' who are like 'us' in being able to use language (*per se*) but whose incompetence in the Symbolic Order reciprocally defines 'our' own power within it" (132). Even granting Purdie's point about the convenience of near neighbours as discursive whipping boys and girls, however, one might still ask whether the Irish boys' and girls' history of immiseration can possibly have played no part in making them whippable to start with. Purdie plausibly criticizes humanist "mythic" conceptions of comedy for exalting the enjoyment derived from comedy's release of vitalist energies while neglecting the power dynamic underlying such humour: "[I]t considerably dignifies the 'mere pleasure' which is the genre's most obvious effect, while evading the issues of sociological power entailed in its creation; if any adverse effects are noted, they can be dismissed as distinct from the universal benevolence of 'true comedy'" (165). I would demur that Purdie's narrowly linguistic view of power relations limits the scope of her own analysis of "adverse effects." Still, her original approach to comedy, though she focuses mainly on informal humour and comic drama, also has much explanatory value as applied to comic fiction.

Starting from premises akin to Purdie's but less single-mindedly discourse-oriented, James English's 1994 *Comic Transactions* applies social analysis to humour in a number of novelists, including Conrad, Woolf, and Wyndham Lewis. Although the writers he examines, with the exception of Salman Rushdie, will not be considered in the present study, English's general line of argument has a direct bearing on my own concerns. English asserts that "[h]umor and laughter have no politics" (17). By this he implies not (as some theorists maintain) that political issues are irrelevant to comedy, but rather that humour has "no automatic hegemonic or oppositional trajectory, no global connection with practices either of domination or subversion" (17). From this "social multiaccentuality" of humour it does not follow that the agendas of comedy are by nature politically neutral. Rather, "Comic practice is always on some level or in some measure an assertion of group against group, an effect and an event of struggle, a form of symbolic violence" (9). English later elaborates on, and qualifies, this somewhat melodramatic formulation: "Since comic transactions invariably draw upon hostilities and resentments of the most unreasoned character, and circulate these among participants in particularly treacherous, multiaccented ways, no joke is entirely innocent of cultural dirty work. And by the same token no joke is simply or wholly 'motivated by ... hatred' of a particular person or group" (230, ellipses in original). Although he coincides with Purdie in his view that humour carries out "cultural dirty work," where for Purdie the dirty work always has a precisely identifiable political bearing English sees the targets of jokes as by nature multiple and elusive: "[W]hile humor seeks to shore up identifications and solidarities, it does so by working on those very contradictions of 'society' which assure that all such identifications and solidarities will be provisional, negotiable, unsettled. If we could always pin down exactly what target group was represented by a particular figure or statement in a joke, exactly where the lines of identity and difference must be drawn, then jokes themselves would cease to exist" (10). Many instances of humour in the texts I will discuss bear out English's provocative thesis. To illustrate his point English himself cites a well-known Monty Python television sketch, "Hell's Grannies," which depicts "gangs of elderly women attacking respectable citizens, beating young men to the ground with their purses, riding their motorbikes through yarn shops, marking their turf with spray-painted slogans such as 'Make Tea Not Love'" (10). By analyzing the sketch English demonstrates that it aims at no single identifiable comic butt, tapping instead into a variety of imputed biases in the viewing audience. He concludes that "the skit's target is not any particular class of criminals (or victims) but the cultural apparatus by means of which criminal classes are constructed in the first place – and, by implication, the group of people (the documentary-watching bourgeoisie) who accept these mythological constructions as reality" (11).

English's reading of the sketch is deft, but he has carefully hand-picked his example to support his thesis concerning comic multiplicity. The Python troupe favoured humour based on arch self-consciousness and abrupt, giddy swerves of direction. Such a comic strategy can hardly be called universal, or even by and large representative. For that matter, many of the Pythons' own sketches are less open to multivalent readings than the "Hell's Grannies" model. One might cite the "Upperclass Twit of the Year" skit, a televised "sporting event" which pits a handful of pedigreed and moneyed imbeciles against one another, requiring them to negotiate a series of absurd or antisocial "challenges": walking along a straight line, shooting tethered rabbits at point-blank range, "Kicking the Beggar," and so on (*Flying Circus* I 156). Such a comedy routine seems natural to interpret from the middle-class perspective congenial to most of the Python performers (given their own origins) and to the probable majority of their audience. There is little room for teasing ambiguity in evaluating the antics of Vivian Smith-Smythe-Smith, Gervaise Brook-Hampster, and their hyphenated fellow twits. The British class system can certainly be called, to use English's term, a "mythological construction," but laughter in this instance is directed only secondarily at the habit of mythologizing and primarily at the all-too-identifiable, privileged beneficiaries of the myth. True, it is possible to locate other satiric targets, such as the inanity of television sports commentary, but these too are secondary; it is the presumed idiocy of the British privileged that is comically foregrounded.[5] The point of a joke may be multiple, but that does not automatically make it indeterminate.

Just as humour at times tends to reinforce social hegemony and at other times to subvert it, so there is no one sweeping principle that can define all humour as either multiaccentual or monologic. The diverse approaches to humour of theorists such as Bergson, Bakhtin, De Sousa, Purdie, and English are all potentially illuminating for my own project. In the chapters to follow I will draw eclectically on their thinking, rather than following single-mindedly the paradigms of one or another. My aim will be to examine heuristically the ideological climate of comedy in a variety of British fictional texts, without placing hermetic conceptual boundaries on my analysis of any of them.

In an age that has witnessed racial and national conflict of unparalleled virulence, laughter itself has sometimes functioned as a potent weapon. My hope is that this study will leave readers with a fuller sense of laughter's power, both to harm and to mend.

PART ONE

Punch Lines

1

Caliban and His Progeny

SHAKESPEARE'S *THE TEMPEST*: MOONCALF AND MAGUS

As a prelude to discussing the treatment of alterity in comic novels, I will first consider a famous earlier work: Shakespeare's *The Tempest.* The play features a famous Other: the "salvage[1] and deformed slave," Caliban, whose problematic relations with his European master, the magus Prospero, prefigure later sites of comedic contention. Beyond that, *The Tempest* strikingly anticipates a key feature of modern comic fiction by foregrounding the moral and psychic dimensions of laughter itself.

With its outlandish setting, its fantastic plot, and its self-consciousness regarding its own status as performance, *The Tempest* incorporates a wealth of material belonging to what Mikhail Bakhtin defined as the carnivalesque mode. The play opens with the carnival trope of "the world turned upside-down," a storm in which royal personages find themselves brusquely ordered about by low-born sailors. In the next scene Caliban, summoned by Prospero as "Thou earth, thou!" (I ii 316), introduces a related motif: the earthiness of the carnival tradition. According to Bakhtin, "Eating and drinking are one of the most significant manifestations of the grotesque body" (*Rabelais* 281). The grotesque Caliban at once strikes his voracious, bodily keynote, "I must eat my dinner" (*Tempest* I ii 332). And yet, defeating carnivalesque expectations, the play finally affirms the hierarchy it threatens initially to subvert. As Bakhtin observes in *The Dialogic Imagination*, "In a patriarchal social structure the ruling class does ... belong to the world of 'fathers'" (15). Prospero's opening speech, assuring his distraught child Miranda that he controls the tempest she thinks has doomed the ship and its passengers, establishes him at once in his dual role of wise father and patriarch commanding the human and the natural elements. The subsequent action decisively confirms his authority.

The Tempest's bearing on the early phases of colonialism has lately become a crux of critical debate. According to Meredith Anne Skura, "Insofar as *The Tempest* does in some way allude to an encounter with a New World native ... it is the very first work of literature to do so." Skura goes on to list other momentous "firsts": "Shakespeare was the first to show one of *us* mistreating a native, the first to represent a native from the inside, the first to allow a native to complain onstage, and the first to make the New World encounter problematic enough to generate the current attention to the play" (307). I would add one more first: *The Tempest* was likely the first literary work to exploit the encounter between Europeans and New World natives for comic purposes.

Traditional interpretations of *The Tempest* dating from the 1950s or earlier have been challenged by revisionist or postcolonial critiques, but they have by no means lost all currency. Frank Kermode, whose introduction to the Arden Edition of *The Tempest* is a well-known example of such readings, sees the antithesis between art and nature as central to the Caliban-Prospero relation. For Kermode, "Caliban is the core of the play" (xxiv) because he embodies raw, unmodified nature. Caliban "represents the natural man. This figure is not, as in pastoral generally, a virtuous shepherd, but a salvage and deformed slave" (xxxviii). Prospero "is ... the representative of Art, as Caliban is of Nature. As a mage he controls nature; as a prince he conquers the passions which had excluded him from his kingdom and overthrown law; as a scholar he repairs his loss of Eden; as a man he learns to temper his passions, an achievement essential to success in any of the other activities" (xlviii).

But not even Prospero's art, for Kermode, is potent enough to refashion Caliban, whose nature is averse to civilization. "Caliban's education was not only useless – on *his* nature, which is nature *tout court*, nurture would never stick – but harmful" (xlvi). Such alterity, by this account, is worlds away from normative conceptions of the human. Nevertheless, Kermode's reading is not reductively lopsided. "There are points in the play," he concedes, "at which Shakespeare uses Caliban to indicate how much baser the corruption of the civilized can be than the bestiality of the natural, and in these places he is using his natural man as a criterion of civilized corruption" (xxxviii).

Where Kermode's Arden introduction says little about Caliban as a comic figure, some recent readings make of the islander's clownishness a central issue, taking it as an index of Shakespeare's attitude toward the interaction between European colonizers and non-European Others.[2] Francis Barker and Peter Hulme, while rejecting Prospero as a trustworthy guide of the audience's judgment, see comedy as Shakespeare's device for shrinking the importance of Caliban's (and thus the colonial subject's) pretensions. They distinguish between "Prospero's play" – that is, his controlling design for all that happens on the island – and *The Tempest* as a dramatic construct independent of Prospero's will. Still, for them "*The Tempest* is ultimately complicit with Prospero's play in treating Caliban's conspiracy in the fully comic mode. Even before it begins, Caliban's attempt to put his political claims into practice is arrested by its implication in the convention of clownish vulgarity represented by the 'low-life' characters of Stephano and Trinculo … [T]he larger play [accedes] ... to the containment of the conspirators in the safely comic mode" (Graff 242).

Paul Brown similarly sees comedy, above all the humorous treatment of Caliban, as Shakespeare's mechanism for defusing threats to the colonialist project. The play refuses to validate Prospero's claim that Caliban is ineducable; the "discursive strategies" contained in his unrepentant replies to Prospero "show that Caliban has indeed mastered enough of the lessons of civility to ensure that its interpellation of him as simply savage ... is inadequate" (Graff 221). As Purdie might put it, Caliban proves himself a sufficiently competent speaker to thwart his positioning as a comic butt. Nevertheless, in Brown's view the alliance of the "masterless" Stephano and Trinculo with the "savage" Caliban results in a misrule that discredits the islander; it "provides an antitype of order, issuing in a revolt requiring chastisement *and ridicule*" (211, emphasis added). At the play's end, the "new solidarity" among the reformed aristocrats, finally reabsorbed into the conscientious governing class, is "underscored by their collective laughter at the chastened revolting plebians" (223). Deborah Willis, however, demonstrates that Brown's stress on the laughter attending Caliban's final entrance is misplaced: "The moment ... is more complex. We are probably drawn to laugh at Caliban – but uneasily. These remarks [by the aristocrats] recall the cynical, sneering humor Sebastian and Antonio have displayed in earlier scenes, reaffirming their sinister character and setting them apart from the 'good' aristocrats" (Graff 267). I will return later to Willis's point; an important one, because it implies that the laughter at Caliban's expense cannot be taken for granted as universal.

Willis herself sees the audience's laughter at Caliban as balanced precariously between contrary alternatives. Caliban is "a composite, possessing qualities of the 'noble savage' as well as the monster" (265). Consequently, "[t]he audience's response to Caliban is likely to have a similarly composite character" (265). "Caliban's credulousness in the scenes with Stephano and Trinculo ... evokes both sympathy and derision. We are invited to laugh at Caliban for his conversion to Stephano and his drunkenness, and yet as the mean-spiritedness of Stephano and Trinculo becomes more evident, Caliban's superiority becomes so as well" (265–6). The strength of Willis's position lies in her analysis of the audience's response as implicated in an ongoing *dramatic process*. For her, Brown's argument identifying Caliban as the menacing colonial Other needs "to take into account the fact that Caliban is not, to the audience, an embodiment of threat. Indeed, Caliban is by turns sympathetic and ridiculous; the play's racism inheres most clearly in its linking of Caliban's 'vile race' to a 'nature' that is conceived of as comically grotesque rather than demonic" (267).

And yet the line between the grotesque and the demonic (as Salman Rushdie has memorably shown) is seldom clear-cut. *Is* Caliban, after all, a threat? His revolt (in league with the drunken, oafish Neapolitans) is too floundering to seem truly dangerous. His own drunkenness casts doubt on Bakhtin's carnivalesque assurances – "Wine liberates from fear and sanctimoniousness" (*Rabelais* 286); his bawling celebration of liberty from patriarchal subjection – "Freedom, high-day! high-day, freedom!" (II ii 186) – only delivers him into a far worse bondage to bullying sots.

Caliban has in the past (by his own gloating avowal) attempted to ravish Miranda, and he contemplates the murder of Prospero with a jubilant gusto that, whatever his grievances, is hardly winning. He is not, like "Bully Bottom" and the other mechanics of *A Midsummer Night's Dream*, merely an affable, officious buffoon. His intermediate position is tersely summed up by Trinculo's quip: "That a monster should be such a natural!" (II ii 30). The paradox implies that Caliban is at once unnatural, a freak or sport, and a natural-born fool; at once strange and familiar. This in-betweenness will characterize a gallery of othered figures in novels to be discussed later: Evelyn Waugh's Emperor Seth, Joyce Cary's Mister Johnson, E.M. Forster's Doctor Aziz and Professor Godbole, and even Rushdie's Saladin Chamcha.

But what above all distinguishes *The Tempest* from other examples of early comedy is its persistence in making a moral issue of laughter itself.[3] Willis's point about Antonio and Sebastian's "cynical, sneering humour" has a direct bearing on that pair's attitudes toward experience, and by extension on other characters' attitudes as well. The wisecracking duo serve as cautionary exemplars, advertising the poverty of one type of laughter. Willis notes that Antonio's "cold, cynical humour" (262) matches his numbness to affection and renders him acidly unengaging. (His is the type of triumphalist wit De Sousa labels "phthonic.") For Willis, his counter-example controls our response to the play's protagonist: "Because Antonio functions so vividly as a threatening 'other,' Shakespeare can display Prospero's imperfections without seriously jeopardizing Prospero's claim to be a 'good master'" (263). Thus, by association, our revulsion from the sneeringly murderous Antonio also colours our response to the howlingly vindictive slave of the "good master," Caliban.

What makes both Antonio and Sebastian such telling foils for the grave Prospero is their callow joking, exemplified by their antiphonal jibes at the counsellor Gonzalo's rhapsody on the Golden Age:

Gon. Had I plantation of this isle, my lord –
Ant. He'd sow't with nettle-seed.
Seb. Or docks, or mallows.
Gon. And were the King on't, what would I do?
Seb. 'Scape being drunk for want of wine.
Gon. I' th' commonwealth I would by contraries
Execute all things ... (II i 139–43)

Gonzalo's famous vision (borrowed from Montaigne's "Of Cannibals") is a utopian fantasy far-fetched enough to provoke the audience to superior smiles. However, James English's postulate concerning the multivalency of humour applies to this exchange: the glib repartee of Antonio and Sebastian causes the two of them to sound more asinine than their butt. Because directed at an aged and well-intentioned fellow castaway, it strikes one not as clever but as shabbily uncouth. In the play's final scene, Prospero addresses the utopian dreamer as "Holy Gonzalo, honourable man" (V i 62); shortly thereafter, he touchingly celebrates their reunion: "Let me embrace thine age" (V i 121). Antonio's jeering at the expense of Gonzalo's honour and age is the precise, aversive antitype of Prospero's welcoming embrace.

In effect, Antonio and Sebastian are programmed to provide what might be called a deliberately botched laugh track, not stimulating but checking our amusement by arousing uneasy tremors. The pair themselves consider laughter so common an item that it serves as the currency of their supercilious gaming. They make bets on which of their fellow castaways, old Gonzalo or the young Adrian, will be next to speak:

Ant. Which, of he or Adrian, for a good wager, first begins to crow?
Seb. The old cock.
Ant. The cockerel.
Seb. Done. The wager?
Ant. A laughter.
Seb. A match!
Adr. Though this island seem to be desert, –
Ant. Ha, ha, ha!
Seb. So: you're paid. (II i 27–36)

The pair's jesting references to their companions as animals harmonize with their readiness to butcher them. In fact, their modus operandi enacts a seamless transition from cold-blooded mirth to cold-blooded murder; soon after their sneering duet, they are conspiring to kill Alonso and Gonzalo, a crime of regicide compounded in Sebastian's case by fratricide. There is an unlovely logic in this progression. Both of the bantering schemers lust for dominion, and malicious joking is only a lighthearted expression of that *wille zur macht*. To alter Purdie's terms, they are proceeding from the mastery of discourse to the mastery of death.

Sebastian laughs out loud once more, in act V when Caliban, along with the dishevelled Stephano and Trinculo, makes his final entrance and exclaims at the sight of Prospero and the other nobles dazzlingly arrayed:

Cal. O Setebos, these be brave spirits indeed!
How fine my master is! I am afraid
He will chastise me.
Seb. Ha, ha!
What things are these, my lord Antonio?
Will money buy 'em?
Ant. Very like; one of them
Is a plain fish, and, no doubt, marketable. (V i 261–6)

One of the pair is still laughing, and both reprise their familiar, derisive lexicon of animality and exchange. Sebastian's laughter reveals that, when others are awestruck or contrite, he clings to any remnant of overlordship he can muster, even if it is exercised only upon a bedraggled mooncalf. But since Caliban on his entrance unconsciously echoes Miranda's artless, moving exclamation – "O brave new world, / That has such people in't!" (v i 183–4) – our own laughter at Caliban's expense must indeed, as Willis maintains, be tempered.

Only one other character in the play expressly laughs aloud: Caliban himself. Caliban chortles – "O ho, O ho! Would't had been done!" (I ii 351) – over his thwarted rape of Miranda. Later, witnessing Stephano beat Trinculo, he laughs with juvenile *schadenfreude*: "Ha, ha, ha!" (III ii 80). Such mirth is hardly more attractive in Caliban than it is in Antonio or Sebastian, though it is so unpremeditated and witless as to be itself comical. It has the paradoxical effect of linking in our minds the raw spawn of nature with the pair of sniggering worldly plotters.

The confederacy of Caliban with the ostensibly "civilized" Europeans, Stephano and Trinculo, enacts a different comic nexus of ethnicity and class. To the play's first, courtly audience, members of the servant order released from their normal due deference might have seemed nearly as outlandish as Shakespeare's monstrous islander. But of course Caliban, even in his fit of murderous greed, retains more shreds of sense than his drunken Neapolitan confederates, and he proves in the end a better learner. And, morosely gleeful as he may be, he garners more sympathy from the audience than do the jeering, homicidal nobles.

There is probably no way to reach a critical consensus about how far Caliban is estranged by Shakespeare's humorous treatment, and conversely how far our laughter itself domesticates him. For Willis, "Ultimately, the play trivializes Caliban's plight" (268). But placing Caliban once and for all as either trivialized or redeemed by the text's humour is a dubious move. Meredith Anne Skura, reluctant to accept the islander as simply an object of burlesque, argues that "[w]hen Prospero finally acknowledges Caliban, although he is a long way from recognizing the equality of racial 'others,' he comes closer than any of Shakespeare's other 'Prosperos' to acknowledging the otherness within, which helps generate all racism – and he comes closer than anyone else in colonialist discourse" (Graff 317–18). Prospero's famous grudging claim to ownership of the mooncalf, "[T]his thing of darkness I / Acknowledge mine" (v i 275–6), to which Skura refers, reinforces her point.

Nonetheless, Prospero's final line in act v, marking the end of his *psychological* exile, his inveterate distance from his fellows – "Please you, draw near" (v i 318) – implicitly excludes Caliban, whom he tersely dismisses ("Go to; away!" (v i 297)). Bakhtin found in Shakespeare, as in

Rabelais, an "essential carnival element"; a "belief in the possibility of a complete exit from the present order of this life" that "determines [his] fearless, sober (yet not cynical) realism and absence of dogmatism" (*Rabelais* 275). *The Tempest* is admirably free from dogmatism, yet it hardly enacts "a complete exit from the present order of this life." Prospero is compelled to exit the established order, but at length he returns to it, having by his signal powers achieved a reordering that affirms and renews the system's constitutive, hierarchical laws of rule and subordination.

In some respects, *The Tempest* subverts dichotomies accepted in its own and later times, the Eurocentric set of distinctions that Abdul JanMohamed calls the "manichean allegory of white and black, good and evil, salvation and damnation, civilization and savagery, superiority and inferiority, intelligence and emotion, self and other, subject and object" (*Manichean Aesthetics* 4). The bland assumption of European superiority, at least, is inventively challenged by Shakespeare's play. As Frank Kermode years ago conceded, Shakespeare's text troubles absolute divisions between the "civilized" and the "savage": "[I]f the natural man is a brute, so much the more terrible is the sin of the nobleman who abases himself below the natural" (liv). If Prospero calls Caliban "A devil, a born devil" (IV i 188), he addresses the party of stranded Italian nobles in a rueful aside: "[S]ome of you there present / Are worse than devils" (III iii 35–6). The advantage, however slim, would seem to rest with the infernal islander. Yet an antinomy not named by JanMohamed – that between artifice and artlessness – is left at bottom undisturbed, if by "artifice" one means not the machinations of the conniving nobles but the marvelous illusionism of a Prospero. Shakespeare, the supreme master of illusion, was perhaps loath to deconstruct the scaffolding of his own artistry; centuries would pass before such self-scrutiny would find its way into European comic imaginings.

COMIC NARRATIVES: LAUGHING STOCKS AND RIEURS

In more modern forms of comedy, a character's "deviancy" from a hypostatized norm regularly provides the mainspring for laughter. While comic novels seldom feature intractable mooncalves, they can display their own fantastic, lunar mutations of human personality. It is the singularity of their makeup, their rare assemblage of personal quirks, that makes such figures funny. The earliest and perhaps greatest of such originals, Cervantes's Don Quixote, conforms to no long-recognizable human type. Yet even the comic "sport" is seldom quite unique. For all his eccentricity, Quixote has fathered a class of quixotic fictional descendants, figures whose extravagant gallantry transgresses the bounds of sanity. Even that strange fish, Caliban, belongs among those who are comic not because of their utter uniqueness but by virtue of their *membership in a comic set*: in his instance the class of outlanders who in mind or body defy European expectations. Although Caliban gains a modicum of self-knowledge by the end of *The Tempest*, for the most part comic *types* have scant leeway ever to achieve seriousness. Bottom the weaver gets magically translated, but his ass's head only renders startlingly visible his untranslatable core of personality.

In narratives of later periods, membership in a disesteemed social group is often a badge of laughability. Nineteenth-century novels most commonly single out working-class types as legitimate comic targets. Even though agricultural and industrial workers formed a numerical majority, they could be construed as Other owing to their removal from the normative "centre": the class of novel readers, presumed to be bourgeois and (by definition) literate. As early as the eighteenth century, however, enrolment in national or racial groups rivalled social class as a source of comic typologies. Being French, as numberless instances attest, confers upon a character both a stigma of untrustworthiness and a passport to risibility. In Fanny Burney's *Evelina* the heroine's scheming French grandmother, Madame Duval, provides an object of easy ridicule throughout the narrative, above all for the heroine's patron, Captain Mirvan, a sadistic xenophobe and incorrigible prankster. An analogous figure from Victorian fiction is the Belgian busybody, Madame Beck, in Charlotte Bronte's *Villette*, headmistress of the school where the heroine, Lucy Snowe, finds employment. Here again, though the foreigner is sharply individualized, her absurdities derive from her membership in a class: that of outwardly observant but "unscrupulous" Roman Catholic Continental females.

Bronte's admired contemporary, Thackeray, was especially given to using alien trespassers on English soil for comic advantage. As his prime targets he favoured the Irish, causing such types as the O'Dowds in *Vanity Fair* and Captain Costigan in *Pendennis* to speak in the broadest of stage brogues, replete with solecisms. Since serious tensions had marred Thackeray's relations with his own Irish in-laws, such caricaturing may have afforded him a gratifying outlet for entrenched grievances, but its main function was to divert Anglo-Saxon "masters of discourse" with an amusing gallery of non-English "defective speakers."

Comic Irishmen and Scotsmen were by Thackeray's day no novelty. Where Thackeray showed a greater, if more distasteful, originality was in his strategic deployment of a non-white character for his satirical ends in *Vanity Fair*. Whereas his ridicule of his brogue-spouters tends to be fairly mild, his portrayal of Amelia Sedley's devoted friend, Rhoda Swartz, is not. The girl, a West Indian heiress, represents a racial portmanteau; as her name suggests, she is of mixed Jewish and black ("swarthy") African ancestry, and thus provides a neatly telescoped comic target. Swartz herself is neither ill-natured nor dishonest; she is, instead, witless and (as Thackeray's own illustrations, with their bulbous "negroid" features, proclaim) grotesquely homely. She is also a painfully inept speaker; one of the few songs she can perform is something she calls *"Fluvy du Tajy"* (255) (properly *"Fleuve du Tage"*), and her English is not noticeably more polished than her fractured French. (Musical proficiency was itself of course a Victorian *sine qua non* of "proper" English femininity.) The satiric point of the portrait is that Swartz, of all girls, solely because of her fortune, is selected by the social-climbing Mr Osborne as the ideal match for his son George, who is in love with the penniless but snow-white Amelia. Thackeray's caustic satire here is aimed at a materialistic social ethos (typified by Osborne Senior's vulgar "climbing"), which crudely privileges raw wealth, however "tainted," over refinement and beauty, the qualities in which Amelia excels. The contrast between George's white swan and her black ugly-duckling rival is registered in George's perceptions of Rhoda on a visit: "Poor Swartz was seated in a place where Emmy [Amelia] had been accustomed to sit. Her bejewelled hands lay sprawling in her amber satin lap. Her tags and ear-rings twinkled, and her big eyes rolled about. She was doing nothing with perfect contentment, and thinking herself charming. Anything so becoming as the satin [George's sycophantic] sisters had never seen" (255). Thackeray's exposé of his society's shallow snobbery focuses, paradoxically, on that snobbery's *levelling* bias, its readiness to overlook Rhoda Swartz's visible alterity, produced by Thackeray as deformity, on the grounds of her fortune, instead of "properly" spurning the girl with cold indifference, or perhaps even with derision matching the author's. The novel's strategy, perverse as it may now seem, works by exploiting its English audience's ingrained racial bias in order to chastise English society's fawning adulation of wealth.[4]

By the early twentieth century, comic treatment of non-white "aliens" was routine in English fiction. Examples crop up even in literature for children, such as Hugh Lofting's immensely popular Dolittle series. In the first volume, *The Story of Doctor Dolittle* (1920), we meet the African prince, Bumpo, a black romantic whose outlook has been addled by his addiction to fairy tales. Bumpo implores the doctor to use his special powers to turn him white; he claims to have chanced upon Sleeping Beauty and to have awakened her with the requisite kiss, only to be spurned on account of his skin colour; "'But you *must* turn this coon white,'" Polynesia the parrot beseeches the doctor (100). Dolittle obligingly contrives to give the young man's face, at least, the desired pallor by applying to it an occult preparation; even Bumpo's formerly "mud-coloured" eyes now turn a "manly gray" (103). As his name suggests, Bumpo is portrayed as a clownish black bumpkin, though the ridicule is bland enough – "'Still, he has a good heart,'" the doctor declares (106) – and though the prince later becomes a trusted aide-de-camp of the doctor in his further adventures, a tractable African Caliban serving the marvelously multitongued white master of discourse.

An earlier and even more widely popular tale for younger children, Helen Bannerman's "classic" *Little Black Sambo* (1899), has in recent years undergone a status shift from canonical to vexed. The book, as everyone knows, is a comic fantasy in which a small boy, Sambo, son of Black Mumbo and Black Jumbo, outwits a pair of ravenous tigers by using articles of his fine new clothing as decoys. Bannerman, who wrote the story to amuse her young daughters when the family was stationed in India, clearly had no conscious intention of denigrating Sambo and company on the grounds of their race. Unlike the *Punch* humorists to be surveyed in the next chapter, she did not expose the black characters to sniggering contempt; instead, she made her little protagonist a feisty and resourceful miniature hero. (Some modern, bowdlerized versions have in fact been retitled "Little *Brave* Sambo.") However, features such as the jocose names and the "golliwog" original illustrations by the author herself have in our time brought *Sambo* into disrepute, even provoking calls for its exclusion from public libraries. Not surprisingly, black North Americans have found it particularly offensive; although the action is apparently set in India, names like Sambo, Mumbo, and Jumbo sound mock-African. (Widely travelled as she was, Bannerman had no compunction about conflating the two "dark continents," a confusion unlikely to trouble the majority of British readers, for whom darkies were simply darkies.) In Carol Talbot's *Growing Up Black in Canada*, the author recalls the unsettling effect reading *Sambo* had on her as a child: "I also remember that I used to often finish my work early and that we could get a book to read when this happened. I really liked the 'Little Black Sambo' book – that stack of pancakes dripping with butter and syrup looked so good – but I did not often indulge in its delights because I didn't want anyone to identify *me* with that thick-lipped, big-eyed, nappy-headed 'jungle' boy. In fact, I didn't even want to take brown bread sandwiches to school, out of fear of the inferences that might be made" (14). Talbot's reminiscence pinpoints the divided response the tale, which combines beguiling charm with crude stereotyping, is apt to elicit.

What is especially revealing about both Bannerman's story and Lofting's is the ease with which non-whites lent themselves to patronizing humorous caricature, even on the part of authors who meant only to provide genial entertainment for young readers. Ronald Firbank's adult but equally fanciful novella of 1924, *Sorrow in Sunlight*, alternately entitled *Prancing Nigger*, can similarly be absolved of malign intent; yet it insistently portrays its principal characters, the Mouth family, as a set of "nigger minstrel" buffoons. Firbank was an influence on Evelyn Waugh's early comic fiction, and there are affinities between the humour of *Sorrow in Sunlight* and that of Waugh's *Black Mischief*. Mrs Mouth, the pretentious, overbearing mother (gender reversal contributes to Firbank's raced humour) insists on moving her family from their home in a rural backwater to the big city. In this town, suggestively named Cuna-Cuna (its population is mostly black), they are exposed to the delights and snares of modern life. They are especially enchanted with the up-to-date plumbing facilities; the name "Mouth" is a metonymy connoting Caliban-like voracity at the expense of other faculties, and their cloacal fixation matches their eagerness for ingestion. (As Richard Dyer observes, white perceptions tend regularly to reduce non-whites to their bodies and bodily functions.) Mother and Father Mouth clash over the wisdom of their decision to abandon the rural simplicities of their old home, Mediavilla (a pun on "medieval") for the sophisticated allure of modernity: "'It's a misfortnit we eber left Mediavilla,' [Mr Mouth] exclaimed uneasily, as a falling star, known as a thief star, sped swiftly down the sky. 'Prancing Nigger,' Mrs Mouth rose, remarking, 'befo' you start to grummle, I leab you alone to your Jereymiads!'" (114). Brigid Brophy has claimed that "[t]he idiom of *Prancing Nigger* is enriched by ... piccaninny English" (555). "Enriched" seems a curious choice of words, since such dialect tends to place its users as clownish "inferior speakers," depleting the sympathetic interest we are likely to take in them.

Still, despite their "piccaninny" pidgin, the Mouths' story has a serious subtext. Firbank's image of the falling star, or "thief star," obliquely reflects on the family's fall from arcadian innocence into the worldly materialism of modern life, which robs them of their Mouth family values. The blackface humour on the one hand appeals to the tastes of the normally bigoted

English reader of the 1920s, always ready to laugh at the antics of "coons"; but on the other it serves as a comic mask screening from plain view the tale's allegorical import, thus avoiding any impression of the straight-faced moralizing that Firbank shunned. Firbank's story is more than an exercise in stock racial joking; but through its use of blackface humour as a vehicle it risks being dismissed as merely that by contemporary readers. Firbank, as a believing Roman Catholic, may mean to imply that we, like the Mouths, are all Calibans, all things of darkness; but his jocose use of literal negritude as a trope for that darkness has by now come to seem dated and tasteless rather than provocative.

Thing of darkness or not, Caliban is a figure who dwells in the limelight; he may be a buffoon, but he is a buffoon with lines to deliver. In English novels before the twentieth century, one finds few racially othered characters playing prominent roles, and even those who come to mind (such as Friday in Defoe's *Robinson Crusoe*) are seldom given substantial treatment of either a comic or serious sort. Only in modern British fiction does the paradigm of the all-white cast get forcibly ruptured; but the Calibans who now begin to infiltrate the scene, like the Congolese natives in Joseph Conrad's *Heart of Darkness*, tend to be relegated to the margins, and are seldom granted as much subjectivity even as Firbank's Mouths. Those exceptional non-whites, like the Mouths, who do occupy more central positions are typically assigned jocose capers to cut.

In Anthony Powell's early comic novels, "exotic" characters, especially Jews and negroes, are positioned on the fringes of the narrative, but have a strong symbolic relevance to those at the centre. The born-yesterday protagonist of *Agents and Patients* (1936), Blore-Smith, boasts an impeccably Anglo-Saxon name and lineage, but he is introduced as "slightly Jewish-looking" (6), a sly hint that he may be susceptible to deflection onto marginal paths. The deflectors soon materialize in the guise of two outrageous, adept confidence men, Chipchase and Maltravers, who fleece Blore-Smith while introducing him to the denizens of a decadent London and Continental demimonde. These include German Jews involved with the burgeoning film industry, among them a certain Herr Roth, vaunted by Maltravers as "'[t]he greatest film-producer in Germany'" (127). As perhaps befits a demimondaine – a "half-worlder" – Roth is of dwarfish stature: "an elderly man about four feet high who wore dark glasses and whose right arm ended in a hook" (126). Powell insistently links racial difference with deformity and stunted growth.

In a prior chapter, Blore-Smith is inveigled into a seedy Paris nightclub, where he is left alone at a table with a negro "who grinned at him and showed his teeth in an alarming manner": "Blore-Smith watched the negro drink a glass or two more of champagne, give a series of contortions with his hips and shoulders as if he were about to have a fit, and then jump up from his chair. For a moment the negro looked wildly around him and then, jerking his elbows and knees violently this way and that, he crossed the floor and was soon dancing with a tiny Jewish blonde" (88). Here again, the murky moral underworld into which Blore-Smith has been lured is adumbrated in the form of racial "outcasts" promiscuously jumbled together. Once more turpitude is symbolized by bodily disfunction (the negro's jerky motions), stunted stature (the tiny Jewish woman), and ethnic dissonance (the Jewish woman's blondness, her fraternizing with a black). What by the end of the century would be perceived as unremarkable racial intermingling registers, in the 1930s, as laughably outré incongruity.

The motif of cosmopolitanism-gone-awry culminates later in a London Chinese restaurant, the Ning-Po, "a dark L-shaped room, full of Asiatic students sitting two or three together, talking and arguing" (173). The clientele also includes two negroes, who are sitting at a table with two (once again) blond girls. A quarrel suddenly erupts between the black men and a member of Blore-Smith's party, the Marquis de la Tour d'Espagne; the Marquis, who has arrived late and inebriated, accuses the negroes of staring at him. Shouting that he "'won't be looked at like that by a black man'" (177), he challenges one of the offending pair to a duel: "Both negroes now stood shoulder-to-shoulder and jabbered in unison. The other blonde began to powder her nose. The owner of the restaurant, a small Chinese, almost a dwarf, had now joined the combatants" (178). The scene's farcical tenor derives from its mingling of absurd, vinous Gallic punctiliousness with African "tribalism" (the two negroes "jabbering" as one), compounded with "oriental" dwarfishness. The tableau vividly signals Blore-Smith's by now near-terminal fall from proper if humdrum British rectitude into a nether world of "foreign" depravity. After the uproar, even the roguishly adaptable Chipchase avers, "'Personally I don't want a Chinese meal much after all this'" (179). The tang of the exotic has turned sour.

Conversely, in the earlier *From a View to a Death* (1933), the protagonist, Arthur Zouch, makes a comically abortive attempt to climb from his usual bohemian milieu into a realm of upper-class British gentility. Zouch, an aspiring painter of less than modest talents, hopes to enter the ranks of the landed gentry by marrying into a well-connected rural family, the Passengers. Although Zouch himself is reputably English, his odd surname stirs tremors of latent foreignness; he is a whoreson zed, an unnecessary last letter. During his stay with the Passengers the tremors are comically intensified by the sudden arrival of his old friend from the city, a raffish, small-time journalist named Fischbein, along with Fischbein's (once again) dwarfish girlfriend. The pair are indulging in the currently faddish hobby of hiking, a fact that strikes the baffled Mr Passenger as impenetrably alien: "'Hikers?' said Mr. Passenger. '*Hikaz*?' The word was evidently unfamiliar to him and he pronounced it as if it belonged to some oriental language" (102). More damaging still, Fischbein himself is made to seem an "oriental" irruption into the bucolic English scene, owing both to his Jewish name and to his sallow, ungentrified appearance: "Fischbein stood in front of Zouch with his hands on his hips. He had a grey face, full of folds and swellings of loose flesh, like a piece of bad realistic sculpture" (103). Through his technique of humorous racial innuendo, Powell turns Fischbein, the hiking Jew, into a harbinger of Zouch's unfitness for the exalted life of the genteel English country house, an unfitness confirmed by the novel's tragicomic dénouement in which Zouch, an inexpert rider, is killed by being thrown from the skittish mount he has been maliciously assigned by his host. If one wishes to qualify as a Passenger, one needs to know how to ride.

Even in more recent fiction, racially "exotic" characters may still be drawn on to provide local amusement. Malcolm Bradbury's academic novel *Eating People Is Wrong* (1959) features an African chieftain attending college in England, Mr Eborebelosa, who is smitten with Emma Fielding, an attractive student, and proposes to make her his fifth wife. When Emma, frantic to discourage him, invents a fictitious fiancé for herself, Eborebelosa gallantly promises to kill his rival. The impasse occasions some facetious dialogue concerning ways in which the tactful Emma might avoid making her rejection of her unwanted suitor seem a racist snub. Bradbury's treatment of trendy anxiety over managing "politically correct" behaviour toward a coloured visitor can at times be archly witty, but it still is founded on a stereotype of Africans as uncouth, polygamous (and even, by implication, cannibalistic) primitives. In Bradbury's later novel *The History Man* (1975) a minor figure, a secretary of East Asian origin, is given the name Miss Minnehaha Ho. The name punningly encodes the presumed laughability of foreignness *per se*. Little wonder if Bradbury commends the fiction of Evelyn Waugh for its boldness in breaching the invidious restraints of "correctness."

The comic positioning of non-whites in British novels, illustrated by texts like Powell's and Bradbury's, raises formal issues of narrative strategy. If humour entails, as Purdie argues, the mastery of discourse, the art of comic fiction hinges on the mastery of laughter, and the two types of mastery are interlinked. A whole repertory of discursive practices helps novelists govern the reader's sense of what is to be laughed at and what is not.

In comic narratives, focalization, the standpoint from which the action is perceived, has much to do with the production of humour. Stage plays seldom draw on such focalizing strategies for the obvious reason that, with rare exceptions, they lack narrators. At most, the spectator may experience an intermittent identification with the perspective of a play's protagonist. The soliloquizing Hamlet is one example of this, and Prospero is another, especially since he does briefly, in *The Tempest*'s opening act, assume the role of diegetic unfolder of past happenings. Usually, however, the spectator's perceptions of events on stage are immediate, rather than mediated by a voice identified with either the author or a character.

By contrast, such mediation tends, in prose narrative, to determine comic delivery. This is one reason why screen versions of comic novels, normally narratorless, often come across as puzzlingly less funny than the printed text. Because humour in such works (as Bergson would insist) generally involves some measure of distance or detachment from the fictional agents and patients, the teller's specific tone and angle of vision have a powerful impact on what we find laughably Other. To take a familiar example: the apparent deadpan detachment of Muriel Spark's narrator in *Memento Mori*, moving fluently from one centre of consciousness to another among her crotchety gallery of octogenarians, radically distances the characters and their tangled intrigues, rendering them inescapably comic by partially stymying the sympathy we might ordinarily extend to the elderly and by stressing their "difference." (Spark's originality resides in the way she complicates and qualifies this othering as the narrative proceeds.) A more equivocal state of affairs obtains in Kingsley Amis's *Lucky Jim*, where the third-person narration locates the reader almost entirely within the consciousness of the protagonist, the scapegrace fledgling academic Jim Dixon. While Dixon is patently a comic figure, this intimate ensconcing of the narrative angle of vision ensures that our laughter at him mostly remains cosily complicit rather than aloof. Such bonding also commonly occurs with first-person narrators, especially in those instances where the teller doubles as protagonist.

A key fact for the study of race-centred comedy is the routine blocking in British fiction of all but "white" perspectives. The issue naturally remains buried in the myriad texts from which racial minorities are simply absent; it emerges baldly, however, in a book like Evelyn Waugh's *Black Mischief*, which hinges on interactions between white Europeans and black Africans. There, after briefly visiting the viewpoint of the beleaguered Azanian Emperor Seth, the centre of consciousness shifts to the white English interloper Basil Seal, who in effect absconds with the reader's investment of interest. The action of Joyce Cary's African novels, even those foregrounding a black native figure like Mister Johnson, similarly unfolds largely through the eyes of white onlookers. The effect is to objectify and estrange the non-whites, making them either menacing or (as with Johnson and Seth) quaintly funny. When, in more recent fiction, non-white characters begin to infiltrate domestic English locales, they are often similarly placed at arm's length. In Amis's *Girl, 20* (1971), the temporizing white first-person narrator, Douglas Yandell, eventually loses his girlfriend to his more purposeful black rival, Gilbert Alexander. Yet Yandell throughout channels the reader's perceptions in a way that invites complicity; Gilbert remains peripheral, eliciting a few snickers because of his prickliness about issues of race. Such a formal marginalizing of non-white perspectives is so routine a feature of twentieth-century British comic fiction as to pass almost unnoticed.

According to Henri Bergson, "Laughter appears to stand in need of an echo" (64). What controls the comic elements in fictional texts is not only whose eyes we are made to look through but whose laughter we are meant to duplicate. In comic novels, humour itself often tends to become thematized, as we have seen happens in *The Tempest*. Just as the raisonneur figure in classic French theatre is assigned the task of guiding the judgments the audience is to make, so in comic fiction certain characters may act as humorous prompters, intimating to us by commentary or example what is fit to be laughed at. Such figures are often masters of discourse; they are invariably masters of mirth. By analogy with the French raisonneur I will call these fictional role models of hilarity *rieurs*. A well-known example is Amis's Dixon. Our normally indulgent amusement at Jim's antics encourages us to feel leagued with him, making us all the more apt to laugh, not indulgently but snidely, at those Jim himself deems ridiculous or obnoxious. The romantic plot of Amis's novel turns, indeed, on the issue of laughter; a *rapprochement* between Dixon and the pretty but initially off-putting Christine Callaghan begins when the two laugh in unison at the havoc Jim has inflicted, while drunk, on his bedroom in the house of their stuffy host, Professor Welch (chapter 6).

Contra Bergson's belief that comic laughter enforces the moral sense of the social majority,[5] a fictional rieur can sometimes act as an independent agent subverting communitarian pieties. Such a rieur – or rieuse – is

Alvina Houghton, heroine of D.H. Lawrence's 1920 novel *The Lost Girl.* Alvina's great task is to escape from the "unchangeable grubby gloom" of Manchester House (143), her family home in the English Midlands; and what above all enables her to defeat that gloom is her progressive acquisition of the capacity to laugh. Throughout Lawrence's narrative, laughter is insistently linked with sensuality, and both of these with the element of encroaching foreignness. The nexus is made manifest in Alvina's thrill of hilarity at the antics of a Swiss travelling player, Louis: "Helpless, inert she lay, in her orgasm of laughter" (147). But it is embodied above all by Alvina's Italian lover, Louis's colleague Ciccio, whose radically instinctual nature prompts even his manageress, Madame Rochard, to describe him in language echoing Prospero's denunciation of Caliban: "'[T]he animal, he wasn't worth all my pains'" (147).[6] Alvina's release into laughter culminates after her father's death, when she engages in boisterous revelry with Ciccio and the other members of the foreign theatrical troupe: "They shouted, positively shouted over their cards, they roared with excitement, expostulation, and laughter" (225). The outrage of Alvina's old duenna, Miss Pinnegar – "'You lost girl!' said Miss Pinnegar, backing out and closing the door" (225) – only spurs the mirth to a tumultuous climax. Alvina's "lostness," betokened equally by her loss of virginity and her boundless laughter, in fact signals her achieved liberation from the emotional bondage in which she has been held by her Midlands community, with its unsmiling Pinnegaresque proprieties.

If Lawrence's Alvina comes to feel "glad to be an outcast" (215), the same cannot be said for Arthur Seaton, the youthful, uninhibited rieur of a later novel also set in the Midlands, Alan Sillitoe's *Saturday Night and Sunday Morning* (1958). Much as he may transgress the prohibitions of his community, cuckolding his closest friend and overturning the occasional small car, Arthur is at bottom comfortably at home there. The novel opens with Arthur's buoyant laughter, even at himself, as he tumbles, intoxicated (an occupational hazard of comic leading men), down a stairway in a pub: "He was laughing to himself as he rolled down the stairs, at the dull bumping going on behind his head and along his spine, as if it were happening miles away, like a vibration on another part of the earth's surface, and he an earthquake-machine on which it was faintly recorded" (6). As the action proceeds, Arthur's sensibility keeps picking up other seismic vibrations that set off his "horse laugh": tremors of social propriety and prudishness defined by this narrative, like Lawrence's, as life-denying. The laugh is Arthur's war cry in his campaign against such restraints, and it proves infectious for the reader.

Arthur is an exceptional rieur by virtue of his working-class status; his laughter genuinely belongs to that popular, transgressive species identified by Bakhtin with carnival and the "grotesque body." At the same time, however, Arthur is normative by virtue of being white. Late in Sillitoe's novel a black African character is introduced, a young visitor to the Midlands named Sam; but Sam is, revealingly, the recipient of laughter rather than its originator. He is the object of bluff joking by the white working-class family that takes him in: "Sitting down to breakfast Bert joked about Sam: 'Hey, man, there's a Zulu in my room'" (214). The humour directed at him is in no sense unwelcoming; rather, he is companionably included in the uproarious festive atmosphere prevailing at the family's Christmas gathering: "'Do you know "Everybody likes Saturday Night" Sam?' Bert shouted from the table, and Sam beamed with happiness at the universal sympathy around him" (213). However, while the young man's consciousness is fleetingly visited to transmit his heartening sense of inclusion, he is kept in a subaltern position that contrasts tellingly with the predominance of Arthur, the alpha rieur.

Fictive rieurs do not invariably perform, however, as unerring touchstones of the laughable. As Patricia Meyer Spacks has convincingly shown, laughter in Jane Austen's novels can serve variously either as a "moral guide" or as an "index of moral failure" (Barreca *Last Laughs* 71). According to Spacks, while in *Pride and Prejudice* the narrator invites us to identify ourselves with Elizabeth Bennet's laughter and even with that of her more acerbic father, attentive reading reveals the amusement of both father and daughter as sometimes misplaced. As Spacks demonstrates, Elizabeth learns through her experiences a "new way of laughter" (74) that betokens the deeper, more mature interpersonal perceptiveness she has gained.

In other English comic novels, what Spacks calls "immediately unattractive kinds of laughter" (73) are often more promptly self-invalidating. Along with rieurs one finds anti-rieurs, characters who, like Antonio and Sebastian in *The Tempest*, by their own ungracious hilarity chill the audience's impulse to laugh instead of whetting it. In *Evelina* the heroine's Holborn cousin, Tom Branghton, proclaims himself a "shoppy" cad by nothing so much as his indiscriminate outbursts of mirth. These complement a repellent coarseness in family relations; when Tom's sisters are justly rebuked by their father for their bad behaviour, "they replied with the utmost pertness and rudeness, while their brother, all the time, laughed aloud" (174). At the suggestion that an indigent young Scotsman may have fallen in love with Evelina, Tom reacts with his typical impropriety:

"'Ha, ha ha! Lord, how I should laugh,' said the son, 'if he should have fell in love with Miss!'" (186). The young man's laughter is as embarrassing a solecism as his grammar. In Burney's fictional world, ruled by the gods of eighteenth-century gentility, the moral quality of humour is inseparable from issues of social class.

Laughter and class stand in a different relation in the work of Burney's older contemporary Henry Fielding, a novelist less awed by his century's codes of propriety. The character of paramount interest in *Joseph Andrews*, Parson Adams, is presented by Fielding as, to all appearances, a ludicrous eccentric. To quote only part of a lengthy description: "It is perhaps not easy to describe the figure of Adams; he had risen in such a violent hurry, that he had on neither breeches nor stockings; nor had he taken from his head a red spotted handkerchief, which by night bound his wig, that was turned inside out, around his head. He had on his torn cassock, and his great-coat; but as the remainder of his cassock hung down below his great-coat, so did a small strip of white, or rather whitish linnen appear below that" (255). If the reader is inclined to smile at the rag-tag old parson, the local grandee, Lady Booby, finds cause for limitless hilarity in the spectacle presented by him and his threadbare brood. Approaching his house, she tells her well-bred companions that "if they pleased she would divert them with one of the most ridiculous sights they had ever seen, which was an old foolish parson who, she said laughing, kept a wife and six brats on a salary of about twenty pounds a year; adding, that there was not such another ragged family in the parish" (293). We are taken aback by the pampered aristocrat's amusement on the score of a clergyman's poverty; our own earlier smiles at Adams's odd appearance are placed in chastening perspective by her callow mirth. We are prompted to recollect that the "old foolish parson," risible as he may at times outwardly seem, has repeatedly proved himself a paragon of Christian wisdom and generosity. One of Lady Booby's key functions in *Joseph Andrews* is to serve as a corrective anti-rieur, reminding us of what is *not* a fit occasion for laughter.[7]

If some fictional characters are constructed as licentious laughers, however, others are bereft of laughter altogether. As Purdie maintains (128–9), the entitlement to make jokes is conventionally withheld from certain target groups. Women have been historically among the foremost of these; as Regina Barreca claims, "There is a long tradition behind the idea of laughter as dangerous, and this condemnation is compounded by the fact that what is dangerous or outrageous for a man is considered even worse in a woman" (*They Used to Call Me Snow White* 47). Barreca adds, "We were taught that only Bad Girls initiated humor" (*Snow White* 50). Non-whites, like women, have been denied the faculty of humour, and in the pages of novels are even more rarely allowed to initiate it. Figures like Thackeray's Rhoda Swartz are constructed as the butts rather than the originators of comedy; until recent times, black rieurs have been a near-invisible species.

If the laughter of non-white characters has been curtailed, so too has their scope for speech. Dialogue assumes an obvious importance in comedy based on nationality and ethnicity. In general, to quote Purdie, "[w]hen it involves actual targets, joking constructs these as *not* fully members of the community of proper speakers, and this involves complex and often strong feelings towards them. The resulting abjection of actual targets in joking forms its most conspicuous and usually debated 'political' effect" (58). Such an effect regularly occurs with speakers of "deviant" dialects, most often Scottish and Irish, in eighteenth- and nineteenth-century novels. In twentieth-century works by writers like Firbank, Waugh, and Cary, the device is applied even more condescendingly to "exotic" variants of English like African pidgins. The imputed aphasia of "primitives" lurks behind the mangled English of numerous *Punch* cartoon captions involving Indians and Africans, as it does behind the speech of caricatured outlanders, like Firbank's Mouths, in period works of comic fiction.

The British reading public of the 1920s and 30s was, however, living in a historical climate that was already starting to make such supercilious treatments of alterity look embarrassingly dated. Over comic narratives of this period, the shadow of the British Empire's dissolution increasingly looms. "During Kipling's lifetime," according to Martin Green, "the modern system crossed the great divide of 1914–1918, after which everyone assumed that the British empire was dying, and everyone in serious literature was openly hostile to it" (*Dreams* 264). While Green's "everyone" is hyperbolic, what he calls "the anxiety of possession" (234) was certainly becoming widely diffused among thoughtful British writers and readers. English notes that, by as early as 1907, "what the modernist novel had to 'manage' or 'defuse' ... was ... fear of a certain 'soft spot' at the heart of the Empire, a growing cavity of degeneration / deterioration / parasitism which was the projection onto the domestic landscape of an essentially global problematic (namely, an emergent legitimation crisis in the colonial order)" (51). According to English, during the interwar period "[s]capegoats that had been discernible but not structurally necessary within the social imaginary of 1900 England – 'the Jews,' 'the Negroes,' 'the Bolsheviks,' 'the feminists,' 'the homosexuals,' 'the young' – now played critical roles in the (still fundamental) ideological fantasy of British 'degeneration'" (68). The implications of this shift for the comic representation of non-whites will emerge in the chapters to follow.

An instructive instance of the defensive role of humour in late-imperial fantasy is Joyce Cary's 1933 novel *An American Visitor*, in which a British administrator, "Monkey" Bewsher, is striving to advance his country's interests in colonial Nigeria. Though a dedicated public servant, Bewsher treats the predicaments of colonial rule with unflagging levity; humour, for him, appears to be a needed emollient to deal with the mounting turbulence of native affairs. He and his American bride, Marie, themselves become choice targets for joking, but since the pair do not take themselves seriously, they remain unscathed. Bewsher treats with respect the black Africans for whom he is responsible; he invariably laughs off personal danger. When he turns up at his house one evening after having supposedly been waylaid by rebellious natives, he is palpably amused: "'Hullo?' he said. 'I hope you haven't waited dinner.' It was obvious that the man was bursting with joy, that he was ready to burst out laughing in their faces" (188). Bewsher plays the role of colonial overseer as a confirmed rieur. Even at the moment of his death, stabbed by native rebels led by a young man he has particularly trusted, he registers wry amusement: "Bewsher fell on his back with a look of ludicrous amazement and indignation. He was heard shouting something again about 'bloody rascals,' in a voice expressive quite as much of surprise as indignation. In fact, Bewsher's own feelings as he lay on the ground with two or three spears in his body, though, of course, full of official indignation, was not empty of a kind of amusement as if some part of his mind were remarking to him, 'Well, old chap, the joke is on you. You're not going to get away with it this time'" (229). Bewsher's pronoun "it" may possibly refer to the humorous bearing he has brought to his duties as an agent of empire. In death, his laughter becomes petrified; his coffin, we are told, contains "Bewsher's smashed and mummified head, a horrible object whose bare-tooth grin made even Stoker [a veteran soldier] feel uncomfortable, and a bagful of his finger-joints. The other bones were probably Birri [local tribespeople] and one femur was certainly goat" (233). The rieur ends up wearing a permanent, gruesome rictus. Bewsher himself, when alive, would doubtless have grinned wryly at such a macabre collage, particularly the goat bone. His capacity for humour has made him a uniquely valuable figure of control and self-control; it does not, however, stop his grinning honour from seeming in the end futile.

By the early decades of the twentieth century, Prospero will need more than a joke book to allay the fury of his unaccountably disaffected Calibans. It is, nevertheless, to the grandfather of British joke books that we must now turn.

2

Inferiority Complexions: The London Charivari

Sometimes when I am asked by young people what the old Colour Bar was like, I suggest they take a look at *Punch* up to the Second World War …

Doris Lessing, *Under My Skin* (229)

Charivari, the name of the Paris magazine from which *Punch, or the London Charivari* drew its subtitle, refers to a popular ritual that Mikhail Bakhtin identifies as closely related to carnival (*Rabelais* 267). A punitive variant of the carnivalesque, charivari was, according to Stallybrass and White, "a rowdy form of crowd behaviour often used against 'unruly women', and ... an overt reminder of patriarchal dominance" (24). While *Punch* in its inaugural years had a socially progressive bent (Henry Mayhew was a co-founder), before long the magazine came to embody the patriarchal attitudes governing its folk model.

For most of its long career as Britain's premier humorous weekly, *Punch* appealed to an affluent, educated readership with conservative social and political leanings but with aspirations to discriminating literary taste. Comic drawings[1] that appeared in its pages over many decades testify to this clientele's interests and recreations: sports such as hunting, fishing, and golf; international travel; and the fashionable London "scene." *Punch* provided urbane entertainment for "ladies" and (above all) "gentlemen," people who wished to be *au fait* with goings-on in their well-appointed, circumscribed world and to learn which books the "smart" set were reading. It is this latter interest that gives the magazine its special relevance to less ephemeral forms of literature. For more than a century *Punch* published work by some of the most distinguished English writers of comic prose. Thackeray had early become a guiding presence; later in the Victorian period the Grossmith brothers' *Diary of a Nobody* was serialized in it. In the twentieth century it printed work by P.G. Wodehouse, Keith Waterhouse, Stella Gibbons (author of *Cold Comfort Farm*), and other notables. The authors discussed in the three chapters to follow – Evelyn Waugh, Joyce Cary, E.M. Forster – were reviewed, often with enthusiasm, in its pages.

Punch humorous drawings and brief literary pieces appealed to its preponderantly white, male, well-to-do readership by encouraging them to define themselves against less worthy Others, who were stereotyped through the use of standardized markers. For many years those regularly caricatured included generic cockneys ("'Arry"), rustic bumpkins ("Jarge"), women of the ultra-fashionable and ultra-unfashionable classes, and children, particularly working-class mites labelled "urchins" or "guttersnipes." Favourite national types, from early on, included comic Scotsmen ("Sandy") and, of course, Irishmen ("Paddy"). For decades in the nineteenth and early twentieth centuries, each half-yearly collected volume would feature a dozen or more Sandy and Paddy joke drawings, fairly evenly divided between the two species. Sandy was, naturally, thrifty to the point of meanness, "canny," rough-edged, and hard-drinking. Paddy shared the latter foible, but was shiftless, impecunious, and given to delicious "Irish" self-contradictions. Both figures performed reassuring, because predictable, roles; both were uncouth in ways that well-bred English readers could contemplate with good-humoured complacency.

According to the American writer E.B. White, "*Punch* is as British as vegetable marrow ... The *Punch* editors not only write the jokes but they help make the laws of England" (qtd in Price 48). Those laws were carefully designed to exclude unEnglish interlopers from the marrow patch. White's own fellow Americans were regularly lampooned as Yankee yokels who began every vapid utterance with the vocable "Say!" Occasionally, however, they were allowed into the patch, as in a cartoon of 20 July 1904, celebrating an upcoming event in which athletes from Harvard and Yale were to meet counterparts from Oxford and Cambridge. The drawing, punningly entitled "The Anglo-Saxon Race," shows a majestic Britannia and an Old Glory-enwrapped Columbia extending a tape across a finish line toward which several wholesomely Aryan young men are sprinting. Britannia says, "Really, my dear, this is the simplest way of settling differences," to which Columbia graciously replies, "Why certainly – if we had any!"

Continental Europeans, who did not share in the allegedly common Anglo-American ethnic stock, were not so warmly welcomed into the race. In the years following 1904, differences with such aliens were to prove far from simple to settle. People of colour, as will be seen, remained still more stringently uninvited. From early on, however, *Punch* jokes involve a complicating overlap between issues of ethnic origin and issues of social class. A drawing of 7 February 1912, picturing a dispute over pennies in a squalid East End greengrocer's shop, is entitled "Unrest in the Near East," and some of the participants are indeed given semi-oriental features. The cockney-speaking shopkeeper, Liza Mullins, is darkly insinuating that a customer has pocketed a missing "tanner." A close acquaintance with vegetable marrows was clearly not enough to ensure wholesome, high-minded Englishness.

Liza Mullins, on the strength of her surname, is probably a transplanted Irishwoman, and in fact for generations of *Punch* wits the Irish were the targets of choice among those excluded from the Anglo-Saxon Race. According to R.F. Foster, Irish people tended to be characterized "as stupid, feckless and idle – a stereotyping that had been very prominent ... since the first colonial interactions between Britain and Ireland" (171). Foster quotes a description of the Irish immigrant "Yahoo" from a *Punch* issue of the 1860s that reads in part: "A creature manifestly between the Gorilla and the Negro is to be met with in some of the lowest districts of London and Liverpool by adventurous explorers ... When conversing with its kind it talks a sort of gibberish" (184). Such rhetoric, however intemperate, is not unusual; for comic purposes Irish figures came to be in effect Africanized in the pages of *Punch*. The stereotyping was exacerbated by subsequent tensions over Irish Home Rule. From late 1879, as Foster attests, nearly every lead (political) cartoon in *Punch* had an Irish referent (186), and this trend was complemented by a spate of humorous "Paddy" drawings, typified by one of 22 April 1893 entitled "A Private View." The cartoon depicts a dishevelled peasant, Murphy, leaning on the gate to his weed patch and gazing at his slatternly, scrawny wife, who has collared a pair of bawling "urchins," one in each hand. Asked by Pat, a decently dressed bystander, what he thinks of the Home-Rule Bill, Murphy answers, "puzzled": "Begorra, if it means staying at Home with the Ould Woman every blessed day, Home Rule won't do for Me at all, at all!" Beyond its overt misogynist point, the joke reiterates an ancient political commonplace: the tawdry *misrule* of Irish home life makes nonsense of the Irish desire to be masters in their own national household. Such "natives," like their African and Indian counterparts later on, are deemed incompetent to direct their own affairs.

By the end of the First World War, *Punch* had begun focusing more single-mindedly on comic butts farther removed from the metropolitan centre. "Sandy" jokes still kept cropping up sporadically for many years;

"Paddy" cartoons, by contrast, vanished almost entirely. Once Ireland (apart from Ulster) divorced itself politically from England, it may have been perceived as a less eligible humorous target. Eccentrics are more enjoyable to mock when they are members of one's family circle. Besides, Irish references might call to mind the painful recent family split, and would thus be less likely to kindle the sort of comfortable laughter *Punch* humour fostered. But whatever the cause of the fading of Paddy and his comic kindred, stereotypes of Africans and other non-whites, already familiar from nineteenth-century cameo appearances, now rush in to fill the vacuum left by the absented Irish butts. Sambo, though excluded from the family inner circle, could be pressed into service as a handy Paddy surrogate.

By and large, the Sambo caricatures tended to be even more dehumanizing than the Paddy jokes. Paddy and Sandy had at least been country cousins, whereas relatively few *Punch* readers were acquainted with individual Africans or Asians, a fact that made even the most absurd stereotypes less vulnerable to skepticism. Familiarity may breed contempt, but unfamiliarity can breed a more facile sort of condescension. In addition, while most of those caricatured might be considered officially members of the "extended" British imperial family, even these tenuous bonds were starting to feel tremors of strain. Although Britain's overseas colonies had not yet, like Ireland, broken away, resistance to foreign rule was gathering momentum, most notably in India. After 1918, casting these subalterns in comic roles could help assuage British anxieties by keeping them, at least psychologically, in their customary abased stations.

While numerous *Punch* illustrators of the 1920s and 30s turned regularly to "native" themes for humorous material, one in particular, Charles Grave, can claim the dubious honour of being the past master of the genre. Bryant's *Dictionary of Twentieth-Century British Cartoonists and Caricaturists* says that Grave "specialized in naval and maritime humour" (96), a euphemistic description that obscures the central focus of Grave's art. In the 1930s, when *Punch* was including on average nearly one racially angled cartoon per issue, Grave's contributions rose in frequency. While he was of course not the originator of the "Sambo" or "golliwog" humorous drawing, he came to be its most assiduous practitioner. After Grave's death in August 1941, the proportion of such material appearing in the magazine dropped off sharply. However, other causes – above all a changed wartime social climate – contributed to the shift.

Grave's work made its debut in *Punch* just before the earlier world war, in 1912, and at first did favour "naval and maritime" subjects. It did not incorporate racial motifs until the final months of the conflict, when Grave produced several joke drawings with Chinese butts. By the mid-1930s, Grave was deploying his exoticizing vein of humour as a specialty in issue after issue. Evidently he made a trip to West Africa (Gambia and Sierra Leone) to obtain more first-hand material; yet, apart from some added visual detail (Grave was a proficient draughtsman), his experiences there had little perceptible impact on the tenor of his cartoons. Such humour derived ultimately not from direct personal observation but from long-standing cultural convention; it was being routinely produced by other *Punch* artists who had never set foot in Africa or Asia.

Xenophobic stereotyping was regularly applied not just to "remote people" but to less remote Continental foreigners. The Charivaria department (weekly collections of one- or two-liners) featured items like this revival of the hoary "French disease" gag, from the 6 July 1932 issue: "A majority of the French medical experts who have been consulted on the question consider it safer to kiss than to shake hands. All the same, we prefer to take the risk of shaking hands with a Frenchman." On occasion *Punch* could display an urbane awareness of the formulaic nature of its own joking targets, as witness this entry from the Charivaria of 26 October 1929: "'British humour is very strange,' says a Frenchman. He would probably see nothing funny in an Aberdonian plumber eating railway buns with his mother-in-law at Wigan." Such arch self-consciousness, it must be said, did little to curtail the number of jokes about the catalogued "funny" items – Scotsmen, manual labourers, Wigan (a famously "plebeian" town), mothers-in-law, and the like – that readers could count on finding in an average issue.

In time, however, people dwelling beyond the bounds of "civilized" Europe came to provide the prime targets of *Punch* witticisms. Oriental names were always considered rich sources of amusement. A particularly leaden entry from Charivaria of 15 May 1918 runs: "Fine Me, a Chinaman, was charged at a London Police Court with keeping opium-smoking utensils. It was a rash thing to do with a name like that." East Indians, for their part, had long been seen as subservient colonials rather than as menaces to "civilization"; still, the bloody Sepoy uprising of 1857 lingered in memory, and Gandhi and his followers were starting to foment serious unrest. In addition, educated Indians, or "babus," sometimes attempted to trespass on genteel white society. Here, again, supposedly ludicrous names could be pressed into service as "clinchers" of presumed white normativity. In a cartoon of 19 April 1911, set in a society drawing room, a young toff tells his flapper sister, "Betty, I want to introduce Mr. Muckergee to you," as an impeccably dressed but conspicuously black-faced young man makes his way toward the settee where Betty is perched. She replies, "Ssh! Algie, he'll hear you!" The joke is coyly multivalent. It is aimed partly at the debutante's provincial ignorance; the London Charivari always relished exposing such "feminine" lapses. However, the name Muckergee is an equally inviting target, suggesting that the "mucker" who bears it is really an incongruous interloper in the white precincts of *bon ton*.

Jews, too, as intruders (like Powell's hiking Fischbein) on the English soiree, were fair comic game for *Punch*, but their status tended to be more equivocal than that of the exotic Muckergees. Though they were not after all "really" Englishmen, they might still, if only in their imputed avarice, resemble Sandy the Scotchman. (A 24 March 1926 cartoon depicts a Scot, who has taken the middle shop between two others labelled "Isaacstein," cannily advising a sign-painter: "No name, laddie. Juist paint up 'Main entrance.'") A motoring cartoon of 25 October 1922, once again focusing on names, hinges on this cultural in-betweenness. A highway patrolman has pulled over a cigar-smoking, hook-nosed driver.[2] The dialogue runs: "What name?" "Abrahams." "Christian name?" "Moses." Modern readers might assume the joke satirizes the ethnocentric narrowness of the report form the officer is filling, but given the social climate of the time such a reading is untenable. The laughter would, instead, have hinged on Moses's eccentric inability to meet the norms of "Christian" officialdom.

Those of black African extraction, who in time became mainstays of *Punch* humour, found it still more difficult to be recognized as "truly" English. In "Punch's Almanack for 1914" a drawing shows a dandified "native of Sierra Leone" accosting a British sailor: "'Ullo, Jack; any news from 'ome?" He receives the scathing answer: "'*Ome*? Wot d'you know about '*ome*? Your 'ome's up that bloomin' palm tree!" Even the native's affected cockney speech is exposed as bogus; his claims to Britishness are trumped by the identification of his actual arboreal (read "simian") origins. A macabre, punning joke drawing from several years earlier (13 March 1907) depicts a similarly dandified "Reformed Cannibal (with a dreadful past)" telling a white man he has encountered on the African plains, "I may be black, Sah, but I've got British blood in ma veins." A black man might assimilate "Britishness" in the baldly implied, gruesome fashion, but he himself had scant hope of being ingested by white Britain.

From well back in the nineteenth century, a dark skin was presumed in *Punch* humour, as in English consciousness at large, to be a risible badge of inferiority. A 7 November 1885 drawing shows two men riding in a third-class railway carriage. One of them, a "Salvation Army Black Man," asks the other, a farmer, "Have you been born again, my friend?" Farmer: "Don't know. Have you?" Black Man: "Yes, I have." Farmer: "Well, then, if I'd bin you, I'd 'a bin born a *White'un*!" The dialogue is followed by the *"Collapse of Black Man."* Evidently, it is futile for the misbegotten to be spiritually reborn; one's fate is indelibly inscribed in one's pigmentation, and there is nothing for it *but* collapse. A Charivaria squib of nearly fifty years later (29 April 1931) runs: "From an article on Ethiopia we learn that bribery and taxation compel the peasant to demand more for his hides and skins in Addis Ababa than they will fetch in Europe. This, of course, increases the Ethiopian's difficulty in changing his skin." The feeble witticism still, after half a century, hinges on the assumption that those unfortunates whose skin is black are (like Hugh Lofting's Prince Bumpo) frantic to change it.

The emphasis on skin colour as a comic motif generally tended to objectify the butts of such humour, eliding the distinction between their humanity and their mere materiality. A cartoon of 22 March 1922 shows a black waiter in a posh restaurant displaying the pastry tray to a dowager. She says, "I'll have that éclair"; he replies, "That, Madam, is my thumb." The joke erases any meaningful difference between the server and the commodity being served. A drawing of a year earlier (16 March 1921; figure 1) by *Punch* stalwart Frank Reynolds reprises the trope of "black collapse." It depicts a boxing ring in which a white pugilist has just toppled a black one; the caption reads: *"Elated Second (as much-fancied negro is floored in the first round).* 'That's knocked a bit of the choclic off!'" The tableau graphically enacts the supremacy of white over black, even as proclaimed by an illiterate stage cockney. The visual configuration here is one persistently repeated in such racialized art: the white boxer is vertical, the black one supine; ready, as it were, to be served up as a "choclic" éclair.[3]

A Charles Grave seasonal cartoon of 30 December 1931 stages a comparable visual "put-down." A large, cigarette-smoking black man is sauntering, hands in pockets, along a path; a cockney "urchin," concealed by a barrel, is grinning while packing a snowball. He gloats to a chum, "This won't 'arf show up on the back of 'is neck." What the lad is up to – targeting an unwitting coloured butt with a white missile – dovetails neatly with what the cartoonist is up to; a complicity is established between artist, subject, and (putatively white) audience. A later Grave drawing of 16 November 1938 ingeniously reverses the "normal" black/white calculus; a massive African woman, about to enter her tropical hut, admonishes her

Figure 1

Elated Second (as much-fancied negro is floored in the first round). "THAT'S KNOCKED A BIT OF THE CHOCLIC OFF!"

broadly grinning son: "If yo' laff at me so much yo' teeth go all black wid de sun." The nonsensical warning is "amusing" because it depicts black subjects clinging to the one precious shred of whiteness they possess. Beyond that, it insinuates that laughter itself is a white prerogative; what is allowed a white cockney "guttersnipe" is off limits for an African boy.

Epitomizing such humour is a Grave drawing of 12 August 1936 (figure 2), showing the interior of a tropical hut, where an (again massive) black "Mammy" prods her husband, slumped glumly at a table, to go for a stroll with his top-hatted friend, visible through the open doorway: "Heah's Hercules Wilberfo'ce wanna yo' to go walkin' wid 'im." "Ah know, Mammy, but ah ain't goin'," the man replies. "His swell hat gives mah an inferiawrity complexion." The speaker's awe before a scuffed remnant of European finery is laughable in itself, but his ignorant mangling of modish Western psychological jargon is meant to be even funnier, because of its unconsciously punning switch of "complexion" with "complex." Although the man does not intend this sense, he does indeed, in snobbish English eyes, have an "inferiority complexion"; his melanin determines his low status. The hut-dwellers' threadbare, "primitive" surroundings are likewise a token of abasement, doubled by their

Figure 2

"Heah's Hercules Wilberfo'ce wanna yo' to go walkin' wid 'im."
"Ah know, Mammy, but ah ain't goin'. His swell hat gives mah an inferiawrity complexion."

"piccaninny," minstrel-show speech. As Purdie argues, imputed linguistic incompetence is a reliable token of comic inferiority.

While it would be worse than pointless to attempt to excuse this sort of humour, such post-World War One items do represent at least a tentative breaching of English insularity, a move (however stilted) to make contact with more variegated locales and peoples. There is often, especially in Grave's work, a willingness to portray "remote" people as at worst harmless rather than menacing, even as clownishly likable. They conform to Joseph Boskin's definition of "the Sambo figure," who "was childish and comical, given to outlandish gestures, physical gyrations and funny clothes

... Irresponsibility was a cardinal characteristic and buffoonery an anticipated act on his part" (252–3). Still, the main point of such joking remains Sambo's inferiority, useful as an unquestioned and therefore consoling reminder of racial preeminence for a war-weary Britain losing its once solid grip on global supremacy. As Michael Adas observes, "The fear that the Europeans' internecine clashes had irreparably broken the spell of the mastery they had long exerted over non-Western peoples was widespread in the decade after World War I" (385). A drawing like Reynolds's emblematic tableau of a white champion flooring a black pretender would have spoken powerfully to English egos frayed by carnage and loss on an unexampled scale. Some such dynamic of compensation, at least, is required to explain the striking frequency with which jokes of this type were featured in *Punch* during the interwar period.

A controlling aim of such humour is to deny the subjectivity of its butts. A revealing instance is a Charles Grave cartoon of 26 May 1937 (figure 3), showing a black African office clerk, tipped back on his stool at a perilous angle, arms wildly akimbo, grinning broadly and explaining to his aghast white superior, "Nothin' wrong, Massa. Sometimes just happiness gets de better of mah." The clerk's epiphanic moment is pictured not as a charming eruption of natural spirits but as "primitive" misrule: a giddy forgetfulness of responsibility. The gushing inkwell and scattered official correspondence his transport has tumbled onto the floor ensure that his spontaneous overflow of feeling will be read as an irksome breach of administrative order. We are invited, above all by the cartoon's visual configuration, to dismiss this Sambo's state of mind as quaintly eccentric rather than to speculate about it. On a larger scale, we will encounter such a humorous evocation of baffling misrule on the part of the "euphoric native employee" in Joyce Cary's *Mister Johnson*.

Admittedly, *Punch* can sometimes find cause for laughter in the behaviour not only of natives but of the British who come in contact with them. The stiff upper lips opposed by travellers and administrators to the trials of colonial life are often a source of amusement, typically, however, mingled with admiration. A cartoon of 4 April 1934 (figure 4) in the series "The British Character," sarcastically subheaded "Adaptability to Foreign Conditions," shows a foursome sitting at a table, the men in formal dress and smoking, playing bridge amid an African jungle. Encircled by lush tropical vegetation and buzzing insects, the quartet are utterly, outrageously imperturbable, absorbed in their "great game." While such unswerving persistence in English routine is clearly presented as comic, the light flooding their card table from above suggests that the players stand

Figure 3

Clerk. "Nothin' wrong, Massa. Sometimes jest happiness gets de better of mah."

for civilization in the midst of Darkest Africa, an idea abetted, through contrast, by the Darkest African – a bulbous-lipped golliwog – bringing them drinks.

In a cartoon of 26 December 1934 showing a choleric colonial administrator, eating a solitary Christmas dinner in the Sahara, the British master growls at an unlucky native servant placing plum pudding in front of him, "What! No holly!" *Punch* readers could chuckle at the lunatic extravagance of the diner's expectations, yet at the same time feel a twinge of respect for so obstinate a resolve to keep home fires burning. But the

Figure 4

THE BRITISH CHARACTER.
"Adaptability to Foreign Conditions."

reduction to ultimate absurdity of this British attachment to cherished domestic forms is a drawing of 24 November 1926, in which a "philosophic colonist" has just had his hut blown away by a tropical storm. While a staggering black servant grasps the vacant tray that had held his master's dinner, the colonist muses, "I suppose one gets used to these hurricanes after a while, but I do wish they wouldn't come at meal-times." Nature, in savage latitudes, has a tiresomely unEnglish habit of flouting cherished proprieties. Such mismatches between British insistence on regularity at all costs and the unruliness of conditions abroad provide a fund of humour in a number of comic novels of this period, like Waugh's *Black Mischief*, in which Lady Courteney struggles with stoic peristence to cultivate her English garden in the face of churlish African inclemency.

But if *Punch* delighted in presenting English travellers and colonial agents "playing by the rules" even to the point of lunacy, it found still keener amusement in showing colonial subjects *not* playing by the rules, or indeed having no rules to play by. Misrule is a governing topos of such humour, as it is of Waugh's and Cary's African comedy. A favourite joke, one tirelessly deployed by Grave, featured the exasperation of

Figure 5

"Has nothing been done about this?"
"Yes, Sah."
"What has been done?"
"Nothin', Sah."

British Prosperos owing to the slackness and incomprehension of their native Caliban subordinates. More often than not the impasse stems from natives' chronic befuddlement by the intricacies of Western mechanisms, as in Grave's drawing of 23 December 1936 (figure 5), showing a supply truck wrecked at a crazy angle in a ditch with a group of native workmen clustered uselessly around it. A starchily erect, white-garbed official interrogates one of them: "Has nothing been done about this?" "Yes, Sah." "What has been done?" "Nothin', Sah." Here a juvenile bit

Figure 6

"The flies don't seem to have bothered you much, Major. What
you do for 'em?"
"Put treacle on my caddie!"

of verbal juggling serves, for the African speaker, as a surrogate for prompt and efficient – i.e., "British" – action.

As in Waugh and Cary, the English in *Punch* jokes are endlessly playing games and sometimes endeavouring to draw confused natives into them. Typically, they show pluck and resourcefulness in keeping up the game under adverse circumstances, like the imperturbable jungle-ensconced bridge foursome. More disturbing is a cartoon of 26 August 1931 (figure 6), in which a bronzed British officer and his golfing partner are shown walking over an African golf course; a small black boy is following at some distance with the officer's clubs, beset by an ugly swarm of insects. The partner observes: "The flies don't seem to have bothered you much, Major. What do you do for 'em?" The major replies jauntily: "Put treacle on my caddie!" One would like to interpret the exchange as a satirical thrust at the sadistic white overlord, but in humour of 1931 such inferences cannot confidently be drawn. While readers of the time may well have found the brutality unnerving, it would probably not have struck them as too cruel to be funny. They recognized, after all, that subalterns were there for the purpose of helping the English masters "play the game" with as few hindrances as possible.

Piquant dissonances between between English game-playing and "savage" unruliness provided an especially rich vein of jokes for *Punch* artists and writers. The theme is elaborately developed in an illustrated piece from the Almanack for 1929 (dated 5 November 1928), one of the long-running Outposts of Empire series, ironically subheaded "Under Local Rules." The narrator's colleague George is rashly attempting to introduce golf to colonial Africa, a novelty at first treated from the natives' perspective: "When at last the time came for George to play himself in, the whole community had gathered to witness this latest manifestation of the white man's undoubted insanity." But the true insanity begins only after George hits his opening drive:

> For a second, two hundred pairs of eyes watched [the ball] as it lifted straight down the middle. Then, while George still stood in a statuesque pose, demonstrating a perfect follow-through, the District gave vent to a concerted roar of delight and, like greyhounds off the leash, dashed away in hot pursuit. Their flying feet thundered as they flowed past the astonished George in two black waves, the crashing of their passage drowning his remonstrances. They felt that the game had really begun. In vain we yelled. Far down the fairway we saw a wild upheaval of gleaming bodies, which fought and wriggled on the ground ...

The obvious joke is on George, with his foolish notion that he can maintain "the etiquette of golf" amid "the primeval jungle that constituted the rough." But the comic follow-through is provided by the riotous spectators, whose uncontrollable physicality and animality ("like greyhounds off the leash") are stressed, along with their gleaming blackness.

Sports that entail a larger component of body contact are even more apt to turn, under *Punch*'s jocular scrutiny, into no-holds-barred mayhem. A 7 November 1928 drawing, captioned "World News: The Chinese have taken up boxing," shows a ring in which homicidal Asian pugilists are variously up-ending, sledge-hammering, and binding one another while impassive spectators go on playing cards, smoking opium, and performing silly pranks. In a similar vein, a Charivaria squib of the same leap year (29 February) notes: "At the conclusion of a football-match in Tunis spectators pelted one another with stones; revolver-shots were fired at one of the captains, and a young girl was slashed with a razor. The absence of any mention of a referee suggests that Tunisians haven't quite grasped

Figure 7

"This is very interesting. Do you fellows often play seven-a-side Rugger?"
"No, Sah. Dere was forty-nine of us when de game began."

the niceties of the game." An entry from the Christmas number of the following year observes, "Cannibal natives of a South Sea island are said to play Rugby. There is a heavy local penalty for biting in the scrums." What purports to be the enforcement of "rules" amounts in fact to a reversion to barbaric misrule. Once again, this "niceties of the game" motif is given its most succinct visual embodiment in a Charles Grave cartoon (7 April 1937; figure 7). On a field in an "outpost of empire" a tattered group of black Africans are scrambling for a football, with improvised goalposts visible in the middle distance. A white colonial official remarks, "This is very interesting. Do you fellows often play seven-a-side rugger?" The answer comes back: "No, Sah. Dere was forty-nine of us when de game began." Here again, the postures of the figures – the white onlooker vertical and alert, the black players contorted at various angles – drive home the standard contrast between upright Anglo-Saxon aplomb and slack, unruly "native" abandon.

According to R.G.G. Price's *History of Punch*, the "impact of European civilization on backward peoples often provided amusing incongruities" for the magazine (132). What was perceived as amusing about the incongruities was, of course, precisely the "backwardness" of the peoples in question. For several centuries technological "progress" has been taken as

Figure 8

AN AFRICAN POTENTATE ON A VISIT TO LONDON IS CHARMED WITH A NEW MUSICAL INSTRUMENT—

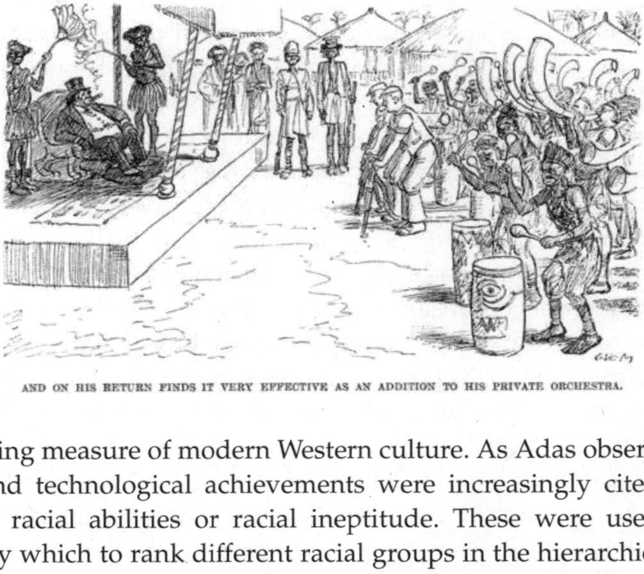

AND ON HIS RETURN FINDS IT VERY EFFECTIVE AS AN ADDITION TO HIS PRIVATE ORCHESTRA.

the defining measure of modern Western culture. As Adas observes, "Scientific and technological achievements were increasingly cited as evidence of racial abilities or racial ineptitude. These were used as key criteria by which to rank different racial groups in the hierarchies of civilized, barbarian, and savage peoples which nineteenth-century thinkers were so fond of constructing" (292). In the twentieth century, imputed backwardness continued to provide a leitmotif pervading Eurocentric humour at the expense of non-Westerners. A telling example is a two-panel cartoon by George Morrow of 19 June 1929 (figure 8). The top panel shows a black chieftain clad in native robes applauding a group of road workers operating jackhammers; the caption reads "An African potentate on a visit to London is charmed with a new musical instrument – "; the bottom panel continues, "And on his return finds it very effective as an addition to his private orchestra." The workmen, hammers and all, have been imported into the domain of the potentate (now togged out in Bond Street finery) to join "musical" forces with his rude minstrelsy of tribal drummers and honkers of ram's-horns. The implied assumptions – that Africans have no grasp of the real function of machinery and that their music is indistinguishable from mechanical noise – would have raised few eyebrows among *Punch* readers.

Such technology-centred humour was just as commonly applied to Asians. A drawing of 11 March 1931 shows a turbaned servant stooping over a lantern next to a seated English sahib. The dialogue runs: Officer "*(after lengthy explanation of how to work newly-acquired acetylene lantern)*": "Now is that quite clear?" Sepoy servant: "Quite, Sahib; only where do you put the paraffin?" Such comic ineptitude, if exasperating, is also reassuring in a member of a group, the Sepoys, who had set much of the British colonial establishment ablaze during the preceding century. An earlier cartoon, from 15 December 1920, features a still more befuddled Indian menial. Faced with an alarming novelty, a ringing telephone, he expostulates, "Oh, Sar, do not be so angry. The Sahib is coming very quickly, I tell you." In the "backward" native mind, modern long-distance communication cannot be dissociated from corporeal presence.

More ambitious attempts by natives to master Western technology are construed as even more laughable. In a Grave drawing of 23 May 1934, an African signal-drummer admonishes a noisy monkey: "Jes' yo stop bangin' dem cokernuts; yo're jammin' my wireless." The native's attempt to exalt his primitive message-system into a "wireless," a pathetic stab at technological climbing, is punctured by visual parody; the monkey in the tree, working his own wireless, bears once again a suggestive resemblance to the frustrated drummer on the ground. A cognate cartoon of 6 March 1936 shows a more "advanced" buffoon in his jungle hut, listening with headphones to a homemade contraption sprouting wires, and exulting to his portly, pipe-smoking mother, "Mammy, Ah bin only five months makin' dis an' it goes. Ah can already hear somebody lettin' off fireworks an' whistlin'."

The recent invention of wireless, which had so marked an impact on the home culture of England, did in fact open new channels of communication with far corners of the empire. A cartoon of 25 January 1928 depicts an African mother fondly holding her infant son in front of a large radio emitting musical notes. The picture is labelled "A Little Cockney of the Niger and His Proud Parents" and bears the gloss: "A Cockney is defined as one 'born within the sound of Bow Bells.'" In theory the drawing might seem to widen the definition of a Londoner, and by extension of an

Englishman, to take in locales thousands of miles from the metropolitan centre, but a glance dispels any such idea. Nothing could be more un-English than the primitives, slovenly in dress and distorted in countenance, shown grouped in their rude, earth-floored shack with its requisite monkey, listening raptly to the sounds cascading from the big horn. The wall calendar proudly displaying a picture of Saint Paul's fails laughably to Anglicize the scene.

The aping of "white" British institutions by "primitives" provides material for humour in other areas as well. Discipline and efficiency, those prime British virtues, are for *Punch* humorists beyond the ken of native administrators. In a Grave cartoon of 25 April 1934, a paunchy, cigar-smoking black boss, gesturing toward a mess of paper and cigar butts littered around a wastebasket beside his desk, growls at a flustered underling: "An' one of yo' chief duties as a commissionaire heah will be to empty the waste-paper basket." The spilled litter amounts, again, to a metonymy for the general mess in the office, including the chief's own disregard for the most elementary rules of hygiene. And here, too, the "piccaninny" dialect scuttles any claim the speaker might have to credible "Western" authority. The implicit question posed by the drawing is: how can such people possibly manage their own affairs, for all their crude mimicry of "white" bureaucratic protocol? What they desperately need is the guiding hand of European administrative expertise, a hand that can be trusted not to litter.

In an Outposts of Empire piece of 16 November 1932, "Richard's Riot Act," Richard, an "Assistant-Deputy Commissioner at a place which had better be nameless," finds himself faced with an incipient revolution by a crowd of unruly, inebriated natives. He easily quells the uprising through his comic mastery of discourse, overawing the dissidents with a garbled pastiche of quotations from Shakespeare and other English canonical texts. He concludes, for good measure, with a threat of brute force. "Within five minutes the revolution had gone in to lunch." In retrospect, the anecdote looks like a laboured piece of wishful thinking on *Punch*'s part. It was the empire, not the revolution, that was destined to go in to lunch.

The examples of *Punch* humour we have been examining date from well before the empire's post-Second World War collapse and the subsequent, unforeseen mass influx of non-white migrants into Britain. When drawings from the prewar period depict the stray African or East Indian visitor to the homeland, like George Morrow's African potentate beguiled by the tunefulness of London jackhammers, the newcomer is typically treated as a comically isolated alien. Fred Pegram's drawing of

Figure 9

Little Girl (in a stage whisper). "MUMMY, THAT GENTLEMAN'S NOT ENTIRELY ENGLISH, IS HE?"

30 October 1929 (figure 9), showing riders in the London "Tube," typifies such humour. A seated, well-dressed white child, who has been eyeing an imposing, turbaned, and mustachioed East Indian standing by a support pole, says "in a stage whisper" to her equally well turned-out mother, "Mummy, that gentleman's not entirely English, is he?" The overt occasion of humour here is the proverbial chagrin caused by small children making all-too-audible personal remarks in public spaces, but a deeper motive for laughter is the naive understatement contained in this child's question. For the real point – an unmissable one for *Punch* readers – is that, let alone "not entirely English," the rider in question is *not remotely* English; respectable, even impressive, as he looks, he remains

irremediably foreign. To drive the point home, Pegram's highlighting and positioning of the stranger forcibly detach him from his metropolitan surroundings.

Southern Europeans in England enjoyed no exemption from *Punch*'s parochial laughter, as witness the Frank Reynolds drawing of 10 March 1920, in which a tall, swaggering policeman accosts a diminutive, swarthy, doubtless Italian street-musician flanked by his (yet again) visually twinned monkey. The "Mayfair Copper" tells the musician, "Now then, get a move on, Tarzan. This ain't a monkey neighbourhood." The elegant, forbidding stone walls and balustrade near which the suddenly Africanized "Tarzan" is stationed drive home the point. More commonly, however, *Punch* cartoons target intruding Tarzans who are more palpably exotic. Almost twenty years later, Reynolds contributed another drawing (6 March 1940) showing the interior of a crowded London bus; the conductor is calling, "Anybody want Lord's Cricket Grahnd?" The joke is that the passengers all look either dowdy, or working-class, or hermetically intellectual; not of the social echelon one might expect to "go in" for cricket. But the eye is led suggestively to one passenger, a youngish black woman wearing Western dress, though her hat evokes a fez. *She*, unmistakably, would be out of her element at Lord's. Even though West and East Indian squads sometimes competed in England, Lord's, like Mayfair, is "not a Monkey neighbourhood."

Even those outlanders who travel to England on official business tend to stand out clownishly, whether they wear native or Western dress. A 6 March 1935 drawing entitled "Jubilee Problems" (figure 10) by Edwin Morrow shows a tribal chieftain attending the Royal Jubilee in grass skirt and gorgeous tribal headdress, bedecked with beads over his bare chest and clutching a massive war club. A stately footman, towering over the jungle monarch, extends a hand, asking, "Can I have your hat and stick, Your Majesty?" It is most obviously the footman's Jeevesian *sang froid* that is the object of humour here, his refusal to modify the standard terminology of court protocol to suit a garishly bizarre version of visiting royalty. The barbaric guest is, however, made to look even more comical; his physique and accoutrements are meant to seem hilariously incongruous amid these impeccably "civilized" surroundings.

But the alternative course – adaptation to occidental modes – gave such pictured visitors no surer shield from ridicule. A cartoon of the following month (17 April 1935), entitled "A Problem of Empire," shows a black dignitary in a London haberdasher's attempting to choose a hat he might suitably wear to round out his Western outfit. The problem is that the visitor,

Figure 10

JUBILEE PROBLEMS.
"Can I have your hat and stick, your Majesty?"

though he tries on model after model, cannot find one that will sit properly on his head, with its high, intractable bush of what was popularly, and demeaningly, referred to as "wool." The drawing (like Morrow's of the preceding month) illustrates a pervasive comic motif connected with such alien types: the theme of *not fitting*. No "civilized" headgear can suit such a figure; what the head requires is a savage bonnet like that worn by Morrow's jungle warlord.

All the same, *Punch* humour of the interwar years consistently assumes that England, whether it fits him or not, is the place "Tarzan" longs to reach. Numerous jokes, most often by the indefatigable Grave, concern stowaways. In Grave's drawing of 22 December 1937, an African kneeling to put a robe in a box informs his friend, "Ah'm packin' to go England." "*You go England!*" the other exclaims. "When you go?" "Ah'm off by de very first ship where de watch ain't watchin'." Africans in their home colonies were reputed to be incorrigibly lazy and shiftless; as Adas comments, "European writers rarely discarded the ethnocentric blunders that made the myth of the lazy African one of the most pervasive and harmful fabrications of the era of Western dominance" (254–5). Paradoxically, though, once in England they were assumed to outdo whites in their zeal for working to the verge of collapse. Whether they were lazy or conscientious, however, it was widely assumed that such newcomers were risibly out of place in Britain. A brief narrative of 10 September 1930, "The Savage" (one of a series called "Simple Stories") concerns the explorer Stanley Higginface's quixotic experiment of transplanting a "savage" to England. Initially the project shows promise; the African leaves off wearing his tribal dress, so that he looks, miraculously, "almost respectable." However, the venture turns sour when the stranger attempts to eat his landlady. The piece, a compendium of stock racial gags, ends with the hoariest cliché of all, when the chastened latter-day Stanley admits that "you couldn't make a silk purse out of a sow's ear."

Throughout the interwar period, however, the main threat that African sows' ears posed to English silk purses was, for *Punch*, not a personal but a cultural invasion. "Negro" jazz music was regularly scoffed at by the magazine; it had little room either for the musical mode or for its typical instruments. According to Charivaria of 30 March 1927, "It is said that the art of saxophone-playing is a secret. The great difficulty is to keep it a secret from the neighbours." A more sweeping dismissal appears in a Charivaria of 15 January of the same year: "'Nigger music comes from the devil,' says a critic. Few people have the courage to interrupt a jazz-band and tell it to go home."

In its facetious campaign against the hellish fad, *Punch* evinced some confidence in the ordinary, sensible Englishman's ability to resist its allure. Those less stalwart, however, risk becoming infected with rank savagery. A cartoon by Reynolds of 1 March 1922 (figure 11), entitled "Manners and Modes: The Spell of the Saxophone," shows a band of golliwog musicians playing saxophones of assorted sizes against a background of potted palms evoking the jungle primeval. The two central figures hold their weird phallic horns at lascivious angles, mirrored by the visibly tranced, dancing white couples on either side of the

Figure 11

MANNERS AND MODES.
THE SPELL OF THE SAXOPHONE.

tableau. Evidently the charms of this sort of music, instead of soothing the savage breast, inflame the civilized one. A kindred drawing of 16 March 1927 by Ernest Shepard (the gentle illustrator of the *Pooh* books), entitled "Dance Imperially – The Kaffir Crawl," inquires, "In the search for a dance to replace the Charleston, cannot we find inspiration in our own native talent?" It depicts elegantly attired white English people on a dance floor cutting alarming, bestial capers, while a mixed band of turbaned Indians and drum-bashing golliwog Africans performs a raucous obbligato.

The danger of contamination from overexposure to "nigger music" is the gist of a short humorous poem of 10 December 1924. Its epigraph quotes a letter to *The Daily Graphic*: "The noisy beats of jazz-bands are merely a disguised and modern form of the tom-toms of old, which incited savages to fury and fired the fierce energy of cannibals." The poem itself runs:

My Phillida, before the jazz
  Began its devastating boom,
My thoughts of you were gentle as
  The tunes that whirled us round the room;
To perfect harmony with grace
  We moved, delighted and content
To smile into each other's face
  With meanings kind and innocent.

Alack! My Phillida, to-day
  The music does not soothe my mind;
In truth I am compelled to say
  My dreams are horrid and unkind;
For, while the bawling niggers biff
  The drums that agitate our feet,
I'm gravely speculating if
    You're really nice enough to eat.

The verses are meant not to echo but to mock the hysterical dread infusing the letter to the *Graphic*; nevertheless, the conviction that sounds produced by "bawling niggers" are not fit entertainment for polite English ladies and gentlemen emerges between the lines. A fear of arousing the latent "cannibalistic" bloodlust masked by the facade of genteel decorum lurks beneath the arch tone; we are not, after all, very far from the comic-macabre world of Evelyn Waugh's Basil Seal and Prudence Courteney, who does turn out to be "nice enough to eat."

The insular jeering of pre-1940s *Punch* was not an exception to a much wider national rule of tolerance. Rather, the magazine habitually deployed, in a comic register, racial attitudes that were endemic in Britain and that often emerged in more sober types of discourse. Nor was *Punch* entirely predictable in its treatment of race; in the 1930s, it published several vitriolic cartoons deploring Hitler's persecution of German Jews. *Punch*, in short, was representative rather than aberrant; its racial humour spoke to the biases of a large and influential sector of British society and drew upon a normative cultural surround that nurtured some of the works of comic fiction we will now examine. The ambivalence at times detectable in *Punch*'s racial joking finds its way, as well, into those works. Writers like Waugh and Cary specialize in types of humour far subtler and more cosmopolitan than the *Punch* examples I have cited. Nevertheless, numerous threads of sensibility connect the magazine's racial humour with more ambitious British literary comedy; and it is these connections that the two following chapters will trace.

3

White Mischief: Evelyn Waugh's African Charivari

According to David Lodge, "The early novels of Evelyn Waugh have probably given more pleasure to more readers than any comparable body of work from the same period of English fiction (1928–1942)" (*Consciousness and the Novel* 161). In what follows, I will consider a well-known early novel by Waugh, *Black Mischief* (1932), in an attempt to determine just what sorts of pleasure it might offer, and to what sorts of readers.

The 14 December 1932 issue of *Punch* contained an enthusiastic review of *Black Mischief*, running in part: "The story is of a black undergraduate (Emperor Seth of Azania) who, going down from Oxford to take over his island empire, is determined to impose upon its rather unequal amenities the advantages of Western civilisation. He is not very successful, poor *Seth*, and in the end his enthusiasms prove fatal; but for the time being the Empire of Azania hums, and to a tune which suits Mr. WAUGH very well ... This novel is the biggest thing that Mr. WAUGH has yet tackled, for its satire is based on a wide and penetrating observation; parts of it are extremely funny in the chromium-callous manner which is his invention." The review, while taking *Punch*'s usual patronizing tone towards African characters, displays a keen appreciation of Waugh's creative originality. To equate Waugh's sensibility summarily with *Punch*'s would, however, be misleading. Waugh's references to the magazine are seldom admiring; the fact that in *Black Mischief* the hopelessly addled British Legation receives eleven copies each week is hardly a tribute. By the 1930s, nearing its centenary, *Punch* was starting to look *vieux jeu*; in Waugh's *Vile Bodies*

(1930) the senescent Colonel Blount props "a morocco-bound volume of *Punch* before his plate" while eating lunch and has another volume brought to his dismayed young visitor, Adam Symes (71). Still, there was an appreciable overlap between Waugh's burgeoning audience and the magazine's public, and much common ground in attitudes toward class and race. Apparently, Waugh did not object to gratifying a widespread taste with which he was intimately familiar, even if he held it in some disdain. As Martin Green observes in *Children of the Sun*, his 1976 study of literary dandyism between the wars, "throughout this period ... English popular taste, even at the level of the popular press, was in alliance with the dandy aesthetes, in one important phase of sensibility, the sense of humor. The snob-aesthete Evelyn Waugh was closer to the mass audience of England than would seem to a foreigner credible" (221). In its sense of humour, *Punch*'s readership hovered midway between mass taste and snob-aestheticism.

What Waugh above all shared with *Punch* was the terrain of "charivari," laughter aimed at those branded as inferior. Such humour figures in Waugh's work from its outset; like *Punch*'s, it targets both "remote people" in their exotic lands and outlanders (like the oafishly pretentious African American "Chokey" in *Decline and Fall*) who dared to crash the gates of the Anglo-Saxon citadel. Waugh's racial comedy displays a sophistication far surpassing *Punch*'s gingerly forays into humorous ambivalence. Nonetheless, as the *Punch* review of *Black Mischief* attests, it appealed to the ethnocentric notions of the laughable favoured by the magazine.

Some readers were not as pleased as *Punch*. A stinging attack on *Black Mischief* was launched by Ernest Oldmeadow, editor of the Catholic *Tablet*, on the ground not of its racial animus but of its alleged indecency and blasphemy: "On [Waugh's] dunghill no lily blooms" (*Critical Heritage* 135). Waugh was stung to compose a heated reply addressed to the Archbishop of Westminster, explaining his aims: "The story deals with the conflict of civilisation, with all its attendant and deplorable ills, and barbarism. The plan of my book throughout was to keep the darker aspects of barbarism continually and unobtrusively present, a black and mischievous background against which the civilized and semi-civilized characters performed their parts: I wished it to be like the continuous, remote throbbing of those hand drums, constantly audible, never visible, which every traveller in Africa will remember as one of his most haunting impressions" (*Letters* 77, letter of May 1933). While the letter was not sent, and remained long unpublished, critical opinion about the book has by and large conformed to the pattern set by Waugh. In a recent study, Frederick L. Beaty writes: "By showing primitive African culture and European civilization existing side by side, [Waugh] brings into bold relief all the bizarre consequences of their interaction, thereby producing some of his sharpest and most intricate ironies" (*Ironic World* 67), a statement that echoes a litany of earlier commentaries. Many of these dwell on the "attendant and deplorable ills" Waugh pinpoints in European civilization; few question the validity of his pair of opposed concepts: the "primitive" or "barbarous" on the one hand and the "civilized" on the other.

Punch certainly did not question those concepts, either in its review of *Black Mischief* or in its comic features, which as we have seen depended heavily on what R.G.G. Price calls the "amusing incongruities" arising from the "impact of European civilisation on backward peoples." It is precisely such incongruities that Waugh exploits for his own comic ends. The comedy he produces, not surprisingly, rests on assumptions akin to those underlying *Punch* "dark continent" jokes, though it is developed with Waugh's characteristic brio.

As one might expect, by the race-tormented 1940s a few voices had begun to express concern about elements of racial condescension in *Black Mischief*. Conor Cruise O'Brien, in a well-known 1946 critique, notes: "Two of [Waugh's] comic novels, *Black Mischief* and *Scoop*, are largely based on a sly appeal to the white man's sense of racial superiority" (*Critical Heritage* 258).[1] A.A. De Vitis, in a 1958 study, concurs: "*Black Mischief*, in picturing the life of a remote African principality, makes its appeal primarily on the basis of snobbery: the white man's racial superiority is the bias that cuts across the novel's action" (29). What is striking, however, is the denial of any such bias by the majority of commentators. Lodge, in his brief 1974 study *Evelyn Waugh*, claims that "[t]he racial snobbery of which Waugh has sometimes been accused may, perhaps, be found in his travel books, but not in the corresponding novels [i.e., *Black Mischief* and *Scoop*], where, if any group survives the author's impartial irony, it is the non-Europeans" (23). In the more recent *Consciousness and the Novel*, Lodge elaborates: "It is easy to mistake this comedy [in a quoted passage] for a display of racial prejudice. There is no doubt that Evelyn Waugh, like most Englishmen of his class and time, harboured a measure of such prejudice. But his imagination was more even-handed. It was the clash of different cultures in colonial and post-colonial Africa, all seeking to exploit each other, that fascinated Waugh, because it generated so many delicious incongruities, absurdities and contradictions in human behaviour" (174–5). As will be seen, Lodge's separation of Waugh's workaday prejudices from his creative imagination becomes untenable when tested against the evidence of the text. Blanket generalities about "human behaviour" and the "clash of different cultures" simply evade the real nature of Waugh's aggressively racialized treatment of individual African characters.

To be fair, Waugh's recorded personal attitudes toward issues of race appear to have been actually more open-minded than those current among "Englishmen of his class and time." According to William Myers, "Waugh was never a racialist in principle" (50). It would be truer to say that Waugh held definite but discordant principles on racial matters and that he could veer from one position to another with giddy abruptness. In his early travel book *Labels* (1930), he asks: "What is it, I wonder, that gives the Anglo-Saxons, alone among the colonists of the world, this ungenerous feeling of superiority over their neighbours? Why did the British residents at Port Said warn me against the hotels which might harbour 'gyppies'?" (187). Soon after, however, describing his return to Britain, he displays a cautiously receptive attitude toward notions of Anglo-Saxon racial preeminence: "And yet, although everything one most loves in one's own country seems only to be the survival of an age one has not oneself seen, and though all that one finds sympathetic and praiseworthy in one's own age seems barely represented at all in one's own country, there still remains an uncontaminated glory in the fact of race, in the very limits and circumscription of language and territorial boundary; so that one does not feel lost and isolated and self-sufficient" (*Labels* 205). In his later narrative of travel in Africa, *Remote People* (1931), Waugh switches even more startlingly from an attitude of liberal tolerance toward Africans to a curiously phrased disclaimer. Discussing the tensions between the white settlers and natives in Kenya, he observes wryly that "the Northern races, confronted with the danger of domination or infection by a coloured race, tend to go a little mad on the subject. The fear of Indians, negroes, Japanese or Chinese obsesses one or other of all the branches of the Nordic race who, by leaving their own sea mists and twilight, have exposed themselves to these strangers. Anglo-Saxons are perhaps worse than any" (*Remote People* 190). Yet he concludes by arguing, in untypically convoluted prose, "It is just worth considering the possibility that there may be something valuable behind the indefensible and inexplicable assumption of superiority by the Anglo-Saxon race" (191). Such vacillation betrays a nagging unease on questions of race, a defensiveness at times detectable below the "chromium-callous" surface of Waugh's fiction.

What the fiction reveals, however, is that, whatever Waugh's inconsistencies, his humour was recognizably the outgrowth of the cultural milieu in which he had been raised. *Black Mischief* restages a broad array of the racial clichés dear to *Punch*: the unbridgeable abyss between civilization (with all its ills) and barbarism, the British resolve to "play the game" in the face of riotous native disorder, the ineptitude of the savage when faced with advanced Western technology and civil institutions. As George Frederickson notes, "The heritage of slavery and beliefs about the savagery of Africa engendered a white supremacist myth that blacks were an inherently unprogressive race, incapable of joining the modern world as efficient and productive people" (94–5). That myth surfaces repeatedly in *Black Mischief*, in details like the wrecked automobile that blocks a broad avenue in Matodi and now serves as a squat for a Sakuyu family, or the locomotive that lurches away from the train taking Seth in triumph back to his capital, leaving the other cars stranded and Seth, who yearns to be "progressive," livid: "This gross incident had bruised his most vulnerable feelings. He had been made ridiculous at a moment of dignity and triumph; he had been disappointed in plans he had made eagerly; his own superiority was compromised by contact with such service" (101). As Michael Adas observes, "More than any other technological innovation, the railway embodied the great material advances associated with the first Industrial Revolution and dramatized the gap which that process had created between the Europeans and all non-Western peoples" (221).

On many other occasions Seth is made to look ridiculous by the failure of his modernizing schemes, all the more so when he is personally implicated in the failure. The neophyte emperor is the novel's prime comic African, the focal point where the main *Punch* motifs converge. Waugh, who in youth had aspired to be a visual artist, contributed several illustrations to *Black Mischief* that strongly recall the *Punch* art sampled in the preceding chapter. Most arresting is the novel's frontispiece (figure 12), a portrait of Seth labelled, improbably, "from the painting by a native artist."[2] The portrait caricatures the black monarch as a "golliwog" bumpkin. Like the *Punch* jungle potentate who imports jackhammers as musical novelties, he is showily togged out in Bond Street clothing. The keynotes struck here are instability and uncontrol, pervasive motifs in the narrative to follow. We see an African ruler unable to sit at ease on the throne of state, or perhaps on any "civilized" chair. The gun – that talisman of Western know-how and command – is firing off crazily at random. As Adas notes, "Perhaps no inventions elicited as much astonishment and respect from Africans as European firearms" (160). The Oxford BA is blazoned as an insignia crazily certifying its owner's freedom from colonial subjection, his own fitness to hold imperial sway. It is a portrait of Caliban masquerading as Prospero, pretending to govern the isle.

Figure 12

H.I.M. Seth of Azania
from the painting by a native artist

The visual ensemble draws upon time-honoured comic modes of presenting authority figures. As Susan Purdie says, "Figures whose public status gives them institutional power are obvious candidates for joking objectification ... In comedy texts, one typical figure of fun is a person who exercises public authority. Texts construct such funny figures in the way we usually need to think of actual authorities – as illegitimately, and therefore ineptly, holding their power" (64–5). However, as Purdie reminds us, joking also typically targets social groups conventionally constructed as "low," such as blacks (128–9). Seth, then, telescopes in a single image two of the classic target types, the "elevated" public authority figure and the "low" black. His overdetermined comic status neatly serves Waugh's ideological premise, confirming that black Africans are laughably unfit to exercise control or authority over themselves. In his terse 1962 preface to *Black Mischief* Waugh speaks of the emergence of self-governing African nations as a puzzling historical conundrum: "Thirty years ago it seemed an anachronism that any part of Africa should be independent of European administration. History has not followed what then seemed its natural course." (That is, "manifest destiny" had seemed to dictate that white colonial rule should spread to become universal in Africa; by the 1960s, of course, the contrary was proving true.) The Emperor Seth, planning a grand banquet to honour two English animal-rights advocates, Dame Mildred Porch and Miss Tin, boasts to Basil Seal, "'You see ... already we Azanians can do much for ourselves'" (166), but his pride is quickly exposed as mere bravado. The banquet is uproariously mislabeled "for Welcoming the English Cruelty to Animals," and the separate courses are listed, through a jocose misprision of the latest European health fad, as "vitamins": "VITAMIN A Tin Sardines, VITAMIN B Roasted Beef, VITAMIN C Small Roasted Sucking Porks," and so on (167).[3] The bearing of the malaprops is transparent: a people unable to produce a dinner menu without collapsing into idiocy can scarcely "do much for themselves"; they need to have much done for them by their cultural and racial betters.

Like a number of his *Punch* African counterparts, Seth has as his leading comic foible a boundless enthusiasm for modern Western "improvements," combined with a blank befuddlement by them. His vagaries along these lines become increasingly laughable as the narrative proceeds. In his eagerness to outfit his army (unsuitably) with up-to-date gear, he backslides atavistically into the rant of despotic tribalism: "'Of course they must have boots. I'll hang any man I see barefooted'" (128). Hearing from the young white opportunist, Basil Seal, about "'[s]omething very modern called birth control,'" he embraces the innovation with manic, self-confounding gusto. "'We must popularize it by propaganda – educate the people in sterility'" (129). Later, he shores up his country's tottering finances by the crank expedient of printing reams of worthless currency, prompting the exasperated Basil to ask, "'What's that black lunatic been up to this time?'" (154). On the verge of remonstrating with Seth, Basil gives up wearily; the lunacy is irremediable, for it is inseparable from the blackness.

Figure 13

Basil

To control the damage caused by such awkward racial overtones, critics have sometimes elected to view the book as enacting a merger of national types, whereby the black potentate Seth and the white adventurer Seal become twinned as alter egos. Thus, Katharyn Crabbe identifies Basil as Seth's "double" (51). She concedes, however, that the two come to play adversarial roles: "It is almost as if Seth and Basil are two competitors for the role of hero, and the minute Basil comes on the scene, Seth begins to disappear" (49). In fact, while (as I will argue) a symbiosis between the two figures is obliquely implied, Seth is never an even faintly credible contender for the hero's role, and the competition between the young men has a foregone conclusion. Waugh's drawing of Basil, leaning suavely in profile against the railing of the ship taking him to Azania (figure 13), contrasts decisively with the straight-on frontispiece portrait of Seth as witless enthroned booby; we see a young white sophisticate, at ease and calmly smoking; an image of poise to set against the harebrained African ruler whose gun is firing off crazily in his black hands. Where Seth, the *soi-disant* "progressive," is ironically shown in a posture that makes him look inertly static, Basil seems in his element as he shares the forward progress of a marvel of Western technological mobility. There is, to be sure, a sly hint of the self-satisfied poseur about Basil as drawn here, but that does not negate the broader contrast. The anarchic nature of Basil's day-to-day life, his helplessness to manage events in Azania as they spiral out of control, may in some measure liken him to Seth, but they do not cancel the profound, basically racial difference intimated by Waugh's illustrations and enforced in the text by countless touches of portraiture.

The narrative's dual structure, centred first on Seth and then on Basil, enacts a paradigmatic process: the supplanting of black by white. If, as Purdie argues, humour hinges on the ownership of discourse, then the defining comic plot of *Black Mischief* can be summarized as Basil's linguistic usurpation of Seth's throne. The book's opening discourse is assigned to Seth, who dictates a proclamation beginning "'We, Seth, Emperor of Azania, Chief of the Chiefs of Sakuyu'" and proceeding in the same bombastic vein (7). After his military triumph, the young ruler becomes still more lavishly voluble: "'We are progress and the New Age. Nothing can stand in our way. *Don't you see?* The world is already ours; it is our world now, because we are of the Present. Seyid and his ramshackle brigands were the Past. Dark barbarism. A cobweb in a garret; dead wood; a whisper echoing in a sunless cave. We are Light and Speed and Strength, Steel and Steam, Youth, Today and Tomorrow.' ... The young darky stood there transfigured; his eyes shining; his head thrown back; tipsy with words" (40). In the mouth of an infatuated "darky," language is a weapon liable to go off half-cocked, like the gun firing randomly in Waugh's frontispiece. By the end, the ownership of language has passed to the more deviously fluent Basil, whose eulogy for Seth trumps all the dead emperor's Westernizing rhetoric by painting him in wholly traditional, and therefore spurious, tribal colours: "'Thousands fell by his right hand ... His virility was inexhaustible, his progeny numerous beyond human computation,'" and – sardonically enough – "'The words of his mouth were like thunder in the hills'" (228). Burying the slain ruler with bogus praise, Basil is stealing Seth's thunder; or, so to speak, cannibalizing him discursively. (This act of linguistic colonization is reinforced by the switch in point-of-view from Seth to Basil: see chapter 1.)

Among admirers determined to absolve *Black Mischief* of racial animus, the most popular argument has it that Waugh's real satiric target is not actually Azania and its black inhabitants but England and its white ones. Jeffrey Heath maintains that "[i]n order to dramatize his conviction that polite cruelty can 'knock the spots off' savagery, Waugh invents the absurd island empire of Azania, which at first glance seems to stand in contrast to England but upon closer inspection proves to be a looking-glass distortion of it" (92). Heath claims that "[a]t its deepest level of meaning, *Black Mischief* could be set in England as easily as in Azania; the exotic setting merely permits a more fanciful elaboration of the theme" (94–5). What close inspection is more apt to reveal, however, is the opposite: Waugh's treatment of the African setting and its inhabitants is more racially implicating than Heath's demure phrase – "more fanciful" – admits. The victorious army of General Connolly is described in terms reminiscent of an "African" tableau by Charles Grave: "fuzzy heads, jolly nigger-minstrel faces, black chests shining through buttonless tunics, pockets bulging with loot" (35). At the great Feast of the Boots (after Basil obliges Connolly to accept a consignment of boots to modernize his barefoot legion, the troops jubilantly eat them), the scene evoked is again a verbal replica of a *Punch* cartoon: "Cook-pots steaming over the wood fires; hand drums beating; bare feet shuffling unforgotten tribal rhythms; a thousand darkies crooning and swaying on their haunches, white teeth flashing in the fire-light" (137). Footwear, that civilized amenity, is devoured in a jungle orgy hilariously anticipating the grisly cannibal feast that will occur later. Seth's own "negritude" too belies his "civilized" Western pretensions, as when the emperor strides into the banquet honouring the English cruelty to animals, "looking neither to right nor left ... white kid gloves, heavily starched linen, neat pearl studs and jet black face" (108). The culminating detail of decor – "*jet* black" – undercuts all the gleaming, pearly Western nattiness. Here, as often, the popular *Punch* trope of "not fitting" governs Waugh's rhetoric.

Complexion melds with gender to produce General Connolly's standard epithet for his doting native wife: Black Bitch. When Seth gratefully bestows a title, Duke of Ukaka, on his victorious general, he is moved to remonstrate about this habitual usage: "'Your name for Mrs Connolly, though suitable as a term of endearment in the home, seems to emphasize the racial distinction between you in a way which might prove disconcerting.'" Connolly replies disarmingly, "'I dare say you're right, Seth. I'll try and remember when we're in company. But I shall always think of her as Black Bitch, somehow'" (43–4). The joke here is of course on the "politically correct" Seth. Connolly's pet name for his lady, even if sexually and racially demeaning, doubtless issues from an affection genuine enough in its fashion. William Myers, conceding that Waugh "does a very thorough job of presenting [Black Bitch] as a kind of likeable monkey," nevertheless argues that the Connollys' domestic bliss exalts the woman above her stereotypic presentation: "[W]e cannot ... allow ourselves to be shocked by personal habits, however crudely drawn, which arouse a man like Connolly to real tenderness" (42). What else her personal habits arouse Connolly to emerges later: "As the time [for her visit to the French Legation] approached, Black Bitch's excitement became almost alarming and her questions on etiquette so searching that the General was obliged to thump her soundly on the head and lock her in a cupboard for some hours before she could be reduced to a condition sufficiently subdued for diplomatic society" (*Black Mischief* 135). Connolly's Taming of the Bitch has repellent racial overtones: the bitch, because black, requires all the more stern a course of taming. But for that matter Waugh's language throughout thumps Mrs Connolly as soundly as the general does; the reader, too, is led "somehow" always to think of the character as Black Bitch, since she is given no other name apart from her absurd scatological title, Duchess of Ukaka.

Again and again in *Black Mischief*, depictions of native Africans, like those in *Punch* cartoons, highlight their skin pigmentation, along with their grossness, unruliness, and animality. On learning that she will have the honour of dining with the wife of the French envoy, Madame Ballon, Black Bitch cannot contain her glee: "[S]he threw back her head, rolled her eyes, and emitting deep gurgles of pleasure began spinning about the room like a teetotum" (134). "'[B]less her black heart,'" Connolly remarks trenchantly (135). Transformed to a spinning object, a top or "teetotum," the woman is in the strictest sense objectified. The scene memorably validates Dyer's thesis that white perceptions reduce coloured people to mere corporeality.[4]

In Waugh's novel, as in *Punch*, attempts by native Africans to ingratiate themselves with Europeans or to conform to Western expectations drive home, by uproarious contrast, the insurmountable truth of their "difference." At the "Cruelty to Animals" banquet, "[All] round the room stood sombre but important figures completely fitted up ... with tail coats, white gloves, starched linen and enamelled studs; only in a few cases were shoes and socks lacking; the unaccustomed attire lent a certain dignified rigidity to their deportment. The ladies had for the most part allowed their choice to fix upon frocks of rather startling colour; aniline greens and violets with elaborations of ostrich feather and sequin. Viscountess Boaz wore a backless frock newly arrived from Cairo combined with the full weight of her ancestral jewellery; the Duchess of Mhomala carried on her woolly head a three-pound tiara of gold and garnets; Baroness Batulle exposed shoulders and back magnificently tattooed and cicatrized with arabesques" (168). Waugh's style here wickedly burlesques an English newspaper "Society Notes" column; the effusive fashion catalogue is punctured by lurid hints of unWestern atavism (the "rather startling colour" of the ladies' frocks, the three-pound bejewelled tiara on the "woolly" head, the Baroness's sarcastically praised "magnificent" tattoos). Much later, at the sinister carnival of Seth's funeral, the primitive reality behind such civilized pretensions emerges more starkly: "Dancing was resumed, faster this time and more clearly oblivious of fatigue. In emulation of the witch doctors, the tribesmen began slashing themselves on chest and arms with their hunting knives; blood and sweat mingled in shining rivulets over their dark skins ... In the shadows, in the extremities of the market-place, black figures sprawled and grunted, alone and in couples" (229). This is the barbaric underside of Black Bitch's whirligig ecstasy.

The ongoing contrast between black and white, savage and civilized, climaxes in the macabre humour of this late scene, where the appalled Basil discovers that he has been feasting on the remains of his girlfriend, Prudence Courteney, in the cannibal ragout. His suspicions are prompted by his sudden recognition of the red beret the girl had been wearing: "The headman of Moshu ... wore an Azanian white robe, splashed with gravy and spirit. His scalp was closely shaven; he nodded down to the lip of the bowl and drank. Then he clumsily offered it to Basil. Basil refused; he gaped and offered it again. Then took another draught himself. Then he nodded again and drew something from his bosom and put it on his head. 'Look, he said. 'Pretty.' It was a beret of pillar-box red" (229). "'Where did you get it?'" Basil uneasily asks the headman. "'Pretty hat,'" he replies. "'It came in the great bird [Prudence's airplane that had been forced to land]. The white woman wore it. On her head like this.' He giggled weakly and pulled it askew over his glistening pate" (230). What is striking here is no subtly implied kinship between the headman and a British dignitary but rather the eloquent colour contrast between the pillar-box red hat, recalling the order and decency of the Royal postal service and the glistening black scalp over which it is slouched askew. To see in such spectacles, as Heath wishes, "a looking-glass distortion of England" is to wilfully disregard the cumulative force of the book's cunningly contrived imagery and action.

Nevertheless, a battalion of critics do choose to ignore that force, engaging in apologetics similar to Heath's. According to Alvin Kernan's 1965 *The Plot of Satire*, "*Black Mischief* is not a caricature of a savage and ludicrous African kingdom but a grotesque image of Western civilization in the twentieth century" (162): "Some elements of racial chauvinism can undoubtedly be found, but the main thrust of the satire is against Western liberals who believe that life can be utterly reformed, anywhere, by increased control over nature and the change of social institutions. Waugh makes this point very cleverly, and very consistently, by juxtaposing similar scenes in Africa and England, showing the same forces at work in both places, and by the cunning use of various kinds of images and inversions. When we see a gigantic savage with the unlikely title of the Earl of Ngumo roaring for raw camel meat in a local restaurant, do we laugh at his pretensions to the title of Earl or do we laugh at the pretensions of certain members of the English aristocracy to be something more than illiterate savages?" (161). There are good reasons why Kernan's concluding rhetorical question may not elicit the answer he obviously expects. Waugh's Earl of Ngumo is not, like Gilbert and Sullivan's family pride-obsessed "Japanese" Pooh Bah, a satirical figure transparently aimed at the British upper class. For one thing, the brief (but amusing) portion of Waugh's narrative set in England contains no aristocrat at all reminiscent of the roaring African Earl. Arguably the closest counterpart would be the overbearing press magnate Lord Monomark; but the contrasts between the characters eclipse any passing resemblance. Monomark's culinary preferences leave scant room for camel meat, raw or cooked; as he lectures a group of admirers at Lady Metroland's party, "'Two raw onions and a plate of oatmeal porridge ... That's all I've taken for luncheon in the last eight months. And I feel two hundred per cent better – physically, intellectually, and ethically'" (72). He bears the full brunt of Waugh's snide satire, but not for being an "illiterate savage"; instead, he is an obtuse, arrogant exemplar of modern Western civilization, whose "attendant and deplorable ills," to quote Waugh's unsent letter, he personifies. He swallows some of the faddish bunk circulated by the print medium he controls; but even this foible requires a high though barren quotient of "civilized" sophistication. To call him savage or barbaric would be an extravagant piece of fancy; it is unlikely that his image will spring unbidden to the minds of those reading about the Earl of Ngumo or the Viscount Boaz. Such comparisons only confirm Waugh's own declaration that *Black Mischief* highlights the *contrasts* (not parallels) between civilization and savagery.

Even if one grants for the sake of argument Kernan's claim that the Earl's ill-breeding mirrors the antics of the English nobility, the benchmark by which savagery is gauged remains African, not English. But in any case Kernan's prediction of readers' responses overlooks the novel's historical and cultural moment. An audience nourished on *Punch*-style humour would have found a gigantic roaring savage funny because he was a gigantic roaring savage, not because he was the spitting image of a British royal. The same applies to William Myers's contention about another incident involving the Earl of Ngumo: "When the Earl of Ngumo threatens 'to dismember any man on his estates' who uses contraceptives ... the 'loud grunts of disapproval' from his peers are notably reminiscent of the noises made by middle-aged dominant males in English county families" (41). "Notably reminiscent," perhaps, to an ingenious critic anxious to redeem Waugh from suspicions of racial snobbery.

Even those who concede that black Africans are patronized by Waugh still insist, like Lodge, that he strikes an acceptable balance by even-handedly targeting white Europeans as well. Crabbe, for example, takes a position along the general lines of Heath's and Kernan's: "If Seth alone had to carry the burden of Waugh's disgust with the mindless pursuit of progress, there might be some justice in considering *Black Mischief* to be a racist book. However, Waugh is at some pains to draw parallels among his ... societies, with the result that Seth's foibles find echoes elsewhere in the novel" (55). But, while Seth is in fact the main African character whose foibles link him to modern English society, such "echoes" do not, as Crabbe supposes, mitigate the charge of racism. Waugh's own countrymen are not exempted from his malicious wit, far from it. The most obvious difference between Waugh's satire and a typical Charles Grave "African" drawing is the gusto Waugh displays in puncturing homegrown absurdities along with foreign ones. Nonetheless, his humour does not trouble the assumption of racial superiority on which *Punch* joking is founded; if his white characters are ridiculed, they are not, like the black ones, ridiculed *on the score of race itself*.

European "progressive" tendencies do indeed, as Kernan and Lodge rightly note, get humorously exploded, but the satiric guns are charged with racial powder. Thus when Seth, in another of his rhapsodies, declares, "'I have seen the great tattoo of Aldershot, the Paris Exhibition, the Oxford

Union. I have read modern books – Shaw, Arlen, Priestley... The whole might of Evolution rides behind [me]; at my stirrups run woman's suffrage, vaccination and vivisection. I am the New Age. I am the Future'" (17), the irony directed at such progressive causes as socialism, feminism, and experimental science gains its bite from the racial abasement of their advocate, a "darky" clown who foolishly lumps together the highbrow Bernard Shaw with the middlebrow Michael Arlen, inoculation against disease with gratuitous cruelty to animals. Waugh, that is, relies on the presumed racial snobbery of his white reader to enlist laughter on the side of misogyny and reaction. Political conservatism rides piggyback on the shoulders of ethnocentric complacency; liberalism is lampooned by being paraded in blackface. Here, as Thackeray had discovered a century earlier, lies the usefulness of racial humour for an aggressive ideological agenda: it provides ready-made rhetorical momentum.

It seems paradoxical that tolerant readers who would dismiss with scorn Grave's golliwog drawings resort to quasi-Thomistic apologetics to excuse analogous humour in Waugh. Waugh, of course, had far more wit and imagination than any *Punch* cartoonist; the racial elements in his work are easier to pass off as but one strand of a broader and richer artistic fabric. Readers who, though themselves tolerant, have grown up with such ungenerous joking as part of their cultural milieu may shrink from condemning so vivacious a literary deployment of it. They may try to sanitize the book's comic action by cordoning that action off from its embedded ideology. Such a critical move is attempted by Lodge, who while conceding that "[t]here *is*, in fact, behind Waugh's fictional world, a consistent point of view – that of a dogmatic Christian anti-humanism," nevertheless insists that "it is not one with which the reader has to identify in order to enjoy the satirical comedy" (*Waugh* 12). Such an argument seems simplistic; if Waugh's comedy is ideological, our amusement conscripts us into at least pro tem complicity with the ideology. As Ronald De Sousa contends, our laughter at a joke normally implies assent to the premises, benign or not, informing it.

What complicates Waugh's ideological agenda is an ambivalence running through *Black Mischief* regarding "savagery" itself. According to Myers, "The main threat to the novel's tonal equilibrium remains ... its dangerous flirtations with barbarism, and it is this which makes *Black Mischief*, for better or worse, a far more serious problem for the reader and critic than either of its predecessors [*Decline and Fall* and *Vile Bodies*]" (44). Unease with "civilization" emerges vividly in Waugh's description of his own return to England in the travel book *Remote People*, in effect a companion piece to *Black*

Mischief. The brief final section, entitled "Third Nightmare" (the other two nightmares concern stays in African locales), recalls a convincingly nightmarish evening spent in a hideous, newly fashionable London nightspot: "I was back in the centre of the Empire, and in the spot where, at the moment, 'everyone' was going. Next day the gossip-writers would chronicle the young M.P.s, peers, and financial magnates who were assembled in that rowdy cellar, hotter than Zanzibar, noisier than the market at Harar, more reckless of the decencies of hospitality than the taverns of Kabalo or Tabora" (*Remote People* 240). Waugh concludes the book sardonically, "I paid the bill in yellow African gold. It seemed just tribute from the weaker races to their mentors" (240).

In *Black Mischief*, cynicism vis-à-vis European civilization colours the career of its slippery, amphibious leading man, Basil Seal. Basil enters the narrative after having spent four days "on a racket" (67), waking disoriented in the flat of resentful strangers who oblige him to leave. This sense of displacement typifies his general relation to his London surroundings, which offer no haven from his *anomie*. Now in his late twenties, he has spent so much of his youth sowing his wild oats that the oats have come to seem tame; he is ready now to sow a new crop of downright savage ones. Even the irregularities of fashionable London bohemia by now strike him as boringly regular, like his parasitic affair with the wealthy, long-suffering Angela Lyne. His friends Alastair and Sonia Trumpington receive a troupe of dubious spongers to whom they absently hand around champagne, while their own dogs foul the bed the couple are lounging in, a scene redolent not of primitive earthiness but of a blasé, aristocratic indifference to the niceties of civilized hygiene. The name "Trumpington" itself suggests the game-playing that pervades such fashionable circles, where the game of choice, "Happy Families," wryly mocks the casual instability of domestic arrangements. Basil himself, who has been playing the game of standing for Parliament in a safe Conservative riding, abruptly withdraws, feeling stalemated. Meanwhile, his anxious mother, Lady Seal, fantasizes with her confidant, Sir Joseph Mannering, about arranging Basil's "moral recuperation" by steering him into a humdrum life as a barrister, a discussion that leaves her "both warm at heart and aglow from their fire-lit, nursery game of 'let's pretend'" (82). Basil welcomes the prospect of an African adventure as a chance to play a more bracing game, one removed from the stultifying pretense and the déjà vu bohemianism of the metropolitan centre.

Throughout his time in Africa, Basil progressively distances himself from British "civilization" and takes on the colouration of the "dark"

Azanian milieu. During the political turmoil that eventuates in Seth's overthrow, he appears at the British Legation pointedly dressed in second-hand Sakuyu clothing (215), and his subsequent behaviour intimates the extent to which he has borrowed native *mores* as well as robes. As I have noted, he delivers a eulogy for Seth couched in traditional terms that would have made the "advanced" young emperor wince. More ruthlessly, he prods Major Joab into avenging Seth's death by assassinating Viscount Boaz, the man responsible for it. Basil then ironically "orders" the feast at which the luckless Prudence is devoured: "'[K]ill your best meat and prepare a feast in the manner of your people'" (226). His part in initiating and then engaging in the cannibal orgy is of course unwitting, but by this point it seems replete with troubling psychological overtones. Figuratively speaking, Basil has made a career of cannibalizing women: the rich and indulgent Angela Lyne; his mother, Lady Seal, whose valuable jewellery he purloins to finance his African venture; Prudence herself, whom he has boorishly used for the sake of sexual pleasure.

And yet what Myers calls Waugh's "dangerous flirtations with barbarism" turn out to be no more than that – flirtations, and consequently not truly dangerous. Basil's own turn toward "savagery" is itself always provisional and performative. Unlike Waugh himself at the end of *Remote People*, Basil does not bring home from Africa an attitude of wholesale skepticism directed toward the pretensions of modern European civilization. Instead, once back in London he recoils from his comic-macabre engagement with the Dark Continent, confessing laconically to Sonia, "'I think I've had enough of barbarism for a bit'" (232). In one sense, the novel could be read as a psychodrama, enacting an exorcism of the hero's (or anti-hero's) latent savagery through his unduly prolonged immersion in the destructive element. The process recalls Stallybrass and White's analysis of the psychological construction of social hierarchy: "A recurrent pattern emerges: the 'top' attempts to reject and eliminate the 'bottom' for reasons of prestige and status, only to discover, not only that it is in some way frequently dependent upon that low-Other ... but also that the top *includes* that low symbolically, as a primary eroticized constituent of its own fantasy life. The result is a mobile, conflictual fusion of power, fear and desire in the construction of subjectivity: a psychological dependence upon precisely those Others which are being rigorously opposed and excluded at the social level. It is for this reason that what is *socially* peripheral is so frequently *symbolically* central" (5). Basil's alliance with the black ruler Seth can be read as such a symbolic identification between the "top" and the "low-Other"; a projection of self into savagery that the white adventurer is unwilling fully to acknowledge and that he must finally annul in order to reintegrate himself into his accustomed, supercivilized social milieu.

If so, however, the exorcism does not complete a wholly successful rite of passage. Despite the exhilaration and horror of Basil's African escapade, he must finally recognize that there is no way of escaping the blasé world-weariness of the modernity from which he has taken a tumultuous leave of absence. He is left in the comic but painful predicament of feeling "fed up" with barbarism but at loose ends amid twentieth-century English civilization. What he never questions is the clear binary opposition between the two; nor – despite all the critical opinion to the contrary – is the reader finally prompted to interrogate it. The Europe of the 1930s that Basil inhabits certainly gave ample evidence of barbarism to attentive observers, but Basil's natural medium is action, not attention. In the 1942 *Put Out More Flags*, which takes up Basil's career on the eve of the Second World War, Waugh shows his aging picaro leaving his safe job at the War Office, where he has been embroiled in his usual raffish schemes, and joining up with an elite corps that will see active combat. As he explains to Angela, "'[T]hat racket [the War Office] was all very well in the winter, when there wasn't any real war. It won't do now. There's only one serious occupation for a chap now, that's killing Germans. I have an idea I shall rather enjoy it'" (221). Thus, having purged himself of the African brand of barbarism, Basil at last heartily embraces the even more murderous modern European variety. Possibly his reasoning is undercut by Waugh's irony, but the irony, if present, seems tenuous. Instead, Basil's resolve to devote himself enjoyably to the task of killing European Others appears seriously meant to mark his long-postponed coming of age.

In his recent essay on Waugh, David Lodge declares that *Black Mischief* is among those "books which I still possess and frequently reread with undiminished pleasure" (*Consciousness* 162). One might respond with a truism and a tautology; there is no disputing tastes, and Waugh's novel can doubtless still be read and enjoyed by those who enjoy it. It seems reasonable to recognize, however, that *Black Mischief* poses problems for contemporary readers that even an ostensible "period piece" like *Vile Bodies* does not. Devotees who would wish away, or whitewash away, the racial burden of Waugh's African novel cannot expect those more skeptical to join in the chorus of absolution. Readers who find the book's humour unpalatable do not deserve to be dismissed, or pitied, as ideologues deprived of a rich literary banquet by their political squeamishness. It is no longer an easy task to manage the necessary, spontaneous complicity with racialized laughter needed to relish joking of a sort taken in stride by urbane British readers of seventy years ago. Like the social assumptions on which it is founded, such humour might be said to have a limited shelf life; and those raised on more egalitarian attitudes may, as De Sousa argues, find it impossible to assume "for the nonce" postures they perceive as outmoded or downright repugnant. For such readers, it is Evelyn Waugh's white mischief – not the faraway people and places that writer exposed to his artful laughter – that now seems remote.

4

Joyce Cary's Tragic African Clown

In *The African Witch*, third in Joyce Cary's sequence of African novels, Aladai, a young Oxford-educated Nigerian prince, pens a note of thanks to Dryas Honeywood, an English girl who has shown him some courtesy when he was snubbed at the local colonial "Scotch club." His acknowledgment of Dryas's offhand kindness is rhapsodic: "It is from that character from which it sprung that I treasure and shall always act upon the advice which you gave me, equally wise and honourable spirit of the noblest and most magnificent not only of your own race but of all humanity; of P. Sidney, E. Burke, F. Nightingale (etc.). Not merely a body but a soul lay dying on that chair [at the club], in an agony beyond what body can suffer, and you gave up for it not merely a cup of water, but the precious draught of your worldly position" (119). Dryas, who "'simply can't get used to black men'" (117), giggles at the florid letter, and her friend Rackham, a British official, quips, "'It's good enough for *Punch*.'" Readers are likely to bridle at the pair's easy amusement; we have seen enough of Aladai to know that he is no Charles Grave "darky" buffoon. He treasures the music of Schubert and the poetry of Wordsworth; however stilted his rhetoric, he has, as he avows, not merely a body but a soul. Like Emperor Seth of Azania, he is an African enamoured of "progress" and Westernization, but he embraces these ideas in a more considered fashion than Waugh's addle-pated puppet. Rackham's earlier barb – "'It's a regular old chestnut, isn't it? – the cannibal chief in the Balliol blazer'" (13) – does not hit home with Aladai as it might have with Waugh's witless Oxford

BA. For once, the educated native is cast not as a fair target for superior European laughter but as a victim of supercilious bigotry.

Or so it would seem. And yet, later, we are startled to find the narrator himself describing Aladai as looking "like the cannibal chief in the comic papers, in his old school blazer" (257). This is no careless slip; by this point, the young man has in effect dwindled to the dimensions of a *Punch* caricature. Evidently the seeds of this degeneration have, from the first, lurked darkly embedded in the African's racial makeup. The novel's enforcement of such logic justifies the Nigerian critic Michael Echeruo's wry conclusion that "the racial bigotry of the white population, though in bad taste, is a natural and civilized response to the racial inadequacies of black humanity" (103). Echeruo's inference has an important bearing on my main concern in this chapter: the last and best-known of Cary's African novels, *Mister Johnson*.

According to Abdul JanMohamed, *Mister Johnson* is "a rather ambivalent novel that combines antipathy [toward the black African protagonist] and guilt" (*Manichean Aesthetics* 47). "Rather ambivalent" is an understatement; the book's implied attitudes bounce dizzyingly back and forth between contrary poles. Critical discussions of it have, as a consequence, themselves been polarized. Some (mostly white European) commentators view Cary as an author whose sympathy with Africans is beyond doubt. In his foreword to the posthumous *Cock Jarvis*, Walter Allen claims flatly that "we know from the African novels that Cary made no distinctions of race and colour" (xi). It is not difficult to locate pronouncements by Cary that support Allen's contention, like the following from *The Case for African Freedom*, where Cary takes issue with "all those who think that the African can never rise to full responsibility. They argue that he is a light-hearted but also light-headed sub-man, a born helot and parasite. Take him out of his tribe and he goes to the devil. Give him money to spend and he drinks himself to death. Teach him to read and write and he becomes an irresponsible demagogue. Put him into trousers and you have a conceited and ill-bred bumpkin who, to prove his worth as a man, pushes everyone else off the pavement. You have turned a savage into a brute" (33–4). Cary goes on: "We need not argue with the racialist. If there is difference in race it is not so great as the difference between individuals. Who could not pick in any European state, thousands of men, stupider, more unfit for responsibility, than the average negro?" (34). Such a statement, despite its tinge of condescension, is patently sincere. And yet one is brought up short by the close correspondence between Cary's most famous fictional African, Johnson, and the pejorative stereotype ("a light-hearted but also light-headed subman, a born helot and parasite") that Cary purports to be disavowing. Whatever can be said for Johnson, the chances are slim that he, or his fictional fellow Africans, might one day "rise to full responsibility."

Critical discussions of *Mister Johnson,* like those of *Black Mischief,* have nonetheless tended to minimize the importance of race as an issue. Cornelia Cook has little to say about Johnson's positioning as a black African, let alone racial humour. She brackets Johnson and Charley Brown, the hero of Cary's next novel, *Charley Is My Darling,* as "representative figures of the two classes [John Stuart] Mill singled out as needing careful guidance – children and primitives" (60). (I will return later to the significance of Cook's coupling of the two categories.) Jacques Bédé, though writing in an African journal, manages to discuss Cary's humour without so much as glancing at its racial import. The African-born Scottish novelist William Boyd, in his introduction to the 1985 Penguin edition of *Mister Johnson,* does address the issue of race squarely, but only to laud Cary for his magisterial treatment of it: "Cary achieved an insight into the mind of the African which avoids sentiment, condescension or paternalistic complacency, attributes which dog even the most well-intentioned accounts of colonial life or, to widen the net, novels about races other than the author's own" (1). In Boyd's view, Cary's achievement hinges on his imaginative freedom from the scruples that hamstring other modern Western versions of Africa and Africans, in which the novelist "sets out with considerable wariness and caution, always assessing his prejudices and deeply sensitive about his cultural conditioning. What right have I, he asks himself repeatedly, to say this is how an African actually thinks and reacts?" (2). By contrast with such navel-gazing, "[t]here is a freedom and forthright vigour about the way [Cary's] imagination ranges through the minds of all his characters that is unimpeded by good liberal reticence and prudent self-awareness" (2). Cary, in short, projects a robust rather than an insipid Africa, one not diluted by sanitizing "correctness."

Other readers, however, have been anything but captivated by Cary's alleged freedom from debilitating scruples. In a three-way conversation with Lewis Nkosi and Wole Soyinka, the Nigerian novelist Chinua Achebe recounts how pique at the portrayal of Johnson actually spurred him to become a writer: "I was very angry with [Cary's] book *Mister Johnson,* which was set in Nigeria. I happened to read this, I think, in my second [university] year, and I said to myself this is absurd. If somebody without any inside knowledge of the people he is trying to describe can get away with it, perhaps I ought to try my hand at it" (13). Achebe's reaction is obviously personal, but it is seconded by less directly implicated commentators. Arnd Witte, in an article comparing *Mister Johnson* with Achebe's novel *No Longer at Ease*, doubts that Cary does in fact "get away with it." Witte passes a caustic judgment on Cary's attitude toward Africans' reluctance to collaborate with British colonizers: "In failing to mention [the] motives for African opposition to 'development' and by characterising African reservations as a childish fear of ghosts, Cary sticks by his own racist convictions and – whether consciously or not – contributes catastrophically to the cultural misconstruction of 'the others'" (Coulson 127). By denying the existence of authentic elements in native African culture and society, Witte argues, "Cary implies that there can only be a negative African identity" (Coulson 133). He makes a provocative connection between this denial and the casting of Johnson as a comic figure: "Johnson, as the personification of [an emerging African] elite, detests 'savage' society, although ironically he is portrayed as not being any different from them: stupid, greedy, arrogant, overly self-conscious and self-centred, but always childishly cheerful because of his complete ignorance, in short: ridiculous. Rudbeck's perception of Johnson as 'a comic' ... pre-empts that of the European readership. In this context it is significant that Johnson has neither a first name nor an African name, which underlines his alienation from both African and European values and makes it easier for Cary to depict the fundamentally 'comical' side of his existence" (Coulson 128). Such a reading of Johnson as stereotypically clownish clashes with Cary's official view of the capabilities of Africans, but much in the novel bears it out. JanMohamed, whose position broadly coincides with Witte's, sees the comic treatment of Johnson and other native characters as a reflex of the distanced stance of Cary's narrator: "In *Mister Johnson* the predominance of this remote point of view allows Cary to portray the protagonist as a ridiculous buffoon. The repeated use of this distancing maneuver relieves the narrator of the burden of seriously describing the pain and frustration that his central African characters might experience because of their colonial predicament" (36–7). An important feature of the novel that JanMohamed ignores, however, is the way the narrator's distance from Johnson, instead of remaining fixed throughout, constantly fluctuates.

Echeruo, while cognizant of the distancing tactic to which JanMohamed objects, locates Cary within the broad context of "the foreign novel of Africa," whose author typically "uses the distanced peoples and lands of his narrative to make assertions of a large and general kind about human life and human values" rather than presenting impartial perceptions of native life (1–2). He notes "the temptation to represent Africa merely as a manifestation of those habits of barbarism beyond which the European mind has progressed" (18) and points out that such presumptions of barbarism inevitably make the figure of "the transitional African" seem absurdly incongruous: "The intermixture of a 'primitive' mind and a 'progressive' European mental attitude was ... bound to produce an absurdity, whether tragic or comic" (20–1). The humour that typically results from such incongruity he calls "the high comedy of the white man's burden" (145). In *Mister Johnson*, the white man's burden bears down oppressively on the shoulders of Cary's leading black comedian.

One hallmark that distinguishes the "civilized" from the "savage" in Cary's African novels is a fixture in the repertory of colonialism: the capacity for humour itself. As I mentioned in an earlier chapter, Bewsher, the dedicated colonial administrator in *An American Visitor*, is an inveterate rieur who treats the predicaments he gets into with jaunty levity. His light-heartedness may finally be his undoing, yet it is also the trait that defines his core of civility. In *The African Witch*, by contrast, Aladai's growing solemnity about his own role as tribal leader charts the somber course of his backsliding into savagery. The more humourless his demeanour, the more vulnerable he becomes to the laughter of the whites. Even the most sympathetic among them, his friend Judy, is amused by his disordered dress when he is attempting to quell, on horseback, a native riot: "Aladai's trousers had worked up his ankles, showing six inches of bright blue sock and the clasp of his suspender. Even a piece of black leg appeared as Aladai, now rounding up the fugitives, wheeled his horse around their front. Judy burst out laughing. 'It's a shame! But what a pity,' she said. 'Royalty ought to avoid such *contretemps*. But I suppose,' she reflected, 'natives don't see it like that at all. He looks quite terribly august to them'" (48). The reader, viewing Aladai's oddly assorted black skin and blue sock from Judy's detached European angle, certainly "sees it" like her, not like the natives. Even though Aladai succeeds handily in subduing the mob, the image presented here clings, reducing the likelihood that he will appear august rather than laughable throughout the ensuing narrative. Other natives, too, and especially the band of religious zealots led by the charismatic Coker, are afflicted with a humour deficit and consequently come to seem both more ridiculous and more menacing. A white forester whose books have been impounded by Coker's insurgents bursts out, "'What good ... is P.G. Wodehouse to these – – .' He swallowed the word in deference to the lady [Dryas]. He was very polite" (258). Civility and the gift of humour are inseparably linked; Coker and his followers are devoid of both. As Echeruo tersely comments, "The fact is that, given the novel's argument, Wodehouse can do little good" (104).

In *Mister Johnson*, the issue of who laughs at whom has an even more central place. Bédé accurately describes the book as the one clearly comic novel among the African group: "The comic element is much more frequent than in the other works, and finds its proper place there" (32; my translation). But besides its frequency, the signal peculiarity of "the comic element" in *Mister Johnson* is its ambivalence. A typical instance is the scene in which Johnson shows off the "lady latrine" he has readied for the newly arrived Celia Rudbeck:

> Johnson catches up a straw pot cover from the floor and puts it over the hole. "You see, Mam – he catch cover you no fit put you foot der in de dark." He rubs his hand along the peeled stick. "I scrape you seat he no fit scratch you legs."
>
> Celia bursts out laughing and says between peals of laughter, "Oh, thanks, Mr. Johnson – I see, it's a beautiful arrangement."
>
> Johnson also laughs. He does not see the joke. He has taken much trouble with the latrine, especially to make the perch firm and give it a smooth stick. He has suffered, like all Nigerians, from rickety perches which collapse at the wrong moment and top bars with bark like sandpaper, splinters like needles, twig ends sharp as chisels. He has set out to compose a masterpiece of sanitary engineering and he is extremely proud of it. But, since Missus Rudbeck laughs, he also laughs. He is delighted by her good humour. (90)

The cultural distance separating the Nigerian and the Englishwoman is gauged by the difference between modes of laughter: hers sophisticated, his imitative but obtuse ("He does not see the joke"). The narrator's tone, with its *Punch*-like condescension toward rude native attempts at technology ("He has set out to compose a masterpiece of sanitary engineering") nudges us to identify with Celia's urbane amusement, while Johnson's monosyllabic pidgin conveys a sense of his comical discursive "inferiority."

After the incident, Celia hits on a racially charged pet name for Johnson: "Rudbeck hears her laughing at six in the morning and asks, 'What's the joke, darling?' 'Only Mr. Wog.' 'He's a comic, isn't he?' 'A perfect quaint'" (92). One understands the couple's laughter, and yet Witte's claim that "Rudbeck's perception of Johnson as 'a comic' ... preempts that of the European readership" oversimplifies the case. In fact, the exchange seems as likely to prompt a reverse reaction; the Rudbecks' humorous patronizing of Johnson is so smugly superior, the "Mr Wog" nickname so dismissive, that readers may well recoil. Even in the funny latrine scene, the narrator has transmitted an intimate awareness of Nigerians' lavatory tribulations that makes Celia's laughter seem glib, even while we uneasily share in it. She performs a curious double role, peculiar to Cary's schizoid brand of humour, as simultaneously rieur and anti-rieur. Soon after, we see her snubbing Johnson unthinkingly: "[O]ne morning when he suggests going to see a fish-hunt in a river pool, she yawns in his face without even knowing her rudeness. Yet she is a most kind and considerate girl" (93). Such details call to mind Forster's *A Passage to India*, imparting a sense of the arrogance that comes with the colonial territory. And yet, even despite these countervailing tugs at the reader's sympathy, one is strongly tempted to see Johnson as, after all, "a perfect quaint." JanMohamed's contention that "Cary is not concerned in this novel with an exploration of the causes and nature of the peculiar combinations in Johnson's personality but only with using him as an object of derision" (32) misses the crosscurrents of identification and detachment that complicate and enrich the reader's feelings toward the native protagonist. Nevertheless, it contains an irreducible kernel of truth.

Predictably, however, in view of Cary's divided treatment of him, other commentators view Johnson as an object not of derision but rather of sympathy, even of adulation. To Cook, "Johnson's actions express a rare personality which, like the creations of the artist, fascinates and influences others" (61). Boyd argues that "Cary's vivid sympathy" for his African protagonist allows us to "see Negative Capability [the Keatsian capacity to empathize with otherness] at work in the novel to a quite remarkable degree" (2); he calls Johnson "the dynamic presence in the novel, an energetic driving force" (3). For Boyd, it is the many-sidedness of the portrait, which includes corruption, mendacity, and violence together with a vibrant élan, that ensures Johnson "can safely take his place beside any of the enduring characters world literature has presented us with": "It is this all-inclusiveness in the portrait ... that refutes any criticism which implies that Mr Johnson is merely a white man's view of an African. Johnson is too diverse, too prodigal an individual to be pinned down by any racial stereotyping. Indeed his race is – paradoxical though it may seem – quite irrelevant" (3). For all Boyd's hyperbolic insistence on Johnson's complexity, his account is as simplistic and unbalanced as JanMohamed's dismissal of the character as a mere racial laughing stock. Boyd's claim that Johnson's race is irrelevant seems more than just paradoxical; it makes nonsense of his own praise of Cary for achieving "an insight into the mind of the African."

True, Johnson does have moments when he seems dynamic enough to transcend incidentals of nation and race. Dealing with the niceties of an office routine he flounders, like one of Grave's feckless African clerks, but teaming up with Rudbeck to put a new road through the territory, he becomes what Boyd considers him, an irresistible, driving force. He manages to turn gruelling manual labour into a carnivalesque spree: "Johnson, in a torn pair of trousers and a carrier's straw hat, is chopping, swearing or singing, improvising and exhorting from before dawn till long after dark. He is always dirty, streaked with layers of sweat and dirt in which the new sweat trickles crookedly like water on a varnished boat, leaving bright, black trails. His cheeks are hollow with tiredness and his eyes are inflamed with wood smoke. But his voice still conveys the most energetic feeling and his legs, body, and arms change every movement from one expressive posture to another, in sympathy with the voice. He is like a witch-doctor possessed by the spirit" (161). The young man seems at such times an embodiment of indomitable energy. Yet "embodiment" is a double-edged term, for the whole vivid evocation dwells on Johnson's physicality, in a way that confirms Dyer's point about stock white perceptions of black people. And the comparison to a witch doctor pointedly underscores the *irrational* nature of Johnson's performance. Even here, the mythic precedent of that uneducable son of a witch, Caliban, lurks in the wings.

In his "Prefatory Essay" to the novel, Cary calls Johnson "a poet who creates for himself a glorious destiny" (iii). Yet Johnson's imagination, however poetic, for the most part produces only puerile illusions, and his eventual destiny, getting shot by his adored white overlord, seems less than glorious. His sense of himself and of others is precarious; witness his confident praise of Celia Rudbeck's beauty, delivered even before he has laid eyes on the woman: "Johnson goes home to lunch and gives Bamu [his wife] a long description from imagination of the beautiful Mrs. Rudbeck who is coming to the station. 'She has hair like the sun falling on the river and her eyes are like the sky on the far side of the sun – her cheeks are as white as your teeth and her breasts are as big as pumpkins. She is the most beautiful woman in England and the King himself wanted to marry her. But she preferred my friend, Judge Rudbeck'" (57). Poetic or not, the young African's epic fantasy is plainly funny, an adolescent vision of pneumatic femininity featuring the compulsory attributes of whiteness and blondeness. To her husband's assurances that this paragon will be her friend, Bamu merely replies, "'My brother Aliu has a bad toe'" (57). The non-sequitur implies that for the native girl her family's well-being is of far more consequence than an unseen, regal Englishwoman's hypothetical friendship. But Johnson's headlong imagination is unequipped to grasp the pragmatic emotional and mental worlds of others. His hyperboles about Celia are soon drolly punctured by Cary's laconic account of the woman's literal appearance: "The next day Rudbeck drives up in his old roaring Bentley to road head, bringing a pale dark little woman with very black eyes" (89).

In a work of postmodernist fiction, Johnson might have figured as an apostle of "performativity," of the drive to invent a persona for oneself in defiance of the constricting, arbitrary confines of the real. But while Cary's treatment of his protagonist sometimes glances in this direction, the glances are regularly countered by deflationary humour. Cook, who commends Johnson as "a triumphant exemplar of the creative power inherent in human nature," speaks of the novel's ending as enacting "a triumph of personal liberation from thwarting or unjust necessity through the fulfilment of an imaginative impulse" (70). More soberly regarded, however, Johnson never succeeds in liberating himself from his delusionary solipsism, and his concluding "triumph" consists in getting himself shot instead of more ignominiously hanged.[1] As Echeruo reasonably observes, "Johnson only exemplifies the creative imagination, not the creative intelligence" (138–9) – and yet how genuinely creative can one call an imagination devoid of intelligence? The climactic moment when Rudbeck blows out Johnson's brains might have more emotional resonance if Cary had taken pains to convince us that his hero possessed brains to blow out.

Throughout the book, Johnson exhibits enough of the stock foibles of *Punch* golliwogs almost to excuse Celia Rudbeck's mocking nickname for him. Some of these lapses manifest themselves in jokes based on discursive incompetence, as when Johnson assures his skeptical friend Ajali (falsely) that he is in the good graces of his superior, Tring: "'If I tell you all ting Mister Tring say for me, you just swell up like a dead goat, bust in tree halves'" (106). Such malaprops, at once colourful and ludicrous, intensify the ambivalence of Johnson's presentation. A similar verbal confusion addles the alibi for his lateness Johnson gives Tring himself, that the office clock "'stop too fast'" (110). More generally, Johnson's erratic time sense corresponds to the ethnocentric stereotype of "natives" described by Michael Adas: "The Europeans' consistently low regard for non-Western timekeeping devices and perceptions of time became more pronounced in the era of industrialization, when what were regarded as African and Asian deficiencies in dealing with time were cited as evidence of the fundamental differences that set Europeans off from the rest of mankind. As manifestations of these deficiencies, essayists and colonial policymakers pointed to the supposedly inherent lack of punctuality exhibited by non-Western peoples, their improvidence and lethargic work habits, and their apparent indifference to time 'lost' or 'wasted' in gossip, meditation, or simply daydreaming" (241–2). The failings Adas lists (with the partial exception of the lethargic work habits) compose an accurate profile of Johnson. Like Caliban's, Johnson's essential clownishness reflects the always implicit power imbalance between the European "natural" master and the non-European "natural" underling. The humour is embedded in the very substructure of colonial relations.

Other items of Johnson's behaviour display an ingrained habit of blank misprision, often linked with the sort of automatic or "mechanical" response Bergson identified as integral to comic action: "The laughable element ... consists of a certain *mechanical inelasticity*, just where one would expect to find the wideawake adaptability and the living pliableness of a human being" (66–7). Having jolted his previous superior, Rudbeck, out of bed at two in the morning with his boisterous singing, "Johnson goes to bed still in a trance of surprise. How, he wonders, should Mr. Rudbeck hear him at two o'clock. How should he be awake at such a time?" (38). Threatened with prison for embezzling funds by yet another superior, Blore, he wakes up in the morning sick: "He groans and says that he is dying" (49). But upon hearing news that Blore himself has fallen ill he makes a miraculous recovery: "Johnson jumps out of bed and calls for his trousers. He can't help laughing" (50). Neither can the reader, but the laughter is patronizing, like that prompted by the black malingerers featured in *Punch* cartoons.

Then, most famously, there is Johnson's unique system of filing-by-free-association:

> [Rudbeck] jerks the file furiously across the table. "Look at that – are you mad – drunk to-day, Johnson? What in the name of Nelson has tobacco, native, got to do with elephant poachers in the Fada Kurmi?"
>
> Johnson stares like a lunatic and tries to discover what the connection was, in his own mind. Suddenly he recollects it. Delighted at actually knowing what the truth is, he cries out," I tink, sah, you say once dem native tobacco – "
>
> "What did I say about it?"
>
> "I tink you say she look like elephant dropping, sah – he all green like elephant dropping." Rudbeck slowly puts down the file and stares at Johnson with wide-opened eyes. (54)

Johnson's behaviour here replicates another paradigm recurrent in *Punch* joke drawings: that of the "illogical native" whose faulty reasoning makes him a laughing stock in his workplace ("Johnson stares like a lunatic"). As JanMohamed argues, "[The] notion of the native as an irrational, hyperemotional being is so thoroughly a part of the colonialist ideology that it becomes the structural principle for the characterization of Mister Johnson" (32).[2] But the valorizing of Western bureaucratic linear reasoning over the clerk's associative thinking, humorously produced here as "eccentric" or "crazy," is itself a proven technique of hegemonic control. According to Stallybrass and White, "It is indeed one of the most powerful ruses of the dominant to pretend that critique can only exist in the language of 'reason', 'pure knowledge' and 'seriousness'. Against this ruse Bakhtin rightly emphasized the logic of the *grotesque*, of excess, of the lower bodily stratum, of the fair. This logic could unsettle 'given' social positions and interrogate the rules of inclusion, exclusion and domination which structured the social ensemble" (43). While Johnson, who is repeatedly associated with the grotesque and the excessive, obviously does not mean to flout Rudbeck's authority, his "illogical" system of filing does pose a latent, carnivalesque threat to the whole regimented hierarchy that the British administrator serves. The "name of Nelson," that legendary issuer of peremptory imperial orders, has an appositeness here that even the name's user, Rudbeck, may not grasp.

Johnson is comic largely because he epitomizes the chronic ambivalence of the "othered" African in British colonial discourse. For JanMohamed that ambivalence resides in "the colonialist prejudice that would like to see Africans simultaneously as naive children and as very cunning and corrupt savages" (40), but in Johnson's case it reflects as well the acute dividedness of Cary's personal feelings. On the one hand, Africans represent for him, more compellingly than they did for Waugh, a seductive alternative to staid official routine, to the tyranny of British rationality, propriety, and inhibition. On the other, they embody the transgressive clownishness of the unruly, unlettered (or at best half-lettered) Caliban. Consequently, a figure like the incorrigible Johnson is sketched with simultaneous derision and indulgence. JanMohamed cites Cary's letters to document his "dislike for blacks" that "was partially based on the paternalism and the European sense of superiority that characterized colonial relations at that time, but ... was further strengthened by Cary's feeling of isolation within a hostile population" (20). He also refers to the paranoia Cary himself later confessed to feeling vis-à-vis the natives who surrounded him (21–2). But while such feelings may well colour Cary's

African novels, they by no means monopolize his imagination. The narratives do not consistently demean their native characters; rather, they by somewhat capricious turns glamorize, demonize, and lampoon them.

As I have mentioned, critics have traced parallels between Johnson and Charley Brown, the protagonist of Cary's 1940 novel *Charley Is My Darling*. But while the two characters do share common traits the differences between them illuminate the besetting bias of Cary's portrayal of Africans. Like Johnson, Charley plays the dual roles of disruptive force and nascent creative artist. He is still in early adolescence, and, as Cary observes in his "Prefatory Essay" to the book, "[E]very ordinary child is by nature a delinquent," and "The child is a born creator."[3] Charley, like Johnson, behaves with arresting spontaneity; he, too, dreams up marvelous, daring schemes that keep landing him in trouble. His enthusiastic work on Mrs Allchin's garden closely recalls Johnson's zealous engagement in Rudbeck's road project. Again like Johnson, Charley upsets those around him by staging noisy "parties," sometimes verging on mayhem. Like Johnson, he explains his misdemeanours by producing funny, baroque fabulations. What the narrator says of Charley – "It was as though a wall of glass stood between him and everything rational" (255) – holds equally true for Johnson. JanMohamed's contention that "when Cary turned his attention to British settings he stopped writing romance and began producing realistic novels" (48) overlooks the romance elements in a novel like *Charley*, whose protagonist is every bit as much a mythic construct as Johnson or as Cary's other Africans.

Cornelia Cook pinpoints the essential distinction between Charley and Johnson when she claims that they represent respectively "children and primitives." Johnson is actually only a few years older than Charley, and both could be said to exhibit the waywardness of adolescent behaviour. Other people call Johnson (and he sometimes calls himself) a "fool chile" (e.g., 61, 70). Yet, even though the narrator of *Charley* considers the difference between children and adults "actually more fundamental than difference of race" (94), it is difference of race that at bottom separates Cary's two teenagers. Cook cites both as embodiments of the "childish nature" that does not connect the past with the present and has no sense of the future. What this implies, however, is that Charley's sensibility functions childishly because he is a child, whereas Johnson's does so because he is a "primitive." In *The Case for African Freedom* Cary makes the connection explicit: "[P]rimitive people are like children ... they do not bear resentment, they do not remember bitterness" (75). Cook herself points out that the events of *Charley Is My Darling* "show the maturing of a character, and define the nature of that character. Charley's consciousness is at first, as Johnson's is and remains, self-centred" (74). But she fails to draw the obvious inference: comparable as Johnson is to his white counterpart, he *cannot* mature because of who and what he is; ultimately, because he springs from a misbegotten continent and culture. ("Maturing," here again, means learning to conform to Anglo-Saxon norms of rationality and composure.) As Adas notes, "The notion of stunted intellectual development in non-Western races was paralleled by the less well articulated but far more pervasive nineteenth-century belief that Africans and Asians thought and behaved like children ... In European writings of this period and well into the twentieth century, Africans were depicted as credulous, emotional, impulsive, and lacking in foresight – all qualities that were associated with childhood" (305). Not coincidentally, they are all qualities associated with Johnson.

Because of these associations the book Johnson dominates has little chance of leading up to the promising openness with which *Charley* concludes. It is no accident that Charley is portrayed in a more inward fashion than Johnson. Although Cary does repeatedly visit Johnson's subjective consciousness, one gets only a rudimentary sense of his interiority; it appears, in fact, that his inner world is underdeveloped, containing little *beyond* the rudimentary. Charley, by contrast, despite his youth and naivety is endowed with a relatively rich and elaborated subjectivity, especially towards the end of the narrative when he has begun to cultivate a less "primitive," more seasoned self-awareness.

Johnson, as Echeruo observes, is "the victim of a conflict of cultures. This judgement is implicit in the differences between Charley and Johnson; in the fact, for example, that Charley is not automatically overwhelmed by the lure of gold in the same way that Johnson is by aspects of European life" (129). "Overwhelmed" is an apt word to describe Johnson's chronic mental state; like Waugh's Emperor Seth, he has internalized as a given the presumption of European superiority. For Johnson, as for Seth, this infatuation has a double effect: it makes him "funny" and it speeds his eventual downfall. Johnson routinely refers to England as his "home"; he promises his wife from the bush, Bamu, that she will have "'cigarettes from home with gold ends'" (118) and later exults (though condemned to be hanged by the "home" authorities) over a bottle of "'whisky ... from England, from home. The best whisky in the world'" (217). In an early scene he extemporizes a song – "England is my country, / Oh, England, my home all on de big water" (36) – in a pidgin that blatantly stamps him as anything *but* English. When, much later, he sings it again, he "dances with the peculiar, loose, boneless step which expresses his patriotic sentiment" (192), but which also, to English eyes, renders his patriotism a farce.

According to JanMohamed, "In order to succeed in presenting Johnson as a buffoon who incongruously and absurdly 'apes' English values and tastes, Cary has to withhold his own sympathy and intellectual understanding from his protagonist's aspirations. By thus distancing himself from his character, Cary is able to portray the hysterical, hyperemotional, and absurd Johnson as the complete antithesis of the typically controlled, calm, and dignified Englishman; the ridiculousness of Johnson's behavior is directly dependent upon the tacit agreement between author and reader that civilized people conduct themselves in a manner diametrically opposed to that of Johnson" (47). Contrary to what JanMohamed implies, "civilized" English calmness, control, and dignity are themselves not exempt from satire in *Mister Johnson*. Still, Johnson's insistence on belonging where he has never set foot and is not wanted does leave him open to the mockery found in *Punch* jokes about England-identifying natives; for example, the cartoon from the Almanack for 1914, in which the cockney sailor rebukes the faux-cockney African: "Your 'ome's up that bloomin' palm tree." Compare the taunts of Johnson's appalling, racist employer, Gollup: "'Home. Haw, haw. Scuse me, Wog – always makes me laugh to 'ear a nig talk of England as 'ome w'en he never see so much as a real chimney pot'" (127). Johnson replies stoutly to this, "'I true Englishman for my heart,'" a declaration at once touching and, with its pidgin solecisms, comically self-undermining.

Like Waugh's Seth, but without even that Anglomane's limited experience of "home," Johnson harbours starry visions of the magical potency of British institutions and commodities. Seconding Gollup's maudlin jingoistic eulogy of the empire ("'You look at our battle honours, from Talavera to the Somme – there isn't a country in the world where we 'aven't laid down our lives for the Empire, and that's for you, Wog, for freedom'"), Johnson paints a euphoric picture of the colonial future: "'I tink some day we English people make freedom for all de worl' – make dem new motor roads, make dem good schools for all people – den all de people learn book, learn to give for each other, make plenty chop'" (130). His words coincide with the advances Cary commends in *The Case for African Freedom* (progress in education, communications, transportation), but his pidgin syntax makes them sound childishly fanciful, and he falters to a lame conclusion concerning "chop." Typically, Cary puts ideas in Johnson's mouth that might be seriously worth advocating, while simultaneously stripping his advocacy of seriousness.

Johnson's speech, however stumbling, voices attitudes that Cary considered normal and proper for Africans. In *The Case* Cary maintains stoutly that "European conquest, with all its faults, has brought incomparably more good than harm to Africa" (19); his case for African freedom is emphatically not a case for Nigerian sovereignty. Cary declares that the African "looks upon Europe and its civilization as things far superior to anything in his own inheritance; and he thinks of the English language as the sign and agent of that superiority; a key to power and prestige" (110–11). A measure of Cary's fixedly ethnocentric vision is his assurance that even colonized "others" are bound to share that vision. In *Mister Johnson*, however, Johnson's deference to such notions of European superiority regularly flounders into bathos, following the familiar comic trajectory of "black collapse." Even by his mimicry of his betters, the colonial subject, as JanMohamed implies, simply likens himself to an ape.

Still, on balance Cary's Johnson emerges as a more likable, less abjectly clownish African than Waugh's black emperor; even his naive utopian simplicities are more engaging than Seth's verbose, self-infatuated paeans to modernity. His most shocking deviation from civility, his murder of Gollup, fails to criminalize or dehumanize him altogether, largely because Gollup himself is a revoltingly brutal racist and bully. The closing pages of *Mister Johnson* give a new lustre to Johnson's personal magnetism by highlighting his comradeship *de profundis* with his guards. Their assurances to him – "'We like you, clerk – you're a nice chap'" (216) – ring true. Such moments, offsetting earlier impressions of Johnson as merely a bumbling fool, provide a rebuttal of sorts to JanMohamed's sweeping condemnation of Cary's Africans, including the doomed clerk: "The absence of perceptual complexity and the denial, through association with idealism and anarchism, of other possible interpretations of African characters and reality result in [a] typical feature of romance: the domination of the text by a single, highly subjective and monolithic viewpoint" (38–9). Where Charley Brown's life is about to broaden at the end of his narrative, Johnson's is rudely curtailed, but our sense of his promise has been unexpectedly enriched. To that extent, our own viewpoint has been broadened by the dialogic complexity that Bakhtin admired in Dostoevsky and that JanMohamed finds lacking in Cary.

Too often, however, the complexity looks embarrassingly like confusion. Johnson himself occupies a hazily defined moral space between the realm of animals (to whom he is repeatedly compared) and the realm of humanity.[4] When under arrest for Gollup's murder, he is called "son of a dog" by a native *dogarai*. Outraged, he "shouts furiously, 'I am not the son of a dog, but an English gentleman'" (200). Even if Johnson on occasion acts like a mindless animal, "son of a dog" is an epithet that cruelly violates the dignity, however stunted, which Cary has accorded him. Yet Johnson's offsetting image of himself as an English gentleman, too, is grotesquely far-fetched. He is exasperated by Bamu and her sister's "juju" talk of devils dwelling in babies, protesting in English, "'Oh, Gawd – oh, Gawd – what do you do with savages like that?'" (109), like a missionary wringing his hands over his backsliding flock. Paradoxically, however, his own behaviour regularly (and laughably) belies his claims to gentlemanly status. Only an hour after his outburst about savages, he is "in paradise; that is to say, entertaining the station" (109), and much of his pleasure comes from the fine appearance the "uncivilized" Bamu makes in the new cloth he has given her.

Johnson's behaviour later, at the orgiastic party he throws during Gollup's absence, contrasts even more bizarrely with that expected of an English gentleman. When Benjamin, who functions throughout as Johnson's more circumspect shadow, adopts his friend's patronizing vocabulary, "'Very savage people ... But I think these people enjoy themselves greatly,'" he elicits a surprising response: "Johnson suddenly crouches down like the dancers, wriggles and skips in that position; then jerks himself three feet into the air, bent backwards at almost a right-angle, with a scream even louder than the old ladies" (133). Benjamin reproves him: "'How can you do so, Johnson? You seem so foolish in your English clothes,'" but for answer Johnson merely "laughs and sings with the dancers" (134). Metaphorically, Johnson's extraverted *joie de vivre* does clash comically with the sober English clothes of his pretensions, but his sheer animal spirits make his "civilized" trappings seem beside the point. At such moments, the novel aligns itself provisionally with the cause of Bakhtinian carnival, valorizing insurgent "African" joyfulness over the unsmiling colonial regimen that it defies.

More often, however, by exposing his "English" pretensions as puerile fantasies, Cary's comic strategy makes Johnson seem anomalous and foolish. An instance is the scene in which Johnson first extols the progressive glories of Rudbeck's road, smugly telling the Emir's skeptical Waziri, "'You are not civilized, Waziri. You don't understand that people must have roads for motors'" (85), and then returns to his hardly civilized wife to sketch castles in the air: "'We shall have parties every day and I shall buy you a motor car, like the gumna's wife'"; Bamu, unimpressed, "listens in silence and then suddenly utters a scream like a parrot" (86). Much of the comic action in fact turns on Johnson's clumsy but tireless efforts to "civilize" or (what for him is synonymous) Anglicize his beauty fresh from the Nigerian bush. As Echeruo observes, "Johnson is using his imagination ... to pursue the beauty of a European or 'civilised' existence," but "[t]he beauty which he apprehends is, predictably, only a paltry version of the real thing" (130).

The clashing views we are given of Johnson throughout the book exemplify the Hobson's choice that, as JanMohamed contends, colonialism imposes on the African native: "If he chooses to be faithful to the indigenous values, he remains, from the colonialist's viewpoint, a 'savage,' and the need to 'civilize' him perpetuates colonialism. If, however, he attempts to espouse Western values, then he is seen as a vacant imitator without a culture of his own. Thus colonialist ideology is designed to confine the native in a confused and subservient position" (5). The novel's denouement intensifies the reader's own confusion, leaving a vertiginous sense of a narrative ideologically at odds with itself. Echeruo sums up the problem cogently: "Because the significance of Johnson's career is complicated ... by his two modes of being, the meaning of this novel is poised between the celebration of Johnson's imaginative vitality and the capacity for devotion on the one hand, and on the other, the portrayal of the burden which his naive devotion to European values places on Rudbeck, the representative of those values. The need to attend to these two demands is responsible for the shift at the end of the novel from Johnson's coming to terms with reality to Rudbeck's growth through the ordeal of executing his protégé" (139). Yet even the two alternatives Echeruo poses – Johnson's facing up to reality and Rudbeck's growth – are themselves questionable. After executing Johnson, Rudbeck returns to his office "insisting with the whole force of his obstinate nature that he has done nothing unusual, that he has taken the obvious, reasonable course" (226), an attitude that gives scant evidence of personal expansion. And on the verge of being executed, Johnson hardly displays a firmer grasp of his own errors, or of his position as a colonial subject, than he has managed all along. The truly striking shift at the end is the makeover Cary bestows on Johnson: after his whole history of comical malfeasance, the young man is at the eleventh hour exalted to the role of tragic victim. Although Cary's account of Johnson's final days is gripping, nothing can make its pathos seem a natural outgrowth of the comic action leading up to it.

Celia Rudbeck's reception of the news of Johnson's death, and of her husband's part in it, suggests an eleventh-hour change in her attitude from amusement at "poor Wog" to a more troubled compassion: "She looks at [Rudbeck] for a moment with the same face as the clerk's [i.e., the same face as that of Montagu, Johnson's successor], astonished and horrified as if at a murderer. Her lips move as if she is going to cry" (227). But the repetition of "as if" is telling; one can only wonder whether the Englishwoman's spontaneous reaction betrays any real, dawning awareness of Johnson's humanity, or of the moral gravity of her husband's action.

Montagu himself is not only a replacement but a foil for Johnson, epitomizing the "European" nattiness and efficiency lacking in his predecessor. In Montagu, however, those virtues seem only a pallid substitute for the dead clerk's troublesome gusto. JanMohamed speaks of "the sense of superiority that Johnson's antics afford the reader" (47), yet the antics also afford something that cannot be so readily defined. What might be called the exoticizing of the African protagonist may distance him from the patronizing Western reader, but it also reflects the fascination Cary himself, in *The Case*, confesses to having felt in Africa: "I had it myself, that love of the picturesque which invites the traveller to delight in anything unfamiliar and racy of the soil; in national government, native costume, native dances; national religious ceremony, even national dirt and poverty, so long as it is different from that which he can see at home" (58). Cary goes on to imply that over time he grew out of this voyeuristic enchantment with "difference," but it is still detectable between the lines of *Mister Johnson*, above all in the treatment of the protagonist, who remains a "perfect quaint," an "unfamiliar and racy" curio, instead of being granted normalizing membership in the human community. Cary concludes his novel on a sombre rather than on a Waugh-like satiric note, yet one is left, as at the end of *Black Mischief*, with a muted nostalgia, a sense that Johnson's disappearance spells the loss of the piquant African unruliness and strangeness. For all that, Cary's comic frame of reference, defensively premised on the superiority of European colonialism's values and institutions, never allows the irrepressible, doomed clerk to grow far beyond the narrow boundaries of *Punch* caricature, to be promoted decisively from "poor Wog" to "poor man." The novel's humour is finally a byproduct of the tension, peculiar to the twilight years of empire, between an embattled faith in the rightness of the colonial project and a nascent suspicion of its fatal flaws. Laughter here serves the cause of a rear-guard struggle to preserve the old imperial control, but one detects mirthless rumblings of panic in the middle distance.

PART TWO

Passages to Elsewhere

5

Forster's Funny Bridge Party: Nation and Humour in *A Passage to India*

No Anglo-Indian will ever deny that India is going to the dogs, or ever has denied it – for India, like *Punch*, never was what it was.

George Orwell, *Burmese Days* (28)

"Forster liked to laugh. In real life he was often melancholy and low-temperature. Then something would catch his fancy and his ragged hedge-row of a moustache would begin to twitch and then he would utter a little cry and begin to laugh – and that is how I remember him, laughing and shaking, and crying out 'Oh! Oh!' as he heard something scandalous, indecent, foolish, silly, but something which confirmed him in his conviction that human beings, absurd and comical as they might be, were all the better for not getting puffed up and trying to be higher than the angels" (Stape 230). Noel Annan's reminiscences will come as no surprise to readers of E.M. Forster; in Forster's work, laughter irresistibly rushes in where angels fear to tread. As Richard Simon notes, the position Forster argued in a 1907 debate on humour, "that 'it was pernicious that the sense of humour could be made to direct our lives; it was not capable of performing such a task'" (215), shows him warily gauging laughter's proper place and boundaries at the outset of his career. Toward its end, in "What I Believe," he lists as the crowning item in his catalogue of traits possessed by natural "aristocrats": "They can take a joke" (*Two Cheers* 73).

Academic critics are not always able to take Forster's jokes. As Vereen Bell comments, "Forster criticism of recent years has tended to overlook the fact that *A Passage to India* is a very funny novel as well as a very serious one" (606). Even a quick survey of the criticism supports Bell's point. For Roger Ebbatson and Catharine Neale, "*A Passage to India* is not a novel one would immediately describe as 'comic'. It does not keep us constantly, or even intermittently, amused" (91). While *A Passage* does contain its share of Forsterian melancholy, "not even intermittently" seems a dour judgment. It is, however, a fashionable one; Forster's novel has of late been almost routinely treated as an unamusing display of the colonial will to subjugate the Other. For Sara Suleri, the book represents "a paradigmatic text of the subterranean desire to replay, in twentieth-century narrative, the increasingly distant history of nineteenth-century domination" (Bloom 107). Edward Said, in *Culture and Imperialism* (1993), contends that it suffers from Forster's ethnocentric refusal to come to grips with Indian nationalism (203–4). According to Lidan Lin's more recent and still harsher assessment, "In [*A Passage*], Forster frequently shows that 'Englishness' is absolutely incompatible with and accordingly superior to 'Indianness'" (135). Ebbatson and Neale argue "that the 'tribal' audience for Forster is a privileged one, and this privilege is everywhere implied in the beautifully held tone of *A Passage to India*" (63).

Bette London detects the aura of privilege in *A Passage*'s omniscient mode of narration, which makes Forster, even against his will, an agent of imperialist ideology: "It offers the narrative a place outside the characters from which to pass judgment and an authoritative base for its claims. Yet it is its very pretense to stand outside its domain – literally above the characters and plot – that implicates the narrative in what it critiques: the colonialist stance. In spite of all its maneuverings, the narrative can never fully escape the characteristic imperialist parts: showman and God" (105–6). Like Ebbatson and Neale, London claims that Forster's intended critique of empire is disabled by the "British" urbanity of its rhetoric: "For the novel reveals the inevitable dominance of the master discourse even as it replicates its hollow tones. It offers no political solutions, but it registers a protest from within the dominant voice – a protest against the very determinateness of discourse it cannot help but represent" (78).

London's analysis recognizes the complexity of the political and aesthetic issues that defeat any attempt to read *A Passage to India* as an ideologically "pure" assault on British hegemony. Many postcolonial critics have, however, taken a less subtle approach to the book. The inadequacies of such readings have been persuasively shown by Paul Armstrong, Brian May, and Judith Scherer Herz, among others. Herz holds that "it is not so much 'collusion' in a civilized critique ... that the text demands of its readers as a willingness to interrogate, as the text itself does, one's cultural assumptions and certainties" (89). Homi K. Bhabha calls *A Passage* "perhaps the greatest of all novels about the complications between oriental bazaars and English clubs" ("On the Irremovable Strangeness" 36).

The complications to which Bhabha alludes provide a wealth of material for comedy, yet postcolonial discussions, when they have not simply ignored the humour arising from transcultural contact, have tended to look at it askance. Abdul JanMohamed, decrying the colonialist strategy of "distancing ... the represented world," argues, "We find the most telling version of this strategy in colonialist humor" ("The Economy of Manichean Allegory" 69). While JanMohamed's Exhibit A is *Mister Johnson*, he implicitly extends his judgment to include *A Passage*. He intimates that racial humour in Forster's novel conduces, as in Cary's, to the abjection of native characters. Said, too, speaks dismissively of Forster's "posturing, comic Indians" (*Culture* 203–4).

A more balanced view of Forster's racial comedy demands the sort of contextual awareness provided by a book like Benita Parry's *Delusions and Discoveries* (1972). Setting Forster's memoir *The Hill of Devi* and his friend J.R. Ackerley's impressions alongside earlier, luridly mythologized British accounts of India, Parry concludes: "Perhaps because both men were critics of their own society, they were able to submit themselves to experiencing India as an enlargement of their perceptions and understanding. Almost alone amongst accounts of living in India in the years before independence it is possible to laugh with them at what they found amusing and to share in their delight" (52). However enlarged, of course, Forster's perceptions could not altogether transcend the horizons set by his own cultural formation, and the comedy he produced inevitably reinscribes those limits. *Contra* Said's criticisms, Rustom Bharucha sensibly argues that "Forster wrote *A Passage to India* as an 'oriental,' which in the context of the book signifies 'a friend of the East.' This does not mean, of course, that he wrote the book as an Indian. How could he? Like any author, his sympathies were circumscribed by his intellectual milieu, his personal and political commitments, and his sense of history – all of which had been unavoidably shaped by his English upbringing, education, and cultural inheritance" (Bloom 102). If, as Bharucha contends, Forster's sensibility was inescapably English, it does not automatically follow that he wrote as a champion, open or unwitting, of British imperialism. His boldness in defying entrenched codes of British racial joking suggests how antipathetic he found the standard colonialist postures.

The way those codes applied to the Indian milieu emerges vividly in period *Punch* cartoons. Their prevailing insularity is epitomized by the 1929 drawing, already discussed, showing a small child who inquires about a turbaned fellow rider on the London Underground: "Mummy, that gentleman's not entirely English, is he?" (see page 66) Smug British amusement at Indian names and complexions abounds in *Punch* drawings from early in the century, like the one in which a young toff introduces the sable-faced Mr Muckergee to his alarmed flapper sister (see pages 51–2).

Although Indians, as Michael Adas has shown, were popularly given more credit for inventiveness and cultural sophistication than Africans, the humour directed at them rests on similar assumptions. Here again, befuddlement by modern technology is a sure symptom of being "not entirely English." Along with the frantic servant of 1920 who implores a ringing telephone not to be angry (see page 64), there is Grave's "knowledgable Lascar" (Indian sailor) of 16 October 1929, who spotting an airplane exclaims excitedly to a ship's officer, "See, Sahib – one steam-chicken walla." Even a native more *au fait* with machinery, like the madly speeding lorry driver in a drawing of 9 June 1920, is made ridiculous both by the havoc he inflicts on his surroundings and by his inflated estimate of his own personal standing. Reprimanded by a haughtily indignant colonial transport officer in an assertive topee – "I told you not to drive fast through the bazaar" – the driver replies, "But, Sahib, these be only very ignorant peoples. ME mota driva! If drive slow, these peoples think me common person." The drawing is entitled, with the obligatory nod to Kipling, "'Oh, East Is East.'" In *A Passage to India*, the breakdown of the Nawab Bahadur's car after it hits a mysterious animal recalls this comic motif of Indian mechanical incompetence but stealthily reverses it. What is hazardous here is not any inept operator of a machine but the brooding Luddite surround of Indian nature. East is East, and it rebukes intrusions by the motorized, speed-demon West.

Apart from their struggles with technology, *Punch* Indians are regularly, and comically, defeated by the intricacies of the English language. In another Grave cartoon, of 2 October 1935, a native secretary replies beamingly to a colonial administrator's friendly inquiry about his brother: "Surr, he is studying Lahore High School; he is very shiny boy, no doubt"; the woozy English raises questions about the point of attempting to educate such babblers. As Adas notes, "[N]umerous British administrators and social thinkers questioned the wisdom of advanced Western education for Indians and other colonized groups" (319). Cartoon Indians are likewise impervious to instruction in the grammar of official procedures. In a maritime drawing of 5 November 1930, responding to an orderly officer's question whether he would throw a life-preserver to a man who had fallen overboard, a "raw Sepoy" sentry primly ventures, "That, Sahib? Never! That's Government property." Meanwhile, the rules by which Indians guide themselves are far from English. To a Western visitor

Figure 14

Babu Teacher. "Number One is called a 'right angle,' and you would naturally suppose that Number Two is a 'left angle.' But by order of Government of India Survey Department this is also a right angle."

who insists on carrying his own suitcase, an incorrigible porter, in a drawing of 15 July 1931, expostulates: "But, Saire, I very poor man. I haf the seven wifes an 'the thirty-two childrens to make support for, not' arf, yes?" The feeble stab at British slang only rubs in the outlandishness of the man's domestic arrangements.

The Indian polygamy gag was to prove durable. A cartoon of 16 August 1939, portrays a turbaned sidewalk artist whose daubs are flanked by a placard announcing "Child & 6 Wives to Support," and the motif did not fade away entirely until many years later. Dr Aziz's impulsive, ill-timed flight from Adela Quested into a Marabar cave after she has asked whether he has one wife or more than one (164) can be explained by the mortifying popularity of this threadbare joke among Europeans.

On political themes, *Punch* ran a number of cautionary cartoons, some of them aimed at Gandhi, often applying stock comic tropes to polemical ends. An example from 5 February 1930, presents two "babus" discussing revolution while murdering English idioms. (First Babu: "This Ghandi [*sic*] making three per centums too low with his shoutings." Second Babu: "I am saying this: we have buttered our bun and we must lie on it." First Babu: "But I am poor man. How shall I keep the cat from the bag?"). Some items have an intriguing relevance to Forster's novel. A drawing that appeared on 23 April 1924, just six weeks before publication of *A Passage*, features a "Babu Teacher" giving a mathematics lecture to a class of young male students (figure 14). Having drawn two opposed ninety-degree angles on his chalkboard, the teacher explains, "Number One is called a 'right angle,' and you would naturally suppose that Number Two is a 'left angle.' But by order of Government of India Survey Department this is also a right angle." The point of the joke is the Indian instructor's misprision of standard mathematical terminology as an inscrutable Western bureaucratic decree. Adas, again, cites a nineteenth-century commentator, John Crawfurd, who "decried the Indians' inability to manufacture the simplest of timepieces and linked this to their general lack of aptitude for mathematics and the sciences" (247). The slightly askew postures of instructor and students underscore their difficulty in measuring up to the demands of no-nonsense British rectilinearity.

Such a contrast is built into the very topography of Forster's novel, but its implications stand at a left angle to those of the *Punch* cartoon. In the opening description of Chandrapore, we learn that in the British Civil Station, pinnacled above the motley sprawl of the town, "the bungalows are disposed along roads that intersect at right angles" (32). Our first impression is one of bureaucratized aridity striving to clamp itself onto the lushness of indigenous life; and soon after we are told that to Doctor Aziz, "[t]he roads, named after victorious generals and intersecting at right angles, were symbolic of the net Great Britain had thrown over India. He felt caught in their meshes" (39). Fittingly, the crisis of Aziz's life stems from his contact with a British woman, the unprepossessing, logical Adela, who has an "angular body" (85).

A more bluntly political cartoon of 12 March 1930 entitled "A Frankenstein of the East" shows a squatting Gandhi admonishing a bare-chested genie whose turban is labelled "Civil Disobedience": "Remember – no violence, just disobedience." The genie replies with an ominous glare, "And what if I disobey *you*?" The point is not *prima facie* unreasonable: with any mass uprising, there is always a risk that avowedly peaceful action may turn destructively violent. It is characteristic of *Punch*-style humour, however, that a foundational Western myth (Frankenstein) gets routinely impressed onto an alien, resistant cultural matrix. What gives the drawing special relevance to *A Passage* is its latent erotic import: both Gandhi and the genie are naked to the waist, but the genie, drawn as much larger (and darker) than his frail master, faces the reader frontally, his black torso radiating a crude, implicitly sexual power. According to Parry's survey of British accounts of India, "Many of the British ideas and images of India suggest that Indians were feared not only as subjects who had once rebelled and who could do so again, but as perverts threatening to seduce and invade the white world" (*Delusions* 4). A parallel "genie" figure in *A Passage to India* is the larger-than-life punkah-wallah who operates a huge fan during the courtroom episode: "Almost naked, and splendidly formed, he sat on a raised platform near the back ... and he seemed to control the proceedings" (220). Suleri reads this character as "an embodiment of [Forster's] homosexual desire" (Tambling 155), but viewed in context his significance is less narrowly personal. What Forster has done is reverse the charge routinely given to the nude native paradigm, converting its associations of male sexual potency from uncontrollable to controlling. This sexual revisionism has a political bearing opposed to that of the *Punch* Frankenstein cartoon. As Frederick McDowell observes, the punkah-wallah is "a symbol of India's natural vitality" (113); it is the British invaders who are perverting that vitality by conscripting it into an alien, rectilinear network of inhibition.

Surprisingly perhaps, *Punch* welcomed *A Passage to India* with open metropolitan arms in its review of 9 July 1924. In "Mr. E.M. Forster's enchanting new novel," it announced, "[t]he Indian scene is set for our delight" (54). What the reviewer fails to mention is that the book's exposé of British colonialism might strike many readers as less than delightful. It is precisely *Punch*-type complacent presumptions of Anglo-Saxon privilege that provide Forster with his primary satiric target. Even the angular Adela, in an early draft of chapter 3, is described as "looking rather scornfully at Punch" (ms. 25), and, while Forster dropped this detail from his final version, his own implied attitude matches Adela's.

What makes the comedy in *A Passage to India* seem more modern than *Punch*'s, or than Waugh's and Cary's, is Forster's searching self-consciousness about the nature of humour itself. As Richard Simon argues, "Forster should be understood not only as a comic novelist, but as a novelist whose subject is the comic" (200). Simon attempts with some success to apply this thesis to Forster's first three novels, but it is actually far more pertinent to his final one. *A Passage* problematizes laughter in ways that vitally engage the book's central concerns.

Forster's alertness to the destructive potency of humour directed at otherness had developed early. It is already evident in a melodramatic short story aptly entitled "The Other Boat," which was begun in 1913 though not finished until late in Forster's life. In it, racist joking operates proleptically to presage the collapse of a transracial homoerotic friendship. The well-bred English protagonist, Captain Lionel March, has begun a love affair with his young Asian cabinmate, "Cocoanut," on a voyage to Bombay. He finds it embarrassing to explain his sharing quarters with a native to his respectable British fellow passengers: "'I got a passage all right,' he brayed, 'but at the cost of sharing my cabin with a wog.' All condoled, and Captain Arbuthnot in the merriest of moods exclaimed, 'Let's hope the blacks don't come off on the sheets,' and Mrs Arbuthnot, wittier still, cried, 'Of course they won't, dear, if it's a wog it'll be the coffees.' Everyone shouted with laughter, the good lady basked in the applause, and Lionel could not understand why he suddenly wanted to throw himself into the sea" (*The Life to Come* 212). In the denouement Lionel does literally throw himself overboard, after first strangling his unsuitable "wog" lover. The racial joking, though it does not directly provoke this violence, embroils Lionel in a self-betraying complicity that makes his betrayal of his friend inevitable. The merry Mrs Arbuthnot's witty discrimination between blacks and coffees points to a deeper, deadlier type of discrimination that quells all hope of transracial intimacy. Such a story grimly exposes what Forster calls, in his essay "Jew Consciousness," the "nasty, sniggering side" of England's character (*Two Cheers* 13).

Sniggering, Arbuthnottian laughter abounds in *A Passage*, normally serving to confirm the British laugher's hegemonic dominance of a subaltern racial group. Equally important, however, is a countervailing type of laughter resembling the egalitarian mirth of carnival celebrated by Bakhtin. One might call this type fraternal, since it establishes a sense of fellowship among people, whether members of the same racial group or not. The opening scene of *A Passage* presents native characters joking together in a relaxed, fraternal fashion: "'Mr Mahmoud Ali, how are you?' 'Thank you, Dr Aziz, I am dying.' 'Dying before your dinner? Oh, poor Mahmoud Ali!' 'Hamidullah here is actually dead. He passed away just as you rode up on your bike.' 'Yes, that is so,' said the other. 'Imagine us both as addressing you from another and a happier world'" (33). Stephen Land has pointed to Forster's departure from orthodox narrative protocol in focalizing the opening of *A Passage* through a figure he calls the "challenger," one who is at odds with the culturally dominant perspective: "*A Passage to India* ... begins with Aziz, and only after his point of view has been firmly established does the narrative move to the conventional world of the Europeans" (206). But what makes this strategy especially arresting is Forster's disruptive tactic of according his native characters, by long convention constructed as humourless, the first laugh. Cary's Mister Johnson is also, of course, immediately marked by his ready laughter, but this proceeds from exuberant animal spirits, and it is as apt to isolate him from his fellows as to unite him with them. Forster's Indians, by contrast, are quickly identified as comprising a compact joking community, and when they at length turn their wit to the shortcomings of their British rulers, we see that humour, as Bakhtin would argue, has the potential for cementing political solidarity as well.[1] At the same time, their banter has disquieting undertones; it flippantly introduces the shadow of death, which broods over the narrative and eventually settles on Mrs Moore.

Later in the same chapter, Aziz enters into a more unexpected (because it transgresses racial and gender boundaries) joking relationship with that lady herself. During their chance meeting at the mosque, laughter confirms the bond between the two that their serious conversation has begun to create: "'I think you ought not to walk at night alone, Mrs Moore. There are bad characters about and leopards may come across from the Marabar Hills. Snakes also.' She exclaimed; she had forgotten the snakes. 'For example, a six-spot beetle,' he continued. 'You pick it up, it bites, you die.' 'But you walk alone yourself.' 'Oh, I am used to it.' 'Used to snakes?' They both laughed. 'I'm a doctor,' he said. 'Snakes don't dare bite me'" (43). Their laughter works as a binding force undeterred by conventional barriers, blithely violating accepted colonial norms of behaviour and sentiment, because it taps into a more deep-seated recognition of shared human vulnerability.

Against such fraternal joking Forster counterpoints the contrary, sniggering type. Such laughter figures prominently in the cultural repertory of the Anglo-Indians, though it is not indulged in by Mrs Moore, Fielding, or Adela Quested. Adela's temperamental disinclination to laugh – McDowell calls her "excessively intellectual and humorless" (122) – militates against any intimacy between her and Dr Aziz of the sort that unites the doctor with Mrs Moore, and also with Fielding. Among Forster's hegemonic British laughers, pride of place belongs to Miss Nancy Derek, who functions, like Antonio and Sebastian in *The Tempest*, as an anti-rieur. Miss Derek's jocularity about all things Indian matches her cavalier attitude toward the native state, Mudkul, whose ruling family she serves after her fashion: "Miss Derek – she companioned a Maharani in a remote Native State. She was genial and gay and made them all laugh about her leave, which she had taken because she felt she deserved it, not because the Maharani said she might go. Now she wanted to take the Maharajah's motor-car as well; it had gone to a Chiefs' Conference at Delhi, and she had a great scheme for burgling it at the junction as it came back in the train. She was also very funny about the Bridge Party – indeed she regarded the entire peninsula as a comic opera. 'If one couldn't see the laughable side of these people one'd be done for,' said Miss Derek" (67). Interestingly, Miss Derek's flippancy echoes Forster's sentiments in a letter of December 1912 describing his first glimpse of Dewas Senior, which he calls "this amazing little state, which can have no parallel except in a Gilbert and Sullivan opera" (*Hill* 29). The Forster of ten years later had outgrown such a stance of complacent, detached amusement; Derek may thus be serving as a fictional surrogate to expiate his own early, facile response to Indian difference. Unlike Forster's, her attitude does not mature over time, as witness her "tearing spirits" at the success of her car-burgling scheme: "Her Maharajah would be awfully sick, but she didn't mind; he could sack her if he liked ... 'He doesn't want the car, silly fool! ... My Maharani's different – my Maharani's a dear. That's her fox-terrier, poor little devil ... Imagine taking dogs to a Chiefs' Conference! As sensible as taking Chiefs, perhaps.' She shrieked with laughter" (106). As Ronald Wallace suggests, "Through Miss Derek, Forster undercuts the English attitude of moral superiority toward Aziz" (45), whom Derek later prompts Adela to accuse of indecent advances. During the lead-up to the trial she goes volubly on with her humorous repartee: "Miss Derek was there too, still making jokes about her comic Maharajah and Rani. Required as a witness at the trial, she had refused to send back the Mudkul car; they would be frightfully sick" (203). The later disclosure of her liaison with McBryde, the police chief, seems apt; two complementary modes of control – supercilious laughter and administrative force – erotically couple.

The amusement of the other Anglo-Indians ("amusement" is a darkly recurrent word in the novel) tends to be similarly dominative. Collector Turton plumes himself on his witty coinage of the term "Bridge Party": "not the game, but a party to bridge the gulf between East and West; the expression was his own invention, and *amused* all who heard it" (49, emphasis added). The supposed verbal wit here serves as a pallid substitute for any generous willingness to reach out to the natives as autonomous subjects; the snide subtext is that Indians are as hopeless at making meaningful contact with Europeans as they are at mastering the esoteric rules of a Western card game. The pathology of English "amusement" comes to a crisis in the trial of Aziz, a blundering attempt to cast the Indian doctor as a lewd Caliban bent on violating the virtue of a white English Miranda. While waiting for the case to be called, Major Callendar, the civil surgeon, titters sadistically about his mutilation of the Nawab Bahadur's handsome grandson, Nureddin: "'His beauty's gone, five upper teeth, two lower and a nostril ... Old Panna Lal brought him the looking-glass yesterday and he blubbered ... I laughed; I laughed, I tell you, and so would you; that used to be one of these buck niggers, I thought, now he's all septic; damn him, blast his soul'" (219; ellipses in original). Beneath the ugly gloating lurks the neurotic fear of Indians as "perverts threatening to seduce and invade the white world."

By the Indians attending the trial, Collector Turton's mirth is instinctively read as a threat: "The Collector made a small official joke as he sat down, at which the entourage smiled, and the Indians, who could not hear what he said, felt that some new cruelty was afoot, otherwise the sahibs would not chuckle" (220). What is actually afoot, however, is the familiar old cruelty, with its customary accompaniment of sniggers. The Collector barely suppresses his mirth at the barrister Amritrao's complaint that Callendar's sharing a dais with Adela would confer unfair authority on the Major: "'Do you object to the Civil Surgeon remaining, Mr Amritrao?' 'I should object. A platform confers authority.' 'Even when it's one foot high; so come along all,' said the Collector, trying not to laugh" (224). Amusement at such moments of tension plays an enabling role allowing the British to pursue their colonial project without qualms: to delete from consciousness the very symbolic markers by which they exercise power.

Discussing the episode, Bette London contends that the trial nullifies the Indian participants, reducing them to feebly gesturing mutes: "In a trial conducted on the British model and adjudicated under Western eyes, the Indians can have no authentic voice. Officially, they speak in borrowed tones; unofficially, they have no voice at all" (76). But this misses the major point of the scene, the Indians' success in coopting an alien judicial model by bringing their own voices to bear on it humorously. If the trial begins with the sneering laughter of the British, before long it is native mouths that are doing the laughing. In Bakhtinian terms, the solemn games played by official authority are subverted by the insouciance of carnival: "Pleader Mahmoud Ali now arose, and asked with ponderous and ill-judged irony whether his client could be accommodated on the platform too: even Indians felt unwell sometimes, though naturally Major Callendar did not think so, being in charge of a Government hospital. 'Another example of their exquisite sense of humour,' sang Miss Derek" (223). As often, the narrator himself is playing a devious game here; the mock solemnity of the stricture on Mahmoud Ali's irony – "ponderous and ill-judged" – leaves it to the reader to infer that the pleader's sarcasm actually hits home. As comedian-in-chief, Miss Derek will of course concede no capacity for wit to the mere natives; joking prerogatives are a chartered imperial monopoly. (Derek does not speak but "sings"; it is now not the natives but the English who are performing comic opera.)

Just a little earlier, an unidentified native spectator has made a more arresting humorous sally. In reply to McBryde's pronouncement on his favourite theme, Oriental Pathology – "'[T]he darker races are physically attracted by the fairer, but not vice versa'" – this heckler slyly inquires, "'Even when the lady is so uglier than the gentleman?'" (222). The question is formulated in faulty "babu" English, but the impact is the reverse of what it might be in a *Punch* drawing. Granting that the interruption is a "more 'authentic' utterance" than those by other Indians in the courtroom, London nevertheless dismisses it as one of several "anonymous utterances – distortions of the master tongue – for which English remains the linguistic base" (76–7). It is of course true that English operates as the discursive medium of the scene; what else could it be in a British colonial trial staged in a novel intended for Anglophone readers? What is notable here is the way the unknown Indian's cruelly devastating remark gains rather than loses force as a result of its unidiomatic form: the question is a doubly impudent breach of English syntax and of British propriety.[2] It is a vivid instance of what Bakhtin calls "the carnivalization of speech, which freed it from the gloomy seriousness of official philosophy as well as from truisms and commonplace ideas" (*Rabelais* 426).

The courtroom incident confirms Elizabeth Barrett's observation that "the Indian-English language in *Passage* exists as an independent structure of the imagination" (90). Barrett cites several occasions "in which a mispronunciation ... indicate[s] an essentially political perception ... bring[ing] into focus the falseness and debasement that characterizes the relationships of colonizer and colonized" (90–1). In the trial scene, the forcible ejection of an unoffending onlooker in place of the mischievous commentator on ugliness sends a further political message, suggesting that humour is a form of dissidence likely to elude official surveillance.

But while British sniggering provides Forster's prime target, Indian humour is not exempt from his ironic gaze. In an early scene, Aziz reacts "with amusement" to bullying by the overbearing Callendar: "When his spirits were up he felt that the English are a comic institution, and he enjoyed being misunderstood by them" (72). Such a response to the colonial predicament is hardly more mature than Miss Derek's view of the peninsula as a comic opera, a fact Aziz himself concedes after his trial. "'My great mistake has been taking our rulers as a joke,'" he tells Hamidullah, who replies with a sigh, "'It is far the wisest way to take them, but not possible in the long run'" (266). As a younger Forster had once argued, it is pernicious to allow the sense of humour to direct our lives. Aziz's own predilection for practical jokes can sometimes seem tasteless, as when, in triumphalist mood after winning his case, he proposes that Fielding join him in a prank on a poor dependent: "'I say, shall we go and pour water onto Mohammed Latif's face? He is so funny when this is done to him asleep'" (250). Aziz's earlier joke on the same unfortunate, nearly causing him to slip off the elephant taking him to the Marabar Caves, is described as "a little piece of court buffoonery" that "distressed only the ladies [Mrs Moore and Adela], whom it was intended to divert" (152).[3]

The narrative lead-up to the sombre Marabar episode is coloured by dubious drollery and embarrassing mishaps. There is a stage direction, "Various pointless jests" (150), again involving the luckless Mohammed Latif. The phrase quietly foreshadows the chilling vision of life itself as a pointless jest that comes in the Caves to Mrs Moore, as well as Adela's pointless charge against Aziz. The whole Caves sequence weirdly travesties familiar "bedroom farce" conventions: the characters blunder in and out of darkness, barging erratically into mistaken chambers; Aziz commits the tragicomic miscue of picking up an incriminating "prop," Adela's abandoned field glasses. Silly prankishness serves as prologue to grim catastrophe.

Elsewhere, however, Indian joking acts as a salve for looming violence rather than as its harbinger. One instance is the self-abjecting buffoonery of Dr Panna Lal, desperate to save his hospital from the fury of a mob howling for the mutilated youth, Nureddin: "Agitated but alert, he saw them smile at his indifferent English, and suddenly he started playing the buffoon, flung down his umbrella, trod through it, and struck himself upon the nose. He knew what he was doing, and so did they. There was nothing pathetic or eternal in the degradation of such a man. Of ignoble origin, Dr Panna Lal possessed nothing that could be disgraced, and he wisely decided to make the other Indians feel like kings, because it would put them into better tempers. When he found they wanted Nureddin, he skipped like a goat, he scuttled like a hen to do their bidding, the hospital was saved, and to the end of his life he could not understand why he had not obtained promotion on the morning's work" (238). Dr Lal's antics are of course remote from Western notions of heroism, and his dreams of reward are ridiculous. All the same, navigating within an unWestern frame of reference that privileges caste, Lal displays resourcefulness in allaying the crowd's rage by stirring them to derisive laughter. He does this at the cost of turning himself into a clown; still, it is better to have the mob rolling in the aisles than wasting them. As Barrett observes, "Buffoonery becomes a conscious and deliberate strategy for dealing with situations that are potentially dangerous" (89). Here, that strategy works perfectly, extinguishing the emotional wildfire of the courtroom scene.

As Barrett also notes, Lal's behaviour does not make him unique: "[T]o a certain extent, all of the Indian characters display a certain tendency towards buffoonery" (86). Other critics judge the "certain tendency" more severely. For Nirad Chaudhuri, who deems Forster's British and Indians alike "insignificant and despicable," Professor Godbole "is not an exponent of Hinduism, he is a clown" (Rutherford 71, 72). Chaudhuri complains that in *A Passage* "Our suffering under British rule ... is deprived of all dignity" (74). For Lionel Trilling, too, Forster's portrait of Dr Aziz reminds us "how lacking in dignity Aziz usually is": "Very possibly this is the effect that Indians make upon even sensitive Westerners ... generations of subjection can diminish the habit of dignity and teach grown men the strategy of the little child" (Rutherford 23–4). Such speculations may now sound jejune, but the question both Trilling and Chaudhuri raise is a pertinent one: does Forster's comic treatment of Indian characters invite laughter that infantilizes them, robbing them of their full humanity? If so, then we may not yet have left the patronizing moral climate of Waugh's Azania, where the runaway locomotive renders Emperor Seth "ridiculous at a moment of dignity and triumph" (*Black Mischief* 101).

Examined more closely, however, the parallel collapses. In *A Passage*, "dignity" is itself an idea that gets wittily interrogated. According to the Collector, Ronny Heaslop possesses that precious quality. Praising Ronny to his mother, Mrs Moore, he tells her: "It wasn't that the young man was particularly good at the games or the lingo, or that he had much notion of the Law, but – apparently a large but – Ronny was dignified" (47). As Herz notes, "[T]he Collector's implied speech mocks its speaker even more than it caricatures Ronny, as it reveals the former's blind indifference to qualifications and his contempt for the language of his subjects" (79–80). In the trial scene, the chairs of the English contingent "preceded them into the court, for it was important that they should look dignified" (220), but such dignity is spurious, merely a matter of furniture arrangement. On the other hand, the Nawab Bahadur's loss of dignity following his car mishap raises more troubling issues, for it threatens the personal stature of a pillar of the local community. Lidan Lin reads it as a calculated slur on the native image: "For Forster ... this scene offers a perfect example of British rational behavior, which is utterly beyond any native Indian ... Both Ronny and Adela ... are presented as rational heroes capable of handling both physical and emotional dilemmas with adroitness and sobriety. The juxtaposition of British rationality and Indian irrationality is clearly meant to be a critique of the latter by the former" (138–9). Lin's inferences seem arbitrary; if anyone is the object of Forster's satiric eye here, it is surely Ronny and Adela. What Forster implies is that the famous British stiff upper lip so prized by Kipling and his admirers betokens a chronic emotional paralysis; it makes kissing painful. In an early draft, Fielding reflects that "Anglo India is unhappy, despite its stiff upper lip and social solidarity"; he concludes that the English in India "never knew 'an' Indian; it <would> \did/ not occur to them to try, because \such/ knowledge is only possible through mutual abandonment, <which> \and this/ their conception of their own *dignity* forbade"[4] (ms. 535; emphasis added). "Dignity" and "knowledge" are here bluntly opposed. Incapable of what T.S. Eliot calls in *The Waste Land* "the awful daring of a moment's surrender, / Which an age of prudence can never retract" (lines 403–4), the "dignified" English are debarred from any infra dig but animating embrace of otherness.

Aziz, snubbed by Major Callendar in an early scene, displays dignity of another sort: "He was offered the use of [Callendar's] house, but was too dignified to enter it" (40). Such pride registers an authentic local protest against habitual colonial arrogance. On other occasions, however, Aziz behaves in a fashion undignified enough to invite superior laughter. As Wallace points out, he is at times "inconsistent, childish, and pompous, a caricature which would seem to justify the British attitude toward Indians" (42). While his conclusion is overstated, Wallace's basic point about Aziz is an arguable one, and it has been advanced provocatively by other commentators as well. According to Armstrong, our doubts about Aziz's mistaken perceptions of Fielding's motives "alienate us from Aziz's perspective even as we inhabit it and thus disturbingly re-create in our relations to him the dissonance between his world and Fielding's" (376), a dissonance that makes Aziz potentially comic, because patently misguided. Quoting the narrator's own condescending judgment on Aziz – "His face grew very tender – the tenderness of one incapable of administration, and unable to grasp that if the poor criminal is let off he will again rob the poor widow" (87–8) – London asks, "[D]oes the [narrator's] voice represent an act of narrative patronage or is it calculated mimicry? Is it a case of slippage into or exposé of the superior British tones; the confident assurance in the legalistic Western mind?" (92–3). One would like to reply "exposé," yet the comment recalls uncomfortably the rhetorical moves made by Waugh and Cary to discredit the notion that mere natives are capable of efficient self-rule. Such condescending "slippages" occur often enough in *A Passage* to raise troubling doubts about the narrator's attitude toward the Indian physician, and they are reinforced by occasional vagaries of the doctor's behaviour.

Aziz's "unBritish" quickness to go to pieces when faced with a crisis makes it sometimes difficult to take him seriously. In a leading character, such vulnerability has more damaging implications than it does in a secondary figure like the Nawab Bahadur. When Fielding arrives just too late to catch the train to the Marabar Caves, Aziz screams, "'Jump on, I must have you,'... beside himself'"; when Fielding misses the jump, he exclaims, "almost in tears," "'Mrs Moore, Miss Quested, our expedition is a ruin.'" To Mrs Moore's remonstrance, "'I see no ruin,'" he replies "piteously, like a child," "'How is that? Oh, explain to me!'" (144). Soon Aziz regains his composure, but, the narrator confides, "if Fielding had come he ... would have remained *in leading-strings*" (145, emphasis added). Evidently, the majestic English male presence has an occult power to infantilize even an experienced Indian physician. After the disastrous expedition, at the even more stressful moment of Aziz's arrest, Fielding must act firmly to prevent his friend from making a foolhardy dash to escape: Fielding "pulled him back before a scandal started, and shook him like a baby" (171). Since Aziz figures as a prime exemplar of "Indianness," such "unmanly" behaviour can again be read as sending the standard colonialist message: Orientals are too childish to manage without Western tutelage.

Such details need, however, to be balanced against others. Childish, impulsive, or undignified as his behaviour can sometimes seem, Aziz never exhibits the bumptious fecklessness of a Johnson. His Indian nationalism may be looked at askance, but he never dreams of England as his "home," never fancies himself a displaced Englishman (not even Hamidullah, though nostalgic about his time in England, does this). After the companionable opening dialogue, as he leaves for his appointment with Callendar, Aziz replies tartly to Hamidullah's query "'Had you better not clean your teeth after pan?'": "'If my teeth are to be cleaned, I don't go at all. I am an Indian, it is an Indian habit to take pan. The Civil Surgeon must put up with it'" (38). Much later he rebuffs Fielding by pointedly snubbing his friend's language: "Speaking in Urdu, that the children might understand, he said: 'Please do not follow us, whomever you marry. I wish no Englishman or Englishwoman to be my friend'" (298).

This pronouncement is, strictly speaking, an evasion; privately Aziz still venerates the dead Englishwoman Mrs Moore and cherishes the memory of his friendship with her, as he discloses soon after to her son, Ralph: "'Yes, your mother was my best friend in all the world.' He was silent, puzzled by his own great gratitude. What did this eternal goodness of Mrs Moore amount to? To nothing, if brought to the test of thought. She had not borne witness in his favour, nor visited him in the prison, yet she had stolen to the depths of his heart, and he always adored her" (306). Superficially this recalls Johnson's adulation of the aloof Rudbeck, whom the African, too, eulogizes as "my best friend in all the world." But the resemblance is misleading; Aziz's reverence for his English patroness cannot be laughed off as a chimera, most obviously because he takes pains to subject his feelings to close scrutiny. This is something his African counterpart never attempts; Johnson is comically unequipped to bring anything "to the test of thought." The narrator's occasional patronage of Aziz, though jarring, is outweighed by evidence of Forster's imaginative engagement with his character's inner life.

Like Johnson, Aziz has a penchant for extravagance, as the lavish entertainment he lays on for his Marabar outing attests. For Aziz, too, largesse can minister to megalomania: "The wings that uplifted him did not falter, because he was a Mogul Emperor who had done his duty" (169). Asked by Fielding, "'Aziz, have you figured out what this picnic will cost you?'" he replies grandly, "'Sh! My dear chap, don't mention that part. Hundreds and hundreds of rupees. The completed account will be too awful; my friends' servants have robbed me right and left, and as for an elephant, she apparently eats gold'" (170). But the spending spree can be seen as merely the reflex of Aziz's customary, impulsive open-handedness, which sets him apart from the parched prudence of a Turton or a Ronny Heaslop. (Johnson's headlong splurging, too, is a symptom of native generosity, but it is more compulsively driven by a self-aggrandizing fantasy life. It is his egocentric disregard of boundaries that makes him boundlessly laughable.)

Aziz does at times display a more subtly comic type of egocentricity. His disparagement of the Bhattacharyas, who have failed to send as promised for Adela and Mrs Moore – "'Slack Hindus – they have no idea of society; I know them very well because of a doctor at the hospital. Such a slack unpunctual fellow!'" (86) – surreptitiously inverts the true history of his own failure to accompany Dr Panna Lal to the "Bridge Party." The retailored version flatters Aziz by making him sinned against rather than sinning, while it secretly gratifies his inveterate sectarian grudge. Still, such mental dodges need to be read not as quaintly "Indian" but as all too familiarly human. The habit of conducting tacit mental repair work on one's own past lapses does not respect national or racial frontiers; dishonesty so globally diffused provokes laughter that might be called *sameing* rather than othering. And even if at times Aziz's reflexes do seem culturally overdetermined in a way that is comically demeaning, his character never hardens into a Bergsonian automatism, as even Johnson's does despite the African's buoyant resilience. In reply to Fielding's charge, "'Your emotions never seem in proportion to their objects, Aziz,'" his indignant rhetorical questions – "'Is emotion a sack of potatoes, so much the pound, to be measured out? Am I a machine?'" (253) – are unanswerable. British calculations of right angles and left angles are misplaced when it comes to the geometry of the feelings.

Even more than his treatment of Aziz, Forster's comic portrayal of the scholarly Brahmin, Professor Narayan Godbole, has provoked clashing critical opinions. Barrett calls Godbole Forster's "most fully developed character of the buffoon" (91), whereas John Drew argues that "the poet" in Forster "identifies himself wholly with Professor Godbole" (John Beer 81). For Kenneth Burke, Godbole effectively unites poet and buffoon; the professor's contribution to "the mystery-muddle pair" of strands in the novel is "the highest form of comedy" (231). To Barbara Rosecrance, the humorous portrayal of the professor normalizes rather than isolates him: "That Godbole's antics are the object of his creator's comic irony reveals him as cast in the same framework of limitation as the other characters" (232). Ebbatson and Neale situate Forster's comic treatment of Godbole as pivotal to the novel's general take on racial difference:

> It is difficult to laugh at a character without introducing an element of condescension into one's attitude. The presentation of Godbole is particularly interesting in this respect. Forster attempts to invite us to laugh at the vagueness and impracticality of Godbole in such matters as his miscalculation of the length of his prayers on the day of the excursion to the caves, and to regard his affliction with piles as amusingly undignified. Yet he is introduced as an emblem of harmony: "as if he had reconciled the products of East and West, mental as well as physical, and could never be discomposed" ... His song is moving and thematically central to the novel, and in his religious ecstasy at the end of the novel there is a combination of humorous presentation and serious authorial intention. The enigma of Professor Godbole, and of how we are to read his role and presence in the novel, is never solved ... [T]here remains the problem of presenting in a comic light a character of another race deemed "inferior" in the historical context of the novel's production and composition. (94)

Others, too, for similar reasons, have been perplexed by the Godbole enigma. As his attire suggests, the professor can be read as either an exemplar of harmony or a wearer of motley. Gillian Beer's epithet, "the holy and infuriating Godbole" (164), nicely captures his contradictoriness, while Stephen K. Land, more charitably, sees "the delightful character of the Professor" as a "masterpiece of ambiguity between the cunning and the naive" (212). Many find Godbole a remote figure, placed at a distance both from the reader and from the other characters. As Rosecrance concedes, Forster's treatment of the Brahmin "is affectionate but detached" (224).

This authorial distancing makes Godbole still more susceptible than Aziz to the othering, injurious type of racial and cultural humour that Ebbatson and Neale rightly raise as an issue. His behaviour at Fielding's tea party – "But he only ate – ate and ate, smiling, never letting his eyes catch sight of his hand" (89) – gives the Indian educator an odd resemblance to one of Ben Jonson's pharisaical comic divines, a stealthy Hindu Zeal-of-the-Land Busy. Yet even his surprising appetite is not in any simple sense laughable. Barrett argues, "[T]he ritualistic act of eating suggests its correspondence to a ritualistic participation in the universe. Comic gluttony, then, however delicately phrased, implies some connection with a largeness, an inclusiveness of spirit" (88). Burke similarly insists: "One must always look upon Professor Godbole's *social aloofness* in terms of ... contrasting *ritual or formal oneness* not only with all mankind, but with the lowliest of things" (231).

Godbole's song at the end of the tea party, "moving and thematically central" as Ebbatson and Neale call it, is presented in a fashion that foregrounds its opaqueness to Western ears along with the foreignness of its ambiance: "This thin voice rose, and gave out one sound after another. At times there seemed rhythm, at times there was the illusion of a Western melody. But the ear, baffled repeatedly, soon lost any clue, and wandered in a maze of noises, none harsh or unpleasant, none intelligible. It was the song of an unknown bird. Only the servants understood it. They began to whisper to one another. The man who was gathering water-chestnut came naked out of the tank, his lips parted with delight, disclosing his scarlet tongue. The sounds continued and ceased after a few moments as casually as they had begun – apparently halfway through a bar, and upon the subdominant" (95). The whole marvelously conjured tableau teeters on the brink of the laughable, but it makes of the professor far too potent a figure to be dismissed as a buffoon. The description vividly locates his singing within an "alien" non-Western scale, but at the same time conveys the powerful *appeal* of the song on its own native cultural grounds.

Here again the narrator is playing one of his sly games with the reader. We feel invited to laugh at specimens of "quaint" Oriental behaviour, but closely considered the invitations reveal themselves as pitfalls, obliging us to interrogate and check the impulse. A striking, sarcastic phrase from an earlier draft describes Godbole, padding back from the festival of Krishna's birth "through the warm mud," as "a ridiculous figure *for those who think such a figure ridiculous*" (ms. 512, emphasis added). Possibly Forster later judged the aside too hectoring to retain, but the novel's final text lays its own traps for those too eager to deal in ridicule.

An instance of such equivocal comedy in which Godbole becomes decidedly holy and infuriating is his exchange with Fielding after Aziz's arrest. Fielding demands certitude:

> "I ask you: did he do it or not? Is that plain? I know he didn't, and from that I start. I mean to get at the true explanation in a couple of days. My last notion is that it's the guide who went round with them. Malice on Miss Quested's part – it couldn't be that, though Hamidullah thinks so. She has certainly had some appalling experience. But you tell me, oh no – because good and evil are the same."
>
> "No, not exactly, please – according to our philosophy. Because nothing can be performed in isolation. All perform a good action, when one is performed, and when an evil action is performed, all perform it. My answer ... is this: that action was performed by Dr Aziz." He stopped and sucked in his thin cheeks. "It was performed by the guide." He stopped again. "It was performed by you." Now he had an air of daring and of coyness. "It was performed by me." He looked shyly down the sleeve of his own coat. "And by my students. It was even performed by the lady herself. When evil occurs, it expresses the whole of the universe. Similarly when good occurs." (185–6)

At first blush, we may deem Godbole's discourse, as Fielding does, a frivolous mystification. Yet what the professor is saying cannot casually be laughed away; his vision of matters of guilt and innocence has a holistic breadth lacking in Fielding's rectilinear, atomistic view of human actions and their consequences. As Ebbatson and Neale comment, "Godbole's slow and almost mischievous manner is presented comically by Forster, as if to underline the pointlessness of Godbole's analysis. Yet Godbole's disquisition emphasizes the communal nature of life and human beings' moral responsibility to one another. Forster certainly lends his authority to this ... " (52). The tension between the overtly comic and the ethically serious prompts repeated double takes concerning the funniness (or unfunniness) of racial and cultural difference, a pattern that applies to the portrayal not only of Godbole but of his Indian fellow characters.

The culminating scene in "Temple" of Godbole's visionary ecstasy features, once again, comic elements; but the joking leaves the professor's inherent seriousness unscathed. To quote Ebbatson and Neale once more, the scene combines "humorous presentation and serious authorial intention." The ceremony of the birth of Krishna assimilates laughter to reverent piety, merging spirituality with the rowdy earthiness Bakhtin admired in carnival. Bakhtin himself might have applauded the festival as an Eastern version of the Rabelaisian mode of the grotesque: "All laughed exultantly at discovering that the divine sense of humour coincided with their own. 'God si love!' There is fun in heaven. God can play practical jokes upon Himself, draw chairs away from beneath His own posteriors, set His own turbans on fire, and steal His own petticoats when He bathes. By sacrificing good taste, this worship achieved what Christianity has shirked: the inclusion of merriment" (286). If there is fun in heaven, there is also fun in the text, as evidenced by Forster's sly antics with capitalization. God here becomes His own Mohammed Latif – a worthier butt of joking than that unfortunate, because not impotent.

The climax of this section is the "funny shipwreck" (311) in which Fielding, Aziz, and Stella and Ralph Moore are all capsized into the water of the tank: "They plunged into the warm, shallow water, and rose struggling into a tornado of noise. The oars, the sacred tray, the letters of Ronny and Adela, broke loose and floated confusedly. Artillery was fired, drums beaten, the elephants trumpeted, and drowning all an immense peal of thunder, unaccompanied by lightning, cracked like a mallet on the dome" (310). In this communal dunking of East and West the twain do at last meet, damply and uproariously. Immersion here is jocosely but benignly baptismal, unlike Aziz's intended prank of pouring water over his long-suffering, decrepit relative. As Wallace claims, through the collision "all of the characters are brought together in a final comic harmony" (47). Transcultural joking relationships again become possible, even if the closing dialogue between Fielding and Aziz is tense and unsmiling rather than facetious. Frances Singh detects in the egalitarian hilarity a topical resonance: it brings the whole ceremony to a resolution "in a very Gandhian way ... for the different groups which are involved with India are joyously united and made equal" (271). *Punch*'s Frankenstein monster of encroaching sectarian violence has been swamped in laughter.

Some critics have read the Temple episode not as a positive vision offsetting or transcending the near-nihilism of the Caves section, but as ironic travesty. According to Reuben Brower, "Forster's account of the ceremony is shot through with comic, sometimes farcical touches, with the result that of all the symbols the Temple seems the most crudely ironic" (195). Generalizing more broadly, Parry contends that "as each positing of universal abstractions is countermanded by perceptions of the specifics in the human condition, so the cosmic is cut down to size by the comic" (Wilde 173). For London, in the Temple section "elements of the facetious continue to intrude, keeping the narrative from entering fully into what it describes. Unable to resist the comic effect, the narrative finally lands itself outside" (104). Citing the mistranscribed English homily "God si love," she argues that "the exuberant energy of the ritual is diminished, subjected to the exposure of an orthographic mistake. Like Ronny, who cannot ignore the absence of Aziz's collar stud, the narrative cannot let pass unnoticed the breach of appropriate form. Corrupting influences, it seems to argue, must be countered where English practices are at stake" (104). What all these readings presuppose is that the visionary and the humorous are mutually inimical; but this is manifestly *not* what the narrative assumes. In *Aspects of the Novel* Forster acknowledges that "the prophetic aspect" demands "the suspension of the sense of humour" but goes on: "Like the schoolchildren in the Bible, one cannot help laughing at a prophet – his bald head is so absurd – but one can discount the laughter and realize that it has no critical value and is merely food for bears" (117).

Those critics for whom the mocking laughter subverts Godbole's mystic vision are behaving, so to speak, bearishly. The laughter, though not simply to be "discounted," only places the transcendent moment within a mediating temporal perspective. Early in the novel the sensible, eminently "English" Mrs Moore has an equivalent moment of transcendence when she addresses a sleeping wasp as "'Pretty dear'" (55). Her vision, too, is by conventional standards laughable, yet it is spiritually profound. Appropriately, Godbole communes mystically with the Englishwoman's perception of the wasp at the height of his own religious ecstasy. Even that shocking solecism "God si love" represents not (as London puts it) a dire "corrupting influence" but rather, in Michael Orange's tactful phrase, "a significant but unimportant abuse of language" (Bloom 73); that is, merely part of the divine "fun." "God si love" is indeed, as London contends, analogous to Aziz's delinquent collar stud, but the analogy points in a direction contrary to hers. Instead of sniping pedantically at Indian inattention to detail, the narrative suggests how little, at bottom, Indian "slackness" about the niceties of English orthography and protocol really matters. Those who sneer at "God si love" are aping the pettiness of a Ronny Heaslop, who sniggers at minor slips like Aziz's (supposed) negligence but stumbles badly over the major question of what love is.

A Passage to India concludes not, like *Black Mischief*, with the dampening imposition of European rule, or, like *Mister Johnson*, with the gruesome enactment of British colonial "justice," but with the poignant deferral of union between the different nations. This difference between closure and open-endedness indicates how nonconformist a comedy of racial encounter Forster's novel is, despite the occasional, uneasy tonal wavering in its presentment of Indians. The nonconformity does not reside simply in the even-handedness of Forster's satire. Wallace proposes that "[b]y laughing at both sides in the conflict of cultures [Forster] hopes to restore right reason and tolerance" (43). While there is doubtless some truth in this serenely Augustan estimate of Forster's aims, it hardly transmits a full sense of how humour functions in *A Passage*, nor, above all, does it register the novel's probing of the manifold connections between laughter and the rude exercise of hegemonic power.

What it was that allowed Forster to revolutionize the comedy of colonialism must remain a mystery nearly as dark as that of the Marabar Caves. Nevertheless, Philip Dodd's tentative move to tie it to Forster's homosexuality has some explanatory force[5]: "One might speculate that what allowed Forster, this quintessential Englishman, to stand at least partly outside this Englishness was his homosexuality. To use the phrase he himself employed to describe another homosexual, the Greek poet C.P. Cavafy, Forster stood at a 'slight angle' to Englishness. And since nowhere in the ideological landscape that was England could he find a place for his own nature, he went elsewhere to find places where that nature might be expressed" (Gatrell 210). In India, as *A Passage* plainly demonstrates, Forster found no secure escape from Englishness, nor did he experience the country as a place where his own slightly angular nature could more than imperfectly be expressed. By the time he was completing the novel, his initial dream of reconciling his native country with his provisionally adopted one had collapsed. As he wrote in a letter of 27 September 1922 to his Indian friend Masood: "When I began the book, I thought of it as a little bridge of sympathy between East and West, but this conception has had to go, my sense of truth forbids anything so comfortable. I think that most Indians, like most English people, are shits, and I am not interested whether they sympathize with one another or not" (qtd in Herz 29). Forster's cynicism, recalling (vocabulary aside) Mrs Moore's post-Marabar disillusionment, reflects his saddened knowledge that the human urge to embrace sniggering myths about Others sooner or later spoils the best-planned bridge parties. He succeeded, however, in a more modest but still impressive project. As McDowell finely says, Forster was "a comic writer alive to the tragic meaning of racial misunderstanding" (100). In *A Passage to India* he builds bridges of laughter between a select few of his characters, and a corresponding bridge between the novel and its readers, even if the bridge of laughter uncomfortably resembles a bridge of sighs.

6

Roman Catholic Carnival: Muriel Spark's Passage to Jerusalem

During the middle decades of the twentieth century, English society underwent changes that had a marked impact on the national sense of humour, and on much else besides. According to Frederick Holmes, these "destabilizing historical forces" included "the social upheaval caused by the immigration into Britain in the 1950s and 1960s of large numbers of people from the West Indies, South Asia, and Africa; the sexual revolution; feminism; and the youth movement, with its emphasis on love, peace, and the expansion of consciousness" ("Comedy" 660). To these I would add another: the collapse of the British Empire and its replacement by its more modest echo, the British Commonwealth. This development was closely linked to the suddenly augmented influx of migrants from former colonies. A popular aphorism cited by Cobena Mercer runs, "[*W*]*e* [*migrants*] *are here because you* [*British colonialists*] *were there*" (7).

The new face of British social life was reflected in *Punch* humour of the time. In the 1960s, under the editorship of the forward-looking Bernard Hollowood, *Punch*'s ideological profile underwent a sea change; eventually, its ties to earlier incarnations of the magazine extended to little more than details of layout. While its audience was always predominantly white and well-to-do, this new *Punch* acknowledged, in its drawings and satirical prose, the revised position of Britain on the global scene, the effects of mass immigration, and, above all, the increasingly contested nature of the concept of "Englishness." In this respect its tendencies ran parallel to those of the new comic fiction of the period, which, if indebted to the achievements of Waugh's generation, departs dramatically from such models. On the level of authorship itself, there were important shifts mirroring the changes in British culture, chief among them a new prominence for female and immigrant voices. Like the homosexual Forster decades earlier, these emerging writers often viewed familiar notions of Englishness from an unaccustomed angle.

The foregoing chapters have been devoted primarily to male authors' comic treatment of racial difference. This gender imbalance is no accident; it reflects the age-old habit of categorizing humorous discourse as a masculine monopoly. Of course, women writers had long persisted in defying that prejudice by producing comic novels, some of them, like Jane Austen's, brilliant; but their comedy had mostly been confined to domestic milieus. When one surveys the body of comic writing set in remote locales, from the novels of Waugh and Cary to more recent examples like J.G. Farrell's 1973 *The Siege of Krishnapur* or William Boyd's 1981 *A Good Man in Africa*, one finds oneself in the smoky confines of a gentlemen's club. This fact is partly explained by practical exigencies. Female authors (aside from a few intrepid spirits like the late-Victorian travel writer Mary Kingsley) have historically had little opportunity to engage in exploration or administration in faraway places. Still, most male *Punch* humourists managed to compose their burlesques of "native" life without retracing the footsteps of Livingstone and Stanley; the repertory of stereotypes available at home sufficed for their comic inventions. Other concerns, ones specific to women's experience, must therefore explain the reluctance of female writers to exploit comic mythologies of race in the fashion of a Waugh or a Cary.

One relevant factor is that, along with other "marginal" types such as Africans, Asians, Jews, and homosexuals like Forster, women have themselves been preferred targets of derisive stereotyping. And there is a more specific parallel between women and colonials noted by Michael Adas: "Especially in the industrial era, science and technology were sources of both Western dominance over African and Asian peoples, male and female, and of males over females in European and American societies … [U]sually it was simply assumed that women knew and cared to know little about mathematics and engineering and that the power derived from superiority in these fields should be monopolized by white males" (14). There are thus reasons why women, white as well as coloured, might be more apt than men to identify with the standard butts of racial joking, and consequently less eager to engage in it themselves. Such an inference is of course speculative, and counter-examples come readily to mind. To mention just one, Stella Gibbons's popular 1932 comic novel *Cold Comfort Farm* contains a character whose name the "smart" young heroine, Flora Poste, first hears as Mybug. Later, upon reading the man's card, she discovers "that his name was not Mybug, but Meyerburg, and that he lived in Charlotte Street – two facts which were not calculated to raise her spirits" (108). It is evidently Meyerburg's implied Jewishness, allied with his pretentious intellectualism (a function of his Bloomsbury address), that is comically dispiriting. All in all, however, such instances of racially tinged comedy on the part of women seem exceptions to the general pattern.

Some feminist theorists have drawn more far-reaching conclusions, claiming that women's styles of humour are *sui generis*. Regina Barreca holds that "women's comedic writings depend on the process, not on the endings," and that "this sets the work of twentieth-century women writers apart from their male counterparts ... The absence of a 'normal' happy ending – as defined by the traditional critics of comedy ... – does not signal that the work is not a comedy. Far from it ... What so often has appeared as submission is really refusal. What has been seen as solemnity is really the heartfelt, limitless nature of women's laughter" (*Last Laughs* 17). Such a claim for women's intuitive rejection of timeworn comic paradigms might account for their lack of enthusiasm for racial caricature. It is, however, open to the charge of essentialist special pleading. Susan Purdie, while reasonably conceding that "since women's experience is socially different from men's, some comic contents and targets are likely to hold more female interest" (141), takes issue not only with Barreca but also with exponents of French *écriture féminine* like Luce Irigaray and Hélène Cixous: "Discourses which disrupt audience expectations at the level of language-use, textual structure or content may well function as oppositional strategies in certain circumstances. Women are likely to be in the forefront of this, as of other oppositions to patriarchy, because we are the people most consistently oppressed by patriarchy. Still, there is no reason or use in labelling it, in comedy writing or elsewhere, *essentially* feminine" (143).

In this chapter and the next, without presuming the existence of "essentially feminine" humour, I will show how comic fictions by three twentieth-century female authors challenge set masculine precedents. Muriel Spark, the subject of the present chapter, is, of course, renowned for honouring no precedents but her own idiosyncratic ones. But while acknowledging her uniqueness, I will argue that in her comedy of racial interplay, the writer Spark most insistently recalls is that equally nonconformist male, E.M. Forster.

BIGOTS AND BELIEVERS: "THE BLACK MADONNA"

"I have inside me a laughter demon without which I would die."
Hubert Mallindaine in Muriel Spark, *The Takeover*, 15

Like her character Hubert Mallindaine, Muriel Spark, that model of cheerful longevity, has inside her a life-sustaining laughter demon. In several respects Spark could be called an outsider vis-à-vis standard Anglo-Saxon attitudes. She is, to begin with, not English but Scottish (though her mother was English born). She is also half-Jewish by ancestry, Roman Catholic by adoption, and, of course, female. She is avowedly a displaced person; in her brief memoir "Edinburgh Born" she declares, "Edinburgh is the place that I, a constitutional exile, am essentially exiled from" (21). Her attitude toward claims for Anglo-Saxon racial superiority is accordingly one of wary diffidence. The Kiplingesque "White Man's Burden" tends to be a laughing matter for her, though Every Man's (and Woman's) burden of sin is not. Her religious orientation, along with her besetting sense of exile, inclines her toward satire: "I'm quite sure that my conversion gave me something to work on as a satirist. The Catholic belief is a norm from which one can depart. It's not a fluctuating thing" ("My Conversion," Hynes 26).

But Spark's pre-conversion experiences in Africa also gave her something to work on as a satirist. They were crucial to her moral and emotional development; in her autobiography *Curriculum Vitae* she says, "It was in Africa that I learned to cope with life" (119). She recounts an anecdote of a small black boy shot dead by a white Rhodesian farmer for daring to peep through a window at his wife while she was nursing their baby: "This story was told me by a smug, self-satisfied South African Dutch woman of about forty-five … The woman seemed to think the farmer was quite right and to regret that things were changing or had changed. I was unable to speak. I simply stared at the woman. She didn't notice this, but went on talking in her self-righteous way. The farmer, she lamented, went to prison for three years" (*Curriculum Vitae* 126–7). In a short story inspired by this incident, "The Curtain Blown by the Breeze," Spark strategically places the self-discrediting monologue in the mouth of the farmer's wife herself: "'It was through that window he was looking. Yere I was sitting yere on the bed feeding the baby and I look up at the window and so help me God it was a blerry nig standing outside with his face at the window. You should of heard me scream. So Jamie got the gun and caught the pic and I hear the bang. So he went too far in his blerry temper so what can you expect?'" (*Collected Stories* 29). In this early treatment of racial callousness, Spark's satiric touch is already assured. The quirks of the dialect combine with the crass bigotry of the vocabulary to lay bare the moral poverty of the attitudes being voiced.

With equal assurance, Spark exposes English hypocrisy on the score of racial difference in a satirical story set closer to home, "The Black Madonna." The action, which involves an upwardly mobile Catholic couple, Raymond and Lou Parker, focuses on the cohabitation of English racial and class snobbery with *bien pensant* religious belief. The Parkers live in a London council flat "not without a self-conscious feeling of being free, in this particular, from the prejudices of that middle class to which they as good as belonged" (*Stories* 40–1). They also show themselves commendably free from prejudice by taking in two young immigrants from Jamaica, Henry Pierce and Oxford St John, both "unmarried, very polite and black" (41). But, as Tom Hubbard observes, Raymond and Lou "pride themselves on a liberal, enlightened outlook which supposedly marks them off from their neighbours; nevertheless, when events take an unforeseen turn, they display their latent prejudices more dramatically than most" (Bold 169).

The pair of West Indians act as catalysts for this exposure. As Hubbard implies, the Parkers' "politically incorrect" English friends end up, ironically, showing more openness to alterity than the Parkers themselves. Lou's fellow Roman Catholic, Tina, offends Lou by using tabooed language:

> Only Tina Farrell, the usherette, had not seemed to understand the quality of these occasions [evenings at the Parkers' flat including the Jamaicans]: "Quite nice chaps, them darkies, when you get to know them."
>
> "You mean Jamaicans," said Lou. "Why shouldn't they be nice? They're no different from anyone else."
>
> "Yes, yes, that's what I mean," said Tina.
>
> "We're all equal,"said Lou. "Don't forget there are black Bishops."
>
> "Jesus, I never said we were the equal of a Bishop," Tina said, very bewildered.
>
> "Well, don't call them darkies."(*Stories* 42)

Unlike the farmer's wife in "The Curtain Blown by the Breeze," Tina uses stock racial epithets without malice; she is merely good-natured but unenlightened. On the other hand, Lou's policing of her friend's discourse points to no heartfelt belief in racial equality; it masks an underlying, unconfessed intolerance from which Tina herself is exempt. Spark subtly intimates Lou's covert preference for "whiteness" in a description of her response to her widowed sister's slatternly household in déclassé Bethnal Green: "Lou looked at the chipped paint, the dirty windows and torn grey-white curtains and was reminded with hopeless clarity of her hopeless childhood in Liverpool from which, miraculously, hope had lifted her, and had come true, for the nuns had got her that job; and she had trained as a nurse among white-painted beds, and white shining walls, and tiles, hot water everywhere and Dettol without stint. When she had first married she had wanted all white-painted furniture that you could wash and liberate from germs ... " (44–5). Lou's life has gone miraculously from hopelessness to hope, without bestowing on her that other cardinal virtue, charity. Her compulsive rejection of anything but pure, antiseptic whiteness implies that lack, while casting doubt on her fitness for a calling that entails an unfastidious eagerness to nurture. Her kindred attachment to the idea of racial "whiteness" surfaces in her resentment of Henry Pierce's condescending remark about her sister:

> "I wonder if she [the sister] tries to raise herself?" said Raymond. "With all those children she could surely get better accommodation if only she – "
>
> "That sort," said Henry, leaning forward from the back of the car, "never moves. It's the slum mentality, man. Take some folks I've seen back home – "
>
> "There's no comparison," Lou snapped suddenly. "This is quite a different case."
>
> Raymond glanced at her in surprise; Henry sat back, offended. Lou was thinking, wildly, what a cheek *him* talking like a snob. At least Elizabeth's white. (46–7)

The "difference" Lou sees between the cases plainly boils down to a mere disparity of complexion. Snobbery, to her snobbish way of thinking, is off limits for black people.

The other Jamaican, Oxford St John, offends Lou for a different reason: not supposed condescension but (by her prudish standards) vulgarity: "He would stand in front of the glass in their kitchen and tell himself, 'Man, you just a big black bugger.' He kept referring to himself as black, which of course he was, Lou thought, but it was not the thing to say. He stood in the doorway with his arms and smile thrown wide: 'I am black but comely, O ye daughters of Jerusalem.' And once, when Raymond was out, Oxford brought the conversation round to that question of being black, *all over*, which made Lou very uncomfortable and she kept looking at the clock and dropped stitches in her knitting" (47). Oxford's sense of humour may be in questionable taste, but at least he possesses one; his earthiness and hearty irreverence bring a breath of carnivalesque fresh air into

Lou's stuffy quasi-bourgeois parlour. Lou's humourlessness, by contrast, matches her refusal to face up honestly to serious issues. When Oxford eventually decamps, she is less willing than her husband to subordinate concerns of propriety to feelings of fellowship: "She was good and tired of Oxford St John with his feet up on her cushions, and calling himself a nigger. 'We'll miss him,' said Raymond, 'he's such a cheery big soul'"(48).

By one of Spark's typical reversals, Raymond absorbs, as if by osmosis, his wife's finicky alertness to the racial overtones of casual speech, while Lou herself drops linguistic stitches in her relief at being rid of the black interlopers: "Their visitors, now, were ordinary white ones. 'Not so colourful,' Raymond said, 'as Henry and Oxford were.' Then he looked embarrassed lest he should seem to be making a joke about the word coloured. 'Do you miss the niggers?' said Tina Farrell, and Lou forgot to correct her" (50). Nonetheless, when fate, or possibly God, plays a practical joke on the couple, and a black baby is miraculously born to them, Raymond, who angrily (though wrongly) suspects infidelity, is as outraged as Lou. Both alike disclaim the child, which the nurses adore: "The nurses were gathered round it, neglecting the squalling whites in the other cots for the sight of their darling black. She was indeed quite black, with a woolly crop and tiny negroid nostrils. She had been baptized that morning, though not in her parents' presence. One of the nurses had stood as godmother" (53–4). The infant's name, Dawn Mary, has meaningful associations. "Mary" of course pays homage to the Madonna, specifically to the revered local Black Madonna whose icon seems to have granted the long-childless couple this baby as a marvelous, though unacceptable, gift. "Dawn" suggests the radiant promise of new life, a promise wasted on the flabbergasted parents. The father declines to dignify the child by bestowing on it his family name. Lou, though herself trained as a nurse, evinces none of the feeling for her own baby lavished on it even by the hospital staff. Even compared with the nurse who stands as godmother for little Dawn Mary, the piously observant Lou, who boycotts the baptism, reveals her lack of trust in God. Her subsequent exchange with the invincibly "incorrect" Tina is equally revealing:

"If that child was mine," said Tina Farrell, "I'd never part with her. I wish we could afford to adopt another. She's the loveliest little darkie in the world."

"You wouldn't think so," said Lou, "if she really was yours. Imagine it for yourself, waking up to find you've had a black baby that everyone thinks has a nigger for its father."

"It *would* be a shock," Tina said, and tittered. (56)

Lou's flaunted pose of "tolerance" has been put to the test by extraordinary events and found wanting. She is now herself using Tina's racially demeaning vocabulary automatically and with an animus of which her friend is innocent. The two upwardly aspiring Parkers' rejection of their exceptional child sets them apart from ordinary, ignorant people of good will; it is at once illiberal, unnatural, and unChristian. The story thus privileges spontaneous fellow-feeling over a merely notional, humourless ideology of tolerance, an emphasis that, again as applied to racial difference, returns in Spark's most ambitious novel.

THE MANDELBAUM GATE: FUNNINESS AND GODLINESS

Of all her works, *The Mandelbaum Gate* (1965) offers Spark's most searching comic scrutiny of English attitudes toward otherness and of the impact non-Europeans can have on English sensibilities. Despite the currents of mistrust and misprision that pervade the narrative, the engagement with alterity is more rewarding for the cosmopolitan major characters than it is for the parochial Lou and Raymond Parker. The book's composition coincided in time with the Vatican II council of the Roman Catholic Church, and reflects that council's ecumenical thrust, but in a carnivalesque fashion unlikely to have been envisaged by the clerics assembled in Saint Peter's basilica.

In Spark's comedy, as in tragic fact, the Holy Land is the site of multiple ethnic and religious fractures, symbolized by the brute barrier of the forbidding Gate itself. As Judy Little observes, "Spark exploits the comedy latent in an area of the world where one culture – an English culture, or an Israeli culture, or an Arab culture – is continually under attack, verbally and militarily, by an opposing counter culture" (141). The novel seeks to move beyond the grim divisions; to transfigure hatred and dread, largely through brave individual gestures of transgression and a dialogic interplay of cultural attitudes. These are frequently connected with humour, or with the theme of comedy itself; there is good reason why the book has repeatedly been compared to Forster's most famous novel. According to William McBrien, "In *The Mandelbaum Gate* the novelist is occupied with personal relationships and her theme and images often have resemblances to *A Passage to India*" (Staley 167). Warner Berthoff points to more specific parallels: "There are in fact conspicuous resemblances [in *The Mandelbaum Gate*] to the scheme of *A Passage to India*. We have the same three-way contrast, within a context of chronic political violence, between transient English and two separate camps of natives: the one group absurdly alien to the life around them and, in their own view, safely immunized from it ... " (Hynes 57).[1] One might add that, as in Forster, the great enemy to be fought is rooted, isolating, and above all humourless tribalism; the prime goal is a generous empathy, typically achieved through liberating, disinterested laughter.

This is not to say that Spark, any more than Forster, writes from an Olympian stance of impartiality. As Peter Kemp argues, "Variously mocking intense commitment to a party or a group, the novel is far from deriding intensity itself. What it advocates is not a tepid caution, low-pressure existence, non-involvement, chary drawing-back from life. On the contrary, and with considerable eloquence, it urges involvement and concern, but channelled always towards the individual, not towards the clan" (104). Other issues apart, Spark's Catholicism, which she says provided her with a non-fluctuating ethical standard, rules out any recourse to a relativist neutrality. Her recorded attitudes toward the major religious groups involved in the action of *The Mandelbaum Gate* can hardly be called dispassionate, as witness the following remarks from an interview in *The Partisan Review*: "What other norm could there be, for someone brought up in the Western world, really wanting something? Whether we like it or not, the Christian-Judaic tradition that grew up around the Mediterranean dictates what we think is good and evil, and defines all of the absolutes that we hold to be important. The idea of Christ as an example, for instance, was terribly important to the whole development of the West – sociologically, morally, even politically. What would the slave liberation movement have been without it? But if you go over to the Islamic side, for instance, what have they got to teach us about love, about pity, about all the things that we hold precious? They've nothing at all. Therefore I hold, perhaps because I talk from within it, to this Judeo-Christian tradition. And looking around at all the splinter groups, like the Church of England, they don't have anything to offer that can at all compare with the Catholic Church" (Frankel 445). Such sentiments spring from the ethnocentrism (here self-conscious but still unblushing) that Forster made a determined effort to shed. An author capable of so sweeping a dismissal of the claims of non-Western creeds seems oddly situated for writing a novel, like *The Mandelbaum Gate*, whose major project is that of transcending sectarianism. Nevertheless, the actual working-out of the narrative itself manages (with exceptions I will discuss later) to keep Spark's latent personal advocacy muted, largely because of the way humour functions as an emollient to the abrasiveness of communalist clashes. As Paul Lewis argues, "If humor allows us to stand back from our pain, rationality, seriousness and fear, then it should contribute to growth by allowing us to bend rather than break" (21).

In *Curriculum Vitae* Spark confides, "I knew that I could never marry Howard [an accountant friend with literary leanings], on the grounds of his deficient sense of humour alone" (181). Humour, for Spark, has always represented not a casual amenity of life but something interfused with its very substance. As Henry Pierce, in "The Black Madonna," tells Lou Parker, "'*Laughter* – hear that, Lou? – *laughter.* That's what the human race was made for. Those folks that go round gloomy, Lou, they – '" Henry's thought is broken off, but the narrative tacitly completes it: they end up renouncing the gift of a beautiful child (*Stories* 42–3). The reader of *The Mandelbaum Gate* might add a corollary: and they entrap themselves in mental prisons of solemn sectarian hatred and violence. Laughter, for Spark as for Lewis, is enabling because it creates a saving distance from fundamentalist rancour and from objects of fierce desire, a position that makes her a literary godmother of that contemporary laughter demon, Salman Rushdie.

In her 1972 address, "The Desegregation of Art," dismissing the currently fashionable literary mode of engaging the audience's sympathy with victims of injustice, Spark says:

Ridicule is the only honorable weapon we have left.

We have all seen on the television those documentaries of the thirties and of the Second World War, where Hitler and his goose-stepping troops advance to their course of liberating, as they called it, some city, some country or other; we have seen the strutting and posturing of Mussolini. It looks like something out of comic opera to us. If the massed populations of those times and in those countries had been moved to break up into helpless laughter at the sight, those tyrants wouldn't have had a chance. And I say we should all be conditioned to regard violence in any form as something to be ruthlessly mocked … I would like to see in all forms of art and letters, ranging from the most sophisticated and high achievements to the placards that the students carry about the street, a less impulsive generosity, a less indignant representation of social injustice, and a more deliberate cunning, a more derisive undermining of what is wrong. (Hynes 35)

The connection Spark makes between laughter and resistance to tyrannical authority aligns her with the thinking of Mikhail Bakhtin, a resemblance that goes far to explain the profusion of carnivalesque elements in a novel like *The Mandelbaum Gate*. Regrettably, as a nostrum for defending democracy against swaggering authoritarianism such a position seems simplistic. To imagine the populace of Poland or Ethiopia splitting their sides and slapping their thighs as the invading legions thundered through is to take refuge in fantasy; the tears streaming down those onlookers' faces were not tears of hilarity. Spark's argument can be challenged, as well, with the counter-example of a writer like Dickens, whose work famously combines "impulsive generosity" with "derisive undermining." Still, the call for "more deliberate cunning" certainly makes a congenial comic agenda for an artful novelist like Spark herself.

Spark's strategy, much like Forster's, entails discriminating among various *types* of laughter, which serve to gauge disparate social attitudes. A solemn commitment to an inflexible dogma can lead to vicious destructiveness, but a stance of mild, dégagé amusement may lead to something little better. Such superior laughter tends here, as in *A Passage*, to characterize British visitors in foreign parts. As Kemp puts it, "[T]he diplomats, relief workers, and tourists generally exercise a milder form of prejudice than most of that raging around them, but are still susceptible to the cosy warmth of shared contempt, capable of surrendering their individuality to freemasonry's heartening complacencies" (99). One such surrender occurs early on, when a waiter on a hotel terrace brings Freddy Hamilton and Barbara Vaughan insufficiently chilled wine: "Freddy smiled at the two glasses on the table. Eventually, they even sipped the lukewarm mixture. 'They simply don't understand about wine at most of these hotels,' Freddy said. Well, it was a relief, at least, that they could have an English giggle about something" (*Gate* 19). The national giggle implies a distance from, even a cool disdain for, the uncouth "foreign" world, and it is no coincidence that, in the ensuing dialogue, the more passionate Barbara quotes the Book of Revelations to accuse Freddy himself of being a "lukewarm mixture": "Being what thou art, lukewarm, neither cold nor hot, thou wilt make me vomit thee out of my mouth" (21). The moment is comic; Barbara's scriptural bombshell drops joltingly into the bland social occasion, and Freddy's discomfiture is funnily acute. (Ultimately, the effect on him is traumatic; he virtually abjures tepid "English giggles" for the remainder of the narrative.)

Yet Barbara herself is capable of using laughter as a tactic of evasion, to chill any impression she may transmit of gauche partisan warmth. Speaking to an Israeli friend of the special importance the Scriptures have for her, "the half-Jew turned Catholic," Barbara, "perceiving that Saul Ephraim was giving serious thought to what she had said, … gave a timid English laugh, and added that of course she realized one could make a fetish of the Scriptures" (26). Here the temporizing national laugh traduces the lived reality of her supranational (and suprarational) devotion. The same self-distorting archness suffuses her relationship with her English friend and colleague Miss Rickward: "Somehow, at some time, an unspoken agreement had been arrived at, to the effect that they shared the same sense of humour and disregard of men" (45). Here, "English laughter" is linked with a compulsion to ward off sexual otherness, a move that masks Barbara's actually strong heterosexual impulses, not to mention Miss Rickward's. "Ricky" eventually reveals herself to be in fact humourless – "Ricky was a good talker, in that she could converse seriously for hours … without any of the far-flung diversions that humour leads to" (154) – but by no means indifferent to men.

Critics sometimes posit an equivalent need for self-protective distancing as the mainspring of Spark's own comedy: "Making people laugh, as many a comedian will confirm, is initially a defensive measure. In Mrs Spark's case, the jokes, like the smooth, invigilated prose, guard against an invasion of privacy or emotional exposure" (Whittaker 145). But, whatever Spark's jokes may be "initially," to dismiss them as "a protective carapace for her feelings" (Whittaker 145) is to unfairly diminish the complex role of humour in her work. In *The Mandelbaum Gate* laughter can grow beyond mere "English giggles"; it can forge a bond between people of profoundly diverse personality types and cultural backgrounds (as it does with Mrs Moore and Dr Aziz in *A Passage*), rather than establishing a sanitizing cordon to separate them. When, on the risky Jordanian leg of her pilgrimage, Barbara is improbably made to pose as Suzi Ramdez's deaf-mute Arab servant, such a bond quickly develops between these two dissimilar women. Waking early in the ancient monk's ramshackle quarters where she has been led, Barbara asks Suzi, "'Where can I wash?'" Suzi replies, "'There's a water-tap downstairs, but you get a big wash tonight, it's not so necessary for you to be washed just now.' And indeed, it mattered so little that Barbara laughed with Suzi, put on the veil, then lifted it so that she could see better to pack the dressing-gown in her suitcase" (187). "Northern" scruples about cleanliness, Barbara suddenly grasps, fade into irrelevance beside her Levantine quest for godliness; and it is the shared, humorous sense of the triviality of hygienic niceties that unites the two women. Suzi's earthiness, as Barbara perceives, coexists easily with urbanity: "Suzi's laughter rippled; it was the laugh of a cultivated woman. Barbara thought then, it's going to be all right, and astonished herself by her confidence in this unknown Arab girl; and it seemed the tone and quality of Suzi's laughter was the reason"

(188). Theirs is the kind of gender solidarity needed to erase the hard-edged masculine boundaries of ethnicity and nation. In her emphasis on the bonding force of such sisterly humour, Spark anticipates Barreca's claim for "the heartfelt, limitless nature of women's laughter."

Such humour is not, however, the exclusive property of one sole sex, class, or nation. Like Shakespeare's great but hardly feminine comedian, Falstaff, Suzi is not only witty in herself, but the cause of wit in a multitude of others. In her, laughter is conjoined with personal force and freedom. Alexandros, her lover, finds that "[s]he made him laugh and feel strong like no other woman. He respected the women of Islam generally, and Christian Arab women, like his wife, were good women. But they did not have the power of provoking laughter as Suzi did; and they made a man feel strong only because they were weak, not because they were free" (209). Suzi's humorous strength proves similarly liberating for Barbara. Laughing with Suzi about her chance encounter with Miss Rickward helps her to break free from that constricting faux-sisterhood with its factitious "shared sense of humour": "And when Barbara next explained that the headmistress was that very one who had tried to speak to her at the Holy Sepulchre, they had both laughed with very much hysteria; Suzi had fallen limp upon Barbara in her laughter, and Barbara had said, 'Don't. You'll catch my scarlet fever'" (220). What turns out to be contagious is not Barbara's fever but Suzi's effervescence, along with her debonair approach to sex:

> "I'm the secret lover of Alexandros, but the more I sleep with Alexandros the more I can sleep with another man. I love Alexandros so much. He gives me the idea of love."
>
> "Have you ever defrosted an old refrigerator?" Barbara said.
>
> "Yes, we have old refrigerators."
>
> "Well, you know how it goes drip, drip, drip, very slowly. I'm like that; only just beginning to defrost, drip, drip, drip."
>
> "Have you ever opened someone else's combination safe?"
>
> "No."
>
> "Me neither, but I know how it's done. Sleeping with Freddy would be like that. One must find the right combination and one has to play around, try this way, try that way, gentle, and listen with the careful ear." (232)

Suzi becomes a catalyst for a process of defrosting that has been stirring in Barbara for months, allowing her to escape from the emotional English winter that had hitherto congealed her life. We will see this metaphorical linkage between northerly latitudes and a state of deathly psychological chill once again in Barbara Pym's late novel *Quartet in Autumn*.

Barbara's thaw apparently dates from the start of her affair with Harry Clegg, whom she thinks of, aptly, as "her humorous lover" (159). It has blossomed in her amusement at her madcap flight with Freddy from the convent where she had been sequestered: "She thought, it was really very funny, that escape from the convent. It would make a good story to tell her cousins on the Vaughan side when they asked her about her visit to the Middle East. And the Vaughan side of herself lay on the camp-bed considering the funny aspect of this affair, since this was what they liked to do; whenever the Vaughans were thrown, provided they managed to pick themselves up, they usually ended by making a good story of it" (164). As a consequence of the adventure, Barbara feels "[f]or the first time since her arrival in the Middle East … all of a piece, Gentile and Jewess, Vaughan and Aaronson" (164). "Funniness" has the saving power not only to bind people together in fellowship but to reassemble the fragments of an individual self. Many of the comic, carnivalesque turns of the narrative serve the purpose of "throwing" Barbara so that she can exhibit her power of "picking herself up" in laughter, establishing her personal superiority to discomfort and danger.

Freddy, if a less resilient figure, makes an even giddier leap from safe sobriety to a laughing readiness for adventure and risk. After blotting from memory his daring, out-of-character exploits in Jordan, he responds to an account of his own forgotten antics in a spirit resembling Barbara's: "'If one wasn't involved, it would be awfully funny. In fact, it is funny. The woman disappears, then it turns out that Clegg has disappeared, and at the same time I disappeared for a few days. It'll make a jolly good story one day if Barbara Vaughan gets out of it alive'" (128–9). And of course she does get out of it, and it does make a jolly good story – the one Spark has been telling us. But even during their nocturnal flight from the convent, the exhilaration of rash action connects Freddy in mirth with his hybrid co-conspirators, the half-Jewish Barbara and Alexandros, the Lebanese-Arab-Orthodox Catholic curio dealer:

> Alexandros said, "Madam, [the nuns] would think something else to see you come with a man and your baggage. Maybe they shall say in the morning that you are a wolf in the raiment of a sheep."
>
> "So I am," Barbara said.
>
> "What a jolly good idea this is," Freddy said, and they all laughed at each other's words with an overflow of relief, success, and the moonlit morning air. (153)

Earlier, in the multicultured Alexandros's elegant sitting room, with its pointedly *eclectic* decor, Freddy has already begun to gain a visceral sense of renewal: "They ate, and Freddy felt Alexandros's eyes upon him and experienced that sense of his own physical qualities, and the qualities of the room, and, most of all, the carpet glowing on the far wall. And he, in turn, perceived large Alexandros in his physical presence, sitting opposite him, fleshy, brown-skinned, thick-jowled with curly black hair, semitic nose, and vital dark eyes" (143). The room and its owner could hardly be more pungently unEnglish, and contact with them warms the normally flaccid Freddy into a vibrancy foreign to his workaday personality. His metamorphosis reverses older patterns of Orientalist comedy; contrast for example Basil Seal's depleting exposure to the foreignness of Azania, which even his comradeship with the roguish Levantine entrepreneur Youkoumian – an Alexandros equivalent – does little to redeem. In Spark, such a baptism in the fire of alterity can lead to a melting of the ice of habit, rather than to the "bust-ups" Youkoumian neurotically dreads.

But it is Suzi Ramdez who acts as the novel's chief unEnglish rieur, its confident guide for the saving Bakhtinian pilgrimage from Lent to Carnival, from inhibition to laughter. Suzi's role in Freddy's thawing extends beyond humorous sexual innuendo to a brief and playful, but decisive, love affair. Freddy's transformation demonstrates how, in this novel, collisions with otherness can be at once comic and enlivening. (True, Suzi and her brother Abdul, though Arabs, count a Norman ancestor in their genealogy. Alterity here turns out to be accommodatingly blue eyed.)

Ethnic hybridity, of which Barbara's half-Jewish half-Gentile inheritance is the leading exemplar, operates as a potent force in *The Mandelbaum Gate*, anticipating the comic fictions by Salman Rushdie and Hanif Kureishi to be considered later. Above all, it fosters a jocular perspective on stony-faced communalist purism. Abdul Ramdez – deemed by his Jewish friend Mendel "far more humorous than most" (106) – epitomizes this genial nonchalance, though it has taken not just a mingled ancestry but an English mistress to equip him with the requisite fund of humour: "Meanwhile, Abdul had acquired from the woman something ineradicable and which was so much part of her nature that she had been herself totally unaware of it: self-humour. It was a form of endowment at the same time that it was a form of corruption. It undid him as a middle-class Arab enemy-hater with a career in the army or a position in business" (96). Evidently, the unaided "Arab mind" lacks the neurons for humour, which only intimacy with Westerners can furnish, along with other "corrupting,"non-Arab attributes.

Thus, Abdul finds in Freddy's philological putterings a "Western" disinterestedness alien to his Arab family ethos: "The ideal reposed in their religion, but somewhere in the long trail of Islam, the knack of disinterestedness had been lost, and with it a large portion of the joy of life" (88). And with it, too, it would seem, the capacity to joke light-heartedly about Arab nationalism. The novel's authoritative and at times noticeably ethnocentric narrator, stationed half-within and half-outside Abdul's private musings, does not concede that some sorts of humour, some sorts of disinterestedness, are functions of one's geopolitical positioning. While she may puncture "English giggles,"she privileges a more generalized type of urbane, detached laughter that unconsciously carries with it a burden of cultural allegiance. The debatable notion that humour exists on a plane transcending ideology governs Spark's comedy and forcibly guides her treatment of character, as her profile of Abdul Ramdez makes plain.

Abdul becomes "[f]rom the histrionic or dramatic point of view … henceforth a spoiled Arab. He could not take any propaganda seriously" (96). Being a "spoiled Arab" translates here as mutating into a dégagé, mirthful cosmopolite. Abdul now frequents a bohemian rendez-vous in the town of Acre that functions as an interfaith joke shop: "[A]t least in the cellar an Arab could laugh at the Arabs or mimic the solemn Israeli guard without being knifed or shot" (101). With his partner-in-comedy Mendel Ephraim he improvises irreverent chants "in colloquial Arabic jargon mixed often with Hebrew":

"My father goes blah O blah O blah for the love of Allah," chanted Abdul.

"My father goes chime chime chime O mine, hard luck, chime," sang Mendel.

"My mother goes quack all day, she goes quack, clack-clack."

"My sister goes tittle-ittle tittle-ill-tee tee goes my sister."

"Eichmann went to battle and killed the children of Israel."

"Mahommed put all the children of Israel to death also, for the love of Allah. There was blood."

"The children of Israel have dispossessed the holy ones of Mohammed. They are refugees. They weep."

"It was a long time ago, my friend. Even yesterday was before our time, it's dead too."

"The past has got nothing to do with you my friend, and nothing to do with me. It's all dead history."

"It's all a long time ago. Great is the God of Israel! Mighty is Allah! We dance and sing and make love with each other, it is better than all that religion and hatred all the day long."(111)

Their vaudeville patter is seditious by design, lampooning the linked values of family, tradition, and religion that have sacrosanct importance for both dominant groups in the region, Jews and Arabs. It proclaims the need to make brotherly love, not fratricidal war.

Such an irreverent, quacking burlesque anticipates Rushdie's larger-scale comic assault on the sacred shibboleths of both East and West in *The Satanic Verses*. And, like Rushdie's more famous (some would say infamous) novel, it has provoked disapproval. Rodney Edgecombe slates the young men's routine, contrasting the duo's performance unfavourably with Barbara's: "Whereas Barbara has been seen exalted on a mountaintop, a traditional place of theophany, Abdul chooses the chemical exaltation of drugs in his effort to forge a meaning for his life, and whereas she attempts to effect a fusion of resistant elements, he and Mendel simply throw them together. Their meaning is in fact the nonmeaning of Absurdism, where sacred chants become the vehicle for juvenile onomatopoeia, and the cadences of the psalms are adapted to accounts of Nazi atrocities against the Jews and of Jewish atrocities against the Arabs" (78). But, while Barbara's experiences do have a moral weight that Mendel's and Abdul's lack, this seems an overly austere reading. The young men's "Absurdism" in fact has a meaning, and a serious one: their zany misrule is a gesture of defiance against the grim iron rule of history. Juvenile onomatopoeia is preferable to mature psychopathology, like Adolf Eichmann's, or to the mutually destructive grudges of tribal zealots. Laughing down the past may appear to be mere adolescent bravado, but in the Middle East it may be the sole available means of living down the past. Abdul Ramdez, for his part, acts consistently in the spirit of Spark's dictum: "I say we should all be conditioned to regard violence in any form as something to be ruthlessly mocked." And the bawling cacophony of Abdul and Mendel's chant actually has much to do with the quest of the "exalted" Barbara, who herself gets "thrown together" capriciously with the most "absurd" and "resistant" elements. Broadly considered, it is in keeping with the carnivalesque strain of the whole narrative. As Judy Little says of Spark's method, "The comic chaos of roles and disguises symbolically suggests the multifaceted possibilities for renewal, for shattering the habit of former identities and former political structures and moving toward new ones" (*Comedy and the Woman Writer* 143). The young men's scoffing heteroglossia is a weapon in their personal campaign to shatter identities and structures that have hardened into straitjackets.

Less spectacularly, Freddy Hamilton's actions, too, show how the armour of fixed identity can be shattered to enable a movement toward renewal and grace. Early on, Freddy comes across not only as "lukewarm" but also as fussily insular. As Edgecombe observes, the diplomat's mentality "trenches more than once on racism. If British institutions and British temperament are fetishized as exemplars of sanity, anything that differs from them must also be dismissed as 'absurd'" (63). The polite little rondeau Freddy composes as a bread-and-butter note is disrupted, to his annoyance, by the chanting of Orthodox Jewish children: "But he could not get his rhythm right against the chanting of these children of the Orient." He walks along mentally "pitting culture against culture" (15). The small incident anticipates the mocking chant of Abdul and Mendel, which in its own jocose way pits culture against culture but which has more chance of "getting the rhythm right" than Freddy's metrical trifling. Just after hearing the children's chant, Freddy bumps into a man in European dress who unexpectedly directs "something in Arabic" at him: "Freddy had thought he was a Jew. You couldn't tell the difference sometimes. Some of them had extremely dark skins, almost jetters. Why couldn't people be moderate?" (11). The Holy Land amusingly mocks Freddy's urge to contain unruly human variety within tidy ethnic envelopes matching his stilted tetrameter couplets.

Even that moderate-seeming Englishwoman, Barbara, upsets Freddy by not conforming to neat racial demarcations. Forgetting that she is half Jewish, he responds to her remark that "'[b]eing a Jew is inherent'" with a regrettable gaffe: "'Yes, I'm afraid so.' Freddy gave a little laugh" (17). Realizing his mistake, he flounders abjectly trying to rectify it: "Freddy felt terrible. He groped for the idea that, being a half-Jew, she might be only half-offended. After all, one might speak in that manner of the Wogs or the Commies, and everyone knew what one meant" (18). Freddy clings foolishly to his cherished, easily resolvable racial and political equations. He has yet to learn that identities, above all in the Middle East, tend to be problematic rather than transparent. In enforcing this truth Spark anticipates Edward Said's insight in *Culture and Imperialism*: "No one today is purely *one* thing. Labels like Indian, or woman, or Muslim, or American are not more than starting-points, which if followed into actual experience for only a moment are quickly left behind" (336).

Barbara herself has come to a comparable view: "'But one doesn't altogether know what one is. There's always more to it than Jew, Gentile, half-Jew, half-Gentile. There's the human soul, the individual. Not 'Jew, Gentile' as one might say 'autumn, winter'. Something unique and unrepeatable'" (*Gate* 37). As Kemp comments, "The novel swarms with instances of people believing what they want to believe, thinking in terms of type not person, the species rather than the individual, and then going on to regard these different groups or categories as alien, potentially or actually hostile" (101). Repeatedly, in *The Mandelbaum Gate*, the reification of abstract typologies leads to a dangerous (but often funny) paranoia. It is Freddy's "moments" of "actual experience" that, in Said's terms, enable him to "leave behind" this culturally incubated pathology. His submerged attraction to the puzzlingly blue-eyed Arab Abdul, and his subsequent, more overtly erotic liaison with Abdul's sister, Suzi, whose "very deep-blue eyes set in her brown face" (216) are emphasized, jar him away from linear, categorical thinking. In a late scene, irritated by Suzi's sudden disappearance that halts their sexual encounter, "Freddy cursed her in his mind for the miserable unspeakable Arab girl that she was" (225); but he soon recants and goes in breathless pursuit of the unspeakable Arab. His staunch insistence, later, that Britain must join the European Common Market – "'We must have our markets abroad and trade with the foreigners'" (247) – intimates his change of outlook. Freddy has by now repudiated British "tight little island" defensiveness in favour of a more worldly openness. His own "trade with the foreigners" has become more vigorous.

Like a reveller celebrating carnival, Barbara masks herself with multiple disguises during the hazardous Jordanian phase of her pilgrimage – an Arab deaf-mute, a Catholic nun – using these to camouflage her inadmissible Jewishness. This protean role-playing helps her to clarify her sense of her own true identity and confirms her undogmatic receptiveness to a broad range of experience. Like the skeptic Abdul she distrusts "isms," especially nationalism, and not least her own British brand. When Freddy offers her the chance to do some ad hoc intelligence gathering because "'there's a possibility of the country being damaged in some way,'" she retorts: "'Which country? This country?' 'Of course not. Ours. What do you think I've been talking about?' 'I smell an ideology, that's all.' Barbara recalled, he had become very amused, he had just about hugged her with joy, and at least he had taken both her hands and looked at her with the affection of one who detested ideologies, too. He said, 'Yes, that's the point'"(262). Barbara, the ecumenical pilgrim, and Freddy, the reconstructed government functionary, have by now both, it would seem, progressed to a standpoint beyond ideology. For a devout Catholic like Barbara, however, the notion of divesting oneself of ideological baggage raises obvious problems. Her final disguise, that of a nun, is patently more meaningful than merely the last change of garb in a carnival gala. To begin with, it also requires Abdul, an Arab who has taken up Christianity for reasons of personal convenience, to pose as a Franciscan friar: "He was an admirable Franciscan" (299). The action is pungently picaresque (to procure Barbara's disguise a bona fide nun has been robbed of her habit), and it terminates raffishly, when Barbara and Abdul manage to cross back safely into Israel, "and the passers-by had stopped to stare at the astonishing thing, a running nun with a monk in pursuit" (300–1). But for all the Boccaccio-like hilarity, the monasticizing of the young Arab has the air of a symbolic ploy, with intrusive overtones of authorial conscription. And Abdul is not the sole conscript; throughout the novel, Orientals show an eyebrow-raising willingness to get enlisted in aiding the foolhardy Westerners, and particularly to serve, at much risk to themselves, as Barbara's chaperones on her pilgrimage. "'With God, everything is possible'" Barbara affirms (244), but with a Catholic novelist pulling the strings everything is cosily providential. A cynic could hardly be blamed for smelling an ideology lurking behind the scenes. Spark would likely insist that a vibrant religious faith like Barbara's (or her own) exists on a different ontological level from a secular political creed; but that itself is an ideological stance.

The novel's lurking sectarian agenda becomes overt in the episode featuring its most raucous transgression of racial and religious bars. The chief transgressor is, surprisingly, Miss Rickward, the middle-aged English headmistress who, after being deflowered by Joe Ramdez, decides to marry him and convert to Islam. Here the limits of Spark's ecumenicism are baldly on display, since Ricky's sexual initiation and her religious conversion are alike presented not as human experiences calling for sympathy but rather as tawdry, comical cartoon clips. The scene where the unsuspecting Barbara discovers Ricky and Ramdez in bed is bawdily slapstick: "[N]ow the man sprang up, wide awake. He seemed enormous, his legs beneath a long white shirt leaping from the bed. Barbara fled back along the corridor and out to the courtyard, pursued by the man, who shouted furiously at her in Arabic, French, English, and some other language" (276). Heteroglossia, which in Mendel and Abdul's satirical pacifist chant was a means of laughing down violence, here instead fuels violence, farcical in tone though it is. Ramdez's gallantries to Ricky before leaping atop her – "'My rose of Islam!' said Joe in admiration, heaving himself into bed beside her. 'Well of sweet waters!'"(247) – evoke a Hollywood travesty of "Eastern" love poetry and are of course jocosely incongruous as applied to a butch Protestant schoolmistress. But, as Barbara later philosophizes, "[I]t was, after all, precisely a woman of virile ways and blunt intellect, and yet of unfathomable emotions, who would respond and ramify most sensuously towards a muscular aging Arab of lordly disposition" (242). What ensues is "Ricky's marriage and her sale of the school in England, her eager embrace of Islam, and the total handing over of her lot to Joe Ramdez" (242). Ricky's eager embrace of Joe is thus inevitably followed by an embrace with more portentous consequences; barnyard sexuality conduces to retrograde religiosity and the mindless relinquishment of female autonomy. At each step Miss Rickward serves as a foil for Barbara Vaughan's erotic connoisseurship, refined Catholic piety, and spirited independence. The aroma of ideology saturates this particular comic strand of the narrative; there are gates through which Spark deems it better not to pass.

Chief among these, perhaps, is the doorway of a mosque; we are not, after all, dealing with the comprehensive spirit of a Mrs Moore. And yet Forster's motto for his earlier novel, *Howards End* – "Only connect" – could arguably fit *The Mandelbaum Gate* equally well. The novel bravely means to bridge those chasms of race, class, nationality, and even religion that separate human beings. As in Forster, the gaps to be mended are not only outward and social but inward and psychological. "Only connect the prose and the passion," Forster's Margaret Schlegel muses, "and both will be exalted, and human love will be seen at its highest. Live in fragments no longer. Only connect, and the beast and the monk, robbed of the isolation that is life to either, will die" (*Howards End* 188). In a more pietistic but compatible spirit, Barbara Vaughan lectures Suzi: "'[E]ither religious faith penetrates everything in life or it doesn't. There are some experiences that seem to make nonsense of all separations of sacred from profane – they seem childish. Either the whole of life is unified under God or everything falls apart. Sex is child's play in the argument'" (*Gate* 283).

Forster might have accepted everything in Barbara's homily except the "under God," but that short phrase touches off a multitude of reverberations. According to Kemp, "In *The Mandelbaum Gate* the whole of the book is unified under the author and everything falls into place" (109). As Kemp shrewdly implies, Spark exerts a godlike control over the disparate strands of her narrative; the problem is that her omnipotence can seem, unlike God's, all too blatantly visible. Towards the conclusion, the rustle of things falling into place becomes a din. As other critics have observed, in its later stages the novel's unity is gained only at the cost of an awkward air of strain. According to Allan Massie, "It comes over one, for once Muriel Spark is not confusing the reader to discourage him from the certainty of an achieved viewpoint; she is herself confused, too close to the action" (72). Instead of consistently unfolding the serious ramifications of her comic plot, Spark increasingly falls back upon laboured "high jinks." As Berthoff argues, "[T]here are contrivances and contrivances – they can intensify the fictive illusion; they can also be used to evade the narrative responsibilities peculiar to that illusion once established – and it is just when Muriel Spark settles down in *The Mandelbaum Gate* to rounding out her ingenious story and resolving her serious themes that dissatisfaction arises ... bald plot management takes over from the ironic counterpointing ... We are asked to believe in too many merely arbitrary and convenient plot developments" (Hynes 60–1).

Against such strictures on Spark's "plot management" Judy Little mounts a plausible defence: "*The Mandelbaum Gate* is often taken too seriously by critics who then criticize it for not being serious enough. Its more or less realistic, fully detailed descriptions and characterizations mislead reviewers into expecting a general realism, and they must then express disappointment at the quite fantastic and coincidental turns in the plot and in the characters' decisions as well" (*Comedy* 144–5). Such a rationale, however, finally deconstructs itself; if the book misleads readers into expecting what they do not get, there would logically seem to be a problem with the book, not simply with the readers. As it happens, Spark herself eventually came to see structural weaknesses in the novel, above all in the ending: "It's out of proportion; the beginning is slow, the end is very rapid" (Frankel 412). At bottom, however, the disproportion has less to do with pace than with broader issues of fictional propriety. While it is unreasonable to "expect a general realism" in this or any other Spark novel, it is natural to expect an overall consistency of mode, rather than a jarring shift from ironic comedy firmly grounded in local particulars to slapdash farce grounded in nothing firmer than authorial caprice.

Ultimately, such inconsistencies stem from the narrative's troubled elision of the ideological splits it attempts to straddle. The facetious treatment of Miss Rickwood's sexual and religious apostasy is a case in point. According to Little, "Ricky's painful and comic transition into nonvirginity, like her subsequent transition into marriage (with Joe Ramdez) and into the Islamic religion, echoes the comedy and anguish in a novel of transitions, some political, some personal" (*Comedy* 145). But actually Ricky's transformation "echoes" all too little: neither the comic nor the painful sides of what Barbara, for one, experiences. It cannot even properly be called a transition; it is rather a free-fall from one condition to an utterly different one. Its fictive function is ideological: to "normalize" by lurid contrast Barbara's own unorthodox sexual and religious transactions. Although Spark's farcical gambits neatly extract Barbara from her personal predicament, enabling, among other things, her marriage within the Church, and training our attention on the underlying sanity of her daredevil pilgrimage, they willy-nilly blur the deeper and more perplexing cultural issues the narrative has negotiated. Consequently, at the close of *The Mandelbaum Gate* we have not the inconclusive, troubling brush between clashing cultures and worldviews that ends *A Passage to India*, but a cluster of more or less "jolly" comic opera pairings: Barbara and Harry united in holy Catholic wedlock; Suzi joined in a not quite so holy union with a Greek Alexandros lookalike; Ricky married for better or (probably) for worse to her Muslim stud, Abdul and Mendel running a café in comfortably remote Tangier, Freddy left solus but thriving on his magically restored memories. The shifty Rupert Gardnor is arrested as an agent for Nasser, and his wife Ruth is banished to Cairo; but as zealots wedded to a smelly ideology they come in for scant sympathy.

It is not surprising that, in her subsequent novels, Spark retreated from the grand scale of *The Mandelbaum Gate*, working in slighter forms where issues of cross-cultural exchange could be kept to a more manageable scale and where her penchant for whimsical plot manipulation could look less inappropriate. Still, Spark achieves in *The Mandelbaum Gate* an impressively original departure from established, patriarchal norms of British racial humour. Berthoff's claim that the novel contains "scenes of strenuous comic confusion that ... bring to mind *A Passage to India* (if not *Scoop* and *Black Mischief*), joining themselves firmly to the enduring English tradition of broad social caricature" (Hynes 59) needs to be qualified. The "English tradition" Berthoff cites is, when seen in perspective, evolving rather than inertly "enduring." At its best, Spark's self-conscious comedy of intercultural relations does, as I have argued, recall Forster's; but then Forster himself represents a notable departure from other past and contemporary English models. As for Evelyn Waugh (with whom Spark has been too often and too casually compared), in its overall comic strategy *The Mandelbaum Gate* provocatively calls into question the Anglo-Saxon attitudes underpinning that writer's racially tinged extravaganzas.[2]

7

The Far and the Near: Pym and Taylor

THE IMPORTANCE OF WARMTH: BARBARA PYM

Throughout her years as editor of the anthropological journal *Africa* Barbara Pym was professionally occupied with the continent in question; yet she never set foot there and evinced little desire to do so. Her comic fiction focuses on how the "outlandish" impinges on staid Englishness; what interests her is not the foreign *per se* but its imponderable impact on the domestic.

Judy Little argues for the subversiveness of Pym's engagement with alterity: "Pym relies on discourses that are not at the center of Western tradition. We are not used to responding to these discourses, we are not even used to perceiving them or their implicit structure. These discourses, although part of the Western symbolic, are among the alternative traditions, linguistic and conceptual formulations that are no longer fashionable" (*Experimental Self* 87). Pym's turn toward unfashionable discourses never, however, entailed a wholehearted embrace of the unBritish. In her early writings, alterity tends to be treated gingerly; unlike Spark, she presents Englishness as too fragile a growth easily to weather exposure to the alien. The posthumous *Civil to Strangers*, written in 1936, as Janice Rossen notes, "stresses English virtues as opposed to dubious foreign ones" (Salwak 158). In Pym's first published novel, *Some Tame Gazelle,*[1] two "English spinsters of uncertain age," Belinda and Harriet Bede, are put at risk by "foreign" incursions that they staunchly repel. The two chief invaders, Bishop Grote, whose diocese is Mbawawa in Africa, and Mr Mold, an Oxford librarian, are both English born and bred, but both are tinged with an aura of "elsewhere." Mold, enamoured of Harriet, is reputed to have "'penetrated the thickest jungles ... where no white man, and certainly no deputy Librarian, has ever set foot before'" (79). Such a statement raises doubts about what else in the Bedes' chaste parish the sexually invasive Mold may penetrate, doubts intensified by his risqué joking at the sisters' dinner party. "In any case," Belinda reflects, "he was certainly not good enough for Harriet, who would soon tire of his florid complexion and facetious humour" (133). When the sisters later learn that the ruddy Mold "has recently left for China, where he was to make a tour of libraries and a special study of the heating systems employed in them" (245), it seems fitting that the rejected aspirant should be banished to obscure furnaces on the far side of the globe.

Bishop Grote is a returning expatriate. Even though in his youth he had served as a curate in the village, "[s]ome had heard that he was black, a real African bishop" (159). He is not black; but, even more than Mold, he personifies the outré alien, an idea driven home by the slide lecture he gives on the customs of the natives in his diocese. According to Robert Emmet Long, Grote's attempt to produce a sound with an African wind instrument demonstrates "[h]is awkwardness in dealing with the primitive": "Nothing could be more foreign to him than this primitive instrument from which he manages to coax a sound but for which he has no natural feeling" (36). More accurately, however, the Bishop is comic not because he has trouble "dealing with the primitive" but because he, an Anglican cleric, displays an uncanonical eagerness to deal with the primitive at all. In the slide-lecture scene, comedy arises from the clash of staid English propriety with "rude" African spontaneity, a conjunction that renders both behaviour patterns laughable. Above all, however, it is Grote's attempted *assimilation* of native, "primitive" modes that ignites laughter. When the Bishop has a slide of a puzzlingly shaped instrument projected, the laughter rises to a prurient climax: "Everyone looked with interest at the curiously shaped object which had now appeared on the screen. It was certainly a very peculiar shape and there was more giggling from the back of the hall. It would hardly be what it seemed to be, thought Belinda doubtfully, though one knew that among primitive peoples one might find almost anything. The anthropologist who went among them must go with an open mind ... The Bishop turned towards the screen and prodded it uncertainly. Then he advanced towards the edge of the platform and said in a loud clear voice, 'I think that slide is upside down'" (180). The chance inversion of the slide serves as a correlative for the overturning of normal restraints on social discourse. For the villagers, such "outlandish" images induce shock, but also a cathartic release. As Glynn-Ellen Fisichelli observes, "[T]he villagers break into gales of laughter when the Bishop dons a tribal mask. He provides them with an exotic respite from 'the trivial round; the common task'" (439). So the alien has its uses, but these are acceptable only when contained within the bounds of an ordered English social occasion; and one means of containment is the safety valve of laughter.

Homegrown though he is, Grote becomes tinged with Africanness by association, and his bid to engross English gentility by marrying Belinda has the force of a tribal takeover. His rejected proposal is central to the design of Pym's novel, which focuses throughout on attempts by the dangerous Other to infiltrate the known, reliable world of village domesticity – the trivial but reassuring round, the common but time-consecrated task. In *Some Tame Gazelle* the intrusive foreign element is doubly repulsed, first by Harriet's rejection of Mold and then by Belinda's of Grote. The novel's conclusion makes the point painstakingly clear: "For now everything would be as it had been before those two disturbing characters, Mr Mold and Bishop Grote, appeared in the village. In the future Belinda would continue to find such consolation as she needed in our greater English poets, when she was not gardening or making vests for the poor in Pimlico" (251–2). The novel's pervasive allusions to "our" English poets, lesser as well as greater, establish the primacy of Englishness itself; one of the most damaging of the Bishop's faux pas in the proposal scene is his confusing of a minor romantic (Hartley Coleridge) with a major one (Wordsworth). He has plainly lived too long in remote parts to be a suitable match for the well-versed Belinda. The sisters' English village is a sanctum that Mold and Grote cannot corrupt. The interlopers' efforts to infiltrate it are rudely mechanical – rebuffed by Belinda, Grote at once switches his attentions to her friend Connie Aspinall – so that their antics seem less menacing than laughable, like the spasmodic movements of Bergson's risible human automatons.

Toward the end of her career, in *Quartet in Autumn*, Pym's presentment of foreignness and its collision with the domestic underwent a decisive shift. Disturbingly alien forces have now invaded the precincts of Englishness in a more serious way; everything will certainly *not* be as it was before their appearance. Foreign elements are no longer limited to quaint imports, like Bishop Grote's naughty slides; otherness has penetrated even London, the centre of metropolitan decency. Penelope Lively has claimed that in *Quartet* social change "is present only in the form of encroaching supermarkets and changed eating-places" (Salwak 49) (as if such developments themselves had no further social resonance), but in fact the encroachments, though casually intimated, go well beyond these. As Annette Weld observes, "Although urban violence has not yet impinged upon the four characters of *Quartet*, they live amidst its growing possibility. Graffiti assault each passer-by with such directives as 'KILL ASIAN SHIT.' A young derelict screams obscenities at her would-be Good Samaritan … The withdrawal from power and empire has created a Britain dense with immigrants" (189). This onrush of alterity touches all of Pym's characters, even if at times unobtrusively; the self-absorbed Marcia is upset to find "an alien brand" among her treasured hoard of United Dairy milk bottles (*Quartet* 55).

Yet, if the alien can be upsetting, it can also be vitalizing in a fashion not found in earlier Pym novels. In *Quartet*, this enlivening power of the intruder is closely associated with warmth, an idea repeatedly contrasted with the motif of "English" chill. Pym's diary entry dated 19 April 1972 may represent the original germ of this contrast: "The ageing white woman in the office. Beside the mysterious depths of the black girls she has nothing, no depths, no mystery, certainly no sexuality. She is all dried up by the mild British sun, in which she may sit in a deck chair, eyes closed against its ravages" (*Very Private Eye* 268). Pym adapted this entry (reminiscent of the contrast between Forster's Adela Quested and Dr Aziz) for an early scene in *Quartet*, where the white office worker, now identified as Letty Crowe, feels "crushed and dried up by the weak British sun" (11). The change from "mild" to "weak" is telling. The British sun can now "ravage" only by its feebleness, a paradox implied in the opening dialogue among the four elderly white colleagues in their London office. One of the two men, Norman, is reading from his newspaper:

> "Hypothermia," he read the word slowly. "Another old person found dead. We want to be careful we don't get hypothermia."
>
> "It isn't a thing you get," said Marcia bossily. "Not like catching an infectious disease."
>
> "Well, if you were found dead of it, like this old woman here, you could say you'd got it, couldn't you?" said Norman, defending his usage.
>
> Letty's hand moved over to the radiator and lingered there. "It's a state or condition, isn't it," she said, "when the body gets cold, loses heat or something like that."
>
> "That's the thing we've got in common then," said Norman, his snappy little voice matching his small spare body. "The chance of being found dead of hypothermia." (9)

Since this is the first reported conversation among the principals of *Quartet*, it forcibly announces the threat of extinction from lack of warmth as a keynote. The danger is more than physical, as emerges in Letty's recollection of some lines from Landor once (mis)quoted by the fourth of the colleagues: "'Nature she loved, and next to Nature, Art,' Edwin had once quoted, even going on to finish the lines about her having warmed both hands before the fire of life – but not too close, mind you. Now the fire was sinking, as it was for all of them, but was she, or were any of them, ready to depart?" (8–9).

The conversation among the office mates provides a cue for the entrance of a youthful black fellow employee, Eulalia, who is only too ready to depart:

> The door opened and a young black girl, provocative, cheeky and bursting with health, entered the room.
>
> "Anything for the post?" she asked.
>
> "Post?" Edwin was the first to speak, echoing her question. "Hardly yet, Eulalia. The post does not have to be collected until half-past three, and it is now" – he consulted his watch – "two-forty-two precisely. Just trying it on," he said, when the girl retired, defeated.
>
> "Hoping to get off early, lazy little so-and-so," said Norman.
>
> Marcia closed her eyes wearily as Norman began to go on about "the blacks". Letty tried to change the subject, for it made her uneasy to criticize Eulalia or to be guilty of any unkindness towards coloured people. Yet the girl was irritating and needed to be disciplined, even though there was no doubt that her exuberant vitality was disturbing, especially to an elderly woman who felt herself in contrast to be greyer than ever, crushed and dried up by the weak British sun. (11)

The interplay of perspectives here is managed with Pym's typical delicacy of touch, but its underlying import is serious. Eulalia (whose name itself sounds exuberant) may lack discipline and may not share Edwin's fussy obsession with timetables, but she possesses warmth galore. She does not dread holding her hands too close to the fire of life and runs no risk of "getting" hypothermia, even by contagion from her unthawed elders. Unlike them, she evidently has a destination beyond the office walls at which she is eager to arrive. The linkage of whiteness with chill and stagnation, blackness with warmth and youth, is thus quickly announced.

The English predisposition to shrink from warmth and to distrust otherness emerges more plainly later, through Letty's exposure to her new landlord, a man who turns out to be, in Letty's euphemistic wording, "a foreigner, if one could put it like that" (49). Letty has been comfortable with her former landlady, a Miss Embrey, who could not be more English but whose very name suggests a dwindling fire. In other ways, too, she sounds like a candidate for hypothermia: "Miss Embrey sat back and folded her hands one over the other, those pale, useless hands exceptionally spotted with brown, and offered more coffee" (49). Her successor, the Nigerian Mr Jacob Olatunde, like Eulalia possesses warmth to spare, manifesting itself in the form of fervid Christian piety. It is precisely this torrid prospect that Letty finds, paradoxically, "cold comfort," as her discussion with her colleagues reveals: "'Of course you won't necessarily have to leave your room in London,' said Edwin. 'The new landlord may be a very good man. A lot of splendid West Africans come to our church and they do very well in the sanctuary. They have a great love of ritual and pageantry.' This was cold comfort to Letty, for it was these very qualities that she feared, the noise and exuberance, all those characteristics exemplified by the black girl in the office which were so different from her own. 'Oh, she'll find their way of life so different,' said Norman, 'the cooking smell and that. I know about bed-sitters, believe me'" (50–1). It is the spectre of difference – of flamboyance, of fervour, of spice – that puts at risk Letty's accustomed "English" sedateness and quietude; and Pym's mastery of tone enables us to sympathize with Letty's dread, even while we sense beneath it a hint of the comically pathological. Letty makes a show of accommodating herself to changed circumstances – "'I may get on very well with Mr Olatunde,' Letty was saying, in a bright, brave tone. 'I certainly shan't do anything in a hurry'" (52) – but her optimism manifestly lacks conviction.

It wilts entirely upon her first exposure to the hubbub of a religious meeting audible from Olatunde's premises, which causes her to sustain an instant culture shock, a bewildering sense of displacement even amid her own familiar London grounds: "Now perhaps Letty really did feel like a drowning man, with the events of her past life unrolling before her, those particular events which had led her to this. How had it come about that she, an English woman born in Malvern in 1914 of middle-class English parents, should find herself in this room in London surrounded by enthusiastic shouting, hymn-singing Nigerians? It must surely be because she had not married. No man had taken her away and immured her in some comfortable suburb where hymn-singing was confined to Sundays and nobody was fired with enthusiasm" (55–6). Groping feebly for explanations, Letty tells herself that her status as an "odd woman," a spinster, has sealed the oddness of her present fate. She bemoans her failure to attain the safety popularly thought to reside in dual numbers, a shared life inside the middle-class matrimonial cocoon. What she cannot grasp is that the date of her birth, 1914, spelled the end of all such fantasies of cosy security and the start of world upheaval, creating a watershed in the history of global migration that would sweep the Olatundes, along with thousands of others, from faraway colonies to the metropolitan citadel ("We are here because you were there"). Letty's plight recalls incidents like one cited by Enoch Powell in his famous 1968 "rivers of blood" speech, concerning the intrusion of two threatening "negroes" who ask to use an aged white woman's telephone. As Paul Gilroy comments, "Their approach suggests the encroachment not just of alien blacks into the national heartland, but of the public sphere in which blacks are defined as being 'at home' into her private, domestic environment" (86). Unlike Powell's anti-immigration speech, however, Pym's treatment of Letty's situation disrupts, instead of reinforcing, facile, received distinctions between "public" and "private."

When she musters the courage to complain about the Nigerian family's noise, Letty is brought up sharply, and amusingly, against the stubborn reality of cultural difference:

"I wonder if you could make a little less noise?" she asked. "Some of us find it rather disturbing."

"Christianity *is* disturbing," said Mr Olatunde.

It was difficult to know how to answer this. Indeed Letty found it impossible so Mr Olatunde continued, smiling, "You are a Christian lady?"

Letty hesitated. Her first instinct had been to say "Yes", for of course she was a Christian lady, even if one would not have put it quite like that. How was she to explain to this vital, ebullient black man her own blend of Christianity – a grey, formal, respectable thing of measured observances and mild general undemanding kindess to all? "I'm sorry," she said, drawing back. "I didn't mean ..." What had she meant? Confronted by these smiling people she felt she could hardly repeat her complaint about the noise.

A handsome woman in a long brightly-coloured dress and head tie stepped forward. "We are having supper now," she said. "You will join us?"

Letty was reminded of Norman as a rich spicy smell was wafted towards her. She thanked the woman politely, saying that she had already eaten.

"I'm afraid you would not like our Nigerian cooking," said Mr Olatunde, with a touch of complacency. (56–7)

The exchange causes Letty to think dejectedly, "'We are not the same'" (57); yet its chief irony is that her "difference" from the Olatundes emerges from their sharing of the same religious creed. In experiential terms, of course, it is not the same; where Olatunde worships (in T.S. Eliot's phrase) Christ the tiger – "Christianity *is* disturbing" – Letty feels more at ease with Christ the tabby cat. What underscores cultural differences is the contrast between personal styles of address: the Olatundes' smiling, expansive directness is set off by Letty's mild, measured obliquity ("a *little* less noise ... *rather* disturbing ... *One* would not have put it *quite like that*"). It is the "uprooted" Africans who embrace life, making themselves at home in a new place and inviting total strangers into their midst, while the native Englishwoman, schooled in her national reticence, keeps life at arm's length. Coming to her Nigerian neighbours on an unwelcoming errand, she is taken aback at being welcomed by them and is left feeling in effect "out in the cold." At the same time, Olatunde reveals himself to be prone to his own brand of cultural exclusiveness; he assumes, "with a touch of complacency," that Letty's insular preference for the blandness of English cooking bars her from relishing Nigerian fare.[2] Pym's African newcomers may embody an element of vibrancy missing from the wan English scene, a Keatsian "beaker full of the warm South," but her even-handed irony, which conjoins strangers and locals as equally prey to minor vanities, keeps her treatment of them unsentimental.

When Edwin finds Letty new lodgings in the house of Mrs Pope, an aged widow living (significantly) in *north* London, he feels "that he had done something pretty good in, as it were, delivering her from Mr Olatunde" (66); but Letty's "deliverance" turns out to be ambiguous at best. Her residence with the prying and austere Mrs Pope (who, true to her name, thinks herself infallible) exposes her to creeping hypothermia. "After the vitality and warmth of Mr Olatunde's house, Mrs Pope's seemed bleak and silent, with its heavy dark furniture and ticking grandfather clock, the kind of tick that would keep one awake until one got used to it" (64–5). Letty's supposed refuge from marauding otherness merely shuts her within a stifling sense of her own life locked in its sameness, edging closer and closer to death: a clock-watching drearily reminiscent of Edwin's. Her second thoughts about her move emerge between the lines of dialogue in which her landlady annouces she will not be visiting her sister over Christmas: "The change of plan was the result of an argument about heating, Mrs Pope's sister apparently being too mean to switch on the storage heaters before January, and the cottage being not only cold but damp and poky as well. 'I shall not go, neither now or ever,' Mrs Pope declared, standing militant by the telephone in the full dignity of her eighty-odd years. 'Warmth is so important,' Letty said, remembering the office conversations about hypothermia" (74). Letty's wistful recognition has a metaphorical aptness reaching beyond the never-to-be-visited cold and damp cottage. Its gravity is confirmed by the chilly Christmas she passes with Mrs Pope militant: "So Letty had no alternative but to listen to Mrs Pope discoursing on her favourite topic of the excessive amount of food most people ate. It was not conducive to an enjoyable meal and Letty could not help feeling that on this occasion she might have done better if she had stayed in her room in Mr Olatunde's house. A jolly Nigerian Christmas would surely have included her, and not for the first time she began to wonder if she had done the right thing by moving. Still, Christmas day had been lived through and was now nearly over, that was the main thing" (75). The idea of the grand Christian festivity as a Lenten ritual to be endured rather than enjoyed makes a depressing contrast with the foreign but convivial Nigerian Christmas Letty has missed. By an ironic capsizing of "normal" expectations, her enjoyment of the warmth and fellowship of her own traditional feast has been sacrificed through her flight from otherness to the dourly hypothermic, remorselessly English Pope. Her removal to north London has brought her "cold comfort" in the most arctic sense.

In the snowy winter months following her retirement Letty seeks the warmth of fellowship by frequenting her local church. "Once Edwin had come to the service and Letty had greeted him so warmly that he must have taken fright, for he had not appeared again" (118). Mrs Pope excuses the behaviour of Letty's former colleague on the grounds that he is a widower and unwilling to commit himself to any particular church (and perhaps, by extension, to any particular relationship). "And he took a lot of trouble finding a room for you when that black man bought the house you were living in. He must think a lot of you – he spoke very warmly.' For Mrs Pope this was going far, but the doubtful prospect of Edwin's 'warmth' did nothing to warm Letty's cold heart" (118). Ironically, Edwin's chivalrous "rescue" of Letty is exposed as merely the gratuitous removal of a lonely woman from a warm hearth, a gesture that leaves her exposed to a desolating, if purely English, emotional chill. In *Quartet in Autumn* there is an implied subliminal connection linking the ideas of warmth, racial otherness, and potential sexual fulfillment. Symbolically, Letty's panicky flight from the Olatundes' household mirrors her lifelong skirting of sexual involvement, her avoidance of "indecent exposure" to the heat of experience in general. However, as Weld suggests, there may be more in Letty's psychological makeup than meets the eye: "Her snooping landlady, approving of her immaculately organised dresser drawers, is surprised only by 'a rather gaily-patterned cotton kimono which seemed not to be in character' … an indication that underneath her predictable exterior Letty still preserves the possibility of a more colorful private life" (187). Once again, it is the hint of the foreign-exotic, the unexplained kimono, that signals the submerged stirrings of an impulse to break through the permafrost of inhibition.

The novel's concluding scene leaves Letty drinking sherry with Edwin and Norman in the kitchen of their recently deceased co-worker, Marcia. By contrast to Mrs Pope's spartan Christmas dinner, this sad occasion becomes a rite of fellowship and tremulous communion. Looking forward to a day in the country with her friend Marjorie and the two men, Letty feels suddenly almost buoyant: "[A]t least it made one realize that life still held infinite possibilities for change" (176). After her earlier panicky flight from change, Letty's sudden welcoming of it betokens a significant shift of gestalt. It also points to the long road Pym herself has traversed from the conservative resolutions of her earliest novels. Still, *infinite* possibilities seems an exaggeration. For the central foursome of *Quartet*, any genuine change of life mode is severely limited by their hesitancy to engage with the new, bewildering "foreign" elements now infiltrating the staid, accustomed British scene – "the trivial round, the common task." One might divide the dramatis personae populating Pym's late novel into two tribes: the coloured and the colourless. Pym's sympathy as narrator is clearly drawn to the homely, etiolated English types, the elderly white generation now being overshadowed and "unhoused" by a more vital and youthful generation of newcomers. Still, while Pym's narrative may identify with her fading quartet, it sends them a clear signal: by shunning the vitality that the black Eulalias and Olatundes have imported into the English scene, the colourless expose themselves to something more ominous: the risk of death by hypothermia.

AN ALIEN'S ENGLISH BIRTHDAY PARTY: ELIZABETH TAYLOR

"[I]n *The Times* I saw that dear Elizabeth Taylor died yesterday," Barbara Pym records regretfully in a diary entry for 20 November 1975 (*Very Private Eye* 284). Even beyond their shared calling as female writers, there were reasons why Pym and Taylor should have felt a sense of close personal and literary communion. Like Pym's, Taylor's work at its most characteristic displays a distinctive flair for social comedy. In a letter to Robert Liddell (also a friend of Pym's) commenting on his 1960 article about her, Taylor says, "I'm awfully glad you think I can be funny. It is not much remarked on. A sense of the incongruity of things is not so unimportant as some people think. Even if it's not used, it's a good piece of equipment to have" (Liddell 71–2). The "good piece of equipment" was in fact repeatedly and brilliantly used by Taylor, as it was by Pym. But an equally important tie was the two women's shared feeling of closeness to their own native grounds. According to Florence Leclerq, "The most striking feature about Elizabeth Taylor is … how deeply English she is" (4). Leclerq quotes Taylor's own testimony: "I love England and it would be painful to me to consider living in any other place. I find so beautiful, harmonious and evocative its landscape, style, tradition, even its climate. I should like to feel that the people in my books are essentially English and set down against a truly English background" (Leclerq 4). These are sentiments that Pym could have warmly seconded.

Owing perhaps to the very depth of her feeling for her country, however, Taylor's work can also manifest an acute self-consciousness about issues of national affiliation. Several of the stories in her late collection *The Devastating Boys* (1972) probe the complexities of being "essentially English," either by setting English characters against a foreign background or by showing "unEnglish" outsiders attempting to negotiate the hazardous terrain of English society. The title story dramatizes the impact – "devastating," but paradoxically positive – two young black boys from a working-class area of London have on a charitable middle-aged white couple who have them as temporary guests in their Oxford home. Another story, "*Crêpes Flambées*," set in Tunisia, sketches a younger English couple's disappointing attempt to re-establish their friendship with a self-promoting local whose café they had frequented on their honeymoon. In both stories, vicissitudes of transracial or transnational contact give Taylor rich opportunities to mine for comic purposes her "sense of the incongruity of things." But it is a third story, "Tall Boy," which focuses on a young Afro-Caribbean newcomer's frustrations in England, that makes the most suggestive connections between humour and race.

A *Punch* cartoon of 15 December 1954 (figure 15) treats the newly topical theme of West Indian immigration to Britain. In the first of two panels composing a "before and after" sequence, a Jamaican man contemplates a poster exhorting its readers: COME TO BRITAIN. ITS FULL EMPLOYMENT ITS NATIONAL HEALTH SERVICE ITS RISING PRODUCTION INDEX. It pictures a factory with a cluster of robustly smoking chimneys. The house wall that bears the poster is cracked, but the scene is bathed in sunlight, a tall palm waves in the background, and a young mother and her child

Figure 15

(perhaps the poster-viewer's own family) look on from an upper window. In the second panel, the same Jamaican, who has duly migrated to England, gazes disconsolately at a matching poster with the legend JAMAICA. ITS SUN ITS RUM ITS MUSIC flanked by a picture of a brilliant sun, palm trees, and a carefree guitar player. The poster is affixed to a wall covered with grime and dismal shadows; beyond, the smokestacks of Blakean dark satanic mills are busy fouling the already filthy air. The migrant shivers in an icy downpour, his hands jammed for warmth into his coat pockets. The house windows are forbiddingly shut; no human face is visible through them; the man stands cheerlessly alone.

The cartoon belongs to the postwar turn away from the patronizing *Punch* humour of the 1920s and 30s. Instead of lofty condescension toward the racially othered newcomer to Britain, its layout implies a rueful sympathy with the disappointed West Indian. The drawing makes England itself look distinctly less appealing than the down-at-heels but warm and sensuous tropical island the migrant has rashly left. His predicament resembles that of the protagonist of Taylor's "Tall Boy," Jasper Jones, a stranger in London who must likewise contend with a sense of displacement and isolation. Jasper, the titular tall boy, is less a devastating boy than a devastated one, and Taylor's story treats the painfulness of his experiences with her distinctive humour and tact.

In the late twentieth-century London patchwork of ethnicities, Jasper is doubly cut off, both from his home island and from other West Indian migrants: "In this part of London, nationalities clung together – Poles in one street, African negroes in the next. This road – Saint Luke's – was mostly Pakistani. Jasper thought he was the only West Indian all the way along it. *His* people were quite distant – in the streets near the railway-bridge, where the markets were, where he had been unable to find a room" (66). The sound of Sunday church bells dispirits Jasper, for in the most poignant meaning of the phrase he belongs to no congregation. Once he has sampled a local church service, but he has been left with a sense of trespassing on alien grounds: "[T]he smell of damp stone, the mumbled, hurried prayers, the unrhythmical rush and gabble of psalms dismayed him. He had decided that this sense of alienation was one he could avoid" (66).

Not only is Jasper, whose home country "had bulged with people" (67), placed out of touch with other men and women of colour; his personal universe seems drained of colour altogether. "The sky was no-colour, too – the no-colour of most of Jasper's Sunday mornings in London" (67). As in Pym's *Quartet in Autumn*, the human scene appears to be portioned out between the coloured and the blanched. The local pub makes Jasper "wonder about Londoners": "There seemed to be inherent in them a wish for punishment he could not understand – a greyness of soul and taste, to match the climate" (68–9). Jasper himself, on the other hand, is capable of exuberant bursts of energy despite his bruising depression: "His arms going like pistons, his knees lifted high, he loped slowly easily. In one way, he loved and welcomed the rain, for giving him the chance to run. He always wanted to run, but people stared when he did so, unless he were running for a bus. Running for running's sake was an oddity" (69). He is a prisoner in a chillingly entropic world, where dynamism gets branded as deviancy.

The spells of "utter desolation" that overwhelm the young man seem to breed in him his own wish for punishment, leading him to perform compulsive rituals meant to provide him with a simulation of human contact: "[H]e got up quietly and began to pad up and down the room; stopping at the far wall from the window, he leant against the wall and rhythmically banged his forehead against it, his eyes shut tight again, his lips parted. Very soon, a sharp rapping came back from the other side – his only human recognition of the day" (71). Such expedients can produce nothing better than a parody of real community; his rhythmic head-pounding is a meagre echo of the much-missed rhythms of his home island, the "human recognition" too anemic to deserve the name. They do not suffice to offset "the silence freezing in his ear-drums." What most oppresses Jasper is not, as one might expect, the hostility of white Londoners but a deeper sense of disaffiliation from his environment: "There was nothing wrong. He was employed. He had a room, and a good suit, and his shoes would soon be dry. There was money going back home to Mam. No one here, in England, called him 'Nigger', or put up their fists to him. That morning, he had sat there in the pub without trouble. There *was* no trouble. Once, at work, they had all laughed at him when he was singing, *I'm Dreaming of a White Christmas*, as he loaded a van; but it was good-natured laughter" (71). In view of the sullen tenor of race relations in late twentieth-century Britain, the young migrant might well consider himself lucky in being the object of nothing worse than good-humoured teasing. Nevertheless, his feeling of dislocation is acute, and Taylor conveys its painfulness through carefully chosen details. Unlike his white co-workers, he has no form of gratification to fill his downtime on weekends: "[W]hatever they did, all were sorry when Monday morning came. They had not longed for it since Friday night as Jasper had" (72). The young man is wretchedly "out of sync" with the healthy, normal pulse of local life.

Taylor is at her funniest and most moving in evoking the odd surrogates for ordinary companionship her urban castaway is driven to improvise. Jasper's birthday signifies to him not a cause for festivity but merely an exacerbation of his solitude. To palliate it he resorts to the emotional onanism of sending himself a greeting card. "He would have liked to sign it, 'From a well-wisher', as if it were to come out of the blue; but this seemed insincere, and he prized sincerity. After a while, he simply wrote, 'With greetings from Mr Jasper Jones', stamped the envelope, and went again to the window to look at his Sunday enemy, the rain" (72). To supplement this anodyne he buys himself the present of a hand-painted, eye-catching necktie. By an amusing irony, this piece of self-indulgence inadvertently proves to be an ingenious ploy, for the faux-gift works as a "tie" in a punning sense, uniting Jasper for once with his English mates when he returns to work: "'Hey, Tall Boy, what the devil you got there?' Buster came over, stared at Jasper's tie, then appeared to be blinded by it, reeling away theatrically, saying 'Strewth!' his hands over his eyes. Some of the others joined in in a wonderful, warm sort of abuse – just how they talked to one another, and which made Jasper so happy, grinning, putting up his fists at them, dancing up and down on his toes like a boxer" (73). This bout of comradely abuse is Jasper's birthday party. Paradoxically, it saves him from the peril of hypothermia, bringing him out of the English chill and into the warmth of group horseplay.

The young immigrant is duly inducted into the male freemasonry of the workplace. His involvement in its sociable rituals releases liberating laughter:

> "So it's his birthday," Dusty said, turning to the others. He advanced slowly, menacingly towards Jasper, stuck out his finger and prodded his tie. "You know what that means, don't you?"
>
> To prolong the delight of being in the middle of it all, Jasper pretended that he did not.
>
> "It means," said Dusty slowly, knocking his fist against Jasper's chest. "It means, Tall Boy, you got to buy the cakes for tea."
>
> "Yeah, that's right," said Buster. "You buy the cakes."
>
> "I know, I know," said Jasper in his sing-song voice. He threw back his head and gave his high, bubbling laugh, and jingled coins in both his pockets. (74)

Through an arresting plot reversal, becoming the target of facetious bullying signifies for the estranged young migrant new "wealth" in his pocket, acceptance into "the middle of it all." Rough joking functions here for once not as a symptom of racial marginalization but as its antidote. Jasper has, by good luck, been welcomed into a fraternal network of joking relationships; humour has an assimilating, empowering effect that enables him, figuratively as well as literally, to "stand tall." Taylor's narrative enacts a triumph of shared working-class sensibility over racial and national divisions, the sort of development longed for by many on the political left in contemporary Britain, but, unfortunately, more easily realized in a fiction like Taylor's than in cold empirical fact.

On a personal level, at least, Jasper is accomplishing the difficult feat of being naturalized in his new country without having to erase or camouflage his own essential "difference." Flaunting his flamboyant neckwear, he has raised a banner declaring his vibrant individuality, which his mates are encouragingly ready to recognize and endorse. Along with that triumph, the young man has begun as if by magic to establish a sense of connection between his beleaguered London self and the radically dissimilar home world that dominates his wistful memories. He is last seen gazing at the photo he has been sent of his three sisters back home, grinning cheekily at him. Braced by this reassurance of his enduring family ties, he feels a surge of confidence about venturing forth into the inhospitable London scene, wearing his own cheeky badge of identity. "The tie had been a good idea. He might give it another airing, this nice, dry evening – stroll among the crowds outside the Odeon and the bowling alley" (76).

Such a conclusion overturns the premises of the 1956 *Punch* cartoon of the Jamaican migrant, which the plight of Taylor's displaced West Indian seems initially to mirror. Although the drawing treats the migrant's disappointment with implicit sympathy, it also seems to foreclose the possibility that such an outlander might some day become an integral part of the English scene into which he has unwarily ventured. The familiar *Punch* theme of "not fitting" still governs the humour. The implied message the cartoon sends to the stranger is: stay on your poor but sunny tropical island and leave cold, gloomy old England to us, who, after all, *belong* here. "Tall Boy" suggests instead that the migrant, however distressed, is not forever doomed to be a misfit; through resourcefulness and spunk he or she may gain a sense of belonging among the dark, satanic mills and the chill, smelly, angelic churches. By the story's end, even the dismal English weather – Jasper's "enemy" – has become friendlier. Where *Punch* simply deploys stock presuppositions about the migrant's plight (and, to be fair, a comic drawing can do little more), Taylor uses her artistry to explore her young West Indian's subjectivity with humour, but also with her rare imaginative outreach.

By the time Taylor was imagining her Tall Boy, however, his real-life counterparts from overseas were already producing their own, very different literary self-portraits. The first such visitor to be considered here is the devastating Trinidadian Samuel Selvon.

PART THREE

The Empire Laughs Back

8

Samuel Selvon and the Carnival of Reverse Colonization

Defining himself before a Caribbean audience in 1979, Samuel Selvon announced: "[W]hat we have here is really an *East Indian Trinidadian West Indian*" (*Foreday Morning* 220). It was clearly the final term – West Indian – that Selvon meant to stress. By ancestry three-quarters East Indian, one-quarter Scottish, he considered himself as thoroughly creolized as any Afro-Trinidadian. In his famous trilogy, *The Lonely Londoners, Moses Ascending,* and *Moses Migrating,* he elected to cast such a black islander, Moses Aloetta, in a trio of major roles: protagonist, narrator (of the latter two novels), and, in some measure, his own alter ego.

For Selvon, situating a black man as his central figure led naturally to comedy. As he says in the "Special Preface" to *Moses Migrating,* "The humor and entertainment that Moses provides sometimes tend to whelm the serious side of his nature. It is a knack that all Black people acquire to survive. In my own years in London, any hardcore material I wrote about Blacks had to have ha-ha" (xiii). Because he pioneered "ha-ha" from a non-white perspective, Selvon has had, claims Elizabeth Ingrams, "a major impact on the evolution of Caribbean and black-British writing, a tradition of writing which still continues to this day with the immense popularity of novels such as *White Teeth* ... by Zadie Smith" (33).

"HERE IS NOT LIKE HOME": *THE LONELY LONDONERS*

Like the "Tall Boy" Jasper in Elizabeth Taylor's story, the Caribbean characters in Selvon's *The Lonely Londoners* are painfully dislocated; their survival in an alien metropolis is precarious. However, where Tall Boy feels himself the sole specimen of his breed amid a sea of strangers, cordoned off from other West Indian newcomers, Selvon's "boys" form a group with at least a provisional sense of solidarity. Harold Barratt lists three factors – alienation, identity, and discrimination – that "inevitably bring Selvon's immigrants together into a noticeably cohesive group" (Nasta *Perspectives* 256). In her afterword to *Moses Migrating*, Susheila Nasta comments that, with the arrival of this black expatriate community, in *The Lonely Londoners* "England begins to be colonized in reverse" (184). The "boys" may be a collection of eccentrics, but they give one another some inkling of a shared existence. If the virtually orphaned Jasper has no option but to scheme at getting absorbed by the mainstream, Selvon's West Indians are less frantically driven to seek white acceptance and, when they do choose to seek it, less apt to gain it.

Individual black newcomers in Pym and Taylor infuse a missing vivacity into the pallid English scene, but Selvon's migrants, however vivacious, need all the vital force they can muster simply to carry on. Rather than casting a warm glow over the frigid northern cityscape, they are themselves chronically at risk of "getting" hypothermia. They must consequently huddle together for moral or even physical warmth. Such conscripted togetherness may, as Barratt argues, take its toll: "The formation of a colony ensures survival of sorts; but it retards the growth of individual strength and maturity" (258). Or, as Gordon Rohlehr puts it, "[T]he 'boys' remain fragmented, partial personalities. They continue to be identifiable in terms of idiosyncracy; they have nicknames, not real names" (41). Still, those who choose to be loners pay a higher price. One of these is the light-skinned Bart: "Many nights he think about how so many West Indians coming, and it gave him more fear than it gave the Englishman, for Bart frighten if they make things hard in Brit'n. If a fellar too black, Bart not accompanying him much, and he don't like to be found in the company of the boys, he always have an embarrass air when he with them in public, he does look around as much as to say: 'I here with these boys, but I not one of them, look at the colour of my skin.' But a few door slam in Bart face, a few English people give him the old diplomacy, and Bart boil down and come like one of the boys" (*Lonely Londoners* 62). Bart's standoffishness is a futile affectation, and his boiling down is predictable. His error lies in assuming that "Englishness" and "foreignness" are matters governed by visible shades of complexion, rather than by more esoteric nuances of attitude. In a milieu that constructs nationality according to elusive but rigid codes, cohesion among the out-group is vital.

Such cohesion is, nonetheless, fragile. The group's members come from a miscellany of origins and pursue divergent personal agendas. While they cluster together, most lead isolated lives, and even the company of family members is not always a blessing. The Jamaican Tolroy regards the surprise arrival of his whole clan not as a windfall but as a deluge: "'Oh Jesus Christ,' Tolroy say, 'what is this at all?'" (16). He can hardly bring himself to acknowledge "that all these people on his hands, in London, in the grim winter, and no place to go to stay" (17). Tolroy's redoubtable Great-Aunt Tanty, however, brings with her the "island" spirit of group solidarity. When a reporter at Waterloo Station asks to photograph her, she refuses to pose alone:

"He want to take photo," Tanty nudge Ma, "where all the children? Tolroy, Agnes, Lewis," she calling out as if she calling out in a backyard in Jamaica, "all you come and take photo, children. The mister want a snapshot."

"One of you alone will be quite sufficient," the reporter say.

"What!" Tanty say, "you can't take me alone. You have to take the whole family." And she went to round up the rest. (19)

Like most of Selvon's West Indians, Tanty is at once a comical and an endearing figure. Her failure to register the altered nature of her surroundings might seem laughably maladaptive, except that she succeeds impressively in adapting the new surroundings to her own requirements. As one of Selvon's most perceptive critics, Mark Looker, observes, Tanty "revers[es] the pattern of the old colonial novel by domesticating her surroundings, turning a few blocks of the city into her own village" (73). While seldom venturing beyond the confines of her London district – "Like how some people live in small village and never go to the city, Tanty settle down in the Harrow Road in the Working Class area" (86) – she manages to recreate a virtual West Indian ambiance.

Still, she can on occasion display a gallant readiness for "foreign" adventure. In one incident, to retrieve a key from Tolroy's mother, who works in a Lyons Corner House in central London, Tanty is obliged to travel by Underground out of her urban "village":

Ma come and give Tanty the key, and ask she how she get to the place.

"I come by tube," Tanty say cool, as if she travelling every day. "How else you think? But I going back by bus."

"Stay and eat a food as you here already," Ma say.

"What!" Tanty say, "eat this English food when I have peas and rice waiting home to cook? You must be mad! But don't let me keep you from your work."

> And Tanty went away, feeling good that she make the trip from Harrow Road at last.
>
> "I hope this bus don't turn over," she tell the conductor, because it didn't have room below and she had to go upstairs.
>
> She was so frighten that she didn't bother to look out of the window and see anything, and when she get off at the Prince of Wales she feel relieved. Now nobody could tell she that she ain't travel by bus and tube in London. (90–1)

By an amusing reversal of historical precedent, Tanty penetrates the heart of the metropolis as English explorers had once ventured into tropical jungles. A jittery Livingstone, she takes in no more of her surroundings than she must (aloft in the alarming double-decker bus she sees as little of the city as she had on her underground journey) and clings to her own time-tested diet and customs. Her feisty determination, however, keeps the reader's laughter from being superior.

The rustic clownishness that might conventionally have coloured Tanty and Ma's dialect speech is modulated here by the narrator's use of the same idiom, an innovation whose importance has been rightly stressed both by Selvon himself and by his critics. Christian Mair speaks of Selvon's "redemption of Creole from its traditional preserve of low comedy" (142). According to Edward Baugh, Selvon established a literary "landmark" by "using the [West Indian] vernacular as his narrative medium" (241). The impact of dialect narration in *The Lonely Londoners* is best suggested by comparison. Selvon's choice of a "standard" rather than Creole-speaking narrator for his later (1970) novel of Trinidad, *The Plains of Caroni*, crucially angles the reader's reception of the text. The action focuses on an ambitious but frustrated East Indian woman, Seeta, and her lofty aspirations for her gifted eldest son, Romesh. The clash between Seeta's fixation on upward mobility and Romesh's allegiance to more intellectual goals generates the major, tragicomic tension of the novel. Seeta is a Creole-speaking Trinidadian whose "efforts at 'proper English,'" as Clement Wyke notes, "result in a comical collision of verbal and grammatical forms" (77). By contrast, the university-educated Romesh resembles the narrator in using rule-book English with effortless fluency. The gulf between mother and son emerges in exchanges like the following: "'You only tried to dominate my life. Thank God I came to my senses in time.' 'If I done that, is only because I love your father so much'" (151). Since Romesh's "proper" speech effectively twins him with the authoritative narrator, the young man seems to act from a preset, unearned position of ascendancy over his rustic, "comical" mother. But by so tipping the scales against Seeta, by all odds the most compelling character in the book, Selvon throws the whole effect of the narrative out of joint. *The Plains of Caroni* thus appears, no doubt inadvertently, to strike an anti-vernacular discursive stance that privileges metropolitan values over indigenous Carribean ones. The vernacular narration of *The Lonely Londoners*, by contrast, discourages any such favoring of the smooth-tongued centre over the "ungrammatical" margin; discursive mastery is dislodged from its accustomed throne.

On the other hand, Selvon's "ha-ha" aimed at male characters raises, more troublingly than the humorous treatment of Tanty or Seeta, the thorny issue of comic stereotyping by a minority writer directed at his own racial group. While the "boys" benefit, like Tanty, from the companionable, creolized narrative voice, their behaviour is more problematic than hers. Their triumphs are typically sexual ones, achieved by (literally) "putting down" white women. Barratt offers an apology for this sexual triumphalism: "Racism … depersonalizes the victim; it reduces him to the status of an object … Selvon's West Indians tend to depersonalize the female – as they themselves have been depersonalized" (253). To comprehend the motives behind the "boys'" opportunistic attitude toward women, however, is not automatically to forgive it, and Selvon persistently raises doubts about black Don Juanism. The Trindidadian newcomer Henry Oliver, dubbed by the cynical Moses "Sir Galahad," exults at having dates with local girls at famous London places. (The episode in question immediately follows Tanty's triumphant tube-and-bus exploit; the juxtaposition puts Galahad's macho bravado in deflating perspective.) More worldly than the incorrigibly insular Tanty, Galahad appears all the more laughable for "buying into" the faded myth of London as metropolitan centre of the globe. He tells Moses, "'I meeting that piece of skin tonight, you know.' And then, as if it not very important, 'She waiting for me by Charing Cross Station.' Jesus Christ, when he say 'Charing Cross,' when he realise that is he, Sir Galahad, who going there, near that place that everybody in the world know about (it even have the name in the dictionary) he feel like a new man. It didn't matter about the woman he going to meet, just to say he was going there make him feel big and important, and even if he was just going to coast a lime, to stand up and watch the white people, still, it would have been something" (91). As Scott Dickinson observes, "Galahad's lived experience in the metropole produces disorientation, chaos and loss at first, rather than the assurance of arrival" (73). His assignations in famous places serve to assure him that he has in fact arrived. The irony is that he gains a sense of renewal from his nearness to the focal points of an empire that had kept his own ancestors in servitude and that has by now itself undergone an irreversible collapse. His imperial sway is exerted over a woman called Daisy, whose main attribute, like the flower's, is her generic whiteness; he evidently prizes the "pieces of skin" he dates chiefly for the gratifying pallor of the skin itself.

The metropolitan field of conquest generates elaborate narcissistic rituals, like Galahad's pre-tryst hair-combing: "That is a big operation for Galahad, because he grow the hair real long and bushy, and it like a clump of grass on the head. First, he wet the hair with some water, then he push his finger in the haircream jar and scoop out some. He rub the cream on his hands, then he rub his hands in his head. The only mirror in the room is a small one that Galahad have tie on to the electric light cord, and the way he have it, it just a little bit higher than he is, so while he combing the grass he have to sort of look up and not forward. So this comb start going through the grass, stumbling across some big knot in Galahad hair, and water flying from the head as the comb make a pass, and Galahad concentrating on the physiognomy, his forehead wrinkled and he turning the head this way and that. Then afterwards he taking the brush and touching the hair like a tonsorial specialist, here and there, and when he finish, the hair comb well" (93–4). At first blush the tone of the description recalls Joyce Cary's satiric evocation of Johnson preening himself for a gala event – Galahad's contortions seem even more absurd than Johnson's – but the resemblance is superficial. Once again, the narrator's mimicry of "island" syntax is crucial; this voice, unlike Cary's, does not rise fastidiously above the character's sociolinguistic horizon. At the same time, the description includes just enough elevated diction ("concentrating on the physiognomy"; "like a tonsorial specialist") to suggest a mock-heroic parody of an ancient topos: the warrior arming himself for battle. The emphasis falls not on the racial "difference" of Galahad's recalcitrant hair, but on his self-infatuated absorption in the process of taming it, so as to avoid creating an impression of "savagery." (Of course, when such a passage is removed from its fictional context and embedded in a text written in conventional critical prose, like the present study, "standard" English exerts its customary normative force, tending artificially to exoticize Selvon's island vernacular.)

Galahad's struggles to make himself "civilized" for his white date are ironically revealed, in retrospect, to be beside the point. As Moses, in a central stream-of-consciousness monologue, comes to recognize, "the cruder you are the more the girls like you you can't put on any English accent for them or play ladeda or tell them you studying medicine in

Oxford or try to be polite and civilise they don't want that sort of thing at all they want you to live up to the films and stories they hear about black people living primitive in the jungles of the world" (124). Cultivating an image of suave elegance is self-defeating when sexual success calls for conformity to a mythos of African uncouthness. On one occasion Moses finds himself marched to a swish Knightsbridge club where society girls begin dancing a risqué can-can: "Moses sit down there wondering how this sort of thing happening in a place where only the high and the mighty is but with all of that they feel they can't get big thrills unless they have a black man in the company and when Moses leave afterwards they push five pounds in his hand and pat him on the back and say that was a jolly good show" (125). The banknote is conscience money paid to the appointed racial Other, his bribe for providing a dash of exoticism to enhance the savour of the chic decadence. Well might a black Londoner feel lonely.

Like the Prufrock of T.S. Eliot, a poet Selvon admired, West Indian expatriates are compelled to prepare a face to meet the faces that they meet; but, if the prepared face is not white, it may not always be deemed meetable. Such warping pressures explain why Galahad, despite his conquest of Daisy and other white metropolitan blossoms, becomes so dissociated from his physicality that he directs a lachrymose address to his own skin colour: "And Galahad watch the colour of his hand, and talk to it, saying, 'Colour, is you that causing all this, you know. Why the hell you can't be blue, or red or green, if you can't be white? You know is you that cause a lot of misery in the world. Is not me, you know, is you! I ain't do anything to infuriate the people and them, is you! Look at you, you so black and innocent, and this time so you causing misery all over the world!'" (97). The effect, again, recalls Mister Johnson's comic self-scolding, but Selvon's tone is as always less condescending than Cary's, and Galahad's dividedness is more painful than Johnson's. As Looker claims, "Although the narrator at times adopts the stance of Horatian satirist, urbane, amused, somewhat distant, that role is continually breaking down, that voice continually being displaced by another one, one more involved, more connected with the lives it has created" (77). The animus of a racist society figuratively flays the young West Indian by detaching him from his own skin; Selvon will not add insult to injury by striking a posture of aloof superiority.

In some of Galahad's fellow expatriates, like Bart, the urge to reject black identity leads to more frantic attempts at taking on the colouration of the British mainstream, and on these the narrator lavishes less indulgence. The prime exemplar is Harris, whose grand "fete" evolves into a pivotal piece of comic business. The humour stems from Harris's attempts to hold a refined soiree for his white guests while struggling to keep "the boys" in check.

Harris is described caustically as a mimic man (to adopt V.S. Naipaul's term) whose efforts to simulate "English" behaviour exceed the mark: "Harris is a fellar who like to play ladeda, and he like English customs and thing, he does be polite and say thank you and he does get up in the bus and the tube to let woman sit down, which is a thing even them Englishmen don't do. And when he dress, you think is some Englishman going to work in the city, bowler and umbrella, and brief case tuck under the arm, with the Times fold up in the pocket so the name would show, and he walking upright like if is he alone who alive in the world. Only thing, Harris face black" (128). Not only the detail (overpunctilious behaviour on London transport, posh newspaper's name prominently blazoned) but the narrative idiom snidely deflates Harris's "English" pose. Though it is a discreetly filtered version of Caribbean speech, Selvon's prose refuses to wear whiteface. As Margaret Joseph observes, "[d]ialect can sometimes be employed as a deliberate subversion of the colonizer's language" (85), a device we have already seen put to strategic use by Forster. Selvon applies "island speech" as a powerful solvent against what Bakhtin calls "already fully formed, officially recognized, reigning languages that are authoritative and reactionary" (*Dialogic* 312).

At the fete, it is Tolroy's irrepressible Tanty whose dialect vernacular sabotages Harris's whiteface decorum:

> "Harris!" Tanty scream out. "You don't know me? You don't remember neighbour who used to live behind you in George Street?"
>
> "I'm afraid –" Harris start to stammer.
>
> "But look how big the boy get!" Tanty bawl. "I didn't believe Tolroy when he tell me. Tolroy say how you living in London for a long time, and that you doing well for yourself. I tell Tolroy: 'Not little Harris what used to run about the barrackyard in shirttail!'" (131–2)

What most mortifies Harris is the public reminder that he has had a childhood in precincts leagues remote from white metropolitan salons. Tanty aggravates this social wound by insisting on dancing with Harris, cutting out his pedigreed young English partner: "'Well,' Harris say, trying hard to keep his temper, 'will you kindly wait until I am finished? We shall dance the next set.' 'You too smart, when the next set come I wouldn't find you,' Tanty say, taking a firm hold of Harris. 'Tell this girl to unlace you: you know what they playing? "Fan Me Saga Boy Fan Me," and that is my favourite calypso. These English girls don't know how to dance calypso, man. Lady, excuse him,' and before Harris know what happening Tanty swing him on the floor, pushing up she fat self against him. The poor fellar can't do anything, in two-twos Tanty had him in the centre of the floor while she swinging she fat bottom left and right" (135–6). With her cheeky bravado, Tanty incarnates the irrepressible "grotesque body" celebrated by Mikhail Bakhtin.

As if getting ambushed by the resurgent Jamaican past, that "fat bottom" he wants to keep locked out of sight, were not painful enough, Harris must contend with unruly behaviour by the "boys," foremost among them the raffishly nicknamed Big City and Five Past Twelve. Their own insistence on Caribbean, carnival boisterousness provokes him to a testy outburst:

> "What time this fete overing, Harris?" Five ask him.
>
> "At the usual time, half-past eleven," Harris say.
>
> "Oh, Christ," Five say. "I don't know why in a big city like London you can't have a fete till morning. Look how it is back home, they have non-stop dance, you dance till you fall down on the ground, the moon go, the sun come, evening come, night come again and still the boys on the floor. Why the arse London Transport can't run bus and tube all night for people to go home?"
>
> "I wish you would watch your language," Harris say. "You don't know it, but there are decent people around you."
>
> "Yes," Big City say, "stop – ing up a good time, Five."
>
> "Take it easy, boys," Moses say.
>
> "Another thing," Harris say, drinking the lemonade and forgetting to speak proper English for a minute, "is when the fete finish and the band playing God Save the Queen, some of you have a habit of walking about as if the fete still going on, and you, Five, the last time you come to one of my dances you was even jocking waist when everybody else was standing at attention." (142–3)

Harris's linguistic cave-in ("you was even jocking waist") marks the collapse of his battle to defend British propriety against Caribbean gusto. For all his efforts to "whiten" his own and his fellows' language, his vernacular roots keep showing.

Much of the comedy of *The Lonely Londoners* arises from the pinning down of characters in a such a crossfire between incongruous cultural impulses: the need to conform to English Lenten norms of propriety and the pull of carnivalesque West Indian ebullience. Even the imperative of simple physical survival can run afoul of English notions of decency. In an episode that follows Harris's fete, Galahad, out of work and hungry, resorts to an unEnglish expedient: "That particular winter, things was so bad with him that he had was to try and catch a pigeon in the park to eat. It does have a lot of them flying about, and the people does feed them with bits of bread" (145). Having secured a bird, Galahad is surprised in the act of putting it down by an outraged elderly matron: "'Oh you cruel, cruel beast!' the woman say, and Galahad head fly back from where he kneeling on the ground to handle the situation better. 'You cruel monster! You killer!' Galahad blood run cold: he see the gallows before him right away and he push the pigeon in his jacket pocket and stand up, and the pigeon still fluttering in the pocket. 'I must find a policeman!' the woman screech, throwing her hands up in the air, and she turn back to the road. Galahad make races through the park, heading down for Lancaster Gate" (146–7). The incident's satiric edge depends on the fact that the woman's words and actions are harshly aggressive in a way that "killer" Galahad's are not. The irony recalls Waugh's *Black Mischief*, where the English animal-rights activists, Dame Mildred Porch and Miss Tin, shower pity on the dogs in Matodi while reviling the famished children who try to grab food away from the animals. In Selvon, however, the burden of comic interest shifts from the English animal-lover to the black reprobate, who is at once clownishly funny and achingly sad.

Sadness is ingrained in the overall impression left by Selvon's comedy of exile; as Wyke says, "an essential part of Selvon's comedy" is "its underlying seriousness" (59), its stress on the bleakness of living as a stranger in a strange land. Yet this mood is not steadily sustained; overall *The Lonely Londoners* embodies a persistent ambivalence toward the move from colonial margin to white metropolitan core. Speaking to Galahad late in the book, Moses delivers a glum verdict: "'Looking at things in general life really hard for the boys in London. This is a lonely, miserable city, if it was that we didn't get together now and then to talk about things back home, we would suffer like hell. Here is not like home where you have friends all about. In the beginning you would think that is a good thing, that nobody minding your business, but after a while you want to get in company, you want to go to somebody house and eat a meal, you want to go on excursion to the sea, you want to go and play football and cricket. Nobody in London does really accept you. They tolerate you, yes, but you can't go in their house and eat or sit down and talk. It ain't have no sort of family life for us here'" (154–5). And yet only a few pages later, the narrator, voicing what sounds like the collective feeling of the "boys," recalls Galahad in his first flush of infatuation with the city: "Oh what it is and where it is and why it is, no one knows, but to have said: 'I walked on Waterloo Bridge,' 'I rendezvoused at Charing Cross,' 'Piccadilly Circus is my playground,' to say these things, to have lived these things, to have lived in the great city of London, centre of the world. To one day lean against the wind walking up the Bayswater Road (destination unknown), to see the leaves swirl and dance and spin on the pavement (sight unseeing), to write a casual letter home beginning: 'Last night, in Trafalgar Square … '" (164).

As the attitude toward London has switched here from plaintive to rhapsodic, so the prose itself has shifted from Moses's Creole to "proper" English, even of a conventionally literary type. The linguistic battle that Harris has lost at his fete gets fought out inconclusively in the text at large. According to Margaret Joseph, the displaced West Indian "has a healthy sense of proportion in [*The Lonely Londoners*], no matter how exiled he feels. Despite his loneliness, his love for London turns the narrator lyrical" (91). But to speak of a "healthy sense of proportion" is to gloss over a besetting problem of inconsistency. The jarring shifts of tone betray an underlying emotional vacillation, an uncertainty that may account for the precarious balance in the narrative between robust "ha-ha" and something more sombre. Tempting as it is to apply Bakhtinian concepts of dialogism and the carnivalesque to *The Lonely Londoners*, as Dickinson (77 and passim) has attempted with *Moses Ascending*, one cannot avoid feeling that some of the tonal acrobatics are less dialogic than simply disjointed.

Moses's concluding reflections strike the sombre tone apocalyptically:

> Under the kiff-kiff laughter, behind the ballad and the episode, the what-happening, the summer-is-hearts, he could see a great aimlessness, a great restless, swaying movement that leaving you standing in the same spot. As if a forlorn shadow of doom fall on all the spades in the country. As if he could see the black faces bobbing up and down in the millions of white, strained faces, everybody hustling along the Strand, the spades jostling in the crowd, bewildered, hopeless. As if, on the surface, things don't look so bad, but when you go down a little, you bounce up a kind of misery and pathos and a frightening – what? He don't know the right word, but he have the right feeling in his heart. As if the boys laughing, but they only laughing because they fraid to cry, they only laughing because to think so much about everything would be a big calamity – like how he here now, the thoughts so heavy like he unable to move his body. (170)

The powerful tableau of black derelicts adrift in London is like a creolized retake of Eliot's *The Waste Land*: "A crowd flowed over London Bridge, so many,. / I had not thought death had undone so many" (lines 62–3). While Selvon's use of black people ("spades") as humorous butts may appear to replicate the racial comedy of Waugh or Cary – to internalize white laughter at non-white "inferiors" – the main force of his laughter is directed elsewhere. If Galahad, Tanty, Harris, and the others seem comic grotesques, Selvon never lets the reader forget that the distorting pressure of English apartheid is what causes their native "island" ways to look deviant. Their attempts to transplant West Indian carnival to London are shown to be, ultimately, a breakwater against tears. As for Moses himself, he is too much the sober raisonneur to be a consistent rieur, to keep up the ha-ha unfalteringly. In *Moses Ascending*, however, where Moses's role shifts from mediating observer to kiff-kiff narrator, the sobriety vanishes.

CRUSOE REVISITED: *MOSES ASCENDING*

Moses Ascending has been called a "novel in which everything is turned upside-down" (Baugh 136). The description recalls Bakhtin's idea of the direction "inherent in all forms of popular-festive merriment and grotesque realism": "[d]own, inside out, vice versa, upside down" (*Rabelais* 370). The ruling principle here is indeed "vice versa"; the narrative concludes with the upwardly mobile Moses forced to move from the top floor to the basement of his own house.[1] It turns upside-down that central Western myth, *Robinson Crusoe*; the black "Crusoe," Moses, acquires the services of a white "Man Friday," the scapegrace Bob. Like his famous original, Bob performs a variety of menial tasks for his lord and master. His devotion, however, is simulated, while his attention to his own gain is heartfelt and eventuates in his getting the upper hand – and the upper storey. As Looker comments, "In parodying the Crusoe-Friday relationship, Selvon not only inverts the hierarchies of colonialism but also subverts the canonical literary tradition, inscribing his own work onto English culture in a parodic claiming of place" (178).

In *Moses Ascending*, as in *Crusoe*, and as in the initial phase of the Prospero-Caliban relationship, master and servant of opposed races enter into a compact based on "fair exchange": the servant goes about odd jobs while the master pursues a "civilizing" project:

[Bob] was a willing worker, eager to learn the ways of the Black man. In no time at all he learn how to cook peas and rice and to make a beef stew. I got him cracking

> because he didn't have no more money to pay rent, and we come to an agreement for him to be my batman and to attend to all the petty details about running the house in lieu … The only thing I didn't like about him was he went out most evenings and came back pissed, drunk like a lord. As we become good friends, or rather Master and Servant, I try to convert him from the evils of alcohol, but it was no use …
>
> And whilst I was indoctrinating him, I also learn a lesson myself, which is that Black and White could live in harmony, for he was loyal and true, and never listened to all that shit you hear about black people. Afterwards he tell me he used to believe it, but since coming under my employ he realize that black people is human too.
>
> I decided to teach him the Bible when I could make the time. (10–11)

This idyll of mutual benefit, racial tolerance, and spiritual edification finally founders owing to submerged conflicts of interest. Moses's hesitation between "good friends" and "Master and Servant" unwittingly pinpoints the ambivalence in the compact, which masks exploitation and rivalry behind a collegial facade. Ultimately, the ways of the black and the white coincide in only one respect: both turn out to be the way of scheming opportunism.

Galahad, by contrast, has abandoned the notion "that Black and White could live in harmony." He unexpectedly materializes in the regalia of a black activist:

> He arrived in his Black Power glad rags. Starting from foot to head, he have on a pair of platforms, yellow socks, purple corduroy trousers, a leather belt about six inches broad with a big heavy brass buckle and some fancy, spiky chunks of metal studded in it. ("That's my weapon. Look." He haul the belt right out of the loops and wield it like a Viking. "I will slaughter a white man one day.") He have on a pink shirt. On both hands, he had on a battery of chunky signet rings, wearing them on unconventional digits. Round his neck he had a heavy chain like what peasants in Trinidad tether their cattle with. And on top of his head, he had on a navy-blue wool cap, pulled down over his ears.
>
> When I opened the door Galahad raise his right hand up in the air making a fist of his fingers as if he going to bust a cuff in my arse, and say, paradoxically, "Peace, brother. Black is beautiful." (16–17)

It is a portrait of an absurdly exaggerated stage activist. Where the sketch of Galahad preening himself in *The Lonely Londoners* betokened at worst self-preoccupied vanity, his appearance here seems an elaborate charade tinged with sinister hints of cruelty. His swaggering bravado contradicts itself; speaking of slaughtering white men, Galahad wields his weapon like a Viking, that snow-whitest of warriors. It is not just Galahad's greeting ("Peace") that is paradoxical.

The power Galahad seeks is a perquisite he and his fellow migrants have been denied by the host society, but his theatrics comically discredit his hopes of self-empowerment. As for the notion that "Black is beautiful," a more plausible case is made by Moses's pretty tenant, the young black English-born militant Brenda. From the skeptical Moses, however, what Brenda's activism elicits is a tribute to the power of black backsides: "Blessed be the coming of this new generation of Black Britons, and blessed be I that I still alive and well to witness their coming of age from piccaninny to black beauty. It is a sight for sore eyes to see them flounce and bounce about the city, even if they capsize on their platforms and trip up in their maxis. Be it bevy or crocodile, Woman's Lib or Woman's Tit, they are on the march, sweeping through the streets … Like how you see an ordinary girl tits jump up and down if she is running, thus a black backside merely pedestrianizing. And it is not only up and down, but sideways, and gyrating in circles, and quivering and shivering in all manner of movement. It is not their coming to look at, but their going" (21). Moses's paean to black women "on the march" shows scant engagement with the cause of gender parity. He casually conflates woman's lib and woman's tit, but for him anatomical detail all too plainly trumps the body politic. As Dickinson says, "The question readers face is how to receive such problematic satire, which often targets women and politically engaged blacks" (84).

The root of the problem is Selvon's own clearly stated preference (like E.M. Forster's) for personal relations over any sort of political commitment. As Selvon says in a 1994 interview, "I never wanted to have anything to do with politics" (*Ariel* 109). Moses's reading of "black is beautiful," crass though it is, functions as a pragmatic antidote to the swaggering of a Galahad and the activist rhetoric of Brenda herself. On the other hand, a tussle between black Brenda and the libidinous white Bob is treated as harmlessly comic because it operates on a purely personal, carnal plane: "You remember how in the old days when they taking photo how the photographer used to go under a big piece of black cloth what cover him and the camera, as if a mystery was happening to get the photo? Well, Brenda had Bob wrap up in the maxi like that, and she was cuffing him. You remember the Black Power signal of the fist in the air? Well Brenda fist wasn't just hovering. It was coming down and going up like a piston. She cuff up Bob with one hand while the other keep the maxi tight around him like a straitjacket so he couldn't move" (30). Brenda has converted gender militancy here from ideological theory to practical technique, pressing an item of female dress into effective martial service. In *Moses Ascending* such personal gestures are more to the point than the incendiary directives – "KILL ALL WHITE PIGS" and so forth (34) – on the placards in the rally in which Brenda and Galahad later take part.

That event, with its clamorous rhetoric and chaotic action, seems more carnival run rampant than sober political protest. When Moses too finds himself swept up in the throng, he witnesses a frightening scene of violence: "And the whole mass cheering and making various sounds of approval, as if they ready to make blood flow instantaneously and slaughter a few pigs as an example. In fact, the incensement was so powerful that a fracas start up right where I standing. Sudden-so men was fighting. It appear that a chap was raising his fist to make the power sign, and he accidentally cuff another in front of him, who turn round and cuff him back. Pandemonium break loose in the square. You know like how you see in those cowboy films how two chaps start a fight in the saloon, and suddenly everybody fighting? Is so this thing was. I find myself in the middle of the milling and confusion. Woman was screaming, men was just thumping out left and right with kick and cuff, and a white supporter went down, and *disappear,* and God alone knows what happen to *he*" (42–3). The Black Power salute, which Selvon uses insistently as a mocking tag, here mutates from a symbol of armed racial solidarity, the concerted will to "slaughter pigs," to a cause of violence directed by blacks against themselves. As Looker observes, in *Moses Ascending* "[t]he 'imagined community, tenuous in *Lonely Londoners* … but still at least potential, has become unimaginable" (187). What was meant as a display of insurgent racial pride morphs scarily into a self-defeating brawl. The resolve to eradicate white authority eventuates only in the erasure of one unlucky white sympathizer ("God alone knows what happen to *he*").

With Moses as his mouthpiece, Selvon produces humour consistently targeting political initiative. Moses's reflections after he has been arrested and jailed, and after Galahad has infuriatingly declined to stand bail, make the point: "I remember lying on my bunk in the cell the night and thinking that if I did keep my arse quiet and stay at home, having a cold beer and looking at the church service on TV, I would not of got myself in this shit. It just goes to show how right I was all the time to have nothing to do with the black brotherhood. And imagine how Galahad

had the gumption to propose that I stay there cooling my heels to put a feather in the Party cap! You see how black man different from white man? Look how, in *Tale of Two Cities*, when that chap was in the Bastille destined for the guillotine, how his friend went and take his place! You think you will ever get a black brother to give you his place in the bus-queue, much less rescue you from the clutches of the law?" (45–6). Here, as often in *Moses Ascending*, the ironies are multiple, extending beyond their ostensible target and rebounding on Selvon's spokesman. By and large the novel supports Moses's skepticism regarding the Black Power movement, an attitude echoed by Selvon's own recorded opinions. In the epilogue to *Foreday Morning*, speaking of the situation in multiracial Trinidad, he says: "Black Power never was for the coloured races as such. It was for the Black man only. Like the White bogey, we now had the Black bogey to contend with. And once again, the strategy of keeping people apart, of creating division, came into operation" (218). Selvon's position as a member of the East Indian minority in Trinidad sensitized him to the fragmenting tendencies of communalist politics. In *Moses Ascending*, such politics even divide Moses from his black "brothers" and indeed for a time from his brothers and sisters of all complexions outside the walls of his jail.

Yet Moses's quietism is not exempted from suspicion. Wishing he had chosen his "better option" of staying home viewing a church service and drinking a beer, Moses is pining for three classic opiates of the masses: organized religion, television, and alcohol. It seems unlikely that this policy of inactivism will ever enable him to advance his own interests, let alone any collective agenda. And the racial distinctions Moses draws ("You see how black man different from white man?") are likewise spurious, based as they are on his analogy, foggily recalled from Dickens, of the eleventh-hour Charles Darnay-Sidney Carton switch. Taking a contrived plot turn from a Victorian novel as a key to racial difference is patently foolish. Indeed, it soon transpires that Galahad, if hardly a samaritan, has at least convinced the "Party" that it is in their own interest to get Moses released from jail. Instead of relenting, Moses is soon provoked by Galahad's ridicule of his projected memoirs to further sniping at his own people: "'[Y]ou could never get a word of encouragement from a black man when you aspire to the arts or philosophy or anything above the low level they set themselves'" (51).

Muttering such racist clichés, Moses begins not unreasonably to fear that he may (as Galahad has foreseen) be losing his sanity. Having corrected Bob's belief in "all that shit you hear about black people," Moses has now grown paranoid enough to take all that shit to heart. Further complicating the ironies directed at Moses, however, is Selvon's own habit of deploying stock racial stereotypes for comic advantage. According to David Dabydeen, "Selvon was so ahead of his time that ... the critics ... didn't know what he was doing. They got caught up in seeing him as a 'trickster', a writer who was duping them with stereotypes which in fact he was exploding, and they got taken in" (qtd in Ingrams, 34). Yet one sometimes wonders whether Selvon is not exploding stereotypes but exploiting them. This applies especially to the novel's central sequence involving Moses's tenant Faizull, a mysterious Pakistani whose business turns out to be smuggling illegal immigrants. In this episode, both Faizull and his contraband flock behave in ways unlikely to dispel the bigotry commonly directed by the English at "Pakis."

Examined more closely, however, Selvon's comic strategy does, even if obliquely, undermine widespread racist assumptions. By mouthing them in crudely caricatured form, Moses himself unwittingly exposes their absurdity. Sounding perversely like an acolyte of Enoch Powell, he panics when faced with Faizull's first consignment of illegals: "The nightmare was now happening for true. It is hard enough to try and fathom one or two with their dark, scowling faces, piercing resentful eyes, and their general inscrutable miens and bearings. When you are faced with a dozen of the best, closely packed together; when is not only men but women too – three females was there; ... when is after midnight and you are in London, a civilized capital metropolis where you do not expect such things to happen – need I go on, dear R? Can you blame me for my tremulous voice and my hollow laughter?" (80). The joke here depends, of course, on having the black West Indian react with white chauvinist outrage to the influx of East Indian "aliens." Even Moses's language loses its island flavour, approaching "standard" speech as he borrows the racial catchphrases of the white "civilized capital metropolis."

The more frantically Moses, abetted by his white Friday, strives to "keep the lid on" his multiracial household, the more the misunderstandings and animosities threaten to boil over. The most bizarre instance is the sheep-slaughtering sequence that provides the narrative's comic pivot. The episode, which begins when Bob calls Moses's attention to a sheep puzzlingly tethered in the grubby yard or "jungle" of the house, soon embroils Moses in arcane details of Islamic ritual. According to Clement Wyke, "Selvon makes us aware of the social situation of the ethnically and culturally different immigrant to Britain. He accomplishes this objective by portraying the religious idiosyncrasies and practices of Pakistani people in an urban society" (107). In fact the sheep episode, as it unfolds, makes a word like Wyke's "idiosyncrasies" seem a sardonic understatement. Moses beholds the slaughter, conducted by Faizull and his butcher friend Farouk, with marked ironic detachment, verging on revulsion:

> Faizull was tying the sheep foots together, two in front and two behind. Farouk start up a oriental chant in one of them strange tongues, Urdu or Punjabi or something.
>
> "What is he saying?" I ask Faisull.
>
> "Shh," he say. "It is a prayer. Try not to make noise. If the sheep becomes excited and nervous, the muscles will get tense and stiff, and the meat will be tough."
>
> "It's the sheep that should be praying," I say.
>
> Then, without further ado, Farouk swivel round on his knees, and before you could say Jack Robinson he lift up the sheep head and administer the death stroke in one clean movement, slitting the throat from ear to ear. It seem to me that he could of gone down an inch more from the head, but that might of meant one inch less neck to share out. (62)

The observer's distancing from "outlandish" practices ("'It's the sheep that should be praying'") could hardly be greater in a *Punch* cartoon or a Waugh novel. Overtones of cruel ritual brutality (the reflection about going down an inch more from the head) abound. Yet even here Moses's sarcastic stance is itself ironically undercut. In his smugness on the score of "them strange tongues" he forgets that he himself is speaking what English readers will likely find a "strange tongue," a rustic patois ("tying the sheep foots together"). And the ironies are compounded by Faizull's cool nonchalance about the niceties of his own faith: "'Is that all?' I [Moses] was disappointed. 'What about all them rites and rituals?' 'Farouk has another job this morning,' Faizull say. 'We can't go through all that rigmarole'" (64).

The one English witness to the slaughter, Bob, reacts in as culturally inscribed a fashion as the migrants. "'I will get the RSPCA to arrest you!' he shout. 'You too, Moses!' Everything was going nice and smooth until this white man run amok: that's why I didn't want him in the first place" (63). Bob's humanitarian frenzy causes him to "run amok" like a tribesman from a lurid jungle-adventure tale. The actors in the scene are all obeying cultural imperatives of crazily diverse sorts, but in each case with a rigid Bergsonian automatism. What results is a flying circus of criss-crossing national obsessions. Bob's English tantrum over the sheep-slaughter is soon allayed by Moses's promise to give him a share of the animal's liver: "'It's good for you,' I say. 'It will make your cock stand up'" (64). Luckily for Moses, he can rely on his English Friday's love for animals yielding to a more powerful animal impulse.

The counterpointed national extravagances of the sheep-slaughtering sequence lie at the heart of Selvon's comedy in *Moses Ascending*. Moses's decaying house, with its motley tenantry, is a ship of fools awash in the social tides of post-imperial London, in which contingents of ill-assorted wanderers from here, there, and everywhere converge. In an anarchic urban world where harassed minorities connive maliciously against each other, Moses's reaction to Faizull is typical: "I wasn't going to let no bloody Paki get the better of me" (66). At best, leagues between representatives of diverse ethnic groups take the form of skulking collusion rather than sincere amity, as when Moses allows himself to be embroiled in Faizull's immigrant-smuggling racket.

In the end, the house that Moses had bought to enable his social "ascent" turns out to be just one more lock-up: "I feel like a prisoner in my own house. I didn't know if I was better off twiddling my thumbs in the basement, or lurking in the hallway upstairs to see if one of the refugees would come out and give me a chance to put my foot in the doorway. It look as if Fate had me shuttling 'tween Pakis and blacks ..." (90). Moses's "Fate" is really the controlling pressure exerted on marginalized minorities by a white majoritarian society. The prison that Moses needs to escape is not literal but figurative: the race-haunted mentality that causes him to picture himself as shuttling between discrete, hermetic enclaves, rather than responding to those who dwell in them as individuals with a claim on his fellowship.

Under such circumstances, Galahad's admonition to Moses – "'If you had stuck to your own kind, you wouldn't of been in this shit'" (86) – is beside the point. In this social context, group affiliations solve little. For one thing, Moses has already landed in "shit" by associating himself with a demonstration sponsored by "his own kind," including Galahad himself. On a deeper level, Moses's real problem, a universal one, is determining what precisely "his own kind" might mean. In a city that offers a carnivalesque assortment of available but mismatched roles, it no easy task to fix on an identity one can confidently live out. Little wonder if the smuggled Pakistanis are so intimidated by their new surroundings that they shrink from moving to the room of the roughneck Bob: "'They think he is a skinhead, and they would be bashed'" (96). Their fear, though actually baseless, takes its due place in the whole comic round-robin of mutual group antipathies and misunderstandings, a state of affairs we will encounter again in Salman Rushdie's *The Satanic Verses*.

At the end of the novel, having been levered out of his "penthouse" by the scheming Bob and his consort Jeannie, Moses issues a disclaimer: "It occurs to me that some black power militants might chose [*sic*] to misconstrue my Memoirs for their own purposes, and put the following moral to defame me, to wit: that after the ballad and the episode, it is the white man who ends up Upstairs and the black man who ends up Downstairs" (149). Since Moses, like it or not, is describing the situation that actually obtains, critics have naturally taken the "moral" Moses rejects as Selvon's implied message about racial dynamics in Britain. According to Looker, "Moses refuse[s] the most logical interpretation of his situation, and even projects it onto his literary enemies" (187). True, the book leaves no doubt in the reader's mind that it is white "natives," and not coloured migrants, who rule the roost in England; still, Moses's denial has a logic of its own. In the world of *Moses Ascending*, any general principle that makes the correlation between race and social positioning seem logical is bound to be worthless. The "ups and downs" of Moses's career are without rhyme or reason, and they tend to blur bewilderingly in retrospect: "I looked out over the back garden, remembering Faizull and the slaughter of the lamb. Them was good days, comparatively speaking. 'There is no god but Mohammed,' I mutter" (147). Stationed as Moses is in London amid a carnival of polycultural perversity, his future path might imaginably take him anywhere, except to a Mecca of clairvoyance and calm.

LAST EXIT TO JAMAICA: *MOSES MIGRATING*

In *Moses Migrating*, Selvon's comedy of recolonization comes full circle. Forgetting the rebuffs heaped on him by his adopted country, Moses has turned into a fervent Anglophile. His devotion to the past glory of empire moves him to revisit his former home, the now-independent Trinidad, on a colonizing mission: a folly nicely timed to coincide with the island's Carnival. As Susheila Nasta observes, "The principle of comic grotesque reversal directs this work as it had directed *Moses Ascending*" (*Perspectives* 6). Moses, like the mimic man Harris in *The Lonely Londoners*, has become more British than the British. Consequently, as Looker says, "In *Moses Migrating*, even more than in *Moses Ascending*, Selvon distances himself from the narrator, and the effect is to replicate in Moses a tourist mentality covertly linked to imperialism and colonialism" (190). Crypto-colonialist though he is, however, Moses remains what Selvon calls him in his preface, a "whitewashed

Black man torn apart by the circumstances of living in a white society" (xii-xiii), one who lacks the white imperialist's cool assurance in approaching a subaltern society.

Troubled by his "desertion" of his transatlantic home, Moses hits on a role that will allow him to feel loyal to Britain while distant from it: he will be "an ambassador not only of goodwill but good manners. The idea put a different complexion on my circumstances. I now had a purpose, which was to show the outlanders in the Carribean that Brit'n was not only still on her feet, but also still the onlyest country in the world where good breeding and culture come before ill-gotten gains and calls of the flesh" (30). On his arrival in Trinidad, he cheers himself with the equally naive notion that "I was going to plant the Union Jack on the land like Raleigh or one of them fellars and get some new subjects for the Queen" (58), failing to notice that the monarch in question is not the radiant first Elizabeth but her lacklustre latter-day namesake.

A more promising brush with the past occurs when Moses stumbles across a familiar islander: Tanty Flora, the childless woman who adopted him when he was a homeless "norphan" and who is now selling oranges at a stall opposite his hotel, the Hilton. (Though she has produced no offspring, her name and her occupation both connote fruitfulness.) Like Tolroy's Tanty in *The Lonely Londoners*, Tanty Flora embodies the rooted steadfastness of Caribbean identity, and talking with her exposes Moses's shaky grasp on his own: "[I]t was as if out here by the Savannah I lose my identity and become prey to incidents and accidents" (65). The first "incident" is Tanty nagging him to get out of the Hilton: "'[I]t must be costing you a pound and a crown! That's for the white tourists-them'" (65). In effect, she is prodding him to reassert his black identity, a thought she soon voices more forthrightly: "'We got no time for white people in Trinidad, Moses, them days is gone forever, praise the Lord. Black is power now,' and as she say that, she sort of make a circle in the air with the sharp knife what she peel the oranges with, a delicate, confident action, nothing like the angry fist in the air, but threatening enough for me to back off" (67). This picture of an ignorant, impoverished old woman as a Black Power activist may provoke smiles, but in fact Tanty Flora makes a more credible militant than Brenda or Galahad, because she is not infatuated with her own militancy. She takes no pains to fabricate the approved, belligerent image. Her version of the Black Power salute, her "delicate, powerful action" with the mundane tool of her trade, contrasts with Galahad's grandiose flourish, or with the misaimed upthrust of a fist that ignited a brawl in *Moses Ascending*. If it threatens Moses, that is only because he sees it as a feint liable to peel away the whiteface mask he now wears. Where Moses views himself as "an ambassador not only of goodwill but of good manners," Tanty upbraids him, "'You come back here with bad money, and bad manners, Moses'" (67). Nettled by this and by further run-ins with local Anglo-skeptics, Moses grumbles pompously: "I could see that I would have a hard time as Jesus with the Pharisees spreading my gospel in Trinidad" (82) – the dubious gospel that Britain has not lost her old supremacy, that white alone is beautiful.

The alternative that Tanty holds out for Moses is that of reintegrating himself in Trinidad by resuming his Creole identity, but this project poses its own problems. For one thing, the island has itself changed during Moses's long expatriation; forces shaking the rest of the world have not bypassed it. Also, Trinidadian identity is itself a troubled concept, given the splintering of island society along racial and class fault-lines. A way out of this racially inflected impasse is offered Moses by Doris, a beauty who epitomizes "the pot-pourri mixture of races that populate the island" (87). As Nasta says in her afterword, "Moses's relationship with Doris is important as it signifies the possibility for Moses of real integration and return" (193). While falling in love with Doris (and with the island itself), however, Moses remains fixated on his whim of impersonating his adored Britannia as a "mas" at the upcoming Carnival, leaving him with the unworkable aim of straddling two incompatible self-concepts simultaneously.

As Moses's Britannia performance takes shape, it withdraws progressively farther from reality. "'This has got to be a dignified mas, man,'" Moses pontificates to Lennard, a young newspaper reporter. "'It got to have solemnity and pride, and pomp and splendour, like when the Queen coronating'" (133). His lust for regal pomp leads Moses to another extravagance: having a tape of "Rule Britannia" playing to dignify his royal progress. Unwilling to stop even at this, Moses decides to have Bob's wife Jeannie accompany him as Britannia's handmaiden, "wafting one of them big feather fans over me like the little black slave boys in them films, in all that hot sun" (137), with Bob to haul the ensemble through the streets: "Gosh, this whole thing might even strike a blow for Race Relations at the same time, with a black man as Britannia, and two white people as his servants!" (137). Moses presumably means to stage a carnivalesque overturning of conventional roles, but unfortunately the "blow for Race Relations" is actually a blow aimed at historical fact. Doris, whose inclusive racial inheritance and good sense make her the book's raisonneur, suggests quietly: "'Quite frankly, I think

Jeannie should play Britannia and let Moses haul the platform. That's the history I learn at school'" (149).

Moses himself either has learned no history, or forgotten the history he once knew. Like Western colonizers both early and late, he is too mesmerized by the glamorous trappings of empire to come to grips with local realities. As Doris remarks, again perceptively, "'Your Carnival will never over, Moses. You are playing mas all the time'" (151). What she means is that her friend's Carnival is a purely personal self-indulgence, a solo "performance" without reference to local traditions. Paradoxically, it is by playing mas in a contrary spirit, by briefly committing himself to his native, communal Carnival, that Moses comes closest to reclaiming his national past and his own roots: "And in truth, I don't know what come over me that morning, if memories of bygone Jouvert return after all my years in stuffy old Brit'n, or if it was that I was in the midst of my countrymen now, the pulse and the sweat and the smell and the hysterical excitement, but my head was giddy with a kind of irresistible exultation like I just got emancipated from slavery … 'Doris!' I scream, 'Doris! Let we get married'" (164–-5). In a rare moment of clairvoyance, Moses recognizes the august Britannia as merely "stuffy old Brit'n"; he is ready to emancipate himself by a change of cultural air. Selvon himself finally came to feel "more comfortable and at ease" away from Britain than "travelling in a place like London, in the underground there, with the stuffy English atmosphere" (Roberts and Thakur 92). For a moment Moses is stirred to play mas in good earnest, pledging himself to Doris, and by extension embracing his Caribbean heritage: the carnivalesque folk tradition, which, according to Bakhtin, allowed participants to enter for a time "the utopian realm of community, freedom, equality, and abundance" (*Rabelais* 9). But Doris never hears his blurted proposal, and when he does literally embrace her, significantly at the Hilton, he is playing mas in the most trivial, egocentric sense, involving no commitment to island values.

Soon enough, he reverts to his obsession with his "Big Moment," his staging of his Britannia spectacular. After performing it (to the applause and laughter of an audience that reads it as an uproarious mockery of British pretensions), his thoughts swerve away from Doris, matrimony, and resettlement to the prospect of his triumphant return to stuffy old Brit'n: "As we left the platform I thank God from the bottom of my heart for my short-lived glory, and for giving me this opportunity to qualify for some distinction of recognition from the British Government. The least they could do, was to inform the Immigration Authorities at Heathrow Airport that I should be welcomed back, without let or hindrance, should

I decide to return" (172). The best Moses can imagine, as a heroically returning prodigal son, is not having the door slammed on his beseeching black face.

As for the other "short-lived glory" of his romance with Doris and Trinidad, Moses tries to avert his thoughts from it. Embarking for sooty London, with Lenten appropriateness on Ash Wednesday, he feels "like Peter must of felt when he deny Christ" (179). If earlier he has worried pointlessly about his "desertion of Brit'n in her hour of need" (25), he has now incurred the guilt of a more dire desertion, that of his own authentic, Trinidadian self. As Margaret Joseph says, he has accepted the role of "the ultimate outsider: he is now exiled from himself as well as from his origins" (102). Selvon's own view of England has darkened over the years since *The Lonely Londoners*; the vibrant comedy of metropolitan life, which in that book had offset the snubs and disappointments, seems to have faded into the shadows. Over all, Selvon's trilogy follows a trajectory leading from cautiously hopeful ambivalence to caustic, disillusioned satire. If Moses is finally left loitering at the glum portals of British Immigration for his destiny – readmission or banishment – to be sealed, his creator was coming to realize that his own future lay in the contrary direction: back across the ocean that Moses has just comically, and painfully, retraversed. The tragicomic, Janus-like predicament of facing both ways across the globe will reappear in the fiction of Samuel Selvon's younger fellow pilgrim, Salman Rushdie.

9

Rerouting the Comic: Salman Rushdie's *The Satanic Verses*

We must find it possible to laugh and wonder as well as rage and weep.

Salman Rushdie, "Outside the Whale"

Because of the global outcry it provoked, *The Satanic Verses* has been widely regarded as an anomalous *cause célèbre*. As Catherine Cundy says, "Since its publication in 1988, the text has all but lost its ability to be judged as an artistic enterprise rather than a cultural and political crisis" (65). A partial exception is *Punch*'s review (7 October 1988), which does assess the novel, though negatively, on the basis of aesthetic values. The reviewer, Adam Lively, finds that it "has the feel of a book in which a style and approach to fiction [magic realism] have reached the point of exhaustion and self-consciousness." For Lively, "The weakest strand in the book concerns the adventures of Chamcha and Gibreel in London." While this judgement may be defensible, *Punch*'s dismissal of just those chapters that expose the racial skeletons in England's closet uncomfortably recalls earlier phases of the magazine. And a *Punch* follow-up about the burning of the novel by Bradford Muslims (3 February 1989) indulges in the sort of sneering at racial otherness that Rushdie's satire targets. Profiling Sayed Abdul Quddus, general secretary of the Council for Mosques, who torched the book at the Bradford rally, Roger Tagholm reports that "[h]e has a moustache and a gangster-style hat, and looks like a cross between Hitler and Al Capone, only with a better tan than either of them."

What Lively (let alone Tagholm) neglects to mention is the comic tenor of Rushdie's novel. This seems an odd omission for a reviewer writing in a humour magazine, but it is by no means isolated. Although Rushdie himself has called *The Satanic Verses* "the most comic of his first four novels" (qtd in Finney 81–2), few critical studies have focused on its humour. To paraphrase Rushdie's apothegm, rage and tears have been privileged over laughter and wonder. Simon Gikandi calls *The Satanic Verses* "the paradigmatic text of postcolonialism" (208); yet when listing the "strategies" Rushdie uses to "unpack the objective metaphors of colonialism and nationalism" (210), he neglects to include comedy. Evidently, even for so sophisticated a critic, humour does not qualify as an important postcolonial paradigm.

Those who do mention the novel's comic mode often see it as a tactical blunder rather than an artistic strength. For Malise Ruthven, "not the least of the problems confronting anyone writing about the Rushdie Affair is that – to put it mildly – Rushdie and a sizeable section of his readers do not share the same sense of humour" (188–9). Levity at the imputed expense of Islam and its Prophet has famously been a cause of outrage to Muslim readers. Ridicule of one's faith can be more offensive than scowling skepticism; any totalizing belief leaves little room for the secularism of laughter. As Jaina Sanga says, "What highlights the impropriety of the novel is partly the narrative tone itself. The novel is at points extremely funny, and Rushdie's exuberant, jocund tone, interspersed with a sense of flippancy dethrones the most somber historical event to a rowdy, pedestrian importance" (110). Or as James English more tersely puts it, "The humor is the real problem: it is not that Rushdie wrote objectionable things, but that he wrote them with a smirk on his face" (229).

Still, it is possible to exaggerate the breadth of Rushdie's smirk. Timothy Brennan's breezy summary of *The Satanic Verses* as "a 500-page parody of Muhammad's life" (144) is a case in point. Actually, the novel's comedy is most acerbically trained not on Gibreel Ferishta's serial dream of the ancient origins of Islam but rather on the waking actions of the contemporary characters, Ferishta included. The Prophet, though humanized and ironized by his subjection to the vernacular medium of prose narrative, is not in fact rudely burlesqued. He is endowed with at least as much gravity as levity; while, as Sanga herself guardedly points out, the book's eccentric gallery of East and West Indians is "not exempt from Rushdie's ridicule" (38). David Myers claims that Mahound, Rushdie's Muhammad-persona, "emerges as a dedicated, patriarchal and even heroic figure particularly when contrasted with the novel's clownish antiheroes, Gibreel Ferishta and Salahuddin Chamcha" (146), a view that perhaps overcompensates for the visceral Islamic outrage. Sara Suleri's assertion that "Rushdie has written a deeply Islamic book … from a cultural point of view, a work of meticulous religious attentiveness" (*Rhetoric* 191) strikes the same note of defensive hyperbole, a maneuver likely only to intensify the ire of the orthodox.[1]

Even those who give the novel's comedy and satire a less nervous reception commonly discuss them only in passing, or at best limit their analysis to technical matters. Rushdie's parodying of prior literature has, for example, received much attention. Nico Israel notes that the book's opening tableau, in which Chamcha and Ferishta fall 29,002 feet from a disintegrating airplane, is "a jet age parody of *Paradise Lost*'s first book" (160), and other proposed models have ranged from the Book of Genesis to *Alice in Wonderland*. Unlike most commentators, Gayatri Spivak points to the fusion of comic and serious elements in the novel: "What we see in process in the greater part of *The satanic verses* is the many fragmented national representations coming together in serious and comic – serious *when* comic and vice versa – figures of resistance" (107). By foregrounding this merger of modes, Spivak illuminates the links between humour and ideological "resistance" in Rushdie's text.

The most ample discussion of comedy in *The Satanic Verses* remains the one by English, who reads Rushdie's humour in the context of contemporary British issues of community. Yet not even English invokes for comparison the raced comedy found in earlier British fiction, like Waugh's, or Cary's, or even Forster's.[2] And while other critics have traced connections between Rushdie and Caribbean writers like V.S. Naipaul or George Lamming, few have mentioned the most richly affiliated comic precursor of *The Satanic Verses*, Samuel Selvon's Moses trilogy.

The differences between Rushdie and Selvon are many and obvious. Besides their disparities in birthdate, upbringing, and countries of origin, the two tend to work in divergent modes. Where Selvon favours a folk-inflected variant of realism, Rushdie has developed his own distinctive vein of globalized, surrealist fantasy. Nevertheless, in both novelists comedy turns on the same basic contemporary phenomenon: the clash between migrant and metropolis. Like Selvon's treatment of Moses Aloetta and his "boys," Rushdie's portrayals of non-white newcomers contending with the mainly white city of London "have to have ha-ha." As Rushdie has recently proclaimed, "The great unheralded battle in the world … is between those who have a sense of humour and those who don't" (Martin, *Globe and Mail*). For Rushdie, laughter is a mode of intelligence and a political force; along with Muriel Spark, he would applaud Bakhtin's comment on the unsmiling "agelasts" : "This old authority and truth pretend to be absolute, to have an extratemporal importance. Therefore, their representatives (the agelasts) are gloomily serious. They cannot and do not wish to laugh; they strut majestically, consider their foes the enemies of eternal truth, and threaten them with eternal punishment. They do not see themselves in the mirror of time, do not perceive their own origin, limitations and end; they do not recognize their own ridiculous faces or the comic nature of their pretensions to eternity and immutability" (*Rabelais* 212–13). This is an exact likeness of the grim, history-denying Imam in *The Satanic Verses*, and Rushdie would no doubt gladly extend it to certain nonfictional Ayatollahs.

What most nearly recalls Selvon's vein of comedy in *The Satanic Verses* is the wealth of humour hinging on incongruity. Suleri remarks colourfully that "the narrative … throw[s] up a pair of Muslim hands at the incongruities that impel its discourse" (*Rhetoric* 192), but one might add that the narrative also laughs out of the corner of its Muslim mouth. Like Waugh's comedy in *Black Mischief*, Rushdie's arises from proliferating transcultural clashes, but here the colliding forces cannot be dualistically defined as "civilization" and "primitivism." As Rushdie has said, "What I've tried to do is to set alongside each other in odd, sometimes raw juxtaposition *all sorts of different bodies of experience* to show what frictions and sparks they make" (*Rushdie File* 9, emphasis added).

Many sparks emanate from the colliding and coalescing of Eastern and Western takes on experience. In *The Satanic Verses* such eerily dissonant comic conjunctions abound. A number depend on clashes between Indian spirituality and Western technology, a point I will amplify later. The ghost of Rekha Merchant, the Bombay matron who killed herself and her children after being jilted by her film-star lover, Gibreel Ferishta, appears to Ferishta floating reproachfully on a flying carpet as the dazed actor strays from station to station of the London Underground. Later, having amassed a fuller experience of London, Ferishta voices to his unreceptive fellow performer Chamcha views that create a Rushdiean "raw juxtaposition": "O, he was in high good humour that day, rubbishing London and the English with much of his old brio. Where Chamcha saw attractively faded grandeur, Gibreel saw a wreck, a Crusoe-city, marooned on the island of its past, and trying, with the help of a Man-Friday underclass, to keep up appearances. Under the gaze of stone lions he chased pigeons, shouting, 'I swear, Spoono, back home these fatties wouldn't last one day; let's take one home for dinner.' Chamcha's Englished soul cringed for shame" (*Verses* 453–4). The contrast between carnivalesque migrant gusto and Lenten, animal-cherishing "Englished" propriety recalls Galahad's tribulations as a pigeon-stalker in *The Lonely Londoners*. The reference to *Robinson Crusoe* brings to mind Moses's topsy-turvy arrangement with

Bob, his "man Friday," in *Moses Ascending*. Admittedly, Gibreel's whole experience of the Crusoe-city involves surreal incongruities unlike anything to be found in Selvon's trilogy.

Like Selvon's, Rushdie's portrayal of migrants draws much of its comic momentum from caricature. Some have objected to the defamiliarizing of Rushdie's principal characters, which proceeds from his unwillingness to endow them with a humanizing depth and complexity. For David Kerr, in this book, as opposed to the earlier *Midnight's Children*, "Rushdie has distanced himself from his circumstances, and to an extent has replaced the sense of shocked horror of the earlier book with bizarre comedy in which it seems that human pain is somewhere else" (170). Ruthven, however, counters the charge that Rushdie has forfeited empathy for the sake of comic impact: "Empathy in fiction … comes more readily with the creation of 'rounded' characters: since Rushdie's thesis appears to be that the migrant's experience leads to the discarding and assuming of identities, to create 'rounded' characters would surely be false to his method: his novel's strength lies in its exuberant two-dimensional qualities, its intense visuality, its way with syntax and astonishing lexical range" (19–20). James English offers a more complex rationale, pointing to the constricted ambit of migrants within the structures of metropolitan society: "What needs to be understood about the comic practice of *The Satanic Verses* … is that its first principle is to subordinate the individual self to the 'characterless plurality' of socially constituted types. Rushdie's characters may strive for an individuality, an authenticity, a unique and sympathetic identity that could be enfolded in an unstereotypic discourse of 'positive images.' But this quest is always obstructed by their prior (and often self-conscious) insertion into a system of social relations which has only the most unoriginal, compromised, and politically dubious subject positions to offer" (233–4). What follows from the socially determined banality of the characters' motivations is, English believes, a Bergsonian comedy depending on automatized, preset reflexes.

But while such defences are cogent, they say little about the strategies by which Rushdie mediates the distancing effect of his comedy. One of the most important of these is his use, recalling Selvon's, of a modified English narrative idiom designed to attune readers to the gap between the migrant's experience and the metropolitan "norm." As Sanga argues, "Rushdie's specific use of language in the novels seeks to reinscribe the colonial English language by Indianizing it. Rushdie's English is very much influenced by … his Indian background, and by appropriating the English language and transforming it, Rushdie's fiction serves subversively to open up a complex area of postcolonial resistance to both colonial cultural and political ideologies, and to the dominant ideologies constructed and perpetuated in the Indian subcontinent" (49). Her claims coincide with what Rushdie himself says in his essay "Imaginary Homelands": "I hope all of us share the view that we can't simply use the language in the way the British did; that it needs remaking for our own purposes. Those of us [Indian writers] who do use English do so in spite of our ambiguity towards it, or perhaps because of that, perhaps because we can find in that linguistic struggle a reflection of other struggles taking place in the real world, struggles between the cultures within ourselves and the influences at work upon our societies" (*Homelands* 17). As I have shown, a broadly similar rationale has been used to defend Selvon's introduction of a dialect-speaking narrator in the Moses trilogy. In fact, however, for all its departures from "standard" English usage Rushdie's narrative voice is never Indianized as thoroughly as Selvon's is creolized. The consequence is a somewhat broader affective gap between narrator and characters in his fiction.

Like Harris in *The Lonely Londoners* and like Moses in *Moses Migrating*, the figure of the mimic Englishman is a mainspring of humour in *The Satanic Verses*. Saladin Chamcha, too, tries to be "more English than," as his friend Zeeny complains (*Verses* 53); he even marries an Englishwoman with a "voice stinking of Yorkshire pudding and hearts of oak, that hearty, rubicund voice of ye olde dream-England which he so desperately wanted to inhabit" (186). He has courted his English rose, Pamela Lovelace, devotedly, feeling "that she had become the custodian of his destiny, that if she did not relent then his entire attempt at metamorphosis would fail" (50). After securing Pamela he completes his ethnic makeover by setting up a passable facsimile of a London bourgeois household and by parroting the jingoistic axioms of the Thatcherite right.[3] According to Spivak, "As migrant, the post-colonial may attempt to become the metropolitan: this is Saladin Chamcha in his first British phase … This self-definition of the migrant as metropolitan is obviously not the book's preferred definition" (107). The book's opening tableau wickedly inverts Chamcha's lust for British propriety by imaging him as a "fastidious shadow falling headfirst in a grey suit with all the jacket buttons done up, arms by his sides, taking for granted the improbability of the bowler hat on his head" (4). We later (421) learn that, improving on Moses's use of a tape of "Rule Britannia" to add patriotic zest to his Carnival "mas," Chamcha during free-fall was singing that same stirring anthem. As Cundy observes, "Saladin's pursuit of Englishness is a repression of his own personal and cultural history. He cuts down the walnut tree planted by his father to celebrate his birth [more accurately, directs his father to cut it down], attempting to excise those years from the narrative of his existence" (78). Indeed, Chamcha's "cutting down" of his own name suggests how his Englishing entails an emasculation of his full selfhood. As Ian Baucom says, "Born Salahuddin Chamchawala, he has contracted himself, torn the difficult syllables from his name and offered himself to his English brethren as a word that can be easily pronounced" (202–3).

Having paid this price for his passport into the English bourgeoisie, Chamcha still faces obstacles, both social and professional, in gaining full membership. In Gikandi's words, "Saladin has no identity except as an entertainer or performer" (215). His theatrical roles themselves spectacularly place him in what English terms compromised subject positions. On a popular children's television show he is cast as the sardonically named "Maxim Alien," and he does the voiceovers for a whole shopping cart full of products: "If you wanted to know how your ketchup bottle should talk in its television commercial, if you were unsure as to the ideal voice for your packet of garlic-flavoured crisps, he was your very man" (60). Whatever the brand Chamcha is promoting, the key to his professional survival is that he himself remain a no-name commodity. To accommodate the ethos of *fin de siècle* British consumerism, he must collude in the elision of his own ethnicity. From this compulsive and compelled denial of his full subjecthood, much of the humour of his strand of the narrative emerges.

During his visit to India with a touring English theatre company Chamcha runs afoul of the linguistic slippage that afflicts Selvon's verbally backsliding Harris. Over the years Chamcha has crafted both a face and a voice to suit his "English" persona: "Mr Saladin Chamcha had constructed this face with care – it had taken him several years to get it just right – and for many years now he had thought of it simply as *his own* – indeed, he had forgotten what he had looked like before it. Furthermore, he had shaped himself a voice to go with the face, a voice whose languid, almost lazy vowels contrasted disconcertingly with the sawn-off abruptness of the consonants" (33). Now, however, exposed to the treacherous Bombay milieu, his mask of the Happy Ethnic Hypocrite begins to slip. After they make love, Zeeny twits him about "'your Angrez [English] accent wrapped around you like a flag, and don't think it's so perfect, it slips, baba, like a false moustache'" (53). Such a mechanical breakdown of a fabricated persona neatly fits the Bergsonian model of automatized comic action. So, too, does Chamcha's later mutation into a goatish, demonic beast at the mercy of its own animal functions; the monster helplessly voiding pellets all over the immigration officers' van obliterates the image of constipated "proper Englishness" that Chamcha had nurtured. From the time of his colossal fall he is manhandled by peremptory forces: "[W]hat had taken him over was the will to live, unadulterated, irresistible, pure, and the first thing it did was to inform him that it wanted nothing to do with his pathetic personality, that half-reconstructed affair of mimicry and voices" (9). To live authentically he must jettison the half-reconstructed affair, whatever the cost in trauma. He must learn to accept the overmastering physical reality of his Bakhtinian "grotesque body"; and Chamcha's new body is as grotesque as anything ever envisioned by the Russian theorist.

The comic point of his goatish metamorphosis lies in the drastic way it forces Chamcha to confront his true "maximum alien" status in English society, which his prior, meticulously honed British persona had allowed him to evade. Once bemonstered, he becomes, in Bhabha's phrase, "the discriminatory sign of a performative, projective British culture of race and racism" (*Location* 228). The convulsive revision of his conventional cognitive maps is, in typical Rushdiean fashion, both agonizing and funny. Paradoxically, Rushdie's surrealism conducts Chamcha to a more "realistic" perception of his essential life predicament. As Rushdie observes *à propos* of Terry Gilliam's futuristic film *Brazil*, "Unreality is the only weapon with which reality can be smashed, so that it may subsequently be reconstructed" (*Homelands* 122). Chamcha's mimicry of a proper bourgeois Englishman has been a false "reality" that his change into a nightmarish beast rudely smashes, freeing him to reconstruct a more genuine reality within which to live.

Chamcha's return as a professional actor to Bombay loosely parallels Moses Aloetta's "recolonizing" visit to his birthplace in *Moses Migrating*. Chamcha, too, travels under British post-imperial auspices, performing a babu part with a white English troupe. Back in Bombay, both on stage and off he is, like Moses, continually "playing mas," strutting and fretting in an assumed role. Chamcha's father Changez, though still living, is in effect a stranger, owing to a bitter quarrel between father and son. All the same, during Chamcha's brief return Changez's passionate attachment to India places him in an admonitory position toward his son recalling the role Moses's Tanty assumes toward her adopted nephew. A closer parallel still links Chamcha's girlfriend Zeeny Vakil and Moses's almost-fiancée Doris. Much as Doris does with Moses, Zeeny urges Chamcha to redeem his castaway status by returning for good to native grounds: "'Salad baba, whatever you call yourself, for Pete's sake *come home*" (62). Zeeny is not, like Doris, an emblematic racial collage, but she is by profession an expert on

Indian artistic eclecticism, and thus stands equally for the principle of hybridity. The invitation she extends is, however, even more problematic than Doris's because of Chamcha's chronic uncertainty about what to call himself and where he belongs. As Una Chaudhuri argues, "[T]he immigrant experience of today interrogates both concepts, home and belonging, and points to a renovation of the general discourse of home" (141). By its close, *The Satanic Verses* accomplishes, however comically and provisionally, such a discursive renovation.

Besides forcing him to reconsider his spurious Englishness, Chamcha's transformation leads him to a more general questioning of stable constructions of ethnicity. His faith in conventional concepts of nation has already been shaken by media magnate Hal Valance's profanely globalizing avowal of love for England: "'I,' Hal Valance announced, 'love this fucking country. That's why I'm going to sell it to the whole goddamn world, Japan, America, fucking Argentina'" (277). It begins to dawn on Saladin that his chief's market-based patriotism "hadn't been Chamcha's way; not his, nor that of the England he had idolized and come to conquer" (279).

Chamcha's subsequent mutation comically transforms not only his bodily shape but his artificial concept of Englishness. Lurking in his lair above the Sufyans' café, he is perplexed by his exchanges with his hosts' teenage daughters Mishal and Anahita: "Conscious of having insulted their hospitality, he tried to explain that he thought of himself, nowadays, as, well, British ... 'What about us?' Anahita wanted to know. 'What do you think we are?' – And Mishal confided, 'Bangladesh in't nothing to me. Just some place Dad and Mum keep banging on about.' – And Anahita, conclusively, 'Bungleditch.' – With a satisfied nod. 'What I call it, anyhow.' But they weren't British, he wanted to tell them, not *really*, not in any way he could recognize. And yet his old certainties were slipping away by the moment, along with his old life" (267). Sanga calls the girls "ostensibly neither Bangladeshi nor British" (38), but she thereby falls into the same taxonomic trap as Chamcha. The Sufyan daughters' names and appearance place them as (in Powellite terms) "foreign," but they feel not the faintest connection with the "old country," for them a faraway ditch filled with banging and bungling, and take cheerfully for granted their bond with England, whether England welcomes them or not.

Baucom, also reluctant to accept the sisters as entirely British, draws a strained analogy between them and their past-haunted mother: "Anahita and Mishal's denial of Bangladesh and their wholesale adoption of a working-class London order of Englishness is not profoundly different from their mother's commitment to the landscape of her youth and her refusal to make contact with the city in which she finds her body if not her self" (205). Baucom's "not profoundly different" blurs the issue: one can hardly deny what one has never possessed; one cannot "adopt wholesale" a culture in which one has been immersed since birth. Paul Gilroy's comment on the children of black migrants exactly fits the junior Sufyans: "Blacks born, nurtured and schooled in this country are, in significant measure, British even as their presence redefines the meaning of the term" (155). In "Imaginary Homelands" Rushdie himself reasonably insists on "a Bradford-born Indian kid's right to be treated as a full member of British society" (*Homelands* 15).[4] The novel contains no funnier juxtaposition than the one between Chamcha's fusty, club-man's model of Englishness and the image presented by the brashly punky second-generation Sufyans. These girls, bored by Chamcha's buttoned-up bowler-wearing notions of English propriety, applaud his carnivalesque incarnation as a smoke-breathing priapic beast; in their eyes he is not menacingly alien but beguilingly "far-out." "'We think you're, you know.' 'Brilliant,' Anahita said and dazzled the bewildered Chamcha with a smile. 'Magic. You know. *Extreme*'" (266). Both the idiom and the attitudes belong to the "extreme" yet unignorable Britain that is supplanting Chamcha's antiquarian house of cards.

But even those who grant that it subverts outmoded concepts of Englishness accuse *The Satanic Verses* of reinscribing stereotypes of East and West Indians, a charge also levelled, as I have noted, at Selvon's trilogy. Debate about this can be waspishly *ad hominem*. James Harrison, granting that Rushdie "has the best of conscious intentions, "argues that "his unconscious attitudes may come through louder and clearer than those he intends to convey. This kind of writing is where an education as 'preppy' and 'ivy league' as is obtainable in Britain can be a handicap" (119). Rushdie's conscious intentions are made plain in his comment on the irony of the book's reception: "I tried to write against stereotypes, and the zealot protests serve to confirm, in the Western mind, all the worst stereotypes of the Muslim world" (*Rushdie File* 75). Nonetheless, Harrison's point deserves serious attention. It is, for example, hard to see how Rushdie's comic treatment of West Indians is "written against stereotypes. "An example is the blackface dialogue stemming from a love-triangle among Caribbean tube employees: "'Get her offa me, Uriah,' Rochelle shouted. 'She mashin up me uniform and all.' Now Uriah, holding the struggling ticket clerk by both wrists, gave out the news: 'I asks her to get marry!' – Whereupon the fight went out of Orphia" (341).

Brennan's claim that "[t]he book's characterisations of West Indians … are often embarrassing and offensive" (164) is hard to refute.

Troubling as their portrayal may be, however, Rushdie's West Indians are peripheral figures. A potentially more damaging charge is that *The Satanic Verses* exploits stock *East* Indian stereotypes, even if less blatantly, for comic advantage. "What conceivable challenge is after all being met," English asks, "what desirable aims could possibly be furthered, by humor that confirms the prejudices of the dominant many against the downtrodden few?" (228). (It is a complaint we will also see levelled against the films and novels of Hanif Kureishi.)

In answer to English's rhetorical question, I would argue that Rushdie's portraits of Indians do not, when closely examined, crudely bolster majority prejudice. Their aim is to expose the comic contradictions dogging migrants whose personalities, as English himself recognizes, are warped by the pressures of confining subject-positions. Hind Sufyan, the mother of Mishal and Anahita, exemplifies this distortion. Uprooted from her friendly Bangladeshi social milieu, she demonizes her strange new home: "[T]hey had come into a demon city in which anything could happen, your windows shattered in the middle of the night without any cause, you were knocked over in the street by invisible hands, in the shops you heard such abuse you felt like your ears would drop off but when you turned in the direction of the words you saw only empty air and smiling faces, and every day you heard about this boy, that girl, beaten up by ghosts" (258). In reaction Hind seals herself within a cocoon spun of filaments from her much-missed, "real" East Indian world. As Baucom comments, Hind "lives in London but turns away from it to inhabit the Bangladesh from which her husband has taken her. Surrounded by the subcontinental foods that she cooks and the Hindi and Bengali movies she rents, she dwells in the absence from which she has migrated" (203). Superficially Hind recalls Tolroy's uprooted Tanty in *The Lonely Londoners*, but she shows none of Tanty's feisty willingness to grapple with the neighbourhood around her, her tube-and-bus-hopping zest for urban adventure. Hind's rejection of England extends even to her two daughters, whose tastes and habits baffle her.

English objects that Rushdie's comic treatment of Hind plays into the hands of white racist preconceptions: "This stereotype of the Asian mother is far from politically neutral; it is a piece of contemporary orientalism which serves the interests of a domestic policing apparatus" (232). According to English, the image of the ghetto-bound Asian woman out of touch with her own second-generation children derives from tired British sociological clichés that feed latent anti-immigrant prejudice. The only answer to this criticism is, I think, that while stereotypes commonly do distort the people to whom they are applied, they can occasionally connect with observable fact. If a woman like Hind shrinks from the forbidding social world encircling her, there is, as Rushdie makes clear, ample reason for her to do so. And her out-of-touchness with her daughters does not need to be explained as an invention of orientalist sociology; painful generational gaps are all too familiar a feature of contemporary life. When such gaps of age are compounded by differences in acculturation, the results can be tragic, but they can also, in the hands of a writer like Rushdie, become acerbically comic.

It is true that Hind Sufyan, as English argues, does not represent a "'positive image' of the Asian mother" (233). But Rushdie is not in the business of manufacturing positive images, and any such image would prevent Hind from fulfilling a key function Rushdie has assigned her: that of comic foil for her tenant Saladin Chamcha. Bhabha claims that Chamcha is positioned midway between two "border conditions" exemplified by his landlady and landlord: "Chamcha stands, quite literally, in-between two border conditions. On the one hand lies his landlady Hind who espouses the cause of gastronomic pluralism, devouring the spiced dishes of Kashmir and the yogurt sauces of Lucknow, turning herself into the wide land mass of the subcontinent itself 'because food passes across any boundary you care to mention'. On Chamcha's other side sits the landlord Sufyan, the secular 'colonial' metropolitan who understands the fate of the migrant in the classical contrast between Lucretius and Ovid" (*Location* 224). Bhabha's argument, though ingeniously developed, is at bottom misleading. Hind's "pluralism" is ironized because it is no more than gastronomic and at best parochial; a mere shadow of the wider social engagement that would permit her to transgress the boundaries of her mind-forged prison. And rather than "in-between, "Chamcha stands at the opposite liminal extreme; as against Hind's border condition of nativist fixation, he represents the contrary border condition of doting, self-negating Anglophilia. In "Imaginary Homelands" Rushdie argues: "[O]f all the many elephant traps lying ahead of us [Asian migrants], the largest and most dangerous pitfall would be the adoption of a ghetto mentality. To forget that there is a world beyond the community to which we belong, to confine ourselves within narrowly defined cultural frontiers, would be, I believe, to go voluntarily into that form of internal exile which in South Africa is called the 'homeland'" (19). Rushdie's words define the homeland-bound Hind Sufyan's situation precisely. Chamcha at least avoids falling into this elephant trap, though he risks running afoul of its equally disabling, assimilationist twin.

Chamcha's yearning to integrate himself into an adoptive community by mimicking its conventions makes him an ape, but still, unlike Hind, an ape with some hope of escaping his cage. By contrast with his deracinated landlady, he is receptive to the cultural stimulus the storied postcolonial metropolis can still offer: "He had been striving ... to be worthy of the challenge represented by the phrase *Civis Britannicus sum*. Empire was no more, but still he knew 'all that was good and living within him' to have been 'made, shaped and quickened' by his encounter with this islet of sensibility, surrounded by the cool sense of the sea. – Of material things, he had given his love to this city, London, preferring it to the city of his birth or to any other; had been creeping up on it, stealthily, with mounting excitement, freezing into a statue when it looked in his direction, dreaming of being the one to possess it and, so, in a sense, *become* it" (412). With its turgid rhetoric and clumps of literary pastiche, Chamcha's tribute to London strikes a comically romanticized note. Yet it also evinces a touching imaginative generosity; the sentiment is not simply sabotaged, like Moses Aloetta's mawkish eulogies of "Brit'n," by sardonic irony. Here, too, Gayatri Spivak's insight applies; much of Rushdie's most effective writing manages a risky tonal equilibrium that is a hybrid of the serious and the comic. Chamcha may by now no longer be pursuing that will-of-the-wisp, "proper" Englishness, but even amid the throes of convulsive identity-reversal he keeps his underlying sense of affinity with London and its ramshackle compositeness: "London, its conglomerate nature mirroring his own, its reticence also his; its gargoyles, the ghostly footfalls in its streets of Roman feet, the honks of its departing migrant geese. Its hospitality – yes! – in spite of immigration laws, and his own recent experience, he still insisted on the truth of that: an imperfect welcome, true, one capable of bigotry, but a real thing, nonetheless" (412). As Rushdie has said, "*The Satanic Verses* celebrates hybridity, impurity, intermingling, the transformation that comes of new and unexpected combinations of human beings, cultures, ideas, politics, movies, songs" (*Homelands* 394). Naive as it may be, Saladin Chamcha's embrace of the mongrel metropole of London is at least a more promising stance than Hind Sufyan's ostrich-posture of shuddering withdrawal.

If by the end of the book Chamcha has lost his urge to say *Civis Britannicus sum*, he does not regret his long exposure to London's hybrid life. He remains an "impure" and staunchly cosmopolitan dweller of a distant but equally conglomerate city, Bombay. By contrast, his alter ego Gibreel Ferishta's exposure to Britain has proved crippling; but for that misadventure it is less Britain that is to blame than Gibreel himself.

Like Chamcha a professional actor, Gibreel personifies what Israel aptly calls "the theatricality of postcolonial subjectivity – a theatricality that Rushdie stages in the arena of post-modernism, on air, on screen, broadcast, as it were, worldwide" (167–8). Gibreel's theatricality leads to a type of clownishness contrary to Chamcha's, a comedy not of mimicry but of cosmic dementia, matching the amplitude of his globalized cinematic image. Gibreel represents, as many have noted, a doppelganger for Chamcha, but his role as an opposite or foil is equally vital. Fantastically transformed, like Chamcha, he assumes an angelic rather than satanic persona. In Baucom's view, Gibreel's halo is well deserved: "If Rushdie desires to elicit the stories of England's hybridity, then Gibreel Ferishta is the servant of that desire. As much as he is an angelic wanderer, Gibreel is a roaming repository of England's narratives. All who come in contact with him surrender to an impulse to reveal themselves, to divulge their tales, to pour their voices into the portals of his semidivine ear. As he wanders through the city of London, he finds himself wandering through a collection of stories whose only connection to one another is that, for all their dissimilarities, they are English" (211). Such a reading of Gibreel's mission unduly flatters the archangel-errant, since none of his metropolitan experiences results in a true clarifying of vision. Ambiguous as Saladin's experience of London may be, it is at any rate more positive than Gibreel's schizoid meandering.

Far from serving Rushdie's "desire to elicit the stories of England's hybridity," Ferishta, as Sanga argues, "must self-destruct by the end of the novel because he is unable to embrace hybridity" (80); he remains, in Rushdie's phrase, "an untranslated man." "Through the final implicit victory of Saladin," according to Simona Sawhney, "the novel suggests that Gibreel's greatest error might well be in his overriding desire for continuity and authenticity" (260); an ironic desire, in view of the hodgepodge of godly masks the actor dons in Indian "theological" films. Qua angel, Gibreel's fatal flaw is his inability to stop looking homeward. Unlike his more seducible satanic opposite, Gibreel austerely resists the equivocations of the metropole: "No more of these England-induced ambiguities, these Biblical-Satanic confusions! – Clarity, clarity, at all costs clarity! … O most slippery, most devilish of cities! – In which such stark, imperative oppositions were drowned beneath an endless drizzle of greys" (364). By glibly equating clarity with "stark, imperative oppositions," Gibreel is succumbing to a mental myopia more dangerous than the confusions he dreads.

Refusing to adapt to his new environment, but more enterprising than Hind Sufyan, Gibreel dreams a nativist reconfiguring of it, comically projecting a "metamorphosis of London into a tropical city" : "'City,' he cried, and his voice rolled over the metropolis like thunder, 'I am going to tropicalize you'" (365). Such an edict ironically echoes Gibreel's dreams of Jahilia; it is a self-infatuated bid to bring the mountain to Muhammad. Gibreel's spiteful trashing of Allie Cone's model mountain collection as he departs her flat reveals the juvenile self-indulgence of his resolve to impose his supernal will on the people and objects around him. As he pursues his angelic mission in the city, he proves himself even more ludicrously at odds with the metropolis than the bemonstered Chamcha. His attempts to reorder townspeople's disordered lives are drolly blundering, as when he identifies a young man on a street corner inspecting a photo of himself as a "lost soul" or "ka" unluckily detached from its body. Hoping to restore the ka to wholeness by planting a seraphic kiss on its mouth, Gibreel receives from it "a most surprising reaction": "'Sod you,' it shouted, 'I may be desperate, mate, but I'm not that desperate,' – after which, manifesting a solidity most unusual in a disembodied spirit, it struck the Archangel of the Lord a resounding blow upon the nose with the very fist in which its image was clasped; – with disconcerting, and bloody, results" (333). Such tongue-in-cheek humour attending blow-on-nose action regularly attends Gibreel's London exploits. It culminates when a "kindly, twinkling lady" he has urged to "repent" offers him "a racist text demanding the 'repatriation' of the country's black citizenry" (336). "'If they came over and filled up wherever you come from,'" she suggests, "'well! You wouldn't like *that*'" (337).

Gibreel's delusional agenda of colonizing the city nearly ends in self-destruction when he attempts, Canute-like, to stem the mechanized swell of London traffic: "He decided to force the issue. The stream of traffic flowed past him. He took a mighty breath, lifted one gigantic foot, and stepped out to face the cars." After this quixotic tilting at automotive windmills he is, predictably, "returned to Allie's doorstep, badly bruised, with many grazes on his arms and face, and jolted into sanity" (347). Generally speaking, Gibreel's daytime delusions reverse his nocturnal dreams of the Prophet's founding of Islam, which graft the relaxed rhythms of modern prose narrative onto the lyricism of prophecy. In his wakeful state, Gibreel tries wildly to inscribe prophetic vision on the vernacular of twentieth-century urban existence. His funny defiance of London traffic presages his mania-driven, unfunny suicide, an act confirming Fawzia Afzal-Khan's dictum that, in this novel, "only those who are flexible survive" (172).

One naturally searches for such reliable keys to interpretation in a narrative in which, as James Harrison puts it, "fact and fiction, fantasy and realism [are] continually and interchangeably shifting and switching like faces on a dance floor under strobe lighting" (114–15). Afzal-Khan herself concedes that Rushdie's narrative is "a mishmash of conflicting genres and modes ... in which the comic and the tragic, the real, the surreal, and the mythic all 'defuse' one another, so no one genre can predominate and 'unify' the others" (154). Yet despite the chaotic impression the book initially creates, overall it enacts a major if unobtrusive forward movement, as the author himself has testified: "[T]he point about *The Satanic Verses* is that it's a novel that begins in a pyrotechnic high-surrealist vein and moves towards a much more emotional, inner writing. That process of putting away the magic noses and cloven hoofs is one the novel itself goes through: *it tells itself*, and by the end it doesn't need that apparatus any more" (*Conversations* 137). Surprisingly few critics have dwelt on the decisive narrative shift Rushdie pinpoints. An exception is David Myers; though Myers's moralistic reading of the novel flattens some of its key ambiguities, he convincingly argues "that Rushdie succeeds, quite improbably, in transforming the novel's final thrust from satiric farce to tragic epiphany ... The closure of *The Satanic Verses* is a self-denial of the remote, supercilious narrator and a neo-romantic yearning to create meaning through the rediscovery of authentic self and the opening out of this self through irrational faith and commitment to the other" (146). The reining in of surrealist elements – magic noses, cloven hoofs – coincides, as Myers implies, with the muting of comedy. In the colossal comic pratfall that opens the narrative, the dual protagonists make their entrances in drastically objectified mode, manipulated by the contrary but equally impersonal forces of "levity" and "gravity." By the end, the narrator's tone toward both characters, and especially Chamcha, has grown markedly more intimate.

The Chamchas' bizarre domestic triangle is at first treated in the vein of surrealist burlesque. As Gikandi says, "[I]f the discourse on Englishness is anchored in the ideal of home and domesticity ..., there is no greater gesture of ironic reversal in the novel than Saladin's return to his English home not as the conquering hero but as 'a figure out of a nightmare or a late-night TV movie, a figure covered in mud and ice and blood, the hairiest creature you ever saw, with the shanks and hoofs of a giant goat'" (221). The text hints slyly at the identity of the legendary hero parodied by Rushdie's nightmarish anti-hero: "Upstairs, at the very top of the house, that is to say in Saladin's 'den', Mrs Pamela Chamcha was writhing in her lover's [Jumpy Joshi's] arms, crying her heart out, and bawling at the top of her voice: 'It isn't true. My husband exploded. No survivors. Do you hear me? I am the widow Chamcha whose spouse is beastly dead'" (194). Readers of Joyce will detect an echo of the moment in *Ulysses* when the bereaved Stephen Dedalus turns angrily on his friend Buck Mulligan for Mulligan's overheard, callous remark: *"O, it's only Dedalus whose mother is beastly dead"* (10). But the echo reverberates beyond Joyce to the titular model for *Ulysses*, the most famous Western exemplar of the hero's return topos: Homer's Odysseus. Parallels exist between the fabulous Greek voyager and Rushdie's luckless Indian migrant: after fantastic and harrowing travels, both return home in mean, unrecognizable guise. The resemblances, however, stop there. Though Odysseus is succored by a goatherd he does not assume the form of a hairy, obscene goatman, and though he finds his long-suffering wife Penelope beset by upstarts, he does not surprise her in bed with one. But while Chamcha is no more than a parodic copy of Odysseus, he has a more fraternal kinship with Joyce's own travestied Ulysses figure, Leopold Bloom, who undergoes, like Chamcha, phantasmagoric mutations and whose wife Molly is also an errant Penelope. In this site of comic return, then, Rushdie is both managing a witty piece of classical parody and obliquely signalling his indebtedness to a great modernist precursor. Above all, however, by making his protagonist at once formidable and absurd, both Odyssean and Bloomian, he provocatively destabilizes the normally accepted boundary between the heroic and the mock-heroic.

When after his cathartic meltdown at the Hot Wax Café (a venue symbolizing the malleability of identity) Chamcha again returns home, now restored to normal human form, his rival Jumpy takes over the role of clownish anti-hero. Learning of Chamcha's reappearance Joshi, living up to his nickname, "leaped ... a good three feet clear of the bed and stood on the pale blue carpet, stark naked and quaking with his thumb stuck in his mouth" (423–4). He exits in furious haste, to the tune of "thumps and crashes" that lead Pamela to think he has fallen downstairs: "'Good,' she screamed after him. 'Chicken, break your neck'" (424). His feeble greeting of the husband he has supplanted – "'Hey, hombre! You're really *well*!'" (424) – marks the reversal of the comic balance of power: now it is the cuckold Chamcha who presides, giving his shrugging go-ahead to the adulterous couple, whose own relations begin to fray. "'What a man!' Jumpy wept at Pamela. 'He's a *prince*, a *saint*!' 'If you don't pack it in,' Pamela Chamcha warned apoplectically, 'I'll set the fucking dog on you'" (424).

As the narrative moves forward, the role of comic butt is thus passed from Chamcha to Joshi, whose stature shrinks to that of a skulking barnyard cackler. Klaus Borner's contention that the pair's liaison offers hope – "Jumpy Joshi's and Pamela's passionate love-affair ... is ... spontaneously satisfactory" (154–5) – ignores the vaudeville limelight in which the affair is bathed. Similarly, the contrast Baucom draws between Chamcha and Joshi in Joshi's favour – "Jumpy Joshi, who attended an English university with Chamcha but did not besot himself with the liquors of Olde England, is the minor hero of Rushdie's text" (207) – ignores Jumpy's abject, thumb-sucking buffoonery. Heroes – even minor ones – are unlikely to be named Jumpy Joshi, or to behave in a manner suiting such a name.

The book's culminating farcical sequence, positioned late in the narrative, puts an effective stop to comedy. The scene is the party on the London-in-miniature film set of an Andrew Lloyd Webber-style feature that commodifies Dickens's *Our Mutual Friend* for mass audiences. The narrator wryly intimates the generic indeterminacy of the action, which again jumbles the heroic with the mock-heroic: "What follows is tragedy. – Or, at the least the echo of tragedy, the full-blooded original being unavailable to modern men and women, so it's said. – A burlesque for our degraded, imitative times, in which clowns re-enact what was first done by heroes and kings" (439). The principal farceurs seem to be imitating not heroes and kings but the Keystone Cops, frantically chasing after and barely missing one another, careening around corners and dashing over bridges of the tiny, simulated metropolis. Rushdie's travesty of heroic and regal exploits conforms to the carnivalesque model of the World Turned Upside Down; the "echo of tragedy" enacts a comic catharsis leading to a genuinely tragic aftermath, the mayhem of the Brickhall race riot. The zany misrule of carnival ushers in the grim bedlam of urban racial strife.

By the time Chamcha returns to Bombay and his father's deathbed the comedy has subsided, and the narrator's distance from Chamcha has narrowed. The narrative voice grows more respectfully familiar with him as he himself becomes more intimate with his dying parent. Chamcha's later *rapprochement* with Zeeny Vakil, for all its aura of magic-lamp wish-fulfillment, is also on the whole given a subdued rather than comic treatment.

Laughter as a narrative event also recedes from centre-stage. In an early exchange, Chamcha, who has pared down his name to render it more Anglo-friendly, makes an easy butt for the wit of Zeeny, the novel's worldly Bombay rieur: "'For Pete's sake,' she added, knifing him with a kiss. '*Chamcha*. I mean, fuck it. You name yourself Mister Toady and you expect us not to laugh'" (55).[5] A more sadistic type of laughter is inflicted on Chamcha later, after his nightmarish return to England as a satanic goat-man, by the immigration officers who indulge in abysmal puns *à propos* of his monstrously enlarged, erect phallus: "'What's this, then?' joked Novak ... giving it a playful tweak. 'Fancy one of us, maybe?' Whereupon ... Joe Bruno slapped his thigh, dug Novak in the ribs, and shouted, 'Nah, that ain't it. Seems like we really got his goat'" (163). In an often-quoted speech, the Manticore in the hospital ward for hideously transformed migrants explains to Chamcha how such metamorphoses work: "'They have the power of description, and we succumb to the pictures they construct'" (174). But demeaning laughter goes hand in hand with deforming description and is equally deadly. Only much later, when Chamcha, restored to his original form, returns to his homeland and resumes his unmutilated name, does he become less susceptible to the crippling hegemony of mirth.

Meanwhile, a parallel shift has affected Gibreel's serial dream of Mahound. In the early phases of the Prophet's ministry he and his followers are vulnerable to Baal's satires and the jeers of the Jahilia populace. Baal titters as he describes the motley apostles of the new faith to his master, Abu Simbel: "Giggling Baal can't stop. 'A revolution of water-carriers, immigrants and slaves ... wow, Grandee, I'm really scared'" (103). In response to his disciple Salman's protest against a doctrinal compromise – "'Nobody will ever take us seriously again'" – Mahound himself urbanely laughs, "genuinely amused. 'Maybe you haven't been here long enough,' he says kindly. 'Haven't you noticed? The people do not take us seriously'" (108). At length, however, as the circumspect Abu Simbel has dimly foreseen, Mahound's ideas prove necessary to take with utter seriousness. It is Baal, now elderly and decrepit, who provokes the Jahilia mob to convulsive laughter when he describes his "marriages" to the twelve prostitutes who have borrowed the names of Mahound's twelve wives: "By the end of his speech the good folk of Jahilia were literally weeping with laughter, unable to restrain themselves, even when soldiers with bullwhips and scimitars threatened them with instant death. 'I'm not kidding!' Baal screeched at the crowd, which hooted yelled slapped its thighs in response. 'It's no joke!' Ha ha ha" (404). Laughter, the terrified Baal finds, has a way of returning to haunt the unwary laugher.

Another focus of the novel's deconstructive laughter, modern technology, holds its own pitfalls for the unwary. Late in the narrative a young Bombay intellectual, Swatilekha, propounds a theory apparently derived from the French philosopher Jean-Francois Lyotard: "Society was orchestrated by what she called *grand narratives*: history, economics, ethics" (551). It is "the oldest of the grand narratives, religious faith," that she fingers as the chief agency of oppression in India. But a less venerable grand narrative, the myth of technological progress, which Rushdie elsewhere defines as "the dream of heaven on earth" (*Homelands* 388), figures in the novel as a secular surrogate for religion. This narrative is also interrogated by *The Satanic Verses* insistently, and with mischievous humour.

The belief in progress, a corollary of Western technological supremacy, has long inspired complacent sniggering at "backward" or "primitive" cultures, as a whole folio of *Punch* cartoons can testify. By the late twentieth century, that belief had been internalized by many non-Westerners. In his 1985 essay "Dynasty," Rushdie names Rajiv Gandhi as a high priest of this "go-ahead" faith: "Rajiv ... has installed a new icon in his quarters: a computer. Already, the image of 'computer kid' Rajiv, leader of the technological revolution, is being polished up. Jawaharlal Nehru once said that India had just entered the age of the bicycle; Rajiv – or, rather, the myth of Rajiv – clearly has other ideas" (*Homelands* 51). These astringent comments foreshadow much that happens in *The Satanic Verses*, starting with its opening mid-air obliteration of an icon of triumphant state-of-the-art technology, a commercial jetliner.

Rushdie's satiric target is, however, not technology per se but the blind worship of it, the "mechanic fundamentalist" dogma of its omnipotence. Rushdie himself, if a technoskeptic, is no Luddite; he speaks with enthusiasm of his switch from typewriter to computer to compose *The Moor's Last Sigh* (Reder 172–3). In *The Satanic Verses*, for the exiled, Khomeini-like Imam technological advance is, after history itself ("the great Shaitan"), one of the chief "lies – progress, science, rights – against which [he] has set his face" (217). Along with much else, the repatriated Imam's cannibalizing of his subjects – "[A]s the people march through the gates he swallows them whole" (221) – hardly prompts one to accept his outlook on such "lies" as sensible or humane. Regarding technological innovation the novel's overall verdict is, however, equivocal. The mechanization of society stirs sinister vibrations when it enables authoritarian control. During the raid on the Club Hot Wax, the coupling of television cameras and police helicopters is starkly dehumanizing: "This is what a television camera sees: less gifted than the human eye, its night vision is limited to what klieg lights will show. A helicopter hovers over the nightclub, urinating light in long golden streams; the camera understands this image. The machine of state bearing down upon its enemies" (469). The Orwellian shudder at the pollution of private space is vividly transmitted by the unexpected "urinating."

Mercedes automobiles crop up repeatedly in *The Satanic Verses*, sometimes though not always in such portentous connections. There is the "unmarked blue Mercedes panel van" (480) carrying the masked men (presumably police operatives) who torch the Brickhall Community Relations Council, liquidating Pamela and Jumpy before they can photocopy documents implicating the authorities. Offsetting that, there is the Mercedes that transports the dying Changez Chamchawala to hospital with some semblance of dignity (544). As a counterweight to the various opulent Mercedes vehicles there is "Zeeny's beaten-up Hindustan," which, though "a car built for a servant culture, the back seat better upholstered than the front" (55), still stands for a more modest, populist, and home-grown technology.

The Mercedes motif figures most tellingly in the powerful embedded narrative of the prophetess Ayesha's pilgrimage to the Arabian Sea, where "Mirza Saeed Akhtar in his olive-green Mercedes-Benz station wagon" (488), fitted with air conditioning, brings up the rear of the procession. As the pilgrimage straggles on, the car becomes tagged as "the station wagon of scepticism" (495), symbolically opposed to the young, butterfly-clad leader's mystical faith. It stands for the "rational" West as opposed to the "devout" East, though as usual in Rushdie these antinomies are not left untroubled. The wagon is fetishized by its owner, Mirza Saeed, as a talisman of modern science, of rationality, of "know-how," and it is also revealed as a token of class snobbery. Saeed's mother-in-law, Mrs Qureishi, the wife of a wealthy banker, initially voices scorn for the car, linking it to the vulgar consumption of globalized Western consumer goods: "'Go and drink your Coke-shoke in your AC vehicle'" (492), she admonishes Saeed when he tries to coax her daughter, his terminally ill wife Mishal, into riding instead of walking. Later, however, Mrs Qureishi herself succumbs to the AC vehicle's allure: "It suddenly seemed wholly unreasonable to her that a person of her breeding should be asked to go barefoot like a common sweeper" (501). The rank of passenger confers not only comfort but social eminence; in the modern commodified culture, technology enables both horizontal and upward mobility. The appointments of the wonder-car give even the elderly, lately bereaved Sarpanch Mohammad Din a vicarious whiff of social empowerment: "He sat on the back seat of the Mercedes as if he were the zamindar and Mirza Saeed the chauffeur, and little by little the leather upholstery and the air-conditioning unit and the whisky-soda cabinet and the electrically operated mirror-glass windows began to teach him hauteur, his nose tilted into the air and he acquired the supercilious expression of a man who can see without being seen" (495). When the already lofty

Mrs Qureishi deigns to enter the car, she comically resents having "to share the back seat with a common man" (504), the toy merchant Srinivas.

In place of the supernatural cure that Mishal Akhtar seeks from Ayesha's pilgrimage, her husband proffers the "miracle" of modern medical science: "'I'll take you to the top clinics in Europe, Canada, the USA. Trust in Western technology. They can do marvels. You always liked gadgets, too'" (499). Mirza Saeed is infuriated by his wife's stoic refusal to be deflected from her pilgrimage; sadly, however, his devout scientific daydreams are no likelier to delay her death than is Ayesha's fantastic trek to the Arabian Sea. Mishal's father pins similar hopes on the wonders of Western medical gadgetry, but upon arriving Qureishi "saw for the first time that his daughter had the mark of death on her forehead and deflated instantly like an inner-tube" (500). His intuitive perception of the truth punctures his faith in the magic of mechanism, as Rushdie's inner-tube simile drives home with poignant wit. Death, as Saladin Chamcha, too, will learn, is an impasse around which no scientific Mercedes can maneuver. Yet Ayesha's unshakeable religious faith, like Professor Godbole's "holy and infuriating," also attempts to swerve mechanically around the brute obstacle of death. Given the chance to save a bastard foundling from being stoned by a fanatical crowd, she intones her standard mantra – "'Everything will be asked of us'" – and the stones fly (511). The rage for transcendence can be cruel.

Inevitably, however, the collision between Ayesha's "Eastern" faith and Mirza Saeed's "Western" cult of gadgetry results in comedy; in Rushdie, Kipling's ever-parted twain do finally meet, and funnily sprawl. At a moment of crisis, when the pilgrims are being assailed by a mob of anti-Islamic zealots and a torrential downpour suddenly engulfs both sides, Mirza Saeed's Mercedes, plunging through a street of basket-makers, zooms to the rescue: "Here he accelerated as hard as he could and charged towards the crossroads, scattering pedestrians and wickerwork stools in all directions. He reached the crossroads immediately after the sea fell out of the sky, and braked violently. Sri Srinivas and Osman leaped out, seized Mishal Akhtar and the prophetess Ayesha, and hauled them into the Mercedes in a flurry of legs, sputum and abuse. Saeed accelerated away from the scene before anybody had managed to get the blinding water out of their eyes. Inside the car bodies heaped in an angry jumble. Mishal Akhtar shouted abuse at her husband from the bottom of the pile: 'Saboteur! Traitor! Scum from somewhere! Mule!' – To which Saeed sarcastically replied, 'Martyrdom is too easy, Mishal. Don't you want to watch the ocean open, like a flower?'" (505–6). Most obviously the slapstick melee produces humour at the expense of the upended pilgrims, swamping any scraps of dignity still clinging to their journey. Yet the vilified Mercedes driver is himself left with scant dignity, and his snide sarcasm is undercut later, when he is dying: "[A]t the instant that his heart broke, he opened" (521). The whole mix-up recalls the funny boat-spill near the end of *A Passage to India*, with its mingling of dissonant nationalities and persuasions; but here differences cannot be, as they are there, dissolved by violent, random comic immersion.

If motorized transport does little to harmonize people of discordant visions, the narrative reveals that "advanced" modes of communication give no better hope of communion. After the catastrophe of Ayesha's pilgrimage, the grieving and embittered Mirza Saeed shuts himself in his house: "He was not interested in the fate of his fellow-survivors; he went to the telephone and ripped it out of the wall" (520). This grim, self-pitying retreat from the modern world sets the scene for Saeed's redemptive "opening" at the moment of his death. Here again, as in the larger, encircling narrative, comic burlesque yields to a more sombre gravity.

Saladin Chamcha's solution to the sort of dilemma faced by Mirza Saeed is neither to become fixated on his cultural and religious "roots," nor conversely to beguile himself with the ephemeral fruits of technology. His return to his natal city of Bombay no more entails an obscurantist rejection of metropolitan modernity than a doting embrace of it. What it does entail is a reaching out for support to other like-minded inhabitants of his recuperated cosmopolitan birthplace. By linking hands with his friends in a "human chain" (a term connoting at once solidarity and restriction) organized by the Indian Communist Party, Chamcha finds for once a way to avoid the clown's gesticulating singularity, to shed the role of Lonely Londoner. "'If you're serious about shaking off your foreignness, Salad baba,'" Zeeny warns him, "'then don't fall into some kind of rootless limbo instead'" (555). Her metaphor recalls Chamcha's and Ferishta's sensational opening fall from the doomed jetliner, an event that leaves both wandering along opposite paths in the rootless limbo of postcolonial England.

According to Israel, at the end of Rushdie's narrative "the horizon of potentialities that transnational migration affords [is] abandoned as a fairy tale, in a somewhat strained attempt at homecoming and reconciliation with father, race, and nation" (174). Such a reading takes an unduly absolute view of what Chamcha's homecoming implies. While Saladin may relinquish his metropolitan ambitions along with his ersatz proper Englishness in order to mend his severed ties with father and fatherland, he does not write off England with the bitter finality of Gibreel, who calls him from no-longer-tropicalized London with the news that he is returning to Bombay "'in the hope that I never have to see her [Allie Cone], or you, or this damn cold city, again in what remains of my life'" (553). Unlike Gibreel, Chamcha is, to quote David Suter, "the emigrant who finds his humanity by accepting his new identity as he lives between two worlds. In doing so, he has opened a forbidden door, as the mullah's reaction to his refusal of the 'holy fabric' at his father's funeral suggests" (73). The close of Gibreel's story is marked not by the opening of doors but by the irreversible drawing down of blinds.

Gikandi observes that the final section of *The Satanic Verses* "has posed problems for many readers because it seems to undermine the whole ideological thrust of Rushdie's project"; that is, it represents "a begrudging affirmation" of the "ideals of home and return" that earlier sections gain their power from questioning (223). But Gikandi's argument, too, hinges on a unitary, purist conception of what Rushdie's ideological project is. To speak of a single, definable "thrust," or, for that matter, a single, definable concept of "home," in a comic novel replete with clashing cross-currents is, unavoidably, to apply a reductive grid. As Rushdie puts it, "In the creative process, many attitudes, many world-views jostle and conflict within the writer, and from these frictions the spark, the work of art, is born. This inner multiplicity, this crowd within, is often very difficult for artists to bear, let alone explain" (*Rushdie Letters* 123). Such a thoroughly Bakhtinian sentiment warns us against taking the experience of any one member of Rushdie's jostling dialogic cast – even Chamcha's – as definitive.

But, if not definitive, Chamcha's experience remains in important ways exemplary. According to Spivak, "In post-coloniality, every metropolitan definition is dislodged. The general mode for the post-colonial is citation, reinscription, re-routeing the historical" (104). The criteria Spivak lists as defining the postcolonial mode all apply to *The Satanic Verses*, but so does another: rerouting the comic. The novel reflects what Rushdie has called his own soul's "mischievous, iconoclastic, out-of-step clown instincts" (*Homelands* 438), instincts that prompt him not to reinscribe but to subvert the normativity of racial humour in older works of English fiction. In his novel, the outsider figure, more specifically Chamcha, is a comic butt not by virtue of his exclusion from "genuine Englishness" but by virtue of his fantasy that such a thing as genuine Englishness exists and is needful to seek. By the close of the book Chamcha's riotous ordeal has shattered his inhibiting shell of glib certainties and evasions. By following his own out-of-step clown instincts he has at last outgrown the motley disguise of postcolonial buffoon. As Rushdie says in *Imaginary Homelands*, "[A]ll the best comedy … contains a truth" (196). Those who have been moved to rage and weeping, rather than laughter and wonder, by *The Satanic Verses* have perhaps merely revealed their unwillingness to absorb the truth (or, better, truths) that its comedy contains.

10

A Funny Kind of Englishman: Hanif Kureishi's Carnival of Ethnicities

"We have class, race, fucking and farce. What more could you want as an evening's entertainment?"

Hanif Kureishi, *The Buddha of Suburbia*

At his own nimble gait, the screenwriter and novelist Hanif Kureishi has followed in Salman Rushdie's satanic footsteps. His mingling of modes and codes has been as audacious as Rushdie's, his humour as impertinent an affront to English propriety. His mixed ancestry, half Asian, half European, itself transgresses accepted boundaries with an impunity not likely to warm the hearts of Enoch Powell and his glum disciples.

Although Kureishi is younger by several years than Rushdie, the indebtedness between the two men is mutual. Kureishi's wide-ranging 1986 essay "The Rainbow Sign"[1] at several points anticipates *The Satanic Verses*; witness his account, stemming from a visit to Pakistan, of a bizarre communal trek to the Arabian Sea: "Then a disturbing incident occurred which seemed to encapsulate the going-away fever [that Kureishi had observed]. An eighteen-year-old girl from a village called Chakwai dreamed that the villagers walked across the Arabian sea to Karbala where they found money and work. Following the dream the village set off one night for the beach which happened to be near my uncle's house, in fashionable Clifton. Here lived politicians and diplomats in LA-style white bungalows with sprinklers on the lawn, a Mercedes in the drive and dogs and watchmen at the gates" (*My Beautiful Laundrette* 84). The incongruities here may have inspired Rushdie's parallel narrative of Ayesha's fantastic pilgrimage (the "Mercedes in the drive" reminds one of Mirza Saeed's air-conditioned Mercedes wagon; most of Kureishi's pilgrims, like Rushdie's, drown after entering the sea). Rushdie develops the anecdote into a baroque parable, interweaving with it the manifold ironies that pervade *The Satanic Verses*.

Kureishi for his part has drawn abundantly on Rushdiean precedents. The borrowing is most overt in his second novel, *The Black Album*, where the Islamic outcry against *The Satanic Verses* provides momentum for the plot. Less obviously, Rushdie's shadow looms over *The Buddha of Suburbia*, Kureishi's debut novel. In his introduction to *London Kills Me*, Kureishi identifies Rushdie's work as a landmark in contemporary English writing: "Until Rushdie wrote *Midnight's Children* and refused to see writing as a purely private activity, there was no one with the moral stature of Sartre or Grass or Gordimer or Baldwin, and not even controversialists like Mailer or Vidal" (x). According to Lee Yu-cheng, "In many ways [*The Buddha of Suburbia*] can be read as Kureishi's attempt to answer the many questions raised by Rushdie" (16). Like Rushdie, Kureishi sees himself as emerging from a phase of British life that was "the end of something – the psychological loosening of the idea of Empire – and the start of something else, which involved violence, the contamination of racism and years of crisis" (*Outskirts* xvi).

The parallels between the two writers can, it is true, be exaggerated. Bart Moore-Gilbert cautions that "the writing of figures like Kureishi needs to be located with care within the paradigm which Rushdie's fiction represents" (193). He notes that "[f]or example the issue of language use as a marker of cultural identity has much less prominence in Kureishi's fiction than [in] Rushdie's, which is characteristically peppered with non-western words and 'untranslatable,' because culture-specific, concepts" (194). Still, even Moore-Gilbert concedes that "there are … areas of overlap between writers like Rushdie and Kureishi, not least because of the consistent pattern of allusion to the work of the former within the latter's corpus" (196). Observing that both writers adopt a "'hybrid' position … *vis-à-vis* colonial discourse" that "can be clearly distinguished from both the 'assimilationist' and the 'cultural nationalist' paradigms of [antecedent] postcolonial writing" (199), he argues "that it is in the context of its discussion of the challenges posed to traditional concepts of identity, ethnicity and Englishness by cultural hybridity that *The Buddha* is most comparable to Rushdie's corpus" (199). Like Moore-Gilbert, Frederick Holmes sees both writers as rejecting an assimilationist stance: "Both Rushdie and Kureishi show that this desired assimilation into a British society defined as exclusively white is untenable in every possible respect" ("Subject" 298). According to Holmes, Kureishi's *The Black Album* "reinscribes some of the main themes of *The Satanic Verses*. Like Rushdie, Kureishi is concerned with the plight of the migrant denied a unitary identity because he is shunted back and forth between two cultures (each of which is itself internally divided and subdivided) and invited to adopt a variety of sometimes contradictory subject positions" ("Subject" 296).

The Black Album concerns the uproar surrounding an unnamed literary figure whose actual identity is an open book; Chili, the brother of the protagonist Shahid, calls him "'that other writer, the one who slags the religion'" (52). In a *New Yorker* piece Fernanda Eberstadt cites Kureishi's offhand explanation of what impelled him to write the novel: "'There were all these blokes who wanted to kill this friend of mine, and I wanted to know why, so I went and found them'" (120). *The Black Album* includes a number of local echoes of *The Satanic Verses*; the college instructor Andrew Brownlow has a stutter recalling the one afflicting Rushdie's film director Sisodia, and like Pamela Chamcha he can voice his leftist views only in a posh accent absorbed from his family background: "Whether he barked, slurred, honked, or ordered, England had honeyed every rotund syllable. Poor Andrew spoke from the very thing he hated" (103–4).

The most provocative echo alludes to Rushdie's much-quoted comment on his loss of religious belief: "Dr Aadam Aziz, the patriarch in my novel *Midnight's Children*, loses his faith and is left with 'a hole inside him, a vacancy in a vital inner chamber.' I, too, possess the same God-shaped hole. Unable to accept the unarguable absolutes of religion, I have tried to fill up the hole with literature" (*Rushdie File* 75). In *The Black Album* an aubergine, hailed by a group of Islamic zealots as miraculous because it contains an arrow mark pointing direly in the direction of the blasphemer Rushdie, becomes a cause of tension and then of risqué banter between Shahid and his girlfriend, the sociology instructor Deedee Osgood. The mystic vegetable's permutations illustrate the ductility of metaphor characteristic of Kureishi's comic method. From its origin as a talisman of religious rage and credulity, it finally morphs into a phallic euphemism. Deedee puts an end to a lovers' tiff about religion with the terse demand, "'Give me your aubergine,'" then adds a plea that burlesques Rushdie's lament about his God-vacuum: "'Fill my cock-shaped hole'" (223). The conversion of Rushdie's crisis of belief into erotic joking typifies Kureishi's free play with Rushdiean precedent. Here the "unarguable absolutes of religion" are blown away by a quarrel culminating in the unarguable absolute of sex.

Deedee's wit and sensuality alike set her in a different sphere from the joke-deficient Muslim activists who exert a contrary tug on Shahid's loyalty. As she tells Shahid, "'When you've been with your friends [the Islamic group] your mouth curls down'" (163). Some of these friends are at least capable of laughter: for example, Shahid "liked Chad [one of the most ardent activists]. Laughter took place all over his body – shoulders, stomach, chest – and his hands quivered like fans, as if someone had activated a motor in his stomach" (20). But in the body of the group's mentor, Shahid's housemate Riaz, no such mirthful motor throbs: "Shahid had taken it for granted that [Riaz's] smile indicated humor, a love of humanity, patience. Yet if you looked closely, it was disdain" (108). Over time, as Shahid's taste for laughter ripens, his qualms intensify: "Shahid didn't like to criticize Riaz, but there was one thing you could say about him: his laughter was always astringent and sardonic. Folly didn't entertain him; he wanted to correct it. Like pornography, religion couldn't admit the comic" (160–1). Shahid's (and perhaps the author's) view of religion is more limiting than Forster's in *A Passage to India*, where the Hindu temple festival genially incorporates patches of ribald jocosity. Riaz himself displays nothing of Godbole's whimsical openness. His idea of a joke is epitomized by his tribute to a friendly Labour MP's support of the Islamist cause: "'This sympathy for our people is as rare as an English virgin.' Riaz giggled at the remark, which he made often" (193). Such laughter issues not from fellowship but from sectarian animus. So does the whole group's gleeful reaction to the burning of Rushdie's novel: "People hooted and clamored as if they were at a fireworks display. Fists were raised at the flaming bouquet of the book. And the former Trevor Buss and Muhammad Shahabuddin Ali-Shah, alias Brother Chad, who was brandishing it at the sky, laughed triumphantly" (236). This is hardly the kind of laughter that Shahid had once found engaging in Chad; and the young man's jubilant playing with fire ends up enveloping his body not in laughter but in flames. When Chad throws a petrol bomb through the window of an offending bookshop, the missile explodes in his face. A bystander reports that "'the boy had his hands and face on fire'" (285).

The Islamic cell's chuckling triumphalism is in fact merely the festive face of their habitual frowning solemnity. Both faces alike betoken their fierce narrowing of the allowable radius of thought and wit. The gap separating them from the undogmatic protagonist is spotlighted in a clash between another youthful group member, Hat, the son of an Indian restaurant proprietor, and Shahid, who has been toying, not with fire but with the wording of some of Riaz's poems he has agreed to copy: "'Hat, please believe me. I was playing – playing with words and ideas.' 'You think you can play with everything, right? I tell you this, some things ain't funny.' 'Usually they're the funniest things,'" Shahid retorts (246). The quarrel between the two young men lies at the heart of *The Black*

Album. Hat's insistence that "some things ain't funny" recalls the stony-faced agelasts (see chapter 9) who, according to Bakhtin, provided a prime satiric target for Rabelais. As Bakhtin argues in his essay "Epic and Novel," "Laughter demolishes fear and piety before an object, before a world, making of it an object of familiar contact and thus clearing the ground for an absolutely free investigation of it" (*Dialogic* 23). An "absolutely free investigation" is the last thing the pious Hat wants, and his intransigence collides head-on with Shahid's refusal to place limits on inquiry or laughter. The collision becomes literal in the ensuing slapstick action: "Almost as if he didn't mean to, Hat pushed Shahid. It wasn't a wholehearted shove, but it was sudden, and Shahid, who wanted to slip away, stumbled and backed into the fridge which contained the drinks. The shelf above containing pickles sprang from the wall and the big jars shot across the floor, breaking open and dumping their shiny contents everywhere. Hat was horrified by his action, particularly when his father ran out of the back room [of his restaurant] and, without even taking in the scene, swiped at Hat's head, slipped on the pickle – kicking his legs in the air as if attempting the can-can – and landed on his backside. He lay, scrabbling in liquid mango, howling oaths" (247–8). The sequence, with its slapstick pratfall, implicitly rebuts Hat's assertion that "some things ain't funny." Hat's humourless Islamic belligerence first causes his stern businessman sire to dance an unIslamic can-can, then floors him in a mess of oozing South Asian condiment.

The entire novel manifests Kureishi's acute self-consciousness about what Bakhtin repeatedly calls the ambivalence of laughter: the power of humour both to demean and to liberate. Humour's liberating force is typified by an earlier moment of mirth that ends the lovers' quarrel over the mystic eggplant: "[Deedee's] cheeks trembled, the corners of her lips lifted, her nose flared. Instinctively her hands went to cover her face ... Laughter exploded in her mouth, a cataract of glee. He started to giggle himself, which set her off again. Each time they looked at one another, and before either of them could begin to pronounce 'aubergine,' they were rolling around the bed, holding on to each other for fear they'd fall off. Tears ran down their faces. They slapped one another and kicked their legs in the air like babies" (222). Such childlike, irreverent laughter, lifting the corners of lips instead of curling them down, is cathartic. It celebrates the uninhibited concord between two rieurs of divergent religion, age, and sex, whose choral leg-kicking makes a pointed contrast with Hat's father's involuntary solo can-can, in which his legs twitch while his mouth howls oaths amid the liquid mango.

As the heir of two separate cultures, Kureishi commands the detachment (or, as John Clement Ball puts it, the semi-detachment) that enables laughter of Shahid's and Deedee's life-warming sort, which transcends the sectarian grudges freezing the faces of hard-bitten agelasts. He would doubtless second Rushdie's dictum: "The great unheralded battle in the world ... is between those who have a sense of humour and those who don't." But he is far from treating laughter per se as an infallible token of enlistment in the ranks of the redeemed.

Elsewhere, he self-consciously highlights the "phthonic," hostile type of laughter favoured by Riaz and Chad, frequently linking it with racial insult. In "The Rainbow Sign" he recounts how, early in his life, mainstream humour at the expense of "Pakis" impelled him to reject the Asian component of his own makeup: "In the mid-1960s, Pakistanis were a risible subject in England, derided on television and exploited by politicians. They had the worst jobs, they were uncomfortable in England, some of them had difficulties with the language. They were despised and out of place. From the start I tried to deny my Pakistani self. I was ashamed. It was a curse and I wanted to be rid of it. I wanted to be like everyone else. I read with understanding a story in a newspaper about a black boy who, when he noticed that burnt skin turned white, jumped into a bath of boiling water" (*Laundrette* 73). As an adult, he retained a troubled awareness of joking as a medium for majoritarian aggression: "Television comics used Pakistanis as the butt of their humour. Their jokes were highly political: they contributed to a way of seeing the world. The enjoyed reduction of racial hatred to a joke did two things: it expressed a collective view (which was sanctioned by being on the BBC), and it was a celebration of contempt in millions of living rooms in England. I was afraid to watch TV because of it; it was too embarrassing, too degrading" (*Laundrette* 76).

The narrator of Kureishi's story "Strangers When We Meet," giving a friend a light-hearted account of how he had "let down" an old flame, muses, "[T]here is nothing as forgiving as a joke" (*Intimacy* 165), but jokes in Kureishi's fiction, like the TV comedy he describes, are often neither forgiving nor forgivable. In *The Buddha of Suburbia,* the narrator Karim Amir's father, Haroon, is the target of joking of an insidious type. Moore-Gilbert comments on "the unthinking everyday racism (characteristically mediated in banter) of the kind suffered by Haroon in his work-place ... While seemingly harmless, such humour is nonetheless important in revealing the widespread fear of difference which Kureishi detects in 'respectable' metropolitan culture" (201). Kureishi's humour, like Rushdie's, often takes the form of counter-thrusts deftly aimed at exposing the absurdity of such fear and its offspring: the war against difference.

And yet, paradoxically, Kureishi's treatment of Asian characters in film and fiction has, like Rushdie's, been blamed for itself abetting prejudice. Such complaints, arising as early as Kureishi's first film, *My Beautiful Laundrette*, which adumbrates many of the themes and character types that recur in his fiction, have dogged his career. As Kobena Mercer observes, "Among British Asian communities, angry reactions [to the film] focussed on the less than favorable depictions of the Asian characters which, when read as emblematic of the community, were seen as replaying certain racist stereotypes. Describing its portrayal of Pakistani shopkeepers and drug-dealers as a form of 'neoorientalism' independent producer Mahmood Jamal argued that this term described 'Asian intellectuals … laundered by the British university system … [who] reinforce stereotypes of their own people for a few cheap laughs'" (73). Kureishi himself puts the case succinctly: "[T]he Asian community think that I'm perpetually throwing shit at them" (qtd in Yousaf 16). Here again, as in Selvon and Rushdie, one encounters the vexed issue of racial stereotyping deployed by a writer who himself belongs to a targeted race. With Kureishi, considering his resentment of Paki jokes in the British media and his avowal of their damage to his own ego, the case seems especially perplexing. A cynical explanation is that Kureishi uses humour deriding his fellow Asians for reasons akin to those prompting the black boy in the news report to jump into scalding water: the urge to make his own skin, figuratively speaking, white. But while some such defence mechanism may lurk behind Kureishi's comedy, to account for it solely on that basis would be reductive. His joking, even when aimed at the racially othered, raises more wide-ranging issues, partly because it is self-interrogating. In his work, even more than in Selvon's or Rushdie's, racial humour itself becomes thematized, figuring as a site of contention.

The Buddha of Suburbia opens with a circumspect thumbnail self-portrait: "My name is Karim Amir, and I am an Englishman born and bred, almost. I am often considered to be a funny kind of Englishman, a new breed as it were, having emerged from two old histories. But I don't care – Englishman I am (though not proud of it), from the South London suburbs and going somewhere" (3). Speaking for himself Kureishi has affirmed his sense of his identity more flatly than Karim: "'Critics have written that I'm caught between two cultures. I'm not … . I'm British, I've made it in England'" (qtd. Kaleta 7). Elsewhere, though, he has made more nuanced judgments: "'My country' isn't a notion that comes easily. It is still difficult to answer the question, where do you come from? I have never wanted to identify with England ... But despite all this, some kind of identification with England remains" (*Laundrette* 99). For Kenneth C. Kaleta, Kureishi's writing "evidences the English sensibility, the English eccentricity, and the English regard for words. It displays the English sense of humor" (2). Kureishi himself might well object that "English" attributes are being too glibly allocated here. Like Karim, he tends to treat the whole question of nationality with ambivalence, a tentativeness detectable in the novel of which Karim is narrator and protagonist.

Cynthia Carey calls *The Buddha of Suburbia* "a rich, profane, carnivalesque novel which relentlessly challenges orthodoxy on every level" (120). Holmes, too, comments on the Bakhtinian transgressiveness of Kureishi's humour: "The novel's comedy is heavily dependent on Karim's flamboyant and vulgar rhetoric, which completely violates bourgeois canons of propriety and decency. He frequently depicts conventionally shocking or disgusting actions and situations in language that highlights their grotesque aspects. Bakhtin's ideas about the carnivalesque are useful when it comes to interpreting the effects and significance of these descriptions. As does the work of Rabelais, Karim's narrations feature what Bakhtin calls 'grotesque realism,' in which 'the material bodily principle, that is, images of the human body with its food, drink, defecation, and sexual life, plays a predominant role. Images of the body are offered, moreover, in an extremely exaggerated form'" ("Comedy" 647). In *The Buddha*, more straightforwardly than in *The Satanic Verses*, the physicality of carnival has a liberating force. Kureishi's carnivalesque mode is more overtly indebted than Rushdie's to older models of English comic fiction, whose influence Kureishi somewhat grudgingly acknowledges: "Looking back on [*The Buddha*] – though I might not like to admit it – I was influenced more by books like *Lucky Jim* and early Evelyn Waugh [than by non-English models like Jack Kerouac's *On the Road*]" (qtd in Kaleta 77). It is all the more ironic that critics, as Kureishi claims, fail to grasp that "people with names like Kureishi or Ishiguro or Rushdie" are "all British too." As a result, "We are still marginalized culturally" (qtd in Kaleta 7).

Karim in *The Buddha of Suburbia* repeatedly grapples with marginalizing misperceptions of his personality. Against Suresht Bald's contention that in the book "Karim claims his origins and thus locates himself," Jamel Oubechou points out "that Karim does not really end up 'claiming his origins', but that he rather becomes aware that identity is problematic, that a re-definition of 'being British' is needed and that this implies a dis/location of this identity and its synthetic reconfiguration and redefinition" (103). According to Moore-Gilbert, Kureishi undertakes such work of reconfiguration as a tactic to combat deep-seated British confusion about identity, which, like his protagonist, he sees as the outgrowth of a "category error evident in metropolitan racism …, radical anti-racism and cultural nationalism alike," that is, the belief "that identity is single and whole, essentially grounded and accessible and expressible in some pure form. By contrast, *The Buddha* argues persistently that identity is constructed, multiply-determined, mixed, provisional and relational" (202). Ball ascribes this position to Kureishi's personal background: "His ethnic hybridity makes him semi-detached (which is to say semi-attached as well) with respect to Britain's traditional racial-national culture and to that of Pakistan and the larger Indian subcontinent" (16). I would add that such (semi-)detachment naturally generates humour at the expense of fixed national allegiances. In Kureishi, clashes between unitary and more flexible views of identity tend to produce comic complications.

Such clashes can, it is true, be anything but comic. In the story (and basis for a later film script) "My Son the Fanatic," Ali, the young Islamic fundamentalist son, tells his skeptical father, Parvez: "'My people have taken enough. If the persecution doesn't stop there will be *jihad*. I, and millions of others, will gladly give our lives for the cause'" (*Love in a Blue Time* 126). To Parvez, "Ali sounded as if he'd swallowed someone else's voice" (126). While the persecution of which Ali speaks is undeniable, the boy's naive acceptance of the abstraction "my people" leads him, as the story's title intimates, into barren fanaticism. It is Ali's embrace of collective identity that explains his father's eerie sense of ventriloquism, for it entails the forfeit of his own unique subjecthood, its dissolution into the flood of those other "millions" of whom he speaks.

Ali's acceptance of a communalist, fixed identity makes him the polar opposite of Karim Amir, who, as Sukhdev Sandhu observes, "becomes an actor, a job which involves the repeated donning and casting aside of costumes and personae" (143). Kureishi began his writing career as a playwright before turning to film, and his later work as a novelist still reflects his sense of the potency of theatrical performance. Commenting on the liberating effect of multiple role-playing in *The Buddha*, Moore-Gilbert postulates a helpful "general rule: the more flexible a character's conception of identity is in the text, the more sympathetic they are to both Karim and the reader" (202). A corollary is that the more *in*flexible a character's conception of identity, the more vulnerable will that character be to Kureishi's corrosive laughter.

An extreme specimen of such rigidity is the father of Karim's pro tem girlfriend Helen, who wants no "wogs" or "blackies" coming to the house: "'If you put one of your black 'ands near my daughter I'll smash it with a 'ammer!" (40). The epithet Karim coins for the father, Hairy Back, seems genuinely funny rather than merely spiteful because it neatly captures the bigot's neanderthal brutishness. The ugly scene of Karim's eviction from Hairy Back's premises is followed by the curious incident of Karim's "rape" by his huge dog ("The dog's breath warmed my neck. I took another step and so did the dog. I knew by now what the dog was up to. The dog was in love with me – quick movements against my arse told me so. Its ears were hot" (41). Holmes comments on the scene's symbolism: "In its virulence, the racism of Helen's father has dehumanized Karim; in effect, it has reduced him to the level of the family's large dog, who has selected him as a sexual partner" ("Comedy" 649). It seems more accurate, however, to say that it is the father whose subhumanity the incident evokes. Compounding racial abuse with animal assault, Kureishi restages Powellite phobias as outrageous farce. The rape becomes a grotesque charade enacting Karim's nickname for the dog's owner; the whole hairy ménage – or menagerie – is driven by crude primal urges.

Karim's "uncle" Anwar, a long-time friend of his father, provides a matching example of Asian rigidity: an unthinking retreat into a communalist compound. Yu-cheng observes that Anwar's story "sadly offers a compelling image of cultural dislocation in diasporic life" (14); but the image is not only sad, it is painfully funny. According to Waddick Doyle, "[A]t the level of both narrative and narration [*The Buddha of Suburbia*] debunks the certainty of ethnic and sub-cultural or indeed any identity. Identity's double game with otherness is played out. Distance rather than identification is what is called for" (118). Here again, the narrative's distanced stance fosters comedy, and Anwar, unable to detach himself from his fetishes, becomes for that very reason ripe for comic treatment. After years in England he is still fettered to South Asian codes of behaviour, most unwisely in forcing his swinger daughter, Jamila, to accept sight unseen an imported Indian husband. Karim, who has been sexually involved with the girl, wryly sums up Anwar's family agenda: "Anwar had told Jamila what he'd decided: she was to marry the Indian and he would come over, slip on his overcoat and his wife and live happily ever after in her muscly arms" (57). (The gender surprise of "muscly" underscores the craziness of the whole operation.) The father's rationale for compelling his distraught family to obey him is hilariously muddled: "'I won't eat. I will die. If Gandhi could shove out the English from India by not eating, I can get my family to obey me by exactly the same'" (60). Anwar's grasp of colonial history is shaky; nothing could less resemble Gandhi's collective drive to expel foreign invaders than Anwar's whim of summoning one displaced Asian to England as his son-in-law. Karim crisply describes Anwar as a prisoner of communalist solipsism: "He'd locked himself in a private room beyond the reach of reason, of persuasion, of evidence" (60).

Even though his daughter Jamila, as Moore-Gilbert claims, "embodies … the conscience of *The Buddha*" (200), the masculinist Anwar disdains to inquire into her subjective life. "He really knew little about Jamila. If someone had asked him who she voted for, what the names of her women friends were, what she liked in life, he couldn't have answered. It was as if, in some strange way, it was beneath his dignity to take an interest in her. He didn't see her" (81). Here, as in "My Son the Fanatic," a humourless male fixation on communal identity leaves no room for more discriminating perception. The revenge Anwar's wife, Jeeta, inflicts on her agelast husband by starving him of laughter is an inspired piece of poetic justice: "[S]he spoke to him, but only occasionally, and made sure not to laugh. He started to suffer the malnutrition of unalloyed seriousness. Someone to whom jokes are never told soon contracts enthusiasm deficiency" (208).

Ultimately, Anwar's jokeless intransigence costs him his life. In a scene of macabre surrealist farce, the old man is "murdered" by his dysfunctional son-in-law Changez, who brains him (albeit in self-defence) with a dildo procured to gratify his Japanese lover, the prostitute Shinko: "As Anwar smacked downwards with his stick, Changez lumbered to one side, just in time, withdrew the knobbly dildo from its paper-bag sheath, and with a Muslim warrior shout – at least, Shinko said it was a Muslim shout, but what would she know? – whacked my uncle smartly over the head with it. Uncle Anwar, who'd come from India to the Old Kent Road to lodge with a dentist, to jangle and gamble, to make his fortune and return home to build a house like my grandfather's on Juhu Beach, could never have guessed all those years ago that late in life he would be knocked unconscious by a sex-aid. No fortune-teller had predicted this. Kipling had written 'to each his own fear', but this was not Anwar's" (210–11). According to Celia Wallhead, "The hilarious episode of Changez 'the Dildo Killer' … is made possible through the contact of the Western and Eastern worlds and at the same time is an ironic reflection on the importance of the penis in both cultures" (76). Carefully examined, however, the comic collisions run along less clear-cut phallic and national lines. Neither the West nor the East is a monolith; Japanese Shinko knows nothing about Muslim warrior shouts, and her Western sex-aid comments sardonically not on the importance but on the insignificance of her Eastern lover's penis. And the humour, finally, hinges on Anwar's ethnic hermeticism: not his contact with other worlds but rather his utter failure to make contact. Karim, the secular relativist, says, "Like many Muslim men – beginning with the Prophet Mohammed himself, whose absolute statements, served up piping hot from God, inevitably gave rise to absolutism – Anwar thought he was right about everything" (172). The mode of Anwar's death is one remote from his own parched field of certainties; his fears have been too narrowly channelled by his Islamic rigour to prepare him for the fate he meets in polymorphously perverse modern London. The "murder weapon," a token of female sexual desire, is another stroke of poetic justice: Jamila's unorthodox sex life is the last thing her father would admit into his blinkered mental universe. This blindness has led him to summon from across the globe an erotically unfit mate for his daughter, and repressed libido now returns to wreak its strange vengeance.

As Sangeeta Ray says, "What is interesting about [*The Buddha*] is the cacophony generated by the multiplicity of heterogeneous positions" on national identity (234). The oddly assorted Asian migrants, Anwar and Haroon, compound the cacophony. For Ball, "Anwar's hunger strike is a sincere act … Anwar's return to his origins is of a different order than … Haroon's. Without leaving the suburbs, he returns 'internally to India' as a way of 'resisting the English here'" (24). Ball argues that, unlike Anwar's, both Haroon's and Karim's returns to native grounds are spurious: "Father and son both become faux-Indians, successfully marketing back to the English warmed-over versions of their own popular appropriations of Indian culture" (23). The label faux-Indian may well apply to Haroon: after most of a lifetime spent camouflaging himself like Saladin Chamcha as an unremarkable Britisher, he suddenly dons orientalist trappings for reasons of personal advantage. A lapsed Muslim improbably posing as a Buddhist guru, he can hardly claim authenticity of any sort. On the other hand, the value of "genuineness" like Anwar's is debatable. Haroon's approach to identity, if duplicitous, is also versatile and creative; he comes across as both droll and formidable. He possesses, unlike Anwar, a performative concept of ethnicity, enabling him to shuttle fluently from one persona to another. Karim describes how, at Eva Kay's meeting, "God" (Karim's facetious nickname for his lordly father) "was hissing his s's and exaggerating his Indian accent. He'd spent years trying to be more of an

Englishman, to be less risibly conspicuous, and now he was putting it back in spadeloads" (21). Complicating the clean division Ball draws between the authentic and the false is the ironic blendedness of Haroon's performance. Wallhead aptly describes him as "set[ting] out on a path with a mixture of sincerity and opportunism, of real wisdom and charlatanism, to become 'the guru from Chislehurst'" (70). The ambiguity is focused by a sharp exchange about Haroon between Karim and his prim Auntie Jean: "'He's been impersonating a Buddhist'" Jean charges; "'He is a Buddhist'" Karim snaps back (44).

Kureishi's comedy thrives on such clashes of dissonant perceptions. As Oubechou argues, "*The Buddha of Suburbia* supports an eclectic view of the world, a hybrid conception of identity which emerges from the juxtaposition of different types of behaviour" (102). While Kureishi offers such a worldview seriously, that does not stop him from exploiting eclecticism as a fund of laughter. In a suggestive analysis of Kureishi's use of collage, Sandhu notes that in his work juxtaposition "often takes a linguistic form" ("Pop Goes the Centre" 144).[2] Haroon's speech and behaviour manifest the humour stemming from such verbal clashes; he is a comic figure not only because his nature, like Anwar's more obviously "Indian" one, conflicts with the Western milieu, but because his *internalized* discords keep oddly surfacing. One instance is the advice he gives his depressive brother-in-law, Ted, on whom he relies for handyman expertise: "'And you're suffering like hell. You're ashamed of it, too. Are people not allowed even to suffer now? Suffer, Ted.' Ted was suffering. He sobbed generously. 'Now,' said Dad, readjusting his priorities, 'what's wrong with this fucking record-player?'" (50). If such verbal hairpin-turns make him funny, Haroon's inconsistency also saves him from entrapment by emotional routine. As Kaleta points out, "The incident [in the novel's opening pages] of Karim watching Haroon standing upside down stripped to his underwear … ridicules the suburban and the enlightened: it embraces and lashes out at stereotypes of suburbia, race, and family" (69). Rather than blindly obeying one unitary set of cultural imperatives, Haroon seizes on diverse roles as they offer themselves, even if they tread clownishly on each other's toes. In his improvisatory brio, he is a fitting father for that theatrical chameleon, his elder son.

Karim, the other faux-Indian, acts performatively in both the literal and figurative senses. As a sexual performer he is flagrantly transgressive, vaulting barriers of gender and race with histrionic abandon to locate erotic partners, cruising from the white male Charlie Kay to the Asian female Jamila to the white upper-class actress Eleanor, deriving his fill of enjoyment and grief from each liaison. As Moore-Gilbert says, "Kureishi … provide[s] a critique of the rigid conception of masculinity which has its roots in Victorian culture (and which is very commonly found in imperial fiction), the legacy of which can be traced at one level in the anti-gay prejudice which Karim observes in society at large. Sexuality in *The Buddha* is, in fact, a key site of resistance to the ethnic dominant" (198). But, above all, Karim is a professional actor, and his vocation becomes another key site of resistance, helping to keep him from hardening into an Anwar-like fixture of single-mindedness. When his mother tells him, "'You're not an Indian. You've never been to India … You're an Englishman, I'm glad to say,'" he flies by the net of nationality by responding, "'I don't care … I'm an actor'" (232).

Ironically, however, his origin and appearance can cause acting to straitjacket him (as it does Saladin Chamcha) within fixed roles rather than liberating him. The painfulness of such typecasting emerges in Karim's debut with the director Shadwell, who gives him the part of Kipling's Mowgli, advising him that he has been "'cast for authenticity and not for experience'" (147). Being "authentic" requires him to fake a stage Indian accent and darken his skin with brown makeup: he ends up looking like "a turd in a bikini-bottom" (146). Discounting Karim's native fluency in English, Shadwell affects to be aghast that the young actor does not understand his "'own language'" (140) and erupts in studied laughter at Karim's supposed decline from the noble savagery of pristine colonial subjects: "He shook his head then and did a series of short barks in his throat. This was him laughing, I was certain. 'Ha, ha, ha, ha, ha!' he went. 'What a breed of people two hundred years of imperialism has given birth to. If the pioneers from the East India Company could see you. What puzzlement there'd be'" (141). Shadwell's laughter is as dogma-driven as Riaz's in *The Black Album*, and it betrays an equivalent moral myopia. His cross-questioning leaves Karim "shaking with embarrassment that he could talk to me in this way at all" (142). In a crucial redirecting of his loyalties, even when about to be taken under Shadwell's patronizing wing, Karim impulsively turns from him to the misfit Changez: "I wanted to dance with him and celebrate the renewal of our friendship. I crept away from Shadwell" (137). Changez may make a shambling dance partner, but he is at least not an overbearing one.

In the end, Karim dodges Shadwell's liberal racist stereotyping by resorting to hyper- performance, playing his graceless role to the hilt: "I started to relax on stage, and to enjoy acting. I sent up the accent and made the audience laugh by suddenly relapsing into cockney at odd times. 'Leave it out, Bagheera,' I'd say" (158). He thus levers his acting to deconstruct Shadwell's sham "authenticity" in two ways: by asserting his own street voice and by humorously flaunting his disengagement. Jamila remains, as usual, unimpressed: "'[I]t was disgusting, the accent and the shit you had smeared over you. You were just pandering to prejudices'" (157). It is not the last time Karim will encounter such strictures.

In his next theatrical venture Karim must contend with a more seductive Svengali, the director Matthew Pyke. Authorized by Pyke to invent his own character, Karim can now put behind him the shaming Jungle Book image foisted on him by Shadwell. He turns for inspiration to actual Indians of his acquaintance: first Anwar, then Changez. What he fails to realize is that he thereby becomes even more perilously enmeshed with stereotypes.

In *The Black Album*, as I have argued, the quality of the characters' laughter provides a key to distinguish tolerance from fanaticism, *joie de vivre* from a lugubrious *joie de mourir*. In *The Buddha of Suburbia*, Kureishi's probing of the moral resonance of humour becomes still more searchingly self-reflexive. In his account of Karim's efforts to prove himself theatrically with Pyke, Kureishi puts on trial his own performance as a writer of comedy.

A moment of embarrassing tension occurs when the young black actress Tracey protests passionately against Karim's dramatic rendering of Anwar's hunger strike:

"I'm afraid it shows black people –"

"Indian people –"

"Black and Asian people –"

"One old Indian man –"

"As being irrational, ridiculous, as being hysterical. And as being fanatical."

"Fanatical?" I appealed to the High Court. Judge Pyke was listening carefully. "It's not a fanatical hunger-strike. It's calmly intended blackmail."

But Judge Pyke signalled for Tracey to go on.

"And that arranged marriage. It worries me. Karim, with respect, it worries me."

I stared at her, saying nothing. She was very disturbed.

"Tell us exactly why it worries you," Eleanor said, sympathetically.

"How can I even begin? Your picture is what white people already think of us. That we're funny, with strange habits and weird customs. To the white man we're already people without humanity, and then you go and have Anwar madly waving his stick at the white boys. I can't believe that anything like this could happen. You show us unorganized aggressors. Why do you hate yourself and all black people so much, Karim?" (180)

One critical juror, Kaleta, finds for the prosecution: "Tracey defines black politically. Anyone who is not white in a racist society is black. The actress is certainly right. In the London of *The Buddha of Suburbia*, power, values, economics, and art are all part of a white person's world" (230). Tracey does indeed have a point, one recalling Kureishi's own complaints about Paki jokes on British television. The issues, however, are too complex to be so easily decided, because they hinge on an unresolvable duality inherent in dramatic portrayal, whereby any character may represent at once a unique individual and a specimen of a broader class. Karim's disclaimer, "One old Indian man," ignores the second, generalizing dimension. Yet Tracey is not "certainly right"; Karim's protest – "'But this sounds like censorship'" (181) – is finally unanswerable. Tracey's dismissal of Karim's performance as "'white truth'" rings hollow, because Karim is, after all, only reproducing what readers, white or black, have already beheld in Kureishi's narrative. Her attack on Karim thus becomes by extension a critique of Kureishi's own comic treatment of Asian characters. Her complaints echo (not coincidentally) those directed against works such as *My Beautiful Laundrette*: Kureishi creates neo-orientalist images of Asians for the sake of "a few cheap laughs." Kureishi's own recorded response to such criticism resembles Karim's: "'I'm not really writing about Asians as a category … We are all people. I don't think because [a character] is Asian I have to be reverential. That would be ridiculous'" (Kaleta 220, ellipses in original). This argument, too, contains an element of evasiveness; we are indeed "all people," but characters in a strongly raced narrative are unlikely to be perceived simply as generic units of humanity. On the other hand, Tracey herself seems lacking in humour; her question "'Why do you hate yourself and all black people so much, Karim?'" is as solemn as it is unwarranted. Karim's laughter is not cheap, and it is not synonymous with hatred.

In "Some Time with Stephen [Frears]," speaking of his film-in-progress *Sammy and Rosie Get Laid*, Kureishi himself has pondered the issues connected with the exploiting of living people for artistic ends: "I can't work out today if the question about the relation between the real people, the real events, and the portrayal is an aesthetic or moral one. In other words, if the acting is good, if the film is well made, if it seems authentic, does that make it all right, is the stealing justified? Will the issue be settled if the experience is successfully distilled into art? Or is the quality of the work irrelevant to the social issue, which is that of middle-class people (albeit dissenting middle-class people) who own and control and have access to the media and money, using minority and working-class material to entertain other middle-class people? Frequently during the making of the film I feel that this is the case, that what we're doing is a kind of social voyeurism" (*London Kills Me* 164–5). By situating artistic practice within an urgent political context, Kureishi bravely raises the possibility that he is annexing for his personal profit the experience of those less fortunate. A corresponding charge of self-serving social voyeurism could obviously be applied to Karim's theft of Anwar for the purpose of advancing his own stage career. Karim's rationale for "taking off" his friend, however, goes beyond a mere racially demeaning opportunism. His intention, at least, is not to lampoon Asians as a group but to satirize a despotic old migrant's senseless clinging to outworn custom amid a new and contrary environment. Such a project parallels Kureishi's program as author throughout *The Buddha of Suburbia*. It does not automatically betoken a hatred of oneself or one's ethnicity in either author or protagonist. Kureishi's treatment of the ill-starred Anwar hardly makes Anwar (in Tracey's phrase) a person without humanity, though it does expose his humanity as laughably stunted.

On the other hand, Karim's impersonation of Changez, though a brilliant success, raises still more disquieting issues, precisely because Changez does not cling as tenaciously as Anwar to communal precedents. As Yu-cheng says, "[W]hen the pure and authentic, symbolised by Changez who comes freshly all the way from India, engages itself in interactions with other elements in diasporic experience, it mixes with others and changes. 'Our way' is simply a way of impossible return" (14). The clownish Changez may consequently not offer as ripe a target for laughter as at first blush would appear. Karim's decision to "do" Changez, though approved by Pyke, is also more open to question because Karim is mocking a human being's congenital deformities and impediments along with his foreignness: "At night, at home, I was working on Changez's shambolic walk and crippled hand, and on the accent, which I knew would sound, to white ears, bizarre, funny and characteristic of India" (188–9). During another tense brainstorming session, Pyke lauds Karim's characterization and airily cuts off the again protesting Tracey on grounds of crass commercial expediency: "'We have class, race, fucking and farce. What more could you want as an evening's entertainment?'" (189). After some rehearsals Pyke praises Karim's portrayal – "'The character you've got going is going to be a big laugh'" – and promises Karim a "'special present,'" his own pliable wife, Marlene (191). In *The Buddha of Suburbia* white reprobates, whether liberal poseurs or hairy-backed bigots, are no safer from Kureishi's corrosive mockery than Asian ones.

As Karim perfects his new role, laughter again becomes a source of tension. Changez has already informed Karim, in an addled babu argot mirroring his cultural in-betweenness: "'You can't be using my character in your acting business ... You love to belittle me, you love to laugh at me and call me a git to the side of my face. One day you will be laughing out of the other side of your neck with me'" (185). But despite the promise Changez extracts from Karim not to steal his personality for theatrical profit, Karim applies himself to the theft with mounting zeal: "There were few jobs I relished as much as the invention of Changez/Tariq. With a beer and notebook on my desk, and concentrating for the first time since childhood on something that absorbed me, my thoughts raced: one idea pulled another behind it, like conjurer's [*sic*] handkerchiefs. I uncovered notions, connections, initiatives I didn't even know were present in my mind" (217). Invention of this sort demands more than mere mechanical copying; Karim's creation of his role entails a substantial investment of self. This, as it happens, is the approach Pyke himself counsels: "What a strange business this acting is, Pyke said; you are trying to convince people that you're someone else, that this is not-me. The way to do it is this ...: when in character, playing not-me, you have to be yourself. To make your not-self real you have to steal from your authentic self" (219). Whether Pyke possesses an "authentic self" is uncertain, but this is at least a more thoughtful view of what acting involves than the trendy Shadwell's.

By the opening performance, Karim has stolen enough from his authentic self to score a professional coup: "[T]he evening was a triumph and I was ... hilarious and honest. At last" (228). To Karim's relief, Changez, of all people, approves: "'I am glad in your part you kept it fundamentally autobiographical and didn't try the leap of invention into my character. You realized clearly that I am not a person who could be successfully impersonated'" (231). Commenting on this amusing non-sequitur, Ray cautions: "Reading this enlightening passage as an instance of Changez's willful blindness is both naive and incorrect" (236). Her judgment passes over Changez's funnily obtuse conviction that his nature is inimitable (he is a grotesque, but grotesquerie can be copied); still, it contains a kernel of truth. Unconsciously, Karim has tapped into common qualities linking him to his peculiar friend from overseas. By projecting himself imaginatively into Changez's shoes, he has made the surprising discovery that they are not an impossible fit. He has begun to laugh out of the other side of his neck. What is more, his presentment of Changez has the unlooked-for effect of altering his perception of his model; he begins to see him not as merely freakish but as endearingly companionable. Visiting his Trotskyite fellow-actor Terry on a day off, Karim thinks of Changez's comic insouciance as a welcome antidote to Terry's rigid ideological obsession: "I wanted to ring Changez and have him walking beside me on his Charlie Chaplin feet" (241). Like the original Chaplin tramp, Changez is the sort of clown who inspires laughter tinged with the warmth of affection.

Comic performance, then, for all its Chaplinesque pitfalls and pratfalls, can be in Kureishi a mode of discovery, indeed of self-discovery. What Karim brings to creating the comic role of Tariq / Changez, a man he has cuckolded and casually teased, is not simply dégagé mockery but empathy. This reorientation feeds into his sentiments at Anwar's funeral: "But I did feel, looking at these strange creatures now – the Indians – that in some way these were my people, and that I'd spent my life denying or avoiding that fact. I felt ashamed and incomplete at the same time, as if half of me were missing, and as if I'd been colluding with my enemies, those whites who wanted Indians to be like them" (212). He partly blames his father, Haroon, for having always failed to cherish his Indian past, "So if I wanted the additional personality bonus of an Indian past, I would have to create it" (213t). His embrace of the concept "my people" is clearly guarded and conditional – he is not auditioning for the role of the young zealot in "My Son the Fanatic" – but it still represents a substantial adjustment of attitude.

By identifying whites, or some of them at least, as enemies (and his cold-fish manipulative director, Pyke, might head the list), Karim appears to be tardily acknowledging the force of Tracey's earnest objections. He still refuses, however, to accept her insistence on grooming impersonations of blacks or Asians so as to spike condescending white laughter. He follows his rueful reflections on missing his Indian heritage with a ribald description of Changez catching in his arms the swooning, grief-stricken Jamila and, in consequence, getting an ill-timed erection. His comic yet empathetic portrayal of Changez on stage hardly constitutes a "positive image," but it allows Karim to claim the bonus of Indian identity for himself by grafting some part of his own personality onto that of an amiable Asian misfit.

Such an enactment of hybrid identity coincides metafictionally with Kureishi's own overall performance in *The Buddha of Suburbia*, a more dialogically structured novel than the subsequent *The Black Album*, written in polemical response to the fundamentalist hounding of Rushdie. Here, as author, Kureishi redeems his humour at the expense of his Indian characters by making the comedy – even that attached to a near-freak like Changez – affectionate and at bottom tolerant rather than hostile. By stealing generously from himself, Kureishi creates a comic discourse of otherness wholly distinct from the supercilious laughter of his avowed model, Evelyn Waugh.[3] Kureishi's first novel enacts an oblique but impressive vindication of its own offbeat ethnic humour. It accomplishes this by allowing no group in an increasingly multiform English society to escape its mocking gaze and by treating laughter as itself a conundrum that the young protagonist's motley experiences teasingly challenge him to solve.

11

Some Subtleties of the Isle: Matthew Kneale's Anti-*Tempest*

You taught me language; and my profit on't
Is, I know how to curse.

Caliban, *The Tempest* (I ii 365–6)

Late in Matthew Kneale's novel *English Passengers*, poised to enter the Tasmanian bush on a demented hunt for the Garden of Eden, the Reverend Geoffrey Wilson reports: "[F]inally we reached a tiny settlement that marked the very edge of civilization, beyond which lay naught but harshest wilderness" (340). Gripped by his mania, Wilson never doubts the distinction between his absolutes – "wilderness" and "civilization" – but it is the comic agenda of Kneale's narrative to trouble such received binaries. What Western thought defines as the "unsettled" Kneale's mixed-race leading man, Peevay, thinks of simply as "the world": the home from which he has been cruelly thrust. Here, as in *The Satanic Verses* and *The Buddha of Suburbia*, such clashes between discordant perceptions of reality have comic repercussions. And here, too, the humour subverts received antinomies between "human" and "alien."

In its work of comic subversion, *English Passengers* consistently draws on Shakespeare's *The Tempest* as an intertext. Though the novel does not allude overtly to the older work, there are numerous implied parallels. Counterposing his narrative against traditional readings of the play as supportive of Prospero and his proto-colonialist agenda, Kneale produces a revisionist version of Shakespeare's fable.[1] Many of the governing motifs in *The Tempest* – ideas of control through art and artifice, or through language, naming, and books – surface anew in Kneale's Victorian recasting, but in inverted form. Key dyads imported from the play, such as reason and error, civilization and savagery, bondage and liberty, undergo sea changes. The themes of travel and exploration and of magic, witchcraft, and the miraculous get similarly transmuted. Kneale's reworking of such elements results in a brilliantly original interrogation of the whole colonizing venture and of the conceptual framework underpinning it.

Whereas in *The Tempest* Prospero and his project provide the main focus of audience attention, in *English Passengers* the distributing of narration among a troupe of monologuists speaking diverse idiolects rules out any such consistent limelighting. In choosing such a dispersed structure for his nineteenth-century story Kneale follows Victorian models like Wilkie Collins's 1868 novel *The Moonstone*.[2] In order to provide a broader perspective on historical process, he interweaves two plot sequences, one starting in the 1820s, the other in 1857. The two strands at length coalesce, linked by the continuing chronicle of the half-aboriginal Peevay. The book's antiphonal structure is designed to challenge the monologic bias ingrained in Eurocentric myths of colonization. "I found it very liberating," Kneale has said, "to be able to jump from one scene and set of characters to another ... I was very concerned to make the voices seem as distinct as possible" (McDonald). The multicentredness enables a comedy deriving from each character's solipsistic tendency to misinterpret the ego systems of the others.

In novels, according to Mikhail Bakhtin, "[t]he incorporated languages and belief systems ... are unmasked and destroyed as something false, hypocritical, greedy, limited, narrowly rationalistic, inadequate to reality. In most cases these languages – already fully formed, officially recognized, reigning languages that are authoritative and reactionary – are (in real life) doomed to death and displacement" (*Dialogic* 311–12). This is as accurate a description as one could wish of the discursive movement of *English Passengers*; the counterpointing of a whole array of distinct idiolects effectively sabotages those that are sanctioned, dominative, "correct," stripping them of their usual mastery and valorizing instead those normally marginalized. The presiding, credible voices are those of "eccentric" speakers, above all Peevay and the Manx ship's captain Illiam Quillian Kewley. (It is relevant that both of the latter are bilingual, and thus capable of a heteroglossia not channeled by the single conceptual groove of "standard" English.[3]) This narrative strategy loosely resembles that of Selvon's Moses trilogy, with its privileging of non-standard Caribbean speech.

Whether this angling of the novel's multiple discourses coincides with "dialogism" in the strictest sense – the polyphonic "plurality of equal consciousnesses and their worlds" that Bakhtin prizes in Dostoevsky's novels (*Problems* 4) – is open to debate. If dialogism implies a free and equal confabulation of diverse voices and viewpoints, that is not what one finds in *English Passengers*, in which some of the monologuists are unmistakably preferred and others, to adopt Bakhtin's own terms, are through their own testimony "unmasked and destroyed." Kneale builds polyphony into his narrative, but he builds in as well unmistakable distinctions between concords and dissonances.

In Kneale's reconceived *Tempest*, the Prospero function is parcelled out among three counterfeit magi: the administrator Robson (who is given no sections to narrate), the Reverend Geoffrey Wilson, and Dr Thomas Potter. This trio's claims to superior wisdom are deftly punctured as the narrative proceeds. "My first interest," Kneale has said, "was in the craziness of the Victorian British mind" (McDonald), and his three faux-Prosperos inhabit cells A, B, and C in his retrospective asylum. Their pretensions to insight and authority make them the most laughable figures in Kneale's cast of characters.

Robson (whose phase of the plot is slightly pre-Victorian) subscribes sanctimoniously to colonialist verities. He pursues the mission of bringing "civilization" to the Tasmanian "savages" much as Prospero has vainly attempted with the "salvage and deformed" Caliban. His official aims are to enlighten his heathen charges with Christian teachings and to keep their endangered race from being expunged altogether. As his admirer, the storekeeper's wife Mrs Price, puts it, he cherishes a "resolve to bring improvement to the unfortunate creatures" (234); his "chief concern" is "to mount nothing less than a crusade to civilize the blacks" (235). As Adas notes, "improvement" is "a term that is ubiquitous in nineteenth-century writings on colonial areas" (196). The word crops up persistently in *English Passengers*, usually with sardonic overtones, and the irony is never more barbed than here. By setting his "blacks" to useful tasks, Robson hopes "with time [to] transform them into something like a happy band of English villagers" (236). To the visiting colonial governor, William Frampton, he confides a still loftier scheme of Prospero-like transmutation: "'This is the Natives' Square … It has been my hope that one day it may be paved, in the manner of an Italian piazza'" (255). More extravagant than Shakespeare's exiled magus, he dreams of creating a mini-Milan on the island, complete with European amenities such as a newspaper and a market. What he manages to create, however, is a gulag; his crusade disturbingly resembles a crucifixion. As Peevay complains, in accents millions of the colonized might echo, "Truly, that was one woeful thing, hateful to behold. I knew most num [whites] were bad scuts better speared dead, yes, but I never did think Robson would tell us piss-awful falsehoods. Robson, who said he was our friend and even spoke to us in our own talking to make us love him" (221).

In his epilogue to *English Passengers* Kneale speaks of "the terrible farce of Flinders Island" (439). Robson, with his fantasies of "improvement," acts as a sinister producer for this dark comedy. Even his idealism is suspect; to Mrs Price, who calls Robson "'a brave man who risked his very life to rescue the aborigines,'" the resident surgeon dryly replies, "'He did well enough from his rescuing, too, as I recall, at five pounds per head'" (244). When exhibiting the Christian knowledge of a native school class Robson asks an aptly renamed child, "'Voltaire, who made me?'" only to receive an unexpected but compelling reply: "'The devil'" (258). The boy endows his white master with the lineage assigned by Prospero to Caliban, a turning of tables that Shakespeare's sorely pinched islander might have relished.

Names and naming have some importance in *The Tempest*; Caliban, to cite a well-known example, says that when Prospero first came he would "teach me how / To name the bigger light, and how the less, / That burn by day and night" (I ii 336–8). The same motif looms larger in *English Passengers*. Robson forcibly "civilizes" the aborigines by renaming them, stamping European nonce-identities (like "Voltaire") on what is assumed to be a mere nameless blank. A relevant parallel is the experience of Peevay's half-brother Tayaleah, who when separated from his tribe is taken in by a settler named Harris. "I decided," reports Harris, "the creature had better have a name. Lucy said he called himself Tayaley or some such nonsense, which was no name at all, so I gave him George, after the King, and then Vandiemen, from his place of birth, making George Vandiemen, which I thought rather clever" (128). (The cleverness consists in giving the little "pickaninny" a label that pays homage to the reigning English imperial monarch and a European colonial administrator.) It is only logical that an indigenous name should be dismissed as "no name at all," since the bearers of such names are deemed by the whites to be no persons at all; merely "creatures."

Mrs Price, who is unconsciously but transparently in love with Robson (such nuances proliferate in Kneale's management of his multiple monologue form) recounts how her idol "suddenly called all the blacks, and the settlement officers, to gather in the open space in front of the school, where he announced – to the amazement of all – that the natives were to be renamed. It seemed a bold notion, and as I watched him call the natives up one by one to receive their new appellations – quite in the manner of a general awarding medals to his soldiers – I was full of admiration. I fully understood the significance of his intention. He meant the aborigines to be begun afresh and reborn as civilized, Christian beings" (238–9). Mrs Price's military analogy unwittingly opens to view the subtext of the ceremony; Robson is indeed acting like a military commandant asserting his supremacy over his subalterns. Far from a benign act of "improvement," such renaming is an act of regimentation. Like the classifying of migrants in *The Satanic Verses*, it is a technique of invasive reshaping. Where Rushdie's aliens are deformed (as the Manticore explains) by being described, Kneale's aborigines are depersonalized by being renamed. The insensitivity of the process is brought home by the sniggering jocularity of the "witty" name choices, relished by the doting Mrs Price: "In some cases I was amused to note that a title concealed some clever sting in its tail. Thus the monstrous female, Walyeric [Peevay's warrior-mother], became Mary, and while this might seem innocent enough, I had little doubt as to which murderous monarch was in Mr Robson's mind. Her half-caste son, Peevay, who had such a curious round mop of blond hair above his little black face, and who insisted on regarding one with such disconcerting seriousness, was now Cromwell, that most sombre of rulers" (239). Since she considers renaming, even with a patronizing sting in its tail, not hurtful but clever, Mrs Price finds it a distressing instance of backsliding that afterwards the natives "secretly continued to address one another by their old, savage appellations" (239). The savages show even more churlish resistance by performing their own surreptitious acts of renaming; the disenchanted Peevay explains that the colony director, whom he had once dreamed of as his own father, now bears the name FAT SCUT ROBSON (222).

The novel works subtly to expose names as by nature fluid and unstable. This applies even to the name of the chief theatre of action, "Van Diemen's Land, or Tasmania, or whatever it was now calling itself," as Captain Kewley derisively puts it (283). And yet, slippery as they may be, names can also contain a potent emotional charge. To Peevay, it is the whites' ignorance of the "real" (i.e., aboriginal) place names – to the colonists "no names at all" – that ensures the futility of their lunge to take possession of the places: "This could never be their place, I did divine. Yes, they could go hither and thither, thinking IT IS MINE NOW, but they would never feel it like my ones did. How could they when they didn't know anywhere's name, or how it got there? Num would never have this place deep inside their breasts, no. They would just be dwelling here" (404). Peevay knows that, humanly speaking, there is more to naming than simply slapping a handy or "witty" label upon a spot or a person as a placard of ownership.

In keeping with the colonizers' forcible renaming is their absolutist approach to discourse. Robson, though one of the few whites who speak the natives' language, reprimands them when he overhears them using it, waving his hand "with a look of cheerful firmness. 'But you must speak English now,' he insisted kindly, 'only English'" (234). This is one way of "bringing improvement" to them, since English (as Joyce Cary confidently believed) is the accepted code of civilization, and their own speech the palaver of barbarism. One recalls Miranda chiding Caliban for his ingratitude: "[W]hen thou didst not, savage, / Know thine own meaning, but wouldst gabble like / A thing most brutish, I endow'd thy purposes / With words that made them known" (I ii 357–60). Human speech itself, then, is a benison granted by the European redeemers to the gabbling brutes. Peevay's first impressions of English speech put that conceit in a startling new perspective, enacting what Bakhtin calls "a relativizing of linguistic consciousness in the perception of language borders – borders created by history and society, and even the most fundamental borders (i.e., those between languages as such)" (*Dialogic* 323). Peevay recalls: "It was interesting to hear white men's talk, yes, as I never heard it before, and I observed it never was said properly but was just murmured, like wombat coughing" (95). Later, having himself mastered the wombat idiom, Peevay concludes with Caliban-like rancour that "I WAS A FOOL TO LEARN WHITE SCUTS' WORDS AND GOD, AS THEY NEVER WERE ANY PISS-POOR USE IN FIGHTING THEM" (331). He now sees that the intruders' language is complicit with their foreign religion as an engine of control and immiseration; that it was never meant to place his own people on an equal footing.

Like the "pains humanely taken" Prospero lavished on Caliban, which have turned out to be "all, all lost, quite lost" (IV i 189–90), Robson's attempts to "improve" the aborigines come to nothing; but Kneale's novel makes it clear that such pains are better lost. A later visitor to Tasmania, Dr Thomas Potter, pompously strikes an attitude recalling Prospero's: "The colonial government made every attempt to improve those blacks who were captured, and to lead them from idleness to civilized ways. One might suppose these efforts would have been received with gratitude, but no, the aborigines showed themselves nothing less than contemptuous of the goodly teaching given them, and, beneath a thin veneer of civilized conduct, they remained quite as savage as before" (392–3). His outrage is mere comic bluster; we know by this point that Robson's schemes for "improvement" deserve a different name and that Potter's own thinking needs desperately to be improved.

The second member of Kneale's trinity of faux-Prosperos is the Reverend Geoffrey Wilson. Though plainly a madman, as the leader of a mission of Christian discovery, Wilson has much in common with the more soberly evangelical Robson. Kneale's dual narrative, with its intertwined chronology, foregrounds the parallel, and Peevay's comment confirms it: "Looking at this Wilson, who was a vicar, I did recollect Smith [another cleric] and Robson from our slow-dying island days" (313). In his introduction to the Arden *Tempest*, Frank Kermode says of Prospero: "As a mage he controls nature; as a prince he conquers the passions which had excluded him from his kingdom and overthrown law; as a scholar he repairs his loss of Eden; as a man he learns to temper his passions" (xlviii). Wilson, point for point a reversed mirror-twin of Prospero, resolves to "repair his loss of Eden" by unearthing the biblical Garden in western Tasmania. Echoing a word recurrent in *The Tempest* and encoded in the name of the heroine, Miranda, he conceives of his crank errand as a "holy quest in search of wonders" (44). Prince Ferdinand, awed by Prospero's prowess as a conjuror, feels that the presence of such a sage "makes this place paradise" (IV i 123–4); Wilson discovers on his antipodean island a paradise inverted, his own personal hell. Fired by his religious zeal to defy the obstacles posed by untamed nature, he is nearly killed by his incapacity to cope with the conditions of the bush, the "world" where Peevay is joyously at home. A rancorous Prospero, he can conquer neither his own nor his companions' passions; his rivalry with Potter goads him to seething hatred, which Wilson (lacking Prospero's self-knowledge) interprets to himself as scrupulous disapproval.

Wilson's crazy Tasmanian dash is meant to shore up the metaphysical foundations of the Victorian worldview, the smug faith underwriting the "civilizing" colonial mission. He frames his bizarre theory concerning the whereabouts of Eden as a buttress to the British imperialist project, equating his expedition with the heroism of the embattled British military during the 1857 Sepoy uprising: "Was not our venture, after its own fashion, every bit as important as their campaigns against murderous rebels? If they were attempting to defend the rule of civilization, we were endeavouring to defend the very rock upon which was built that civilization, the Scriptures themselves" (41). To the vicar's dismay, that rock has shown signs of crumbling from exposure to the solvent of advanced nineteenth-century scientific findings. Near the end of his trek, his scriptural roadmap in tatters, he is left stranded, bereft of invisible means of support: "All at once I felt haunted by a terrible vision, of a world without guidance: a kind of emptiness, where all was ruled by the madness of chance. How could one endure such a place, where all significance was lost? I myself would mean nothing, but would merely be a kind of self-invention, a speck upon the wind, calling itself Wilson. I felt my spirit waver, as if it were toppling into the abyss before me" (358). What the vicar shrinks from as unthinkable is, of course, the abyss of modernity, the unscripted, non-scriptural universe that will be a commonplace of the advanced thought and literature of the century following his own. It is also the universe posited by the whole fragmented structure of Kneale's narrative frame, whereby a gallery of self-inventing egos strive to impose their various constructions of experience on the void confronting them all.

Closely considered, however, some of these versions of reality have more cogency than others. When Wilson's priestly platitudes are exposed to the skepticism of native Tasmanians, the outcome is decisive. Searching for a guide among the aborigines gathered at the governor's Christmas banquet, the vicar unexpectedly finds himself in a doctrinal colloquy with Walyeric (AKA Mary), Peevay's ferocious, pipe-smoking mother, who inquires blandly whether God is everywhere. Peevay recounts the ensuing exchange:

> Wilson was surprised by her pipe, but he smiled still. I could see he never surmised Mother at all. "Everywhere. God is in sky and deepest places of the sea. He is in mountains and trees. He is in birds and animals and fishes too. Most of all, he is in us."
>
> Mother lit her pipe. "Then he is in you?"
>
> He smiled very much. "Of course. And he is in every one of you, too."
>
> Mother gave her dangerous look. I suppose I divined she must do something heinous soon.
>
> "And he is everywhere inside you?"
>
> Wilson nodded. "Most certainly."
>
> "So he must be in your dirty stinking arse, Vicar? Poor old bugger God, isn't he, stuck inside there?" (314)

The vicar is of course taken aback by Walyeric's "heinous" behaviour; but her language, unseemly as it is, compensates for her own heinous treatment by a succession of ungodly white marauders, starting with her abduction and rape by the brutal convict Jack Harp. That rape figures as the novel's central symbolic act, a "fall" prefiguring the whole traumatic European violation of the aborigines and their way of life: their uprooting from their home territory; the removal of their traditional means of subsistence; their exposure to novel and wasting diseases; their indoctrination with alien religious beliefs, like Wilson's; even their arrogant renaming.

Walyeric's "magic words," as Peevay wryly calls them (314), have in fact a magical effect, challenging the whites to confront, for once, the arbitrariness of their own sanitized conceptual universe. They produce the further miraculous result of at last uniting Walyeric and Peevay, after years of estrangement, in shared, insurgent laughter: "So a strange thing happened. Mother heard my laughing and now she looked at me, which was the first time that day. Then she smiled. This was sudden, almost as if it was just some mishap she never did intend, but still it was interesting to me, because it was the first smile I got from her in all those many years ... I was so surprised that I smiled too. So it was I felt as if some hateful ache stopped, at long last" (315). Frederick Holmes's Bakhtinian commentary on "grotesque realism" in *The Buddha of Suburbia,* in which "the material bodily principle, that is, images of the human body with its food, drink, defecation, and sexual life, plays a predominant role" ("Comedy" 647; see chapter 10), applies equally to Kneale's revisionist *Tempest*. In Shakespeare's play such grotesque realism is confined to "low" action involving the bibulous clowns. In scenes dominated by Prospero, formality and propriety are privileged over the body and its gross, unruly attributes. Various elements enforce this preference: the measured gravitas of Prospero's verse; the for once punctilious observance of the unities of place and time; Prospero's caution to Ferdinand against unchastity – "If thou dost break [Miranda's] virgin-knot before / All sanctimonious ceremonies may / With full and holy rite be minister'd, / No sweet aspersion shall the heavens let fall / To make this contract grow" (IV i 15–19); the ornate pageantry of Prospero's masque, shattered by the rowdy cabal of the murderous buffoons. In *English Passengers,* Kneale inverts the Shakespearean hierarchy in the interest of Bakhtinian comic boisterousness. Kewley lodges a pointed complaint against Anglo-Saxon standards of shipboard decorum: "Man Island being too small for the formal" (39). Tasmania, though a far larger island, is likewise too small. Walyeric's words to Wilson are of course an outrage to social decency, but they do the necessary job of switching attention from the vicar's vapid Victorian pieties to the smelly but incontrovertible facts of bodily life. In *The Tempest* Prospero observes that the ethereal Ariel was "a spirit too delicate" to act Sycorax's "earthy and abhorr'd commands" (I ii 272–3), but in *English Passengers* to be earthy is not ipso facto to be abhorrent. And, as in Kureishi's *Buddha,* the novel's revision of the racial hierarchy works in tandem with its transvaluation of moral values and social codes on the island.

Islands, in *English Passengers,* persistently suggest myopic self-enclosure. It is symbolically right that Wilson ends his calamitous Pilgrim's Progress on another island, Wight, enwrapped in mental fogs, believing himself the Messiah but "too bereft of wits to repeat his own name" (431). That fate carries a keenly ironic sting in its tail; for once it is not the aboriginal underling but the white master who suffers the humiliating erasure of his name, and thus of his identity.

Doctor Thomas Potter, the third of Kneale's spurious magi, is a savant with grand but twisted "scientific" ambitions. His elaborate scheme of racial hierarchy is a mere shabby parody of Prospero's ordered vision. George Alder, an early governor of Van Diemen's Land, affirms that "[t]he blacks … have no comprehension of what I may term *system*" (97); the claim is false, but beyond that *English Passengers* interrogates the whole Western notion of system-making as an index of intelligence. Where Robson and Wilson both worship a sacred text, the Christian scriptures, the systematizing Potter busies himself compiling his own secular scripture, *The Destiny of Nations*, which codifies his pseudo-empirical findings and which closely resembles the popular theories of racial difference mentioned in this book's introduction.[4] Potter is at once Wilson's twin and his antitype. His scientific scheme, like Wilson's religious one, is meant as a theoretical prop for the grand narrative of Britain's empire. According to the scheme, the view of imperium as the mere "consequence of chance … could hardly be more misleading. There is, in truth, no finer manifestation of the destiny of men than this mighty institution of imperial conquest. Here we see the stolid and fearless Saxon Type, his nature revealed as never before as he strides forth in his great quest, subduing and scattering inferior nations – the Hindoo, the American Indian, the aboriginal race of Australia – and replacing these with his own stalwart sons" (271). Not only is Potter's rhetoric bombastic, he does not even abide consistently by his own terms. His racial categories keep getting adjusted to accommodate new pieces of information that embarrassingly discredit them and, incidentally, to vent his own spleen (since Potter, too, lacks Prospero's powers of self-command): the loathed Wilson, to cite the prime example, is pigeonholed as a parasitical "Norman" *untermensch*. Potter is consistent, however, in his refusal to accord full human status to non-whites. To quote a pertinent statement by Adas, "The more extreme advocates of European global hegemony, who adhered to a survival-of-the-fittest world view, went so far as to argue with Frederic W. Farrar that scientific and technological backwardness explained and justified the decimation or (in the case of the Tasmanians) the utter extermination of 'primitive peoples' who had not 'added one iota to the knowledge, the arts, the sciences, the manufactures, the morals of the world'" (204). Potter would heartily endorse such tawdry debasements of Darwinism.

Under Potter's objectifying, clinical lens, all native people, dead or living, are relegated to the status of "specimens." After sequestering Walyeric's remains, the doctor reports in his crabbed shorthand, "Self pleased to see specimen = *excellent* + far better than those from *Flinders*, which all = damaged or incomplete" (329). Potter's attitude not just to the natives but to his fellow human beings in general exhibits a cold, voyeuristic curiosity. It receives its apt comeuppance from the half-caste Port Arthur prisoner, Black O'Donnell, who jabs his finger smartly into the doctor's peering eye (294). His prize "collectible" is Walyeric's cadaver, which he acquires through an unHippocratic act of bodysnatching. He thus brings to its sad completion the European assault upon the native woman's integrity initiated years earlier by the convict Jack Harp. In Peevay's judgement Potter's action is more demeaning even than crude physical brutality: "Killing was better, yes, as that is being hateful and afraid, which is some esteem, while this cutting and playing was just a scornful thing, odious as could be. This was making her small, into nothing at all, not even dirt" (330–1).

In his career's macabre aftermath, Potter's own remains, salvaged from the wreckage of the *Sincerity*, are made small by a scientific malaprop. As Kewley reports, the skeleton is "all arranged on a handsome metal frame, and spliced together tidy as could be," with a brass plate inscribed: "UNKNOWN MALE PRESUMED TASMANIAN ABORIGINE POSSIBLE VICTIM OF HUMAN SACRIFICE" (438). The doctor thus becomes a misfiled Exhibit A in his foolish system of classification by racial "type," a skeleton in his own taxonomic closet. Metaphorically, however, the inscription speaks the truth: Potter is indeed a human sacrifice, having given up his life to the pursuit of his cruel and empty obsession.

Peevay, who has dealings with all three pseudo-Prosperos, might be termed a Nabilac: a Caliban whose meaning has been reversed. Unlike his famous precursor he is a hybrid not of devil and witch but of a depraved English convict and an aboriginal amazon warrior, an equally problematic inheritance. Jack Harp, who regularly abducts and rapes native women, makes a passable devil, though his own monologues convey some sense of the way penal servitude has diabolized him. As for Peevay's fierce mother, Walyeric might reasonably claim sisterhood with the witch Sycorax. Even the hooligan Jack finds abducting her no mean feat: "Well, she was trouble, that piece, yelling and biting like some raw animal, and getting the others after me, too" (47). She afterward manages to elude Harp's clutches by working her witch's "spell" on his lecherous mate, Ned: "Once she'd got him thirsting for her strong she must've witched him into opening up her lock and letting her free, and then, while he was busy getting his rewards, she'd have given him a tap with that stone" (48). By fastidious lady colonists she is deemed "monstrous" and "unfeminine": Mrs Price calls her "that monster of a creature, undeserving of the title female, about whom such dreadful stories are told, and who answers the kindliest smile with a glower of insolence" (235). While she may not deserve the title female, she certainly deserves the title rebel; she vividly embodies the principle of the subaltern's rooted resistance to colonial rule. After her death Peevay, "ponder[ing] the life she got," perceives her not as monstrous but as marvelous: "No, she could not get her dearest desire to vanquish num white men, and make them go away, because this was some impossible thing, but she had her mob and fought her war, and lived bravely and never cared what anybody else said, which was some wonder" (387). In Peevay's eyes, his mother's indomitable resolve makes her more worthy of admiration than a colonialist "wonder" like Shakespeare's Miranda.

Peevay himself, like Caliban, is persistently cast as a monster. A dark-skinned, blond-haired hybrid, he is perceived as eerily deviant by both parent groups, whites and natives. Initially he accepts this monstrous image of himself, but what prompts him to do so is his *white* inheritance, which estranges him from his Palawa comrades. As a child, he is appalled, like Frankenstein's hominoid, by his own reflection: "Just there in the water, you see, all at once there was a stranger, and this stranger was like a monster. His face was almost ordinary but that just made him worse because his hair was so wrong" (49). Once he has glimpsed a group of whites, however, he is consoled by the difference between his appearance and theirs: "At least my skin was human colour" (60). Kneale's use of multiple centres of perception to relativize accepted terms – "monstrous," "ordinary," and above all "human" – contributes much to his novel's power to jolt Western readers from their accustomed, comfortable frame of reference.

For most of the narrative Peevay is ill at ease with his own hybridity; only toward the close does he become reconciled to it. Here, as in the work of Rushdie and Kureishi, such ethnic and cultural crossings can lead to self-punishing splits. In *English Passengers* Peevay's brother Tayaleah, educated in England, is fatally at war with himself. With his typical pungency, Peevay diagnoses his brother's fatal fall from a tree as the consequence of his riven identity: "Ever since he came to Flinders Island on Robson's boat I saw Tayaleah was like some fellow who is snared between his awake and his dreamings, and is pulled by both, stronger and stronger, never knowing what is true, till he is torn like paper. Tear got too big, so he jumped" (265). Peevay himself manages to avoid such tearing, but only by the drastic step of shunning white culture and, finally, integrating himself with his newfound company of fellow hybrids, "Peevay's Mob." Hybridity is an idea Potter's purist taxonomy rejects; the doctor maintains "that separate races *cannot* and *will not intermix*" (198). When this dogma becomes untenable he predictably invents "Potter's Law," finding "proof that *when two types = unnaturally mixed, characteristics of lower type shall always prevail*" (344). Peevay's history powerfully exposes the hollowness of Potter's Victorian polarities: "higher"/"lower" and "natural"/"unnatural."

Unlike the feuding Victorian Tweedledum and Tweedledee, Potter and Wilson, Kneale's aboriginal protagonist is not portrayed as intrinsically comic. Although he is sometimes amusingly naive, and can be alarmingly violent, his monologues reveal him as sensitive and humanly identifiable; far from a "salvage and deformed" clown of Caliban's stamp. Kneale can make his reversed Caliban an at times engagingly funny figure, but he does not make of him a figure of fun. If Peevay is sometimes, like Caliban, murderous, he has demonstrable cause; he picks off Potter's minions one by one, but then they have tried to murder him, and Potter himself has dishonoured Peevay's mother's remains. He is, within his means, giving tit for tat, repaying the long drawn-out ethnic cleansing inflicted on his people by methodically wiping clean his white enemies-slate.

Shakespeare's Prospero, exasperated, calls Caliban ineducable; he is "A devil, a born devil, on whose nature / Nurture can never stick" (IV i 188–9). Caliban learns to speak his masters' language but famously claims that its benefits have been overrated: "You taught me language; and my profit on't / Is, I know how to curse. The red plague rid you / For learning me your language!" (I ii 365–7). As Houston Baker comments, "Not 'self' discovery, but the impossibility of feeling anything other than cursed by language is the sense of Caliban's utterance" (53). As we have seen, recent critics cite the fact of Caliban's dispossession to justify his dissidence, but the text does not yield conclusive support for this reading. Bestial as well as thankless, Caliban sought to rape the young and virginal Miranda. Peevay instead, rather than a thwarted rapist, is himself the hapless outcome of a rape. He is a quick learner; though possessing a perfectly adequate native lexicon of his own, he gains a command of English, and, while he too finds English cursing useful, he profits in other ways as well. Nonetheless, the presumed civilizing benefits of a European education are questioned more strenuously by Kneale than by Shakespeare. The notion that an acquaintance with English books is "improving" comes in for an especially skeptical cross-examination.

Commandant Darling, who is mildly friendly toward the aborigines, calls his pet parakeet Shakespeare (227), but Darling is the official who segregates the Tasmanians on the "dying island" of Flinders, and Shakespeare has no more relevance to the perishing remnant than a twittering bird. Another colonist, the catechist Smith, gives Peevay an edifying book entitled *Two Little Orphans* (268), but though at first captivated by it Peevay comes to see that (like Prospero's book of magic) it is merely a mechanism of control, keeping the aborigines "in their place." "[A]ll of a sudden I could discern what Smith's TWO LITTLE ORPHANS book really said. No, it never was some kindness at all, but just a clever trap to catch me when I was despairing and easy. It was shaming to me, yes, that I got so caught. What the book said was, GO ON, LITTLE BLACKFELLOW, DIE SWEETLY NOW, DIE QUIET AND SMILING AND THANKFUL, AS THIS IS YOUR LAST TASK FOR US" (269–70). Here, as often, the unidiomatic "oddness" of Peevay's discourse only highlights the sharpness of his perception.

If not a comic figure, Peevay is frequently a source of amusement, both because of the attitudes he expresses and the style in which they are expressed. Among all the characters in the novel, with the exception of Kewley, he has the keenest insight into the covert motives of others, both aboriginal and white. He surmises (as he would put it) the psychology informing Western notions of white "know-how" as contrasted with native "backwardness": "White men like to think you're stupid when you don't know some new thing he has, but in fact that's just his foolishness. He doesn't want to know that our ones can learn his cleverness quick as he can, because deep down inside his breast white man WANTS our ones to be stupid" (103).

Mrs Denton, the governor's wife, finds that Peevay writes "in a most peculiar style, using long words most strangely … only too suggestive of a disordered mind" (303), but her critique only confirms her snobbishness; she manifestly does *want* Peevay to be disordered. As regards the "most peculiar style," Kneale explains: "For Peevay I looked at the one surviving dictionary of the Tasmanian aboriginals, then mixed in Victorianisms, a few swear words, and any metaphors that I felt he might have come up with from the natural world he knew … I'd had some feedback from Australian friends who pointed out that Peevay sounded very different from the mainland aboriginal style of speaking English of today. That was fine by me – I wanted Peevay to sound quite different, as he came from another place and time" (McDonald). Peevay's idiom is thus an amalgam, not a simulation of any historical person's actual speech patterns, but all the more effective an expressive vehicle for his own hybridity. His unique blend of the scriptural, the juridical, the natural, and the obscene causes his English to seem at once outlandish and intimately familiar, and thus potentially double-sided in its affective charge, evoking both laughter and pathos. Its very quirkiness, raciness, and profanity (there are more than just "a few swear words") endow it with a surprisingly authentic ring, especially by comparison with the "correct" but wooden inflections of the other characters' idiolects.

What Peevay's idiom most strikingly conveys is the radical innocence of his perceptions. The candour of his gaze and speech allows Kneale to "make strange" – to relativize – the key myths that Westerners have naturalized as part of the very fabric of civilization. The majestic march of European wisdom is destabilized by the freshness of Peevay's testimony; he is a Caliban transmuted from comic object to reflective subject. An instance is his first view of whites: "Then twigs were breaking, telling us this something coming was clumsy. In fact it was three somethings. No, I had never seen creatures so strange, I do recollect. They were the shape of men but only this. Their skin was not like skin at all but was the colour of stone, and loose, so it flapped. Even their feet were ugly, too big and with no toes. Worse, though, were their faces. These were coloured like raw meat, with no alive look in them" (55). Peevay's sense of the whites' weirdness derives amusingly from his unfamiliarity with Western customs; the flapping "skin" and ugly "feet" are of course Western body coverings: i.e., clothing and boots. Yet his image of the "somethings" contains a residual truth that separates it from a mere comic misprision, like Caliban's deluded belief that the drunken numskulls, Stephano and Trinculo, have dropped from the heavens, or like Mister Johnson's misreadings of his white superiors' motives. For Westerners accustomed to think of aborigines as clumsy, hideous, and unnatural, Peevay's untutored perception of Europeans as exactly that – clumsy, hideous, and unnatural – comes as a salutary minor shock.

Another shock to English complacency has a less remote source. Throughout the novel, Kewley and his crew of Manxmen, though nominally British, are bound by an unstated affinity to Peevay and the Palawa. Kneale broadens his assault on colonialist myths by opening a second front, manned by a white "Nabilac" garrison. The Manxmen, too, are island people who treasure their own history, customs, and language and who resent English "scuts" as bitterly as Peevay. Their language and nationality also have been put at risk by the scythe of imperial expansion.

Kneale has expressed his regret for the depletion of their native speech: "I'm fascinated by languages, and feel very sad that so many are presently disappearing. In some ways it seems almost like the loss of biodiversity" (McDonald). For Kewley Englishness signifies those qualities he most detests: stiff-necked propriety, petty "cleverness," a niggling rule-book mentality. "Truly, there's no overestimating the foolishness of Englishmen," he grumbles, "especially brainy ones like these [Wilson, Potter, and Timothy Renshaw]" (285). Later he adds: "Englishmen [are] the kind that love laws sooner than their own flesh and blood" (379). Kewley views the Manx as, like other colonials, an invaded and subjugated nation. Chronically at odds with prying British customs inspectors, he sides with the enraged Sepoys in their insurrection: "There's no bad losers like Englishmen, especially Englishmen in uniform. No wonder all those Indian Hindoos had mutinied against them" (33). In the Cape Col ony he is struck by the self-effacing demeanour of the local Indians and black Africans, "Nor was this surprising, I dare say, seeing as the Dutchman and Englishman Africans treated them like proper dirts, sneering and yelling at them in a way that wasn't pretty to watch" (166). Kewley's personal idiom, like Peevay's, contrasts pungently with the cut-and-dried correctness of most of the other monologuists' idiolects. A smuggler, thief, and fluent liar, Kewley relies on duplicity (his double-hulled vessel is puckishly named the *Sincerity*) to elude the single-minded English patrol of shipping. Nevertheless, he retains his core of humanity, obstinately rescuing Wilson, Potter, and the other "Garden of Eden" castaways even against his own interests.

Kewley, however, is no idealist; his downright hard-headedness exposes the hollowness of the Englishmen's preoccupation with "higher things." Unwittingly, he saves from the wreck of the *Sincerity* Potter's treatise, the Destiny of Nations, which he judges accurately to be "purest gibberish, being all about types and characteristics and other nonsense. I couldn't think why Potter had been hanging on to it so" (426). He is meanwhile stunned to find that Potter has not "hung on to" something of undeniable value: the bag of smuggler's gold that has been staring him in the face throughout his mutiny: "It looked like he'd never even troubled himself to open the thing and see what was inside" (425). The doctor's peering "scientific" curiosity has been trained on absurdly irrelevant objects.

For misdirection, however, the prize belongs to Wilson's search for Eden in the Tasmanian bush. What makes the irony poignant is that the territory Wilson invades to find the fabled Garden does actually represent, to Peevay, a lost paradise. True, Peevay's remembered early "world" was by his own account no Eden; it was occupied by warring tribes, and his own group was vexed by internal tensions. Still, it seems edenic compared with the dystopia the colonizers have installed. Prospero imports into his island only his book, his staff, and certain "utensils," and he departs leaving, apparently, few traces of his occupancy. His Victorian successors tote more sinister luggage, and the scars they leave are enduring. Firearms are a ubiquitous, ugly presence in *English Passengers;* even the Eden expedition, though ostentatiously Christian, is equipped by its pious backer, Childs, with state-of-the-art weaponry. The Reverend Wilson himself admires these utensils of bloodshed: "The lure of guns. I confess I myself felt it, though all my teaching warned me otherwise" (29–30). Less devout English colonists have already spent decades following, without pious qualms, equally unholy lures. The outcome has been the wanton decimation of the native inhabitants, their forcible confinement, and the wholesale rape of their women. In addition, the island has been converted into a penal colony that punishes home-bred British Calibans without mercy. What Wilson never suspects is that his fancied site for the biblical Eden is a place where his countrymen have made a hell. Kewley rubs in the irony with terse Manx understatement when he rescues the bedraggled castaways: "I could only suppose they'd had no great luck finding paradise after all" (378).[5]

A feature of colonization dramatized by Kneale's novel, its divisiveness, plays a major role in unparadising the island. Governor Alder's solution to the conflict between settlers and natives is chillingly simple and, to modern eyes, chillingly familiar: it is "to divide the colony into two entirely separate realms" (98). The boundary establishing this de facto apartheid is named, aptly, the "Black Line" (133). The consequences of this administrative divisiveness reach further; the colony is fragmented along faultlines that are by no means only racial. On a domestic level, the Hobart surgeon's wife, Mrs Seaton, believes that her husband's former colleague Potter is "threatening to create a division between us – a distance – when there had been none before" (324). And, of course, there are the walls, physical and psychological, shutting off Port Arthur convicts from "respectable" settlers like the Seatons. Still, it is the racial divisions that are most insidious, extending to small but telling details like the screen that segregates the forlorn remnant of natives from the white guests at the finicky Mrs Denton's Christmas feast. Insulting in itself, the barrier irresistibly recalls the lethal isolation of the aborigines on their "dying island" of Flinders.

The principle of separation is taken to its appalling limit in the Separate Prison at Port Arthur (291) where transported convicts are "corrected" by being masked and isolated, a penitentiary of the sort conjured up by Michel Foucault in his discussion of the Benthamite Panopticon.[6] Here the act of renaming encompasses the ultimate violation of personal identity: the replacement of inmates' names with numbers. Running throughout the novel, a buried parallel links convicts and aborigines, both alike chained to imperialist engines of oppression. Even the brutal Jack Harp, Peevay's "white scut" father, is a degraded brother of the natives he victimizes. Just as Robson's work on Flinders is supposed to "improve" the confined natives by "civilizing" them, so Governor Alder sees the "machinery of punishment" as representing for the convicts "a mighty engine of betterment, designed to bring the happiness that follows improvement" (130). Unlike Prospero's psychotherapeutic project of bettering his former enemies through artifice that fosters recollection and self-scrutiny, neither Alder's scheme nor Robson's stimulates its objects to anything but sullen hatred and despair.

The sole Englishman who does manage to locate an Eden of sorts is perhaps the unlikeliest: Timothy Renshaw. The young man, who frustrates his family's haughty expectations, happily lacks their killjoy Victorian high-mindedness. His occupations are desultory; on the sea voyage he shows energy principally in his nocturnal masturbatory activities, which puzzle and vex Wilson: "[F]requently during the night I would be disturbed by the sound of his fidgeting with his person in some curious, twitching way, quite as if he had some ailment" (110). If his fixations are less portentous than those of Wilson and Potter, he seems almost as self-preoccupied. Yet at the end, after passionately renouncing his ties with his family in the metropolitan centre, he discovers his own modest, pastoral paradise on the very fringes of empire. Unlike the disenchanted Wilson, he gains an edenic vision of the Garden, angels and all: "Dropping the mule bag, I hobbled forward, until, uttering a kind of giggle, I pushed open a gate and found myself in a garden, all brightest colours, such as I had hardly looked upon for all these many weeks. How strange it was, though. Everywhere I looked, you see – on walls, atop stones and stood upon the lawn – were winged angels, dozens of them, all regarding me with smiling grey faces" (391). It is the owner of this bucolic garden, a farmer fittingly named Sheppard, who turns out to have carved the stone angels. After recovering from the injuries sustained during his trek Renshaw falls in love with Sheppard's daughter Liz, a rustic Eve. Even her confession that her father is an ex-convict, a Port Arthur man, does not render either the locale or its occupants less paradisal: "There was something about this place that made me feel alive in a way I never had done back in London" (429–30). By stooping socially, and becoming literally covered in muck while helping with the lambing (that pastoral activity), Renshaw finds an authentic part to play and abandons the role of clownish upper-class idler he had been performing. As Liz laughingly says, seeing him dishevelled and dusty, "'You look like a real Tasmanian'" (430).

A critical step in Renshaw's progressive naturalization is his contact with that eminently real Tasmanian, Peevay. By stopping Potter's minion Hooper from murdering the native guide, Renshaw affirms their common humanity and breaches the colonial etiquette of white solidarity. Later, when Peevay comes to the aid of the injured and abandoned young Englishman, there occurs a brief, moving moment of communion between the two. Renshaw recounts how Peevay "sat down in front of me, directing me a strange, almost quizzical look. 'You must tell me this one thing. Why did you fight Hooper so?' It seemed a strange sort of question. 'I could hardly let him shoot you.' A frown passed across his face, almost as if he were enduring some pain, or struggling with confusion. He reached out and, just for a moment, touched my arm with his finger, murmuring, 'Renshaw'" (362). Peevay's look of pained confusion is natural; nothing in his experience explains why a white man would intervene on his behalf against a fellow white. The slight physical contact can hardly be called a bonding, but it is one of the few instances of genuine sympathy between races in the entire narrative – a recognition signalled, for once, by the grateful pronouncing of a name. More typical is Peevay's response to Wilson's question, "'Was it you who smote down Ben Fiddler [one of the mule drivers Peevay has killed]?'": "He let out a low laugh and I [Wilson] was certain I was right" (369–70).

In *English Passengers*, as so often in other comic novels, laughter itself has vital and sometimes disquieting repercussions. Peevay's "low laugh" over his vengeful liquidation of Fiddler belongs to the disquieting type. A more horrifying instance of such vindictive mirth occurs in the narrative segment by George Baines, a young employee of the New World Land Company, who reports that when some stockkeepers are asked about their gratuitous killing of blacks, one of them, Sutton, jokes about "shooting crows," "and this evoked a foul laugh from the rest" (68). Baines is even more scandalized when he later overhears his superior, Mr Charles, who has promised to discipline the murderers, laughing with one of them: "It is a trifling thing, I dare say. Try as I may, though, I simply have not been able to rid it from my thoughts" (74). Such heartless amusement is no "trifling thing"; it typifies the dehumanizing force of British dealings with the natives whose territorial rights have been laughingly usurped. The transported English convicts, along with their defenders, are exposed to a similar chuckling abjection. The reformer Julius Crane, arguing for a more humane treatment of prisoners against his sneering opponent Knowles, reflects that there is "little so poisonous to debate as laughter" (191–2).

Peevay himself repeatedly complains that he and his mother serve for the white colonists as poisonous "jokes to amuse." That is why his and Walyeric's shared, ribald laughter at the Reverend Wilson's expense marks for both of them a momentous turning of the racial tables. For once, Caliban and Sycorax become rieurs and give Prospero his snickering comeuppance, making the white overlord their laughing stock. Laughter may be double-edged; still, it remains a potent, inalienable weapon in the meagre arsenal of the dispossessed. Unfortunately for the aborigines, their oppressors retain an overwhelming supremacy in other, more tangible weaponry; the White Man's Burden entails much shouldering of weighty arms.

At the end, coming accidentally upon his "mob" of fellow mixed-race islanders, Peevay finds a life-enhancing means of warding off isolation and extinction. Unlike Caliban at the close of *The Tempest*, he will not be left to fade away on his island, solitary and aimless. While he cannot forgive his father, he can now view the white marauder's original sin, the rape of Walyeric, as a kind of fortunate fall: "Yes, he was some heinous scut with no good in him, but good came from him, even if this was just some foolish mischance he never did intend. See, he made me, and now he gave me my tribe, too. That was some mystery to confound" (433). So Kneale, like Rushdie and Kureishi, ultimately affirms the value of hybridity, linked though it may be with histories of sexual violation and personal anguish.

English Passengers enacts a tour de force of historical revisionism by turning inside-out colonialist assumptions embedded in *The Tempest* and handed down to modernity in the form of humorous literary and pictorial treatments of "primitives." Kneale thus deconstructs Abdul JanMohamed's "manichean allegory of white and black, good and evil, salvation and damnation, civilization and savagery, superiority and inferiority, intelligence and emotion, self and other, subject and object" (*Manichean Aesthetics* 4; see chapter 1). One might object that the novel simply enacts a reversed version of that manicheanism, giving the colonized a monopoly on virtue and their alien victimizers a lion's share of vice. Kneale's primary exponents of white adventurism, Robson, Wilson, and Potter, are endowed with little more depth than the stereotypic Africans of Waugh and Cary; they are generally "flat" exemplars of hypocrisy, greed, arrogance, and sheer lunacy. One answer to such a critique might be that Kneale needed to skew his treatment of colonial issues in order to redress the historic imbalance exposed by JanMohamed and others; it was high time for the pendulum of humour to swing in the opposite direction. But the book can be defended on more solid grounds, for, more closely examined, *English Passengers* does not in fact reverse ethnocentric commonplaces in a naively mechanical fashion. Kneale's aborigines, especially Peevay and the fierce Walyeric, may be engaging but they are far from being "noble savages"; their "world" of pre-conquest Tasmania is not projected as idyllic, though it enabled them to sustain a satisfactory way of life. The systemic abuses inflicted by the British conquerors are horrifying in aggregate, but the colonists themselves are portrayed as varying in their attitudes toward the colonial project and its attendant indecencies. Kneale's use of a whole chorus of voices for his narrative framework creates a discursive polyphony that complicates the overall impression the book leaves. Whether this structural innovation forms part of a more widespread advance in the comic fiction of interracial contact is a question best left to a concluding chapter.

12

The Empire Laughs Last

They made such a fuss with my trunk. "You mind if we just throw
the damn thing out of the window?" Gilbert asked me. He had
managed to carry it up all the stairs all those weeks ago but
now it was too hard to get it down. I opened my mouth to cuss
him when he said, "What, you still don't know what is a joke?"
"Oh, yes," I told him, "a joke is something that is funny."

Andrea Levy, *Small Island* (Hortense's narrative)

A *Punch* cartoon of 24 May 1967 shows a white vacationer gazing glumly at a crowd of young coloured people playing strenuous beach games. The man grumbles to his wife, "If I had my way, I'd send 'em all back to where they come from – Brum, Bradford, Brixton." Ruefully acknowledging that he cannot bracket the youngsters as immigrants, the disgruntled one must lamely adjust outmoded Powellite slogans to the demographics of the new Britain. The exotic lands where "remote people" used to dwell have invaded the familiar urban enclaves of home. The formerly watertight boundaries between here and there, far and near, even "us" and "them," have become porous; jokes premised on such stock binaries now have a way of falling flat.

Because it is responsive to shifting social realities, humour has a history; it may not progress, but it evolves. The evolution I have traced from the racialized amusement of interwar *Punch*, Waugh, and Cary to more recent comedy observes laws of natural selection. While sometimes taking hints from older fictional models, current British comic novelists pursue styles of joking better adapted to the environment in which they live and write. The realm of national complacencies has been shaken by a stealthy regime change; the balance of humorous power has shifted. Such changes do not take place in a vacuum; they reflect alterations in Britain's standing in the world, in its people's sense of themselves relative to others, and in the makeup of its home populace. As I have argued throughout this study, joking inevitably presupposes attitudes. The shift in the conceptualizing of race from a Doctor Potter-like paradigm of "higher" and "lower" to one of manifold equivalences has had far-reaching consequences for comedy. This is not to say that older, insulting types of racial mockery have magically vanished, or that recent comic fiction ranks higher on some celestial scoreboard than what came before. The least one can say, though, is that the newer comedy of racial difference speaks far more compellingly to the sensibilities of contemporary readers.

Three widely acclaimed twenty-first century novels by young writers of mixed ancestry, Zadie Smith's *White Teeth* (2000), Hari Kunzru's *The Impressionist* (2002), and Andrea Levy's *Small Island* (2004), represent several of the varied directions the new style of racial comedy can take. Levy's book is plainly indebted to Samuel Selvon's Moses trilogy; the other two owe more to the precedents of Rushdie and Kureishi. Sukhdev Sandhu has said, "A belief in contingency, in the tricksy messiness of our lives, aligns *White Teeth* with a novel such as *The Satanic Verses*" ("Excremental Children" 21), while Kunzru has observed that Kureishi's groundbreaking work has enabled younger second-generation writers like Smith (and by implication himself) to find authentic voices of their own (Kunzru, website review). All three writers derive humour from the dissolving of boundaries once seemingly impermeable: those of gender, nation, and ethnicity.

An eloquent spokeswoman for this porousness is Alsana Iqbal, a Bengali woman featured in the sprawling multicultural cast of *White Teeth*. Alsana has been taken to task by her pontificating husband, Samad, for wearing sneakers and African headscarves with a sari, a promiscuity of dress that flouts "pure" communal tradition. At length, after reading out an encyclopedia entry tracing Bengalis back to Indo-Aryan migrants who over time "mixed within Bengal with indigenous groups of various racial stocks," she bursts out: "'Oi, mister! Indo-*Aryans* … It looks like I am Western after all! Maybe I should listen to Tina Turner, wear the itsy-bitsy leather skirts. Pah. It just goes to show,' said Alsana, revealing her English tongue, 'you go back and back and back and it's still easier to find the correct Hoover bag than to find one pure person, one pure faith, on the globe. Do you think anybody is English? Really English? It's a fairy-tale!'" (236). Alsana's tirade sums up the novel's implied position on racial identity; but instead of seeming heavily didactic, it sounds amusingly of a piece with the irate woman who utters it. Smith has much to say on Alsana's pet topic, but she says it through comedy, suddenly revealing the long-suffering wife as the family's redoubtable master of discourse and endowing her English tongue with a racy cosmopolitan edge.

Like Kneale's *English Passengers*, *White Teeth* and *The Impressionist* both exploit the instability of names and the vagaries of naming to subvert ideas of identity as transparently definable and fixed. In the London of *White Teeth* promiscuous intermingling of all types, and its attendant heteroglossia, defeat purist monologic investments. Smith's crew of youthful Rushdie-bashing London Muslims (recalling the Islamic clique in Kureishi's *The Black Album*) give themselves a corporate name meant to trumpet jihad: the Keepers of the Eternal and Victorious Islamic Nation. But the linguistic tide they must navigate asserts its own obstinate pressure; their fiery communalist title yields the damply Anglo-Saxon acronym KEVIN. In Smith, as in Rushdie and Kureishi, a distinct culture refuses to be sealed hermetically within an ideological cocoon; stray, dialogic vibrations from the ambient space insist, comically, on infiltrating.

Kunzru's mixed-race protagonist in *The Impressionist* can claim no one determinate name but only, in effect, a series of aliases bestowed on him by others; he is at various times called Pran Nath Razdan, Rukhsana, Clive, Bobby, Chandra, and lastly – as far as we know – Jonathan Bridgeman (for brevity's sake I will normally refer to him as Pran). The narrative is accordingly marked by repeated brusque shifts of scene and circumstance; the non-sequitur could be called, paradoxically, its sole unifying principle. Identity in Kunzru's novel seems endlessly malleable, a truth impressed on the adolescent Pran (here given the female persona of Rukhsana) by the khwaja-sara, chief hijra of the Indian state of Fatehpur: "'You may think you are singular. You may think you are incapable of change. But we are all as mutable as the air! Release yourself, release your body, and you can be a myriad! An army! There are no names for it, Rukhsana. Names are just the foolishness of language. Why try to stop a river? Why try to freeze a cloud?'" (66). The khwaja-sara holds out to Pran a model of Heraclitean flux as a promise of release into a no-name realm of transcendent freedom, but in this time and place (a feudal principality in 1920s colonial India) the promise merely sugarcoats the bitter pill actually in store for the boy: gelding, and a job as a Fatehpur palace eunuch.

Namelessness is thus a two-edged sword, enlarging the boundaries of the self while at the same time threatening to mutilate it. In Pran's subsequent career ironies arising from this ambivalence proliferate. If Pran recoils from the proffered "female" identity, he goes on recklessly to embrace mutability in regard to nation and race; Elspeth Mcfarlane, the missionary's wife who shelters him in Bombay, thinks of him aptly as "such a chameleon" (165). When he first learns that his biological father was English and finds himself expelled from the house of his presumptive Indian father, he is crushed by a desolating sense of homelessness. Several years later, however, when he purloins the papers and the identity of a dead Englishman, Jonathan Bridgeman, his outlook on homelessness swerves toward the Heraclitean views of the khwaja-sara: "How easy it is to slough off one life and take up another! Easy when there is nothing to anchor you. He marvels at the existence of people who can know themselves by kneeling down and picking up a handful of soil" (227–8).

In his Bridgemanian phase Pran matriculates first at an English public school and later at an Oxford college, turning himself into a perfect faux-Englishman, a "Maxim Alien" like Saladin Chamcha, with the added advantage, denied to Rushdie's would-be chameleon, that his non-European origins are undetectable. He falls in love with a coquettish young siren, Astarte Chapel, who, like Chamcha's flame Pamela Lovelace, represents "the very essence of the English girl" (279). As Kunzru wryly puts it, "He is starting to coincide with his shadow" (254). Such protean adaptability at first enables Pran/Jonathan to elude the confining effects of fixed racial and national categories that more rooted characters unthinkingly accept. Ironically, however, he allows himself to become entrapped in his own improvised white Anglo-Saxon mask. In India, trained by the Scottish missionary Andrew Macfarlane, Pran has internalized his tutor's crank scheme of racial classification based on divergent cranial capacities, a system closely recalling Dr Potter's in Matthew Kneale's novel of two years earlier. According to Macfarlane's measurements British skulls turn out unsurprisingly to be the most capacious, a fact betokening, of course, inborn superiority and a God-given entitlement to rule.

Pran's tragicomic error lies in allowing himself to be imprisoned by the "shadow" with which he coincides, the "purely English" persona of Bridgeman. So extreme is his horror of his own "taint" of black blood that he recoils from the sight of African tribesmen at the Wembley empire exposition as if they were fecal waste: "It is like staring into the toilet bowl, looking at what he has expelled from himself" (303). Predictably, his fragile self-image crumbles when he discovers that his white goddess, Astarte, loves an African-American jazz musician, "Sweets." The crowning irony is that the frantically conformist "Jonathan" is too bland a British paleface to captivate her: "'Sweets is different ... You're the most conventional person I know, Johnny'" (330). Having accepted the racial hierarchy drilled into him by Macfarlane, he is dismayed to find the system turned on its head by his love fiasco. "When you have organized your whole life as a ladder (with, for example, something shining and white at the top, and sticky blackness at the bottom), there are consequences when someone kicks it away. Jonathan is in a state of collapse" (332). Because his faux-identity has been purely performative and driven by spurious distinctions of race, he is left with a terrifying sense of his own lack of real existence. His predicament is adumbrated by the art of the nightclub impressionist from whom the novel takes its title: "In between each impression, just at the moment when one [imitated] person falls away and the next has yet to take possession, the impressionist is completely blank. There is nothing there at all" (333).[1]

The book's conclusion, in which Pran joins a scientific expedition researching a remote African tribe, the Fotse, slyly reverses the *dénouement* of Waugh's *Black Mischief*. When the news of his planned excursion first circulates, "a student magazine prints a cartoon of him in a cooking pot, surrounded by grinning cannibals" (317), a joke recalling numerous *Punch* African drawings as well as the climactic cannibal orgy in Waugh's novel. Pran feels flattered to think that he is now a "celebrity," the iconic white adventurer, as it were a Basil Seal daring to penetrate the perilous haunts of black maneaters. His actual fate, however, is the opposite of Basil's. Where after horrifying African adventures Basil returns to England purged of his "savage" impulses, convinced that he has "had enough of barbarism," Pran's parallel ordeal of purgation rids him of his obsession with whiteness, his awed allegiance to European standards of "civilization." The elderly Fotse who attends him tells him that "he has been possessed by a European spirit" and that, while the other whites will be killed, "he can draw the spirit out" of Pran, though only through an arduous rite of exorcism (378). Like the people whose existence Pran had marveled at earlier in the novel, the Fotse "can know themselves by kneeling down and picking up a handful of soil." As for Pran, he has by now reached the point of readiness for such a release. He asks himself: "What if, long ago, he got lost? What if he got lost from himself, and could never get back again?" (373). No Fotse exorcism can restore him to any originary self; he cannot return to being Pran Nath Razdan any more than he can go on being Jonathan Bridgeman. However, he is now free to assume a new name, a new identity, that will be neither Indian nor European, neither "black" nor "white," but authentic because *sui generis*. He ends, mysteriously clad in a burnous, riding a camel across the desert: "For now the journey is everything. He has no thoughts of arriving anywhere" (383).

The plot of *White Teeth* is contemporary rather than (like *The Impressionist*'s) historical, yet its comedy, too, hinges on journeys in quest of identity. Here again ethnic "roots," while significant, do not suffice to define the individual self; myths of origin are repeatedly deflated by funny non-sequiturs. For Smith, a fixation on the dark backward and abysm of time can only widen the abysses that sever one generation from its successor. To the half-Jamaican Irie Jones, the glamour of the Chalfens, the English-Jewish family of intellectuals who befriend her and her idol Millat Iqbal, lies not only in their supposed Englishness but in their refusal to be bound by the past or to stay locked within air-tight generational cells. Like Kunzru's Pran they seem to have the knack, precious in this fragmented late-twentieth-century society, of crossing arbitrarily drawn boundary lines. Irie admires the Chalfens because in their house they "let speech flow freely from adult to child, child to adult, as if the channel of communication between these two tribes was untrammelled, unblocked by history" (319). But even the Chalfens' empathy is constricted by their parochial notions concerning the history of post-imperial migration, their insistence on exoticizing native-born non-whites. Irie's warm thoughts about her new friends are cooled by a series of conversational double-takes hinging on what Kureishi, in "The Rainbow Sign," calls the difficult question, "Where do you come from?":

"Well," said Joyce [Chalfen] … . "Where are you from, if you don't mind me asking?"

"Willesden," said Irie and Millat simultaneously.

"Yes, yes, of course, but where *originally*?"

"Oh," said Millat, putting on what he called a *bud-bud ding-ding* accent. "You are meaning where from am I *originally*."

Joyce looked confused. "Yes, *originally*."

"Whitechapel," said Millat, pulling out a fag. "Via the Royal London Hospital and the 207 bus."

All the Chalfens milling through the kitchen, Marcus, Josh, Benjamin, Jack, exploded into laughter. Joyce obediently followed suit.

"Chill out, man," said Millat, suspicious. "It wasn't that fucking funny." (319)

Smith is of course not the first writer to puncture naive British assumptions about those with dark, "unBritish" skins and the insular compulsion to identify them with their "origins," even if these turn out to be merely Brum, Bradford, Brixton; the novelty lies in making the ostensible alien himself the satirist. It is Millat, the London-raised son of Bengali migrants, who acts as the final arbiter of laughter, deciding how "fucking funny" his own joke is. Wickedly mimicking East Indian English, he lampoons the automatic tendency of his white friends to impose a foreign identity upon him. As Susan Purdie argues, "[B]ecause [joking's] transgressions are attended to as linguistic constructs and their marking as such is intrinsic to the experience of joking pleasure, all jokers construct themselves as *discursively* central" (127). By his casual use of slang and obscenity ("chill out, man"; "It wasn't that fucking funny"), Millat lays claim to a street-smart centrality that trumps Joyce Chalfen's white bourgeois inquisitiveness about his "eccentric" origins.

But, in a fashion typical of Smith, this humorous reversal involves further complexities, because Millat's sense of his own identity is (like Pran's) itself chronically troubled. Millat's identical twin, Magid, has been spirited off to Bangladesh to be raised as an orthodox Muslim believer; instead, by the perverse logic governing cultural affiliation in *White Teeth*, he becomes a fervent apostle of Western scientific rationalism. It is the Willesden-bred Millat who heartily embraces Islam, going so far as to join the inauspiciously named KEVIN clique. Yet even his commitment to this non-Western cause is suspect, an outgrowth of his yearning to live up to the tough-guy image projected by Hollywood stars like Al Pacino. In his dividedness, he epitomizes the predicament of Smith's whole cast of migrant parents and children: "[Millat] stood schizophrenic, one foot in Bengal and one in Willesden. In his mind he was as much there as he was here. He did not require a passport to live in two places at once, he needed no visa to live his brother's life and his own" (219). His awkward straddling posture captures both the pathos and the humour of the migrant's in-between condition.

This dividedness is enacted in one of the novel's most bizarre sequences, wherein Irie Jones has sexual relations in quick succession with both "Easternized" Millat Iqbal and his Westernized twin Magid and becomes pregnant with a child of hybrid but undecidable paternity. For all the pain attending such splits, however, Smith's treatment of the multicultural panorama she unfolds is finally hopeful. She has said that in *White Teeth* she "wanted to show people making an effort to understand each other, despite their cultural differences" (Farry). The gap between effort and achievement often produces humour, but the effort is not itself ridiculed. In Smith the collision and coalescence of cultures and ethnicities issue in laughter, but also in promise. She could certainly endorse Cobena Mercer's suggestion "that the emerging *cultures of hybridity*, forged among the overlapping African, Asian and Caribbean diasporas, that constitute our common home, must be seen as crucial and vital efforts to answer the 'possibility and necessity of creating a new culture': *so that you can live*" (3–4). Like Kunzru, Smith is well placed to appreciate the "paradox" Mercer proposes: that "the national peculiarities of Britain's postimperial condition provided unique conditions of possibility for diasporic ways of seeing that sought to move beyond 'nation' as a necessary category of thought" (24).

Moving beyond nation is also the agenda of Andrea Levy's *Small Island*, whose ambiguous title may refer variously to England, Jamaica, or any number of still smaller Caribbean islands. Metaphorically, it can also refer to any of the central quartet of the novel – the English Queenie and Bernard, and the Jamaican Hortense and Gilbert – since the egocentricity of each isolates him or her from the others. An apt alternate title for the book might have been *Four Solitudes*. Though her cast of speakers is smaller, Levy employs a monologue-based structure similar to Kneale's in *English Passengers* and broadly comparable in its aims. The book's conclusion, in which Hortense and Gilbert agree to adopt Queenie's mixed-race baby, dramatizes the perils but also the promise of hybridity in an England just emerging from the turmoil of a world war.

Beyond the delicate ironies of Levy's use of monologue form, what especially distinguishes *Small Island* is its nuanced exploration of racialized laughter itself. In its self-consciousness, the book extends comic innovations deployed earlier by Forster and Spark, and more recently by Kureishi. The comedy, like Smith's, is kaleidoscopic and perspectival; characters who at first glance seem flat ethnic cardboard cutouts are gradually revealed to be multilayered. Gilbert Joseph initially recalls Selvon's West Indian "boys," an even more hapless version of Galahad from the Moses trilogy, but we later penetrate beyond his surface clownishness to his equally genuine sensitivity and generosity. (The half-Afro-Caribbean, half-Jewish Gilbert might stand as a twenty-first-century reply to Thackeray's abject, hybrid West Indian heiress, Rhoda Swartz.) Bernard Bligh seems as stiff and intolerant as a Forsterian Turton or Heaslop; returning to England from India after his war service and finding it full of "blasted coloured colonials," he says, "I've nothing against them in their place. But their place isn't here" (469). Yet despite the crashing banality of such sentiments, even Bernard is more than a walking cliché, as we see when he implores his wife Queenie to keep her baby, the child of an unknown (to him) "blasted coloured colonial" father. We are all, Levy implies, in some measure stereotypes, because we are all formed, or deformed, by our exposure to the imperatives of our parent cultures. In *Small Island* the interplay of such socially inscribed responses produces comedy, but humour also stems from less predictable quirks of individual behaviour.

Levy's novel dramatizes with remarkable vividness the virulent force of crude racial joking. When Gilbert, who has obtained a precarious job with the British Post Office as a delivery boy, seeks help from some railway workers concerning which packages he is to pick up, they respond with the expected slurs: "'When are you going back to the jungle?' Oh, man, this is the best joke these four men had heard today. They all laugh at this. A coon. The jungle. What a lark. Two of them light up cigarettes. Man, I am better than a tea-break. While the hands on the clock keep moving, I pick up another sack. 'Oi, darkie, you ain't answered me. When are you going back to where you belong?'" (317). Levy here empowers Gilbert, as Smith empowers Millat, by making him the arbiter of funniness, exposing moronic racist wisecracks to his acerb private sarcasm. Yet Gilbert's practical power is limited. To protect his employment he must restrain his impulse to retaliate physically or even verbally; he is thus obliged, ruefully, to swallow humiliation.

Elsewhere, however, humour can serve as a more supportive source of power for Levy's coloured migrants. When Gilbert's wife Hortense attempts to get work as a teacher in London, the woman interviewing her tells her, "'You're not qualified to teach here in England,'" and compounds this injury with insulting laughter: "'Miss, I'm afraid there really is no point your sitting there arguing with me.' And she giggled. The untimely chortle made my mouth gape" (454). Hortense's rather baroque expression "untimely chortle" may make the reader smile, but it still captures the sheer nastiness of the interviewer's amusement. Worse, when the dismayed and confused Hortense tries to leave through the door of a closet, the other women on the interviewing panel begin to laugh: "All three were giggling when I emerged from the dark of the closet. One behind a hand, another with a sheet of paper lifted up so I might not see" (455). But Gilbert, hearing the story from the devastated Hortense, superimposes his own idiosyncratic brand of humour on it:

> "Why you do that?" I asked her.
>
> "I thought it was the door to leave by."
>
> "Oh dear," I said.
>
> "But it was a cupboard and the women all laugh on me."
>
> My mind conjured the scene but instead of laughing hearty on the joke of this proud woman's humiliation, my heart snapped in two. "And tell me," I said, "what was this cupboard like?"

Her expression flashed. "What is this fool man saying?" but she answered, "There was a bucket and perhaps a mop."

"Ah. Now, that was a broom cupboard. I have walked into many broom cupboards."

Reddened and moistened with tears, her eyes gazed upon me. And I believe this was the first time they looked on me without scorn. Two breaths I skipped before I could carry on. "It's true! I walk into broom cupboard, stationery cupboard …"

"This one had paper in also."

"Interesting cupboard," I told her. "You say it have broom and paper." And then it happen.

She smiled. (459–60)

Stifling the impulse to engage in detached, heartless laughter of his own, Gilbert uses compassionate, whimsical humour to soothe the smart of the "untimely chortles" inflicted on Hortense by the white women. It is a catalytic narrative moment, sparking the conversion of the marriage of Gilbert and Hortense, until now merely nominal, into a real relationship. It is crucial for the reader as well, for it balances the racist laughter of rejection against the unraced laughter of sympathy – and awards the victory to the second. Gilbert here qualifies as the triumphant rieur, whereas the giggling functionaries are firmly typed as obnoxious anti-rieurs. A special distinction of Levy's novel is this ongoing, self-conscious *weighing* of various types of humour. We are repeatedly invited to laugh at the principal characters – this is, after all, a comic work, despite its sombre elements – but we are again and again compelled also to interrogate, and sometimes to regret, our amusement. This cross-questioning of laughter itself, recalling Kureishi's *Buddha of Suburbia* but even more far-reaching, makes such writing virtually a distinct subgenre, one related to late-twentieth-century postmodernist self-reflexivity. On the analogy of "metafiction," it might be given the cumbersome label "racial metacomedy."

It is a piquant irony that, after *Punch* stopped publication in 1992, it was briefly resuscitated by the Egyptian magnate Mohammed Al Fayed, a man who might once have been a butt of the magazine's knowing laughter on the score of his ethnic origins but who was moved to save it by his fondness for venerable British institutions. Such ironies naturally proceed from the sudden porousness of the boundaries of British nationhood; the presence en masse of those who had formerly been objects of urbane condescension. Evelyn Waugh's "Remote People" have unexpectedly thronged the portals of home; "Englishness" and a "sense of belonging" are no longer birthrights to be taken for granted but riddles to be scrutinized.

During the latter part of the twentieth century, British humour of race and nation underwent radical changes. Far from being a passing caprice, this is a symptom of a seismic shift in the national imaginary. Once the Outposts of Empire had invaded the metropolis in force, joking about origins, customs, or speech acquired a different context and new, often grating, overtones. On one level, racial humour became more widespread and more virulent: witness the plethora of Paki jokes that plagued Kureishi's childhood and adolescence or the routines of Bernard Manning that send nightclub spectators (or some, at least) into stitches. Citing a 1983 Policy Studies Institute survey of London police, Paul Gilroy reports the following banter between two constables about the death of thirteen young blacks in a fire in Deptford: "1st PC 'Do you know what they've renamed Deptford?' 2nd PC 'No, what have they renamed it?' 1st PC 'Blackfriars'" (102). Rather than acting therapeutically – "letting the pus run," in Howard Jacobson's phrase – such callous and tasteless joking is likelier to aggravate wounds already festering.

In contemporary works of comic fiction like Smith's, Kunzru's, and Levy's, "English giggles" at the expense of the not entirely English have yielded to a cosmopolitan amusement better suited to the new England's unexampled cultural diversity. This does not mean that in their novels Waugh's unbridled comic gusto has been replaced by a bland "political correctness"; "bland" is the last adjective that would occur to most readers of these recent works. Rather, in place of the stock assumptions that underlay older types of racial humour, whether Waugh's or Cary's or *Punch*'s, these writers rely on ironies of situation and paradoxical clashes of individual perspective. As we have seen repeatedly in earlier chapters of this study, comedy involving race, no matter how enlightened or sophisticated, is always apt to draw on embedded stereotypes of one sort or another. The very act of putting an individual into a particular ethnic slot may entail automatic assumptions about group features and foibles. Novels like the three discussed in this chapter, however, gain their humorous force largely from the inventiveness and brio with which they explode such assumptions.

Such an imaginatively self-conscious approach to the comedy of race is all the more welcome, because the future is unlikely to bring a comic "happy ending": a Britain free of interracial strife, the sort of egalitarian utopia wistfully envisioned by Gilroy, "a world in which 'race' will no longer be a meaningful device for the categorization of human beings, where work will no longer be servitude and law will be disassociated from dominion" (218). What Gilroy himself, among others, has called "the new racism" – defined by George Frederickson as "a way of thinking about difference that reifies and essentializes culture rather than genetic endowment, or in other words makes culture do the work of race" (141) – poses an ongoing challenge to multicultural peace. There are frequent flare-ups of communalist anger, sometimes accompanied by violence, on the part of jostling ethnic and national groups. The sensational terrorist attacks in Britain, the United States, and elsewhere have exposed Muslims in particular to animosity proceeding from "the new racism," an attitude that can take more insidious forms than crude racist jokes. The political slogan floated by the Conservative Party in the 2005 British election – "Are you thinking what we're thinking?" – was meant to play provocatively on the fear and resentment harboured by white "real English" voters toward allegedly intruding "others." Troubling as that catchphrase was, what is perhaps more significant is that it backfired, in part because it quickly became the target of impolite parodies ("Are you drinking what we're drinking?"; "Are you thinking that we're stinking?"; and so on). While the wit may have been less than brilliant, the jokes were damaging enough to cause the slogan to be hastily retired. Humour remains in twenty-first-century Britain a serviceable weapon in the war on bigotry.

In the most accomplished comic fiction of the new century, laughter seldom gets directed from "high" to "low," from those presumed to occupy the cultural core toward those stranded on the margin. Instead, literary humour has itself migrated to the periphery. The writers who produce such comedy may or may not be more gifted than an Evelyn Waugh, but they are more inclusive, in that their humour attunes us to the manifold othernesses of the motley inhabitants of their works, and of our world. The artistic task they set themselves coincides with what the anthropologist Clifford Geertz defines as "the job of ethnography": "to provide … narratives and scenarios to refocus our attention; not, however, ones that render us acceptable to ourselves by representing others as gathered into worlds we don't want and can't arrive at, but ones which make us visible to ourselves by representing us and everyone else as cast into the midst of a world full of irremovable strangenesses we can't keep clear of" (*Available Light* 84). While Geertz is an American, his words have a resonance not contained by national boundaries. By refocusing its readers' attention, contemporary British comic fiction transfigures their laughter, making it what Walter Benjamin believed laughter ought to be: the best start for thinking.

Notes

INTRODUCTION

1 All italicized phrases in citations appear thus in the original text unless otherwise noted.

2 Act I Scene 5. What complicates the situation is that the call to arms is a ruse, invented in the interest of a wager upon the girls' fidelity between the young men and Don Alfonso.

3 Compare John Bruns: "We should applaud Bergson for having the wisdom to acknowledge human motives as complex and contradictory, but we should also recognize a confined and confining style in his description of the affect system. Rather than imagine pity as 'silenced,' why not see it as comfortably cohabiting with laughter?" (9).

4 Explicit awareness of the connection between humour and the venting of hostility dates back at least as far as the seventeenth-century philosopher Thomas Hobbes. There is no space in the present discussion to trace in detail the development of the concept.

5 In the famous "Dead Parrot" sketch, in which an irate customer returns a defunct bird to a pet shop, class is again an issue. Here, however, laughter is directed "downward," since both the daft customer and the shady shop-keeper speak broad cockney. The viewer, in Purdie's terms, enjoys a sense of empowerment through an imputed superior "mastery of discourse."

CHAPTER ONE

1 "Salvage" is spelled thus in the First Folio's "Names of the Characters" list. Modern editions frequently normalize the spelling to "savage." Frank Kermode, however, keeps "salvage" in the Arden Edition of the play; see his discussion on xxxix of his introduction.

2 For a concise survey of Octave Mannoni's and later commentators' revaluations of *The Tempest* in the light of decolonization, see also Garry Wills's review-article "Goodbye, Columbus" in *The New York Review of Books*, 22 November 1990, 6–10.

3 Compare, however, Lewis's illuminating commentary on Shakespeare's use of contrasting modes of laughter to distinguish between "Christian" and "Jewish" attitudes toward experience in *The Merchant of Venice*, *Comic Effects* 40–7: "*Merchant* is built around distinct interests and world views competing for our support for their assumptions about what is amusing and what is no laughing matter" (40).

4 Not all Victorian novelists shared Thackeray's assumption that non-whiteness automatically made one laughable. In one of the American interludes of his 1844 novel *Martin Chuzzlewit*, Charles Dickens caustically satirizes that assumption. The protagonist, young Martin, who has been introduced to a New York family of *soi-disant* abolitionists named Norris, voices his sympathy with the brutalized African slaves. He is surprised by the reception of his views: "Now, one of the young ladies – the prettiest and most delicate – was mightily amused at the earnestness with which he spoke; and on his craving leave to ask her why, was quite unable for a time to speak for laughing. As soon however as she could, she told him that the negroes were such a funny people, so excessively ludicrous in their manners and appearance, that it was wholly impossible for those who knew them well, to associate any serious ideas with such a very absurd part of the creation. Mr Norris the father, and Mrs Norris the mother, and Miss Norris the sister, and Mr Norris Junior the brother, and even Mrs Norris Senior the grandmother, were all of this opinion, and laid it down as an absolute matter of fact. As if there were nothing in suffering and slavery, grim enough to cast a solemn air on any human animal; though it were as ridiculous, physically, as the most grotesque of apes, or, morally, as the mildest Nimrod among tuft-hunting republicans!" (351). In a novel in which laughter of various moral shades often functions as an index to character, the Norris family's mirth at the expense of negroes marks the nadir of unseemliness. Compare Houston A. Baker's reference to "Joel Chandler Harris and all white spokesmen who would make the Negro merely the 'funny man' of American life" (87).

5 "The man who withdraws into himself is liable to ridicule, because the comic is largely made up of this very withdrawal. This accounts for the comic being

so frequently dependent on the manners or ideas, or, to put it bluntly, on the prejudices, of a society." (Bergson 150)

6 Cf. *The Tempest* IV i 188–90: "A devil, a born devil ... on whom my pains / Humanely taken, all, all lost, quite lost."

7 A more extended and subtle shift in the presumed "comic" status of a fictional character occurs in Flaubert's *Madame Bovary*. The novel opens with Charles Bovary's introduction as a new student in a schoolroom; his monstrosity of a cap and his mangling of his own name as "*Charbovari*" (2) immediately place him as a comic misfit and induce hilarity in his classmates: "A loud burst of laughter from the other pupils threw the poor boy into such a state of confusion that he did not know whether to hold his cap in his hand, leave it on the floor or put it on his head" (2). Over time, however, we gain a more intimate knowledge of Charles's emotional life and finally come to view Charles not as a comic but as a tragic figure, or at least as close to one as Flaubert's austere vision permits. The book concludes with a meeting between Charles and Rodolphe, the man who (as Charles knows) has cuckolded him with his late wife, Emma. Charles tells Rodolphe, "'Only fate is to blame'"; Rodolphe judges him "to be extremely meek for a man in his position – comical, even, and a little contemptible'" (302). The cuckolder's shallow misreading of Charles's grief as "comical" reveals him to be an insensitive anti-rieur and more than a little contemptible.

CHAPTER TWO

1 *Punch* itself introduced the term "cartoon" in 1843 but restricted it then and later to full-page political satiric drawings. Graphic jokes of any other sort were referred to simply as "drawings and sketches." (I am indebted for this information to Nick Roberts of the *Punch* Cartoon Library.) For the sake of simplicity, I will use the terms "cartoon," "humorous drawing," and "joke drawing" interchangeably in my text.

2 The cigar as a standard prop for comic caricatures of Jews found its way into serious literature as well. See T.S. Eliot's minor poem, "Burbank with a Baedeker: Bleistein with a Cigar."

3 The metaphor linking black skin with chocolate still retained some currency at least as late as 1983, the date of a Greater London Council poster reproduced by Paul Gilroy (140) headed "Which Slice of the Cake Are You Getting?" and showing a wedge of chocolate cake inserted into a white cake frosted with the London skyline. Although intended as a positive contribution to an anti-racism campaign, the image, as Gilroy points out, unwittingly reinforces the stereotyped notion of coloured people "not fitting in."

CHAPTER THREE

1 Much of what I say about the racial humour in *Black Mischief* also applies to the later *Scoop* (1938). In some ways, however, the comic treatment of African politics in *Scoop* is more nuanced than that in the earlier novel.

2 The travel book *Remote People* had a matching frontispiece portraying the newly enthroned Emperor Haile Selassie, shown full-face in a posture closely resembling Seth's, labelled with equal implausibility "from the painting by a native artist." Unlike the one in *Black Mischief*, this illustration is ostensibly serious in intent. The objects associated with Selassie (small table with vase of flowers, sceptre of rule, and so on) have no comic charge. However, because the decor overshadows his diminutive figure, the impression given of Selassie is generally miniaturizing, so that the subscript "King of the Kings of Ethiopia" becomes inevitably tinged with irony.

3 *Punch* had already sent up the vitamin fad with features like "The Vitamins: A Scientific Song" (22 June 1927), which makes its facetious point by means of whimsical doggerel: "Of 'C' with frank delight I sing; / For 'C''s the pretty Vitamin / Who makes and minds that schoolgirl skin / And stops us coming out in lots / Of horrid, horrid little spots" – ringing the changes from "A" through to "D" at more than ample length.

4 Compare Harriet Beecher Stowe's description in *Uncle Tom's Cabin* of the black girl Topsy, who has been asked to sing and dance: "The black, glassy eyes glittered with a kind of wicked drollery, and the thing struck up, in a clear shrill voice, an old negro melody, to which she kept time with her hands and feet, spinning round, clapping her hands, knocking her knees together, in a wild, fantastic sort of time, and producing in her throat all those odd guttural sounds which distinguish the native music of her race; and finally, turning a somerset or two, and giving a prolonged closing note, as odd and unearthly as that of a steam whistle, she came suddenly down on the carpet" (qtd in Baker 24). The white reducing of black characters to crazily gyrating mechanisms has, evidently, a long history, of which Waugh's whirligig Black Bitch is a latter-day manifestation.

CHAPTER FOUR

1 Admittedly, Johnson does thereby contrive at least to have his death represent a *personal* connection, of however meagre a sort, rather than a mere judicial proceeding.

2 Bédé, without alluding to its racial overtones, calls Cary's humour in a scene like the exchange about filing "un peu éléphantin" (28); the pun may be unintentional.

3 For Cary there was always a close natural link between artistic creativity and anti-social behaviour, the painter Gulley Jimson in the Trilogy representing the best-known example.

4 JanMohamed has noted "the equation of the African to various animals" (32) in Cary's fiction.

CHAPTER FIVE

1 One should mention that Forster's position as a visitor to India differed markedly from Cary's as a colonial official in Africa. Cary, isolated among people with whom he could not easily communicate but for whom he was administratively responsible, tended to find "natives" at once remote and menacing. Making his fictional Africans both violent and laughable was arguably for him a means of coping with his recollected sense of danger and unease. Forster, by contrast, first travelled to India on the strength of his close prior friendship with an Indian, Syed Ross Masood. Years later, when serving as a functionary in the small state of Dewas Senior, he, too, was isolated; but he was able to communicate in English with many of the people among whom he lived. He had few administrative duties and was free to associate casually with local people on a day-to-day basis. Consequently, while he was frequently amused by features of Indian life that still struck him as strange, he felt for the most part unthreatened.

2 Elsewhere, Forster goes out of his way to emphasize the Indians' *control* of their rulers' alien speech; Fielding, for example, has been "struck by the liveliness with which the younger generation handled a foreign tongue. They altered the idiom, but they could say whatever they wanted to say quickly; there were none of the babuisms ascribed to them up at the Club" (76). By damaging contrast, Mrs Turton's grasp of Urdu extends to "none of the politer forms, and of the verbs [she knew] only the imperative mood" (56).

3 "Court buffoonery" is a phrase rooted in personal history. During his first visit to Dewas Senior in early 1913 Forster himself had been distressed rather than diverted by the antics of the Subedhar, the ruler's buffoon: "[His Highness] is always translating his droll speeches and I can't see their drollery: sometimes his turban is set on fire, which makes me wretched" (*Hill* 39).

4 Editors' markings in citations from the manuscript versions of *A Passage to India* indicate Forster's erasures and alternate wordings in the cited passages.

5 Forster's homosexuality is obviously not by itself a sufficient explanation of his tolerant attitude toward racial otherness and the general avoidance in his work of racially demeaning humour. Ronald Firbank, a writer whose sexual orientation was equivalent to Forster's (and whose writing Forster, like

Waugh, admired) had, as I have noted, no compunction about exploiting "piccaninny" stereotypes for their purported comic value.

CHAPTER SIX

1 Cf. also Norman Page (56 and 60) and Patrick Swindon (Hynes 68), among others.

2 Spark does, as I have implied, share Waugh's general tendency to privilege Roman Catholic characters and their experiences. This is, however, an issue separate from the two writers' handling of specifically racial humour.

CHAPTER SEVEN

1 Although the completed manuscript of *Civil to Strangers* antedates the publication of *Some Tame Gazelle*, Pym began to compose the latter novel first. By the time she submitted it for publication, however, it had been extensively reworked.

2 In the novel's earlier typescript version the complacency had been ascribed to *Mrs* Olatunde (ms. Pym 34); by making the husband the complacent party, Pym imbues the more prominent exponent of African vitality with a sobering shade of common, comic human smugness.

CHAPTER EIGHT

1 In her essay "Blacks Next Door" (*Punch* 29 January 1964), Elspeth Huxley writes: "If there is one thing on which all immigrants agree it is that, almost to a man, they mean to buy a house. To them it represents the very thing they've left home to find – security" (155). An ironic dimension of *Moses Ascending* is that Moses, who has hoped to find security through his purchase of a London house, instead lands himself in a position of radical instability.

CHAPTER NINE

1 Perhaps the most cogent attack on Rushdie's novel by a non-Muslim is Richard Webster's 1990 *A Brief History of Blasphemy: Liberalism, Censorship and "The Satanic Verses."* Webster displays an unusually sympathetic understanding of Muslim objections to the book. He points out that, for believers, "[t]he Koran remains the essential and only sanctuary of God and of the Prophet Muhammad, and any attempt to tamper with that sanctuary or to abuse its holiness is seen as an attempt to destroy religion itself" (30). However, while accusing Rushdie of

"insulting the sacred tradition of the Koran" (134), Webster for the most part cites specific complaints by Muslim critics rather than carefully analyzing Rushdie's text to assess the exact nature and gravity of the supposed insults. Ultimately, the outrage to Muslim belief may simply derive from the author's temerity in including the Prophet Muhammad as a character in a novel, and a comic novel at that. Fiction, even if non-realistic, has an inherent tendency to humanize and thus desacralize hieratic figures; one might theorize that, as a product of Western skeptical secularism, the novel as a form carries with it its own inescapable ethnocentric burden. Including an inviolable religious icon among the cast of characters must thus *ipso facto* amount to an act of sacrilege – one that, it seems safe to predict, will not soon be repeated.

2 English does provide an illuminating comparison between Rushdie's satire on British immigration authorities and Waugh's zany send-up of pettifogging customs officials in *Vile Bodies*. See *Comic Transactions* 216–18.

3 Broadly speaking, Chamcha's romantic attitude toward "Englishness" resembles that of Tony Last, the protagonist of Waugh's *A Handful of Dust*. Unlike Rushdie's Indian migrant, Last is genuinely the descendant of an upper-class British country family; but he attempts to act out a personal vision of traditional English, baronial life that is every bit as fanciful a construction as Chamcha's and that leads equally to comic disaster.

4 The sentence reads in full: "And we are not willing to be excluded from any part of our heritage; which heritage includes both a Bradford-born Indian kid's right to be treated as a full member of British society, and also the right of any member of this post-diaspora community to draw on its roots for its art, just as all the world's community of displaced writers has always done" (*Homelands* 15). Rushdie's concept of national heritage is obviously more capacious and complex than that of the Sufyan sisters, who are simply not equipped to recognize "roots" that extend beyond the turf of the London they have always known.

5 "Toady" is the slang translation of "Chamcha."

CHAPTER TEN

1 Included in *My Beautiful Laundrette*; the section quoted also appeared separately in *Granta*.

2 Holmes makes the point that "Kureishi's comedy is ... a product of words as well as of characters and scenes" ("Comedy" 645).

3 In his memoir *My Ear at His Heart*, Kureishi recounts an anecdote concerning his Uncle Achoo, who lived in Somerset near Evelyn Waugh's house: "Achoo met him once, locally, and offered him his hand; Waugh – a writer I still

admire for his prose – offered not his hand but a finger" (103). The incident obliquely suggests the racially inflected distance separating Kureishi from Waugh, despite his appreciation of Waugh's style.

CHAPTER ELEVEN

1 Kneale's is by no means the first modern, dissident reimagining of Shakespeare's play. An influential prior example is Aimé Césaire's 1969 *Tempête*, a dramatic reworking in which "Ariel became a mulatto 'house slave' and Caliban a black 'field slave'" (Wills *NYRB*). Also, starting with Jonathan Miller's 1970 production of the original *Tempest*, staged versions have tended to present Caliban in a relatively favourable light, Prospero in an unfavourable one.

2 Like several of Kneale's narrators (but unlike Kneale himself) Collins treats the inhabitants of Britain's overseas colonies, represented by a trio of shadowy, sinister Indians, as potentially criminal exotics. Recent criticism has, however, challenged this reading of *The Moonstone* as an example of conventional Victorian orientalism.

3 The colonialist Robson has learned the Palawa people's language, but since he resolutely discourages them from speaking it he makes a poor representative of the principle of heteroglossia.

4 As Kneale explains in his epilogue, he modeled Potter's book on the bestselling 1850 work of pseudo-science, *The Races of Men*, by "a disgraced surgeon named Robert Knox" (440).

5 By a further historical irony, current publicity promoting Tasmania as a prime tourist destination insists on calling it an "unspoiled island paradise" and "one of the last remaining unspoiled places on earth," conveniently overlooking the ethnic cleansing and the brutal confinement of prisoners that have marred the island's history.

6 See Michel Foucault, *Discipline and Punish*, 195–308. Foucault explains that, in this type of correctional institution, "[t]he crowd, a compact mass, a locus of multiple exchanges, individualities merging together, a collective effect, is abolished and replaced by a collection of separated individualities. From the point of view of the guardian, it is replaced by a multiplicity that can be numbered and supervised; from the point of view of the inmates, by a sequestered and observed solitude" (201). Kneale's Separate Prison foregrounds the psychological effect of the prisoners' numbering and isolation. The effect of continual possible surveillance, which Foucault stresses, is given less prominence.

CHAPTER TWELVE

1 Possibly the most extreme recent elaboration of the mutable-identity topos occurs in Hanif Kureishi's 2002 science-fiction fantasy *The Body*. The protagonist, a well-known playwright named Adam, is offered the opportunity to exchange his aging body for a youthful one through the transplanting of his own brain into the preserved cadaver of a young man. Here again identity shifts entail a change of name: Adam chooses to be called "Leo Raphael Adams." Identity now becomes a matter of aesthetic preference; the "guy" Adam chooses has the attributes he deems desirable: "Stocky and as classically handsome as any sculpture in the British Museum, he was neither white nor dark but lightly toasted, with a fine, thick penis and heavy balls" (27). Although racial hybridity is intimated here, the novel does not foreground it; after *The Black Album* ethnicity has, in fact, become a subordinate concern in Kureishi's fiction. Instead, youth, aesthetic appeal, and robust masculinity are the featured attractions of the protagonist's new physical self. Despite the obvious advantages of life as a "Newbody," Adam(s) ends up trapped, more inexorably than Kunzru's Pran, in the identity he has selected, which turns out ironically to be the negation of identity: "I was a stranger on the earth, a nobody with nothing, belonging nowhere, a body alone, condemned to begin again, in the nightmare of eternal life" (149).

Bibliography

Achebe, Chinua. "Conversation with Chinua Achebe." *Africa Report*. July 1964, 19–21.

Adas, Michael. *Machines as the Measure of Men*. Ithaca and London: Cornell University Press, 1989.

Afzal-Khan, Fawzia. *Cultural Imperialism and the Indo-English Novel*. University Park: Pennsylvania State University Press, 1993.

Allen, Walter. Foreword. Cary, Joyce. *Cock Jarvis*. Alan Bishop, ed. London: Michael Joseph, 1974.

amazon.com: *The Story of Little Black Sambo*. www.amazon.com/exec/obidos/tg/detail/-/0397300069/002-9373958–6915212?v=g … 20 October 2003.

Amis, Kingsley. *Girl, 20*. Harmondsworth: Penguin, 1980 [1971].

– *Lucky Jim*. Harmondsworth: Penguin, 1992 [1954].

Appignanesi, Lisa and Sara Maitland, eds. *The Rushdie File*. London: Fourth Estate Limited, 1989.

Apte, Mahadev L. *Humor and Laughter: An Anthropological Approach*. Ithaca and London: Cornell University Press, 1985.

Armstrong, Paul B. "Reading India: E.M. Forster and the Politics of Interpretation." *Twentieth Century Literature* 38:4, Winter 1992, 365–85.

Baker, Houston A., Jr. *Modernism and the Harlem Renaissance*. Chicago and London: University of Chicago Press, 1987.

Bakhtin, Mikhail. *The Dialogic Imagination*. Austin: University of Texas Press, 1981.

– *Problems of Dostoevsky's Poetics*. NP: Ardis, 1973 [1929].

– *Rabelais and His World*. Cambridge MA and London: Massachusetts Institute of Technology Press, 1968 [1965].

Ball, John Clement. "The Semi-Detached Metropolis: Hanif Kureishi's London." *ARIEL* 27:4. October 1996, 7–27.

Barker, Francis and Peter Hulme. "Nymphs and Reapers Heavily Vanish: The Discursive Con-texts of *The Tempest*. Gerald Graff and James Phelan, eds. *William Shakespeare, "The Tempest": A Case Study in Critical Controversy.* Boston and New York: Bedford / St Martin's: 2000, 229–45.

Barratt, Harold. "From Colony to Colony: Selvon's Expatriate West Indians." Susheila Nasta, ed. *Critical Perspectives on Sam Selvon*. Washington: Three Continents, 1988, 250–9.

Barreca, Regina, ed. *Last Laughs: Perspectives on Women and Comedy.* New York etc.: Gordon and Breach, 1988.

– *They Used to Call Me Snow White ... But I Drifted: Women's Strategic Use of Humor.* New York etc.: Penguin, 1991.

Barrett, Eliabeth. "Comedy, Courtesy, and *A Passage to India.*" *English Studies in Canada* 10:1, l984, 77–93.

Baucom, Ian. *Out of Place*. Durham: Duke University Press, 1999.

Baugh, Edward. "Friday in Crusoe's City: The Question of Language in Two West Indian Novels of Exile." Susheila Nasta, ed. *Critical Perspectives on Sam Selvon.* Washington: Three Continents, 1988, 240–9.

Beaty, Frederick L. *The Ironic World of Evelyn Waugh.* DeKalb: Northern Illinois University Press, 1992.

Bédé, Jacques. "Le comique et l'humeur dans les romans africains de Joyce Cary." *Cameroon Studies in English and French.* 1976, 1, 21–36.

Beer, Gillian. "Negation in *A Passage to India.*" *Essays in Criticism* 30, 1980, 151–66.

Beer, John, ed. *"A Passage to India": Essays in Interpretation*. Totowa NJ: Barnes & Noble, 1986.

Bell, Vereen M. "Comic Seriousness in *A Passage to India.*" 66, 1967, *The South Atlantic Quarterly,* 606–17.

Benjamin, Walter. "The Author as Producer." *Reflections: Essays, Aphorisms, Autobiographical Writings*. Trans. Edmund Jephcott. New York and London: Harcourt Brace Jovanovich, 1978.

Bergson, Henri. *Laughter.* [1900] Wylie Sypher, ed. *Comedy.* Baltimore and London: Johns Hopkins University Press, 1980 [1956].

Berthoff, Warner. [From "Fortunes of the Novel: Muriel Spark and Iris Murdoch."] Joseph Hynes, ed. *Critical Essays on Muriel Spark*. New York: G.K. Hall and Macmillan, and Don Mills, Ontario: Maxwell Macmillan Canada, 1992, 55–64.

Bhabha, Homi K. *The Location of Culture*. London and New York: Routledge, 1994.

– "On the Irremovable Strangeness of Being Different." *PMLA* 113:1, January 1998, 34–9.

Bharucha, Rustom. "Forster's Friends." *E.M. Forster's "A Passage to India,"* Harold Bloom, ed. New York, New Haven, Philadelphia: Chelsea House, 1987, 91–106.

Bloom, Harold, ed. *E.M. Forster's "A Passage to India."* New York, New Haven, Philadelphia: Chelsea House, 1987.

Bold, Alan, ed. *Muriel Spark: An Odd Capacity for Vision*. London: Vision Press, and Totawa: Barnes and Noble, 1984.

Borner, Klaus H. "Salman Rushdie, *The Satanic Verses*: Observations on Cultural Hybridity." *Proceedings of the Conference of the German Association of University Professors of English*, v. 15, 15–62.

Boskin, Joseph. "The Complicity of Humor: The Life and Death of Sambo." John Morreal, ed. *The Philosophy of Laughter and Humor.* Albany: State University of New York Press, 1987, 250–63.

Boyd, William. Introduction. Cary, Joyce. *Mister Johnson.* Harmondsworth: Penguin, 1985.

Bradbury, Malcolm. "Desperate Laughter." *The Independent*. 12 June 1995.

– *Eating People Is Wrong*. London: Penguin, 1962 [1959].

– *The History Man*. London: Penguin, 1975.

Brennan, Timothy. *Salman Rushdie and the Third World*. New York: St Martin's, 1989.

Brophy, Brigid. *Prancing Novelist*. London: Macmillan, 1973.

Brower, Reuben A. *The Fields of Light.* New York: Oxford University Press, 1951.

Brown, Paul. "'This Thing of Darkness I Acknowledge Mine': *The Tempest* and the Discourse of Colonialism." Gerald Graff and James Phelan, eds. *William Shakespeare, "The Tempest": A Case Study in Critical Controversy.* Boston and New York: Bedford / St Martin's, 2000, 205–28.

Bruns, John. "Laughter in the Aisles: Affect and Power in Contemporary Theoretical and Cultural Discourse." *Studies in American Humor,* New Series, 7 March 2000, 5–23.

Bryant, Mark. *Dictionary of Twentieth-Century British Cartoonists and Caricaturists.* Aldershot: Ashgate, 2000.

Burke, Kenneth. *Language as Symbolic Action.* Berkeley and Los Angeles: University of California Press, 1966.

Burney, Fanny. *Evelina*. Oxford: Oxford World's Classics, 1982. [1778]

Carey, Cynthia. "Hanif Kureishi's *The Buddha of Suburbia* as a Post-Colonial Novel." *Commonwealth Essays and Studies* 4. 1997, 119–25.

Cary, Joyce. *The African Witch*. London: Michael Joseph, 1951 [1936].

– *An American Visitor.* London: Michael Joseph, 1933.

– *The Case for African Freedom*. Austin: University of Texas Press, 1962 [1941].

– *Charley Is My Darling*. London: Sphere Books, 1990 [1940].

– *Cock Jarvis*. Alan Bishop, ed. London: Michael Joseph, 1974.

– *Mister Johnson*. Introduction by William Boyd. Harmondsworth: Penguin, 1985.

– *Mister Johnson*. New York: New Directions, 1989 [1939].

Chapman, Graham et al. *Monty Python's Flying Circus: Just the Words*. Vol. 1. London: Mandarin, 1990 [1989].

Chaucer, Geoffrey. *The Complete Works of Geoffrey Chaucer*. New York: Oxford University Press, nd.

Chaudhuri, Nirad C. "Passage to and from India." *Twentieth Century Interpretations of "A Passage to India,"* Andrew Rutherford, ed. Englewood Cliffs: Prentice-Hall, 1970, 168–77.

Chaudhuri, Una. "The Poetics of Exile and the Politics of Home." Patrick Colm Hogan and Lalita Pandit, eds. *Literary India: Comparative Studies in Aesthetics, Colonialism, and Culture*. Albany: State University of New York Press, 1995, 141–9.

Chrisman, Laura and Benita Parry, eds. *Essays and Studies 1999: Postcolonial Theory and Criticism*. Cambridge: D.S. Brewer, 2000.

Coleman, Daniel. *Masculine Migrations*. Toronto, Buffalo, London: University of Toronto Press, 1998.

Cook, Cornelia. *Joyce Cary: Liberal Principles*. London and Totawa: Vision and Barnes and Noble, 1981.

Coulson, Anthony, ed. *Exiles and Migrants: Crossing Thresholds in European Culture and Society*. Brighton: Sussex Academic Press, 1997.

Crabbe, Katharyn. *Evelyn Waugh*. New York: Continuum, 1988.

Cundy, Catherine. *Salman Rushdie*. Manchester: Manchester University Press, 1996.

Daniel, W.O. *Racial Discrimination in England*. Harmondsworth: Penguin, 1968.

Da Ponte, Lorenzo and W.A. Mozart, *Così Fan Tutte* (Libretto). New York: Schirmer, 1951.

De Sousa, Ronald. "The Ethics of Laughter and Humor." John Morreal ed. *The Philosophy of Laughter and Humor*. Albany: State University of New York Press, 1987, 226–49.

De Vitis, A.A. *Roman Holiday: The Catholic Novels of Evelyn Waugh*. London: Vision, 1958.

Dickens, Charles. *Martin Chuzzlewit*. Harmondsworth: Penguin, 1968 [1843–4].

Dickinson, Swift. "Sam Selvon's 'Harlequin Costume': *Moses Ascending*, Masquerade, and the Bacchanal of Self-Creolization." *Melus*. Fall 1996, 21:3, 69–106.

Dodd, Philip. "England, Englishness, and the Other in E.M. Forster." *The Ends of the Earth 1876–1918*, Simon Gatrell, ed. London and Atlantic Highlands NJ: The Ashfield Press, 1992, 205–17.

Doyle, Waddick. "The Space between Identity and Otherness in Hanif Kureishi's *The Buddha of Suburbia*. *Commonwealth Essays and Studies* 4, 1997, 110–18.

Drew, John. "The Spirit Behind the Frieze?" *"A Passage to India": Essays in Interpretation*. John Beer, ed. Totowa NJ: Barnes & Noble, 1986, 81–103.

Dryden, John. Translator's Preface to C.A. Du Fresnoy, *De Arte Graphica. The Works of John Dryden*, Vol. 20. Berkeley and Los Angeles: University of California Press, 1989.

Dyer, Richard. *White*. London and New York: Routledge, 1997.

Ebbatson, Roger, and Catharine Neale. *E.M. Forster "A Passage to India": A Critical Study.* Harmondsworth: Penguin, 1986.

Eberstadt, Fernanda. "Rebel, Rebel: For Allah and England." *The New Yorker*, Vol. 71, August 21 and 28, 1995.

Echeruo, Michael J.C. *Joyce Cary and the Novel of Africa*. London: Longman, 1973.

Edgecombe, Rodney Stenning. *Vocation and Identity in the Fiction of Muriel Spark*. Columbia and London: University of Missouri Press, 1990.

Eliot, T.S. *The Complete Poems and Plays*. New York: Harcourt Brace, 1950.

English, James F. *Comic Transactions: Literature, Humor, and the Politics of Community in Twentieth-Century Britain*. Ithaca and London: Cornell University Press, 1994.

Farry, Eithne. Interview with Zadie Smith, 2 October 2001. www.amazon.co.uk/exec/obidos/tg/feature/-/25895/026-1609358–3272454.

Fielding, Henry. *Joseph Andrews*. London: Penguin, 1977. [1742]

Finney, Brian. "Demonizing Discourse in Salman Rushdie's *The Satanic Verses*." *ARIEL* 29:3, July 1998, 67–93.

Firbank, Ronald. *Sorrow in Sunlight. Valmouth and Other Stories.* Ware: Wordsworth, 1996 [1924].

Fisichelli, Glen-Ellen. "The Novelist as Anthropologist – Barbara Pym's Fiction: Fieldwork Done at Home." *Papers on Language and Literature*. Fall 1988, 24:4, 436–45.

Flaubert, Gustave. *Madame Bovary*. Trans. Lowell Blair. Toronto, New York, etc.: Bantam, 1981 [1857].

Forster, E.M. *Abinger Harvest*. Elizabeth Heine, ed. London: Andre Deutsch, 1996.

– *Aspects of the Novel*. Oliver Stallybrass, ed Harmondsworth: Penguin, 1990 [1927].

– *The Hill of Devi*. New York: Harcourt, Brace, 1953.

– *Howards End*. London: Penguin, 1985 [1910].

– *The Life to Come*. Harmondsworth: Penguin, 1975 [1972].

– *The Manuscripts of "A Passage to India,"* Oliver Stallybrass, ed. New York: Holmes and Meier, 1979.

– *A Passage to India*. Oliver Stallybrass, ed. Harmondsworth: Penguin, 1989 [1924].

– *Two Cheers for Democracy*. New York: Harcourt, Brace, 1951.

Foster, R.F. *Paddy and Mr Punch: Connections in Irish and English History.* London: Penguin, 1993.

Foucault, Michel. *Discipline and Punish*. Trans. Alan Sheridan. New York: Vintage, 1979 [1975].

Frankel, Sara. "An Interview with Muriel Spark." *Partisan Review.* Summer 1987, 25:2, 443–57.

Frederickson, George M. *Racism: A Short History.* Princeton: Princeton University Press, 2002.

Freud, Sigmund. *Wit and Its Relation to the Unconscious.* New York: Dover, 1993 [1916].

Geertz, Clifford. *Available Light.* Princeton: Princeton University Press, 2000.

Gibbons, Stella. *Cold Comfort Farm.* London: Penguin, 1938 [1932].

Gikandi, Simon. *Maps of Englishness: Writing Identity in the Culture of Colonialism.* New York and Chichester: Columbia University Press, 1993.

Gilroy, Paul. *There Ain't No Black in the Union Jack.* London, Melbourne, etc.: Hutchinson, 1987.

Graff, Gerald and James Phelan, eds. *William Shakespeare, "The Tempest": A Case Study in Critical Controversy.* Boston and New York: Bedford / St Martin's, 2000.

Green, Martin. *Children of the Sun.* New York: Basic Books, 1976.

– *Dreams of Adventure, Deeds of Empire.* London and Henley: Routledge and Kegan Paul, 1980.

Harrison, James. *Salman Rushdie.* New York: Twayne, 1992.

Heath, Jeffrey. *The Picturesque Prison: Evelyn Waugh and His Writing.* Kingston and Montreal: McGill-Queen's University Press, 1982.

Heilman, Robert Bechtold. *The Ways of the World: Comedy and Society.* Seattle and London: University of Washington Press, 1978.

Herz, Judith Scherer. *"A Passage to India": Nation and Narration.* New York: Twayne, 1993.

Holmes, Frederick M. "Comedy, the Carnivalesque, and the Depiction of English Society in Hanif Kureishi's *The Buddha of Suburbia* and Kingsley Amis's *Lucky Jim.*" *English Studies in Canada* 28.4, December 2002, 645–66.

– "The Postcolonial Subject Divided between East and West: Kureishi's *The Black Album* as an Intertext of Rushdie's *The Satanic Verses. Papers on Language and Literature* 37 (3), Summer 2001, 296–313.

Hynes, Joseph, ed. *Critical Essays on Muriel Spark.* New York: G.K. Hall and Macmillan, and Don Mills, Ontario: Maxwell Macmillan Canada, 1992.

Ingrams, Elizabeth. "The Lonely Londoners: Sam Selvon and the Literary Heritage." *Wasafiri.* 2001 Spring, 33, 33–6.

Israel, Nico. *Outlandish: Writing between Exile and Diaspora.* Stanford: Stanford University Press, 2000.

Jacobson, Howard. *Seriously Funny: From the Ridiculous to the Sublime.* London: Viking Penguin, 1997.

JanMohamed, Abdul. "The Economy of Manichean Allegory: The Function of Racial Difference in Colonialist Literature." *Critical Inquiry* 12, Autumn 1985, 59–87.

– *Manichean Aesthetics: The Politics of Literature in Colonial Africa*. Amherst: University of Massachusetts Press, 1983.

Joseph, Margaret Paul. *Caliban in Exile: The Outsider in Caribbean Fiction*. Westport: Greenwood, 1992.

Joyce, James. *Ulysses*. New York: The Modern Library, 1934.

Kaleta, Kenneth C. *Hanif Kureishi: Postcolonial Storyteller*. Austin: University of Texas Press, 1998.

Kemp, Peter. *Muriel Spark*. New York: Barnes and Noble, 1975 [1974].

Kermode, Frank. Introduction. Shakespeare, William. *The Tempest*. Frank Kermode, ed. London: Methuen, 1954 [1611].

Kernan, Alvin B. *The Plot of Satire*. New Haven: Yale University Press, 1965.

Kerr, David. "Migration and the Human Spirit in Salman Rushdie's The Satanic Verses." *The Commonwealth Review* 2: 1–2, 1990–91, 168–80.

Kneale, Matthew. *English Passengers*. NP: Vintage Canada, 2001 [2000].

Kunzru, Hari. *The Impressionist*. New York, London etc.: Dutton, 2002.

– Website Review of Smith, *White Teeth*. (Review commissioned but not printed by *The London Review of Books*.) www.harikunzru.com/hari/whiteteeth.htm.

Kureishi, Hanif. *The Black Album*. New York: Scribner, 1995.

– *The Body*. New York, London, etc.: Scribner, 2004 [2002].

– *The Buddha of Suburbia*. Harmondsworth: Penguin, 1990.

– *Intimacy* and *Midnight All Day*. New York: Scribner, 2001 [1998 and 1999].

– *London Kills Me*. London: Penguin, 1992.

– *Love in a Blue Time*. New York: Scribner, 1997.

– *My Beautiful Laundrette and Other Writings*. London: Faber and Faber, 1996.

– *My Ear at His Heart: Reading My Father*. London: Faber and Faber, 2004.

– *Outskirts and Other Plays*. London and Boston: Faber and Faber, 1992.

Land, Stephen K. *Challenge and Conventionality in the Fiction of E.M. Forster*. New York: A.M.S. Press, 1992.

Lawrence, D.H. *The Lost Girl*. Cambridge etc.: Cambridge University Press, 1981 [1920].

Leclerq, Florence. *Elizabeth Taylor*. Boston: Twayne, 1985.

Lessing, Doris. *Under My Skin*. London: HarperCollins, 1994.

Levy, Andrea. *Small Island*. London: Headline, 2004.

Lewis, Paul. *Comic Effects*. Albany: State University of New York Press, 1989.

Liddell, Robert. *Elizabeth and Ivy*. London: Peter Owen, 1986.

Lin, Lidan. "The Irony of Colonial Humanism: *A Passage to India* and the Politics of Posthumanism." *ARIEL* 28: 4, October 1997, 133–53.

Little, Judy. *Comedy and the Woman Writer: Woolf, Spark, and Feminism*. Lincoln and London: University of Nebraska Press, 1983.

– *The Experimental Self: Dialogic Subjectivity in Woolf, Pym, and Brooke-Rose*. Carbondale and Edwardsville: Southern Illinois University Press, 1996.

Lively, Penelope. "The World of Barbara Pym." Dale Salwak, ed. *The Life and Work of Barbara Pym*. Iowa City: University of Iowa Press, 1987, 45–9.

Lodge, David. *Consciousness and the Novel*. London, New York, etc.: Penguin, 2003 [2002].

– *Evelyn Waugh*. New York and London: Columbia University Press, 1971.

Lofting, Hugh. *The Story of Doctor Dolittle*. Canada: McLelland and Stewart, 1923.

London, Bette. *The Appropriated Voice: Narrative Authority in Conrad, Forster, and Woolf*. Ann Arbor: University of Michigan Press, 1990.

Long, Robert Emmet. *Barbara Pym*. New York: Ungar, 1986.

Looker, Mark. *Atlantic Passages: History, Community and Language in the Fiction of Sam Selvon*. New York, Washington, etc.: Peter Lang, 1996.

Mair, Christian. "Naipaul's Miguel Street and Selvon's Lonely Londoners: Two Approaches to the Use of Caribbean Creole in Fiction." *The Journal of Commonwealth Literature*. 1989, 24:1 138–54.

Martin, Sandra. "Salman Rushdie, Speaking Volumes." *Globe and Mail*. September 21, 2002.

Massie, Allan. *Muriel Spark*. Edinburgh: The Ramsay Head Press, 1979.

May, Brian. *The Modernist as Pragmatist: E.M. Forster and the Fate of Liberalism*. Columbia and London: University of Missouri Press, 1997.

McBrien, William. "Muriel Spark: The Novelist as Dandy." Thomas F. Staley, ed. *Twentieth-Century Women Novelists*. London: Macmillan, 1982, 153–78.

McDonald, Sean. "A Conversation with Matthew Kneale." Boldtype. www/randomhouse.com/boldtype/0400/kneale/interview.html.

McDowell, Frederick P.W. *E.M. Forster*. New York: Twayne, 1969.

Mercer, Cobena. *Welcome to the Jungle: New Positions in Black Cultural Studies*. New York and London: Routledge, 1994.

Moore-Gilbert, Bart. "Hanif Kureishi's *The Buddha of Suburbia*: Hybridity in Contemporary Cultural Theory and Artistic Practice." *Q/W/E/R/T/Y* 7, October 1997, 191–207.

Morreal, John, ed. *The Philosophy of Laughter and Humor*. Albany: State University of New York Press, 1987.

Myers, David. "From Satiric Farce to Tragic Epiphany: Salman Rushdie's *The Satanic Verses*." *The Commonwealth Review* 2:1–2 1990–91, 144–67.

Myers, William. "Potential Recruits: Evelyn Waugh and the Reader of *Black Mischief*." *Renaissance and Modern Studies* 21 (1977), 40–51.

Nasta, Susheila. Afterword to Selvon, *Moses Migrating*. Washington: Three Continents, 1992 [1983].

– ed. *Critical Perspectives on Sam Selvon*. Washington: Three Continents, 1988.

Olson, Elder. *The Theory of Comedy*. Bloomington and London: Indiana University Press, 1968.

Orange, Michael. "Language and Silence in *A Passage to India*." *E.M. Forster's "A Passage to India."* Harold Bloom, ed. New York, New Haven, Philadelphia: Chelsea House, 1987, 57–74.

Orwell, George. *Burmese Days*. Harmondsworth: Penguin, 1967 [1934].

– *The Collected Essays, Journalism and Letters of George Orwell*, Vol. 3. Harmondsworth: Penguin, 1970 [1968].

Oubechou, Jamel. "'The Barbarians and Philistines' in *The Buddha of Suburbia*: Dis/Locating Culture." *Commonwealth Essays and Studies* 4. 1997, 101–9.

Page, Norman. *Muriel Spark*. Basingstoke: Macmillan, 1990.

Parry, Benita. *Delusions and Discoveries: Studies on India in the British Imagination 1880–1930*. London: Allen Lane / The Penguin Press, 1972.

Powell, Anthony. *Agents and Patients*. London: Mandarin, 1992 [1936].

– *From a View to a Death*. London: Mardarin, 1992 [1933].

Price, R.G.G. *A History of Punch*. London: Collins, 1957.

Punch: Or the London Charivari. London, 1841–2002.

Purdie, Susan. *Comedy: The Mastery of Discourse*. Toronto and Buffalo: University of Toronto Press, 1993.

Pym, Barbara. *Civil to Strangers and Other Writings*. New York: Plume, 1989.

– Ms. Pym 34. Bodleian Library.

– *Quartet in Autumn*. London: Panther, 1980 [1977].

– *Some Tame Gazelle*. Frogmore, St Albans: Granada, 1981 [1950].

– *A Very Private Eye*. Hazel Holt and Hilary Pym, eds. New York: E.P. Dutton, 1984.

Ray, Sangeeta. "The Nation in Performance: Bhabha, Mukherjee, and Kureishi." Monika Fludernik, ed. *Hybridity and Postcolonialism*. Tubingen: Stauffenburg Verlag, 1998, 219–38.

Reder, Michael R., ed. *Conversations with Salman Rushdie*. Jackson: University Press of Mississippi, 2000.

Roberts, Kevin and Andra Thakur. "Christened with Snow: A Conversation with Sam Selvon." *ARIEL* 27:2, April 1996, 89–115.

Rohlehr, F. Gordon. "The Folk in Caribbean Literature." Susheila Nasta, ed. *Critical Perspectives on Sam Selvon*. Washington: Three Continents, 1988, 29–43.

Rosecrance, Barbara. *Forster's Narrative Vision*. Ithaca and London: Cornell University Press, 1982.

Ross, Alison. *The Language of Humour*. London and New York: Routledge Intertext, 1998.

Rossen, Janice. "The Pym Papers." Dale Salwak, ed. *The Life and Work of Barbara Pym*. Iowa City: University of Iowa Press, 1987, 156–67.

Rushdie, Salman. *East, West*. Toronto: Vintage Canada, 1996 [1994].

– *Imaginary Homelands*. London: Granta Books, 1992 [1991].

– *The Satanic Verses*. Toronto: Vintage Canada, 1997 [1988].

Rutherford, Andrew, ed. *Twentieth Century Interpretations of "A Passage to India."* Englewood Cliffs: Prentice-Hall, 1970.

Ruthven, Malise. *A Satanic Affair: Salman Rushdie and the Wrath of Islam*. London: Hogarth, 1991.

Said, Edward W. *Culture and Imperialism*. New York: Vintage, 1994.

– *Orientalism*. New York: Pantheon, 1978.

Salwak, Dale, ed. *The Life and Work of Barbara Pym*. Iowa City: University of Iowa Press, 1987.

Sandhu, Sukhdev. "Excremental Children." Review of Smith, *White Teeth*. TLS January 21, 2000, 21.

– "Pop Goes the Centre: Hanif Kureishi's London." Chrisman, Laura and Benita Parry, eds. *Essays and Studies 1999: Postcolonial Theory and Criticism*. Cambridge: D.S. Brewer, 2000, 133–54.

Sanga, Jaina C. *Salman Rushdie's Postcolonial Metaphors*. Westport: Greenwood, 2001.

Sawhney, Simona. "Satanic Choices: Poetry and Prophecy in Rushdie's Novel." *Twentieth Century Literature*, Fall 1999, 45:3, 253–77.

Selvon, Samuel. *Foreday Morning*. Essex: Longman, 1989.

– *The Lonely Londoners*. New York: St Martin's, 1956.

– *Moses Ascending*. London: Davis-Poynter, 1975.

– *Moses Migrating*. Afterword by Susheila Nasta. Washington: Three Continents, 1992. [1983]

– *The Plains of Caroni*. London: MacGibbon & Kee, 1970.

Shakespeare, William. *The Tempest*. Frank Kermode, ed. ("The Arden Edition"). London: Methuen, 1954 [1611].

Sillitoe, Alan. *Saturday Night and Sunday Morning*. New York, London etc.: Penguin/Plume, 1992 [1958].

Simon, Richard Keller. "E.M. Forster's Critique of Laughter and the Comic: The First Three Novels as Dialectic." *Twentieth Century Literature* 31: 2–3, Summer-Fall 1985, 199–220.

Singh, Frances. "*A Passage to India*, the National Movement, and Independence." *Twentieth Century Literature* 31:2–3, Summer-Fall 1985, 265–78.

Skura, Meredith Anne. "Discourse and the Individual: The Case of Colonialism in *The Tempest*." Gerald Graff and James Phelan, eds. *William Shakespeare, "The Tempest": A Case Study in Critical Controversy*. Boston and New York: Bedford / St Martin's, 2000, 286–322.

Smith, Zadie. *White Teeth*. London, New York etc.: Penguin, 2001 [2000].

Solomos, John. *Race and Racism in Britain*. 2nd ed. New York: St Martin's, 1993.

Spacks, Patricia Meyer. "Austen's Laughter." Regina Barreca, ed. *Last Laughs: Perspectives on Women and Comedy*. New York etc.: Gordon and Breach, 1988, 71–85.

Spark, Muriel. *The Collected Stories*. London: Penguin, 1994.
– *Curriculum Vitae*. London: Constable, 1992.
– "The Desegregation of Art." [1971] Joseph Hynes, ed. *Critical Essays on Muriel Spark*. New York: G.K. Hall and Macmillan, and Don Mills, Ontario: Maxwell Macmillan Canada, 1992, 33–7.
– "Edinburgh Born." Joseph Hynes, ed. *Critical Essays on Muriel Spark*. New York: G.K. Hall and Macmillan, and Don Mills, Ontario: Maxwell Macmillan Canada, 1992, 21–3.
– *The Mandelbaum Gate*. London: Penguin, 1967 [1965].
– "My Conversion." Joseph Hynes, ed. *Critical Essays on Muriel Spark*. New York: G.K. Hall and Macmillan, and Don Mills, Ontario: Maxwell Macmillan Canada, 1992, 24–8.
– *The Takeover.* London: Penguin, 1978 [1976].
Spivak, Gayatri C. "Reading The Satanic Verses." Maurice Biriotti and Nicola Miller, eds. *What Is an Author?* Manchester: Manchester University Press, 1993, 104–34.
Stallybrass, Peter, and Allon White. *The Politics and Poetics of Transgression.* Ithaca: Cornell University Press, 1986.
Stannard, Martin, ed. *Evelyn Waugh: The Critical Heritage.* London, Boston, etc.: Routledge and Kegan Paul, 1984.
Stape, J.H. *E.M. Forster: Interviews and Recollections*. New York: St Martin's, 1993.
Street, Brian V. *The Savage in Literature*. London and Boston: Routledge and Kegan Paul, 1975.
Suleri [Goodyear], Sara. "Forster's Imperial Erotic." *E.M. Forster.* Jeremy Tambling, ed. Basingstoke: Macmillan, 1995, 151–70.
– "The Geography of *A Passage to India.*" *E.M. Forster's "A Passage to India."* Harold Bloom, ed. New York, New Haven, Philadelphia: Chelsea House, 1987, 107–13.
– *The Rhetoric of English India*. Chicago and London: University of Chicago Press, 1992.
Suter, David W. "Of the Devil's Party: The Marriage of Heaven and Hell in Satanic Verses." *South Asian Review*, 16 January 1992: 13, 38–47.
Swindon, Patrick. ["Spark's Plots"] [excerpted from *Unofficial Selves*, 1973]. Joseph Hynes, ed. *Critical Essays on Muriel Spark.* New York: G.K. Hall and Macmillan, and Don Mills, Ontario: Maxwell Macmillan Canada, 1992, 65–73.
Sypher, Wylie, ed. *Comedy.* Baltimore and London: Johns Hopkins Paperbacks, 1980 [1956].
Talbot, Carol. *Growing up Black in Canada*. Toronto: Williams-Wallace, 1984.
Tambling, Jeremy, ed. *E.M. Forster.* Basingstoke: Macmillan, 1995.
Taylor, Elizabeth. *The Devastating Boys*. London: Virago, 1984 [1972].

Thackeray, William Makepeace. *Vanity Fair.* Oxford: Oxford University Press (Oxford World's Classics), 1983 [1847–48].

Trilling, Lionel. "*A Passage to India.*" *Twentieth Century Interpretations of "A Passage to India."* Andrew Rutherford, ed. Englewood Cliffs: Prentice-Hall, 1970, 17–32.

Wallace, Ronald. "The Inclusion of Merriment" Comedy in *A Passage to India.*" *Essays in Literature* 4, 1977, 37–48.

Wallhead, Celia M. "Paradigms of Diversity in Hanif Kureishi's *The Buddha of Suburbia.*" *Revista Canaria de Estudios Ingleses*, no. 28. April 1994, 65–79.

Waugh, Evelyn. *Black Mischief.* London: Penguin, 1965 [1932].

– *A Handful of Dust*. London: Penguin, 1951 [1934].

– *Labels*. London: Duckworth, 1930.

– *The Letters of Evelyn Waugh*. Mark Amory, ed. London: Weidenfeld and Nicolson, 1980.

– *Put Out More Flags*. London: Penguin, 1943 [1942].

– *Remote People*. London: Duckworth, 1931.

Webster, Richard. *A Concise History of Blasphemy: Liberalism, Censorship and "The Satanic Verses."* Southwold: The Orwell Press, 1990.

Weld, Annette. *Barbara Pym and the Novel of Manners*. Basingstoke and London: Macmillan, 1992.

Whittaker, Ruth. *The Faith and Fiction of Muriel Spark*. London: Macmillan, 1982.

Willis, Deborah. "Shakespeare's *Tempest* and the Discourse of Colonialism." Gerald Graff and James Phelan, eds. *William Shakespeare, "The Tempest": A Case Study in Critical Controversy.* Boston and New York: Bedford / St Martin's, 2000, 256–67.

Wills, Garry. "Goodbye, Columbus." *The New York Review of Books*, 22 November 1990, 6–10.

Witte, Arnd. "Things Fall Apart: The Portrayal of African Identity in Joyce Cary's *Mister Johnson* and Chinua Achebe's *No Longer at Ease.*" Anthony Coulson, ed. *Exiles and Migrants: Crossing Thresholds in European Culture and Society.* Brighton: Sussex Academic Press, 1997, 125–35.

Wyke, Clement H. *Sam Selvon's Dialectical Style and Fictional Strategy.* Vancouver: University of British Columbia Press, 1991.

Yu-cheng, Lee. "Expropriating the Authentic: Cultural Politics in Hanif Kureishi's *The Buddha of Suburbia.*" *EurAmerica* 26:3, 1996, 1–19.

Index